𝕾𝖙𝖆𝖓𝖉𝖆𝖗𝖉 𝕷𝖎𝖇𝖗𝖆𝖗𝖞 𝕰𝖉𝖎𝖙𝖎𝖔𝖓

THE WRITINGS OF

BRET HARTE

WITH INTRODUCTIONS, GLOSSARY, AND INDEXES

ILLUSTRATED BY PHOTOGRAVURES

VOLUME V

The Writings of Bret Harte

STANDARD LIBRARY EDITION

HOUGHTON MIFFLIN COMPANY

MARUJA

AND OTHER TALES

BY

BRET HARTE

BOSTON AND NEW YORK

HOUGHTON MIFFLIN COMPANY

The Riverside Press Cambridge

CONTENTS

LIST OF ILLUSTRATIONS

MARUJA AND OTHER TALES

MARUJA

CHAPTER I

MORNING was breaking on the highroad to San José. The long lines of dusty, level track were beginning to extend their vanishing point in the growing light; on either side the awakening fields of wheat and oats were stretching out and broadening to the sky. In the east and south the stars were receding before the coming day; in the west a few still glimmered, caught among the bosky hills of the cañada del Raimundo, where night seemed to linger. Thither some obscure, low-flying birds were slowly winging; thither a gray coyote, overtaken by the morning, was awkwardly limping. And thither a tramping wayfarer turned, ploughing through the dust of the highway still unslaked by the dewless night, to climb the fence and likewise seek the distant cover.

For some moments man and beast kept an equal pace and gait with a strange similarity of appearance and expression; the coyote bearing that resemblance to his more civilized and harmless congener, the dog, which the tramp bore to the ordinary pedestrians, but both exhibiting the same characteristics of lazy vagabondage and semi-lawlessness; the coyote's slouching amble and uneasy stealthiness being

repeated in the tramp's shuffling step and sidelong glances.
Both were young, and physically vigorous, but both displayed the same vacillating and awkward disinclination to
direct effort. They continued thus half a mile apart unconscious of each other, until the superior faculties of the
brute warned him of the contiguity of aggressive civilization, and he cantered off suddenly to the right, fully five
minutes before the barking of dogs caused the man to make
a détour to the left to avoid entrance upon a cultivated
domain that lay before him.

The trail he took led to one of the scant watercourses
that issued, half spent, from the cañada, to fade out utterly
on the hot June plain. It was thickly bordered with willows and alders, that made an arbored and feasible path
through the dense woods and undergrowth. He continued
along it as if aimlessly ; stopping from time to time to look
at different objects in a dull mechanical fashion, as if rather
to prolong his useless hours, than from any curious instinct,
and to occasionally dip in the unfrequent pools of water
the few crusts of bread he had taken from his pocket.
Even this appeared to be suggested more by coincidence of
material in the bread and water, than from the promptings
of hunger. At last he reached a cuplike hollow in the
hills lined with wild clover and thick with resinous odors.
Here he crept under a manzanita bush and disposed himself
to sleep. The act showed he was already familiar with the
local habits of his class, who used the unfailing dry starlit
nights for their wanderings, and spent the hours of glaring
sunshine asleep or resting in some wayside shadow.

Meanwhile the light quickened, and gradually disclosed
the form and outline of the adjacent domain. An avenue
cut through a parklike wood, carefully cleared of the undergrowth of gigantic ferns peculiar to the locality, led to
the entrance of the cañada. Here began a vast terrace of
lawn, broken up by enormous bouquets of flower-beds be-

wildering in color and profusion, from which again rose the
flowering vines and trailing shrubs that hid pillars, veranda,
and even the long façade of a great and dominant mansion.
But the delicacy of floral outlines running to the capitals
of columns and at times mounting to the pediment of the
roof, the opulence of flashing color or the massing of trop-
ical foliage, could not deprive it of the imperious dignity
of size and space. Much of this was due to the fact that
the original casa — an adobe house of no mean pretensions,
dating back to the early Spanish occupation — had been
kept intact, sheathed in a shell of dark red wood, and still
retaining its patio, or inner courtyard, surrounded by low
galleries, while additions, greater in extent than the main
building, had been erected — not as wings and projections,
but massed upon it on either side, changing its rigid square
outlines to a vague parallelogram. While the patio retained
the Spanish conception of *al-fresco* seclusion, a vast colonnade of veranda on the southern side was a concession to
American taste, and its breadth gave that depth of shadow
to the inner rooms which had been lost in the thinner shell
of the new erection. Its cloistered gloom was lightened
by the fires of cardinal flowers dropping from the roof, by
the yellow sunshine of the jessamine creeping up the columns, by billows of heliotropes breaking over its base as a
purple sea. Nowhere else did the opulence of this climate
of blossoms show itself as vividly. Even the Castilian
roses, that grew as vines along the east front, the fuchsias,
that attained the dignity of trees, in the patio, or the four
or five monster passion-vines that bestarred the low western
wall, and told over and over again their mystic story, paled
before the sensuous glory of the south veranda.

As the sun arose, that part of the quiet house first
touched by its light seemed to waken. A few lounging
peons and servants made their appearance at the entrance
of the patio, occasionally reinforced by an earlier life from

the gardens and stables. But the south façade of the
building had not apparently gone to bed at all: lights
were still burning dimly in the large ballroom; a tray
with glasses stood upon the veranda near one of the open
French windows, and further on, a half-shut yellow fan
lay like a fallen leaf. The sound of carriage-wheels on the
gravel terrace brought with it voices and laughter and the
swiftly passing vision of a char-à-bancs filled with muffled
figures bending low to avoid the direct advances of the sun.

As the carriage rolled away, four men lounged out of
a window on the veranda, shading their eyes against the
level beams. One was still in evening dress, and one
in the uniform of a captain of artillery; the others had
already changed their gala attire, the elder of the party
having assumed those extravagant tweeds which the tour-
ist from Great Britain usually offers as a gentle concession
to inferior yet more florid civilization. Nevertheless, he
beamed back heartily on the sun, and remarked, in a pleasant Scotch accent, that: Did they know it was very extraordinary how clear the morning was, so free from clouds
and mist and fog? The young man in evening dress flu-
ently agreed to the facts, and suggested, in idiomatic French-
English, that one comprehended that the bed was an insult
to one's higher nature and an ingratitude to their gracious
hostess, who had spread out this lovely garden and walks
for their pleasure; that nothing was more beautiful than
the dew sparkling on the rose, or the matin song of the
little birds.

The other young man here felt called upon to point out
the fact that there was no dew in California, and that the
birds did not sing in that part of the country. The foreign young gentleman received this statement with pain
and astonishment as to the fact, with passionate remorse as
to his own ignorance. But still, as it was a charming day,
would not his gallant friend, the Captain here, accept the

challenge of the brave Englishman, and "walk him" for the glory of his flag and a thousand pounds?

The gallant Captain, unfortunately, believed that if he walked out in his uniform he would suffer some delay from being interrogated by wayfarers as to the locality of the circus he would be pleasantly supposed to represent, even if he escaped being shot as a rare California bird by the foreign sporting contingent. In these circumstances, he would simply lounge around the house until his carriage was ready.

Much as it pained him to withdraw from such amusing companions, the foreign young gentleman here felt that he, too, would retire for the present to change his garments, and glided back through the window at the same moment that the young officer carelessly stepped from the veranda and lounged towards the shrubbery.

"They've been watching each other for the last hour. I wonder what's up?" said the young man who remained.

The remark, without being confidential, was so clearly the first sentence of natural conversation, that the Scotchman, although relieved, said, "Eh, man?" a little cautiously.

"It's as clear as this sunshine that Captain Carroll and Garnier are each particularly anxious to know what the other is doing or intends to do this morning."

"Why did they separate, then?" asked the other.

"That's a mere blind. Garnier's looking through his window at Carroll, and Carroll is aware of it."

"Eh!" said the Scotchman, with good-humored curiosity. "Is it a quarrel? Nothing serious, I hope. No revolvers and bowie-knives, man, before breakfast, eh?"

"No," laughed the younger man. "No! To do Maruja justice, she generally makes a fellow too preposterous to fight. I see you don't understand. You're a stranger; I'm an old habitué of the house — let me explain. Both of these men are in love with Maruja; or, worse than that, they firmly believe her to be in love with *them*."

"But Miss Maruja is the eldest daughter of our hostess, is she not?" said the Scotchman; "and I understood from one of the young ladies that the Captain had come down from the Fort particularly to pay court to Miss Amita, the beauty."

"Possibly. But that would n't prevent Maruja from flirting with him."

"Eh! but are you not mistaken, Mr. Raymond? Certainly a more quiet, modest, and demure young lassie I never met."

"That's because she sat out two waltzes with you, and let you do the talking, while she simply listened."

The elder man's fresh color for an instant heightened, but he recovered himself with a good-humored laugh. "Likely — likely. She's a capital good listener."

"You're not the first man that found her eloquent. Stanton, your banking friend, who never talks of anything but mines and stocks, says she's the only woman who has any conversation; and we can all swear that she never said two words to him the whole time she sat next to him at dinner. But she *looked* at him as if she had. Why, man, woman, and child all give her credit for any grace that pleases themselves. And why? Because she's clever enough not to practice any one of them — as graces. I don't know the girl that claims less and gets more. For instance, you don't call her pretty?"

"Wait a bit. Ye 'll not get on so fast, my young friend; I 'm not prepared to say that she's not," returned the Scotchman, with good-humored yet serious caution.

"But you would have been prepared yesterday, and have said it. She can produce the effect of the prettiest girl here, and without challenging comparison. Nobody thinks of her — everybody experiences her."

"You 're an enthusiast, Mr. Raymond. As an habitué of the house, of course, you " —

"Oh, my time came with the rest," laughed the young man, with unaffected frankness. "It's about two years ago now."

"I see — you were not a marrying man."

"Pardon me — it was because I was."

The Scotchman looked at him curiously.

"Maruja is an heiress. I am a mining engineer."

"But, my dear fellow, I thought that in your country " —

"In *my* country, yes. But we are standing on a bit of old Spain. This land was given to Doña Maria Saltonstall's ancestors by Charles V. Look around you. This veranda, this larger shell of the ancient casa, is the work of the old Salem whaling captain that she married, and is all that is American here. But the heart of the house, as well as the life that circles around the old patio, is Spanish. The Doña's family, the Estudillos and Guitierrez, always looked down upon this alliance with the Yankee captain, though it brought improvement to the land, and increased its value forty-fold, and since his death ever opposed any further foreign intervention. Not that that would weigh much with Maruja if she took a fancy to any one; Spanish as she is throughout, in thought and grace and feature, there is enough of the old Salem witches' blood in her to defy law and authority in following an unhallowed worship. There are no sons; she is the sole heiress of the house and estate — though, according to the native custom, her sisters will be separately portioned from the other property, which is very large."

"Then the Captain might still make a pretty penny on Amita," said the Scotchman.

"If he did not risk and lose it all on Maruja. There is enough of the old Spanish jealousy in the blood to make even the gentle Amita never forgive his momentary defection."

Something in his manner made the Scotchman think that

Raymond spoke from baleful experience. How else could this attractive young fellow, educated abroad and a rising man in his profession, have failed to profit by his contiguity to such advantages, and the fact of his being an evident favorite ?

" But with this opposition on the part of the relatives to any further alliances with your countrymen, why does our hostess expose her daughters to their fascinating influence ? " said the elder man, glancing at his companion. " The girls seem to have the usual American freedom."

" Perhaps they are therefore the less likely to give it up to the first man who asks them. But the Spanish duenna still survives in the family — the more awful because invisible. It 's a mysterious fact that as soon as a fellow becomes particularly attached to any one — except Maruja — he receives some intimation from Pereo."

" What ! the butler ? That Indian-looking fellow ? A servant ? "

" Pardon me — the major-domo. The old confidential servitor who stands in *loco parentis*. No one knows what he says. If the victim appeals to the mistress, she is indisposed ; you know she has such bad health. If in his madness he makes a confidante of Maruja, that finishes him."

" How ? "

" Why, he ends by transferring his young affections to her — with the usual result."

" Then you don't think our friend the Captain has had this confidential butler ask his intentions yet ? "

" I don't think it will be necessary," said the other dryly.

" Umph ! Meantime, the Captain has just vanished through yon shrubbery. I suppose that 's the end of the mysterious espionage you have discovered. No ! De'il take it ! but there 's that Frenchman popping out of the myrtle bush. How did the fellow get there ? And, bless me ! here 's our lassie, too ! "

She halted a few paces off

"Yes!" said Raymond in a changed voice, "it's Maruja!"

She had approached so noiselessly along the bank that bordered the veranda, gliding from pillar to pillar as she paused before each to search for some particular flower, that both men felt an uneasy consciousness. But she betrayed no indication of their presence by look or gesture. So absorbed and abstracted she seemed that, by a common instinct, they both drew nearer the window, and silently waited for her to pass or recognize them.

She halted a few paces off to fasten a flower in her girdle. A small youthful figure, in a pale yellow dress, lacking even the maturity of womanly outline. The full oval of her face, the straight line of her back, a slight boyishness in the contour of her hips, the infantine smallness of her sandaled feet and narrow hands, were all suggestive of fresh, innocent, amiable youth — and nothing more.

Forgetting himself, the elder man mischievously crushed his companion against the wall in mock virtuous indignation. "Eh, sir," he whispered, with an accent that broadened with his feelings. "Eh, but look at the puir wee lassie! Will ye no be ashamed o' yerself for putting the tricks of a Circe on sic a honest gentle bairn? Why, man, you'll be seein' the sign of a limb of Satan in a bit thing with the mother's milk not yet out of her! She a flirt, speerin' at men, with that modest downcast air? I'm ashamed of ye, Mister Raymond. She's only thinking of her breakfast, puir thing, and not of yon callant. Another sacrilegious word and I'll expose you to her. Have ye no pity on youth and innocence?"

"Let me up," groaned Raymond feebly, "and I'll tell you how old she is. Hush — she's looking."

The two men straightened themselves. She had, indeed, lifted her eyes towards the window. They were beautiful eyes, and charged with something more than their own beauty. With a deep brunette setting even to the darkened cornea, the pupils were blue as the sky above them. But they were lit with another intelligence. The soul of the Salem whaler looked out of the passion-darkened orbits of the mother, and was resistless.

She smiled recognition of the two men with sedate girlishness and a foreign inclination of the head over the flowers she was holding. Her straight, curveless mouth became suddenly charming with the parting of her lips over her white teeth, and left the impress of the smile in a lighting of the whole face even after it had passed. Then she moved away. At the same moment Garnier approached her.

" Come away, man, and have our walk," said the Scotchman, seizing Raymond's arm. " We'll not spoil that fellow's sport."

" No ; but she will, I fear. Look, Mr. Buchanan, if she has n't given him her flowers to carry to the house while she waits here for the Captain ! "

" Come away, scoffer ! " said Buchanan good humoredly, locking his arm in the young man's and dragging him from the veranda towards the avenue, " and keep your observations for breakfast."

CHAPTER II

In the mean time, the young officer, who had disappeared in the shrubbery, whether he had or had not been a spectator of the scene, exhibited some signs of agitation. He walked rapidly on, occasionally switching the air with a wand of willow, from which he had impatiently plucked the leaves, through an alley of ceanothus, until he reached a little thicket of evergreens, which seemed to oppose his further progress. Turning to one side, however, he quickly found an entrance to a labyrinthine walk, which led him at last to an open space and a rustic summer-house that stood beneath a gnarled and venerable pear-tree. The summer-house was a quaint stockade of dark madroño boughs thatched with redwood bark, strongly suggestive of deeper woodland shadow. But in strange contrast, the floor, table, and benches were thickly strewn with faded rose leaves, scattered as if in some riotous play of children. Captain Carroll brushed them aside hurriedly with his impatient foot, glanced around hastily, then threw himself on the rustic bench at full length, and twisted his mustache between his nervous fingers. Then he rose as suddenly, with a few white petals impaled on his gilded spurs, and stepped quickly into the open sunlight.

He must have been mistaken! Everything was quiet around him, the far-off sound of wheels in the avenue came faintly, but nothing more.

His eye fell upon the pear-tree, and even in his preoccupation he was struck with the signs of its extraordinary age. Twisted out of all proportion, and knotted with ex-

crescences, it was supported by iron bands and heavy stakes,
as if to prop up its senile decay. He tried to interest himself in the various initials and symbols deeply carved in
bark, now swollen and half obliterated. As he turned
back to the summer-house, he for the first time noticed that
the ground rose behind it into a long undulation, on the
crest of which the same singular profusion of rose leaves
was scattered. It struck him as being strangely like a
gigantic grave, and that the same idea had occurred to the
fantastic dispenser of the withered flowers. He was still
looking at it, when a rustle in the undergrowth made his
heart beat expectantly. A slinking gray shadow crossed
the undulation and disappeared in the thicket. It was a
coyote. At any other time the extraordinary appearance
of this vivid impersonation of the wilderness, so near a
centre of human civilization and habitation, would have
filled him with wonder. But he had room for only a single
thought now. Would *she* come?

Five minutes passed. He no longer waited in the summer-house, but paced impatiently before the entrance to
the labyrinth. Another five minutes. He was deceived,
undoubtedly. She and her sisters were probably waiting
for him and laughing at him on the lawn. He ground his
heel into the clover, and threw his switch into the thicket.
Yet he would give her *one* — only one moment more.

"Captain Carroll!"

The voice had been and was to *him* the sweetest in the
world; but even a stranger could not have resisted the
spell of its musical inflection. He turned quickly. She
was advancing towards him from the summer-house.

"Did you think I was coming that way — where everybody could follow me?" she laughed softly. "No; I
came through the thicket over there," indicating the direction with her flexible shoulder, "and nearly lost my slipper and my eyes — look!" She threw back the insepara-

ble lace shawl from her blonde head, and showed a spray of myrtle clinging like a broken wreath to her forehead. The young officer remained gazing at her silently.

"I like to hear you speak my name," he said, with a slight hesitation in his breath. "Say it again."

"Car-roll, Car-roll, Car-roll," she murmured gently to herself two or three times, as if enjoying her own native trilling of the r's. "It's a pretty name. It sounds like a song. Don Carroll, eh! El Capitan Don Carroll."

"But my first name is Henry," he said faintly.

"'Enry — that's not so good. Don Enrico will do. But El Capitan Carroll is best of all. I must have it always: El Capitan Carroll!"

"Always?" He colored like a boy.

"Why not?" He was confusedly trying to look through her brown lashes; she was parrying him with the steel of her father's glance. "Come! Well! Captain Carroll! It was not to tell me your name — that I knew already was pretty — Car-roll!" she murmured again, caressing him with her lashes; "it was not for this that you asked me to meet you face to face in this — cold" — she made a movement of drawing her lace over her shoulders — "cold daylight. That belonged to the lights and the dance and the music of last night. It is not for this you expect me to leave my guests, to run away from Monsieur Garnier, who pays compliments, but whose name is not pretty — from Mr. Raymond, who talks *of* me when he can't talk *to* me. They will say This Captain Carroll could say all that before them."

"But if they knew," said the young officer, drawing closer to her with a paling face but brightening eyes, "if they knew I had anything else to say, Miss Saltonstall — something — pardon me — did I hurt your hand? — something for *her* alone — is there one of them that would have the right to object? Do not think me foolish, Miss Saltonstall — but — I beg — I implore you to tell me before I say more."

" Who would have a right ? " said Maruja, withdrawing
her hand but not her dangerous eyes. " Who would dare
forbid you talking to me of my sister ? I have told you
that Amita is free — as we all are."

Captain Carroll fell back a few steps and gazed at her with
a troubled face. " Is it possible that you have misunderstood,
Miss Saltonstall ? " he faltered. " Do you still think it is
Amita that I " — He stopped, and added passionately, " Do
you remember what I told you ? — have you forgotten last
night ? "

" Last night was — last night ! " said Maruja, slightly
lifting her shoulders. " One makes love at night — one
marries in daylight. In the music, in the flowers, in the
moonlight, one says everything ; in the morning one has
breakfast — when one is not asked to have councils of war
with captains and commandantes. You would speak of my
sister, Captain Car-roll — go on. Doña Amita Carroll sounds
very, very pretty. I shall not object." She held out both
her hands to him, threw her head back, and smiled.

He seized her hands passionately. " No, no ! you shall
hear me — you shall understand me. I love *you*, Maruja
— you, and you alone. God knows I would not help it if
I could. Hear me. I will be calm. No one can hear us
where we stand. I am not mad. I am not a traitor ! I
frankly admired your sister. I came here to see her. Beyond that, I swear to you, I am guiltless to her — to you.
Even she knows no more of me than that. I saw you, Maruja. From that moment I have thought of nothing —
dreamed of nothing else."

" That is — three, four, five days and one afternoon ago !
You see I remember. And now you want — what ? "

" To let me love you, and you only. To let me be with
you. To let me win you in time, as you should be won.
I am not mad, though I am desperate. I know what is due
to your station and mine — even while I dare to say I love
you. Let me hope, Maruja, I only ask to hope."

She looked at him until she had absorbed all the burning fever of his eyes, until her ears tingled with his passionate voice, and then — she shook her head.

"It cannot be, Carroll — no ! never ! "

He drew himself up under the blow with such simple and manly dignity that her eyes dropped for the moment. "There is another, then ? " he said sadly.

"There is no one I care for better than you. No ! Do not be foolish. Let me go. I tell you that because you can be nothing to me — you understand, to *me*. To my sister Amita, yes."

The young soldier raised his head coldly. "I have pressed you hard, Miss Saltonstall — too hard, I know, for a man who has already had his answer ; but I did not deserve this. Good-by."

"Stop," she said gently. "I meant not to hurt you, Captain Carroll. If I had, it is not thus I would have done. I need not have met you here. Would you have loved me the less if I had avoided this meeting ? "

He could not reply. In the depths of his miserable heart, he knew that he would have loved her the same.

"Come," she said, laying her hand softly on his arm, "do not be angry with me for putting you back only five days to where you were when you first entered our house. Five days is not much of happiness or sorrow to forget, is it, Carroll — Captain Carroll ? " Her voice died away in a faint sigh. "Do not be angry with me, if — knowing you could be nothing more — I wanted you to love my sister, and my sister to love you. We should have been good friends — such good friends."

"Why do you say, 'Knowing it could be nothing more' ? " said Carroll, grasping her hand suddenly. "In the name of Heaven, tell me what you mean ! "

"I mean I cannot marry unless I marry one of my mother's race. That is my mother's wish, and the will of her relations.   You are an American, not of Spanish blood."

"But surely this is not your determination?"

She shrugged her shoulders.   "What would you?   It is the determination of my people."

"But knowing this" — he stopped; the quick blood rose to his face.

"Go on, Captain Carroll.   You would say, Knowing this, why did I not warn you?   Why did I not say to you when we first met, 'You have come to address my sister; do not fall in love with me — I cannot marry a foreigner.'"

"You are cruel, Maruja.   But, if that is all, surely this prejudice can be removed?   Why, your mother married a foreigner — an American."

"Perhaps that is why," said the girl quietly.   She cast down her long lashes, and with the point of her satin slipper smoothed out the soft leaves of the clover at her feet.   "Listen; shall I tell you the story of our house? Stop! some one is coming.   Don't move; remain as you are.   If you care for me, Carroll, collect yourself, and don't let that man think he has found *us* ridiculous."   Her voice changed from its tone of slight caressing pleading to one of suppressed pride.   "*He* will not laugh much, Captain Carroll; truly, no."

The figure of Garnier, bright, self-possessed, courteous, appeared at the opening of the labyrinth.   Too well-bred to suggest, even in complimentary raillery, a possible sentimental situation, his politeness went further.   It was so kind in them to guide an awkward stranger by their voices to the places where he could not stupidly intrude!

"You are just in time to interrupt or to hear a story that I have been threatening to tell," she said composedly; "an old Spanish legend of this house.   You are in the majority now, you two, and can stop me if you choose. Thank you.   I warn you it is stupid; it isn't new; but

it has the excuse of being suggested by this very spot."
She cast a quick look of subtle meaning at Carroll, and
throughout her recital appealed more directly to him, in a
manner delicately yet sufficiently marked to partly soothe
his troubled spirit.

"Far back, in the very old times, Caballeros," said
Maruja, standing by the table in mock solemnity, and rapping upon it with her fan, "this place was the home of
the coyote. Big and little, father and mother, Señor and
Señora Coyotes, and the little muchacho coyotes had their
home in the dark cañada, and came out over these fields,
yellow with wild oats and red with poppies, to seek their
prey. They were happy. For why? They were the
first; they had no history, you comprehend, no tradition.
They married as they liked" (with a glance at Carroll),
"nobody objected; they increased and multiplied. But
the plains were fertile; the game was plentiful; it was
not fit that it should be for the beasts alone. And so, in
the course of time, an Indian chief, a heathen, Koorotora,
built his wigwam here."

"I beg your pardon," said Garnier in apparent distress,
"but I caught the gentleman's name imperfectly."

Fully aware that the questioner only wished to hear
again her musical enunciation of the consonants, she repeated "Koorotora," with an apologetic glance at Carroll,
and went on. "This gentleman had no history or tradition to bother him, either; whatever Señor Coyote thought
of the matter, he contented himself with robbing Señor
Koorotora's wigwam when he could, and skulking around
the Indian's camp at night. The old chief prospered, and
made many journeys round the country, but always kept
his camp here. This lasted until the time when the holy
Fathers came from the South, and Portala, as you have all
read, uplifted the wooden Cross on the seacoast over there,
and left it for the heathens to wonder at. Koorotora saw

it on one of his journeys, and came back to the cañada full of this wonder. Now, Koorotora had a wife."

"Ah, we shall commence now. We are at the beginning. This is better than Señora Coyota," said Garnier cheerfully.

"Naturally, she was anxious to see the wonderful object. She saw it, and she saw the holy Fathers, and they converted her against the superstitious heathenish wishes of her husband. And more than that, they came here " —

"And converted the land also; is it not so? It was a lovely site for a mission," interpolated Garnier politely.

"They built a mission and brought as many of Koorotora's people as they could into the sacred fold. They brought them in in a queer fashion sometimes, it is said; dragoons from the Presidio, Captain Carroll, lassoing them and bringing them in at the tails of their horses. All except Koorotora. He defied them; he cursed them and his wife in his wicked heathenish fashion, and said that they too should lose the mission through the treachery of some woman, and that the coyote should yet prowl through the ruined walls of the church. The holy Fathers pitied the wicked man — and built themselves a lovely garden. Look at that pear-tree! There is all that is left of it!"

She turned with a mock heroic gesture, and pointed her fan to the pear-tree. Garnier lifted his hands in equally simulated wonder. A sudden recollection of the coyote of the morning recurred to Carroll uneasily. "And the Indians," he said, with an effort to shake off the feeling; "they, too, have vanished."

"All that remained of them is in yonder mound. It is the grave of the chief and his people. He never lived to see the fulfillment of his prophecy. For it was a year after his death that our ancestor, Manuel Guitierrez, came from old Spain to the Presidio with a grant of twenty leagues to settle where he chose. Doña Maria Guitierrez took a fancy to the cañada. But it was a site already in possession of the Holy Church. One night, through treachery, it was said, the guards were withdrawn and the Indians entered the mission, slaughtered the lay brethren, and drove away the priests. The Commandant at the Presidio retook the place from the heathen, but on representation to the Governor that it was indefensible for the peaceful Fathers without a large military guard, the official ordered the removal of the mission to Santa Cruz, and Don Manuel settled his twenty leagues grant in the cañada. Whether he or Doña Maria had anything to do with the Indian uprising, no one knows; but Father Pedro never forgave them. He is said to have declared at the foot of the altar that the curse of the Church was on the land, and that it should always pass into the hands of the stranger."

"And that was long ago, and the property is still in the family," said Carroll hurriedly, answering Maruja's eyes.

"In the last hundred years there have been no male heirs," continued Maruja, still regarding Carroll. "When my mother, who was the eldest daughter, married Don José Saltonstall against the wishes of the family, it was said that the curse would fall. Sure enough, Caballeros, it was that year that the forged grants of Micheltorrena were discovered; and in our lawsuit your government, Captain, handed over ten leagues of the llano land to the Dr. West, our neighbor."

"Ah, the gray-headed gentleman who lunched here the other day? You are friends, then? You bear no malice?" said Garnier.

"What would you?" said Maruja, with a slight shrug of her shoulders. "He paid his money to the forger. Your corregidores upheld him, and said it was no forgery," she continued, to Carroll.

In spite of the implied reproach, Carroll felt relieved. He began to be impatient of Garnier's presence, and longed

to renew his suit.   Perhaps his face showed something of
this, for Maruja added, with mock demureness, "It's always
dreadful to be the eldest sister ; but think what it is to be
in the direct line of a curse ! Now, there's Amita — *she's*
free to do as she likes, with no family responsibility; while
poor me ! "   She dropped her eyes, but not until they had
again sought and half reproved the brightening eyes of
Carroll.

"But," said Garnier, with a sudden change from his easy
security and courteous indifference to an almost harsh impatience, "you do not mean to say, Mademoiselle, that you have
the least belief in this rubbish, this ridiculous canard ? "

Maruja's straight mouth quickly tightened over her
teeth.   She shot a significant glance at Carroll, but instantly resumed her former manner.

"It matters little what a foolish girl like myself believes.
The rest of the family, even the servants and children, all
believe it.   It is a part of their religion.   Look at these
flowers around the pear-tree, and scattered on that Indian
mound.   They regularly find their way there on saints'
days and festas.   *They* are not rubbish, Monsieur Garnier ;
they are propitiatory sacrifices.   Pereo would believe that a
temblor would swallow up the casa if we should ever forego
these customary rites.   Is it a mere absurdity that forced
my father to build these modern additions around the heart
of the old adobe house, leaving it untouched, so that the
curse might not be fulfilled even by implication ? "

She had assumed an air of such pretty earnestness and
passion ; her satin face was illuminated as by some softly
sensuous light within, more bewildering than mere color,
that Garnier, all devoted eyes and courteous blandishment,
broke out : "But this curse must fall harmlessly before the
incarnation of blessing ; Miss Saltonstall has no more to
fear than the angels.   She is the one predestined through
her charm, through her goodness, to lift it forever."

Carroll could not have helped echoing the aspirations of his rival, had not the next words of his mistress thrilled him with superstitious terror.

" A thousand thanks, Señor. Who knows? But I shall have warning when it falls. A day or two before the awful invader arrives, a coyote suddenly appears in broad daylight mysteriously, near the casa. This midnight marauder, now banished to the thickest cañon, comes again to prowl around the home of his ancestors. Caramba! Señor Captain, what are you staring at? You frighten me! Stop it, I say ! "

She had turned upon him, stamping her little foot in quite a frightened, childlike way.

" Nothing," laughed Carroll, the quick blood returning to his cheek. " But you must not be angry with one for being quite carried away with your dramatic intensity. By Jove! I thought I could see the *whole* thing while you were speaking — the old Indian, the priest, and the coyote ! " His eyes sparkled. The wild thought had occurred to him that perhaps, in spite of himself, he was the young woman's predestined fate; and in the very selfishness of his passion he smiled at the mere material loss of lands and prestige that would follow it. " Then the coyote has always preceded some change in the family fortunes ? " he asked boldly.

" On my mother's wedding-day," said Maurja in a lower voice, "after the party had come from church to supper in the casa, my father asked, 'What dog is that under the table ? ' When they lifted the cloth to look, a coyote rushed from the very midst of the guests and dashed out across the patio. No one knew how or when he entered."

" Heaven grant that we do not find he has eaten our breakfast ! " said Garnier gayly, " for I judge it is waiting us. I hear your sister's voice among the others crossing the lawn. Shall we tear ourselves away from the tombs of our ancestors, and join them ? "

"Not as I am looking now, thank you," said Maruja, throwing the lace over her head. "I shall not submit myself to a comparison of their fresher faces and toilets by you two gentlemen. Go you both and join them. I shall wait and say an Ave for the soul of Koorotora, and slip back alone the way I came."

She had steadily evaded the pleading glance of Carroll, and though her bright face and unblemished toilet showed the inefficiency of her excuse, it was evident that her wish to be alone was genuine and without coquetry. They could only lift their hats and turn regretfully away.

As the red cap of the young officer disappeared amidst the evergreen foliage, the young woman uttered a faint sigh, which she repeated a moment after as a slight nervous yawn. Then she opened and shut her fan once or twice, striking the sticks against her little pale palm, and then, gathering the lace under her oval chin with one hand, and catching her fan and skirt with the other, bent her head and dipped into the bushes. She came out on the other side near a low fence, that separated the park from a narrow lane which communicated with the highroad beyond. As she neared the fence, a slinking figure limped along the lane before her. It was the tramp of the early morning.

They raised their heads at the same moment and their eyes met. The tramp, in that clearer light, showed a spare, but bent figure, roughly clad in a miner's shirt and canvas trousers, splashed and streaked with soil, and half hidden in a ragged blue cast-off army overcoat lazily hanging from one shoulder. His thin sunburnt face was not without a certain sullen, suspicious intelligence, and a look of half-sneering defiance. He stopped, as a startled, surly animal might have stopped at some unusual object, but did not exhibit any other discomposure. Maruja stopped at the same moment on her side of the fence.

The tramp looked at her deliberately, and then slowly

lowered his eyes. "I'm looking for the San José road, hereabouts. Ye don't happen to know it?" he said, addressing himself to the top of the fence.

It had been said that it was not Maruja's way to encounter man, woman, or child, old or young, without an attempt at subjugation. Strong in her power and salient with fascination, she leaned gently over the fence, and with the fan raised to her delicate ear, made him repeat his question under the soft fire of her fringed eyes. He did so, but incompletely, and with querulous laziness.

"Lookin'—for—San José road—here'bouts."

"The road to San José," said Maruja, with gentle slowness, as if not unwilling to protract the conversation, "is about two miles from here. It is the highroad to the left fronting the plain. There is another way, if"—

"Don't want it! Mornin'."

He dropped his head suddenly forward, and limped away in the sunlight.

CHAPTER III

BREAKFAST, usually a movable feast at La Mision Perdida, had been prolonged until past midday; the last of
the dance guests had flown, and the home party — with the
exception of Captain Carroll, who had returned to duty at
his distant post — were dispersing; some as riding caval-
cades to neighboring points of interest; some to visit certain
notable mansions which the wealth of a rapid civilization
had erected in that fertile valley. One of these in particular, the work of a breathless millionaire, was famous for the
spontaneity of its growth and the reckless extravagance of
its appointments.

"If you go to Aladdin's Palace," said Maruja, from the
top step of the south porch, to a wagonette of guests,
"after you 've seen the stables with mahogany fittings for
one hundred horses, ask Aladdin to show you the enchanted
chamber, inlaid with California woods and paved with gold
quartz."

"We would have a better chance if the Princess of China
would only go with us," pleaded Garnier gallantly.

"The Princess will stay at home with her mother, like a
good girl," returned Maruja demurely.

"A bad shot of Garnier's this time," whispered Raymond to Buchanan, as the vehicle rolled away with them.
"The Princess is not likely to visit Aladdin again."

"Why ? "

"The last time she was there, Aladdin was a little too
Persian in his extravagance; offered her his house, stables,
and himself."

" Not a bad catch; why, he 's worth two millions, I hear."

" Yes ; but his wife is as extravagant as himself."

" His *wife*, eh ?   Ah, are you serious; or must you say something derogatory of the lassie's admirers too ? " said Buchanan, playfully threatening him with his cane.   " Another word, and I 'll throw you from the wagon."

After their departure, the outer shell of the great house fell into a profound silence, so hollow and deserted that one might have thought the curse of Koorotora had already descended upon it.   Dead leaves of roses and fallen blossoms from the long line of vine-wreathed columns lay thick on the empty stretch of brown veranda, or rustled and crept against the sides of the house, where the regular breath of the afternoon " trades " began to arise.   A few cardinal flowers fell like drops of blood before the open windows of the vacant ballroom, in which the step of a solitary servant echoed faintly.   It was Maruja's maid, bringing a note to her young mistress, who, in a flounced morning dress, leaned against the window.   Maruja took it, glanced at it quietly, folded it in a long fold, and put it openly in her belt. Captain Carroll, from whom it came, might have carried one of his dispatches as methodically.   The waiting-woman noticed the act, and was moved to suggest some more exciting confidences.

" The Doña Maruja has, without doubt, noticed the bouquet on her dressing-room table from the Señor Garnier ? "

The Doña Maruja had. The Doña Maruja had also learned with pain that, bribed by Judas-like coin, Faquita had betrayed the secrets of her wardrobe to the extent of furnishing a ribbon from a certain yellow dress to the Señor Buchanan to match with a Chinese fan.   This was intolerable !

Faquita writhed in remorse, and averred that through this solitary act she had dishonored her family.

The Doña Maruja, however, since it was so, felt that the

only thing left to do was to give her the polluted dress, and
trust that the Devil might not fly away with her.

Leaving the perfectly consoled Faquita, Maruja crossed
the large hall, and, opening a small door, entered a dark
passage through the thick adobe wall of the old casa, and
apparently left the present century behind her.   A peaceful
atmosphere of the past surrounded her not only in the low
vaulted halls terminating in grilles or barred windows; not
only in the square chambers whose dark, rich, but scanty
furniture was only a foil to the central elegance of the lace-
bordered bed and pillows; but in a certain mysterious odor
of dried and desiccated religious respectability that penetrated
everywhere, and made the grateful twilight redolent of the
generations of forgotten Guitierrez who had quietly exhaled
in the old house.   A mist as of incense and flowers that had
lost their first bloom veiled the vista of the long corridor,
and made the staring blue sky, seen through narrow windows
and loopholes, glitter like mirrors let into the walls.   The
chamber assigned to the young ladies seemed half oratory
and half sleeping-room, with a strange mingling of the con-
vent in the bare white walls, hung only with crucifixes and
religious emblems, and of the seraglio in the glimpses of
lazy figures, reclining in the deshabille of short silken saya,
low camisa, and dropping slippers.   In a broad angle of the
corridor giving upon the patio, its balustrade hung with
brightly colored serapes and shawls, surrounded by voluble
domestics and relations, the mistress of the casa half reclined
in a hammock and gave her noonday audience.

Maruja pushed her way through the clustered stools and
cushions to her mother's side, kissed her on the forehead,
and then lightly perched herself like a white dove on the
railing.   Mrs. Saltonstall, a dark, corpulent woman, redeemed
only from coarseness by a certain softness of expression and
refinement of gesture, raised her heavy brown eyes to her
daughter's face.

"You have not been to bed, Mara?"

"No, dear. Do I look it?"

"You must lie down presently. They tell me that Captain Carroll returned suddenly this morning."

"Do you care?"

"Who knows? Amita does not seem to fancy José, Estéban, Jorge, or any of her cousins. She won't look at Juan Estudillo. The Captain is not bad. He is of the government. He is" —

"Not more than ten leagues from here," said Maruja, playing with the Captain's note in her belt. "You can send for him, dear little mother. He will be glad."

"You will ever talk lightly — like your father! She was not then grieved — our Amita — eh?"

"She and Dorotea and the two Wilsons went off with Raymond and your Scotch friend in the wagonette. She did not cry — to Raymond."

"Good," said Mrs. Saltonstall, leaning back in her hammock. "Raymond is an old friend. You had better take your siesta now, child, to be bright for dinner. I expect a visitor this afternoon — Dr. West."

"Again! What will Pereo say, little mother?"

"Pereo," said the widow, sitting up again in her hammock, with impatience, "Pereo is becoming intolerable. The man is as mad as Don Quixote; it is impossible to conceal his eccentric impertinence and interference from strangers, who cannot understand his confidential position in our house or his long service. There are no more major-domos, child. The Vallejos, the Briones, the Castros, do without them now. Dr. West says, wisely, they are ridiculous survivals of the patriarchal system."

"And can be replaced by intelligent strangers," interrupted Maruja demurely.

"The more easily if the patriarchal system has not been able to preserve the respect due from children to parents.

No, Maruja! No; I am offended. Do not touch me! And your hair is coming down, and your eyes have rings like owls. You uphold this fanatical Pereo because he leaves *you* alone and stalks your poor sisters and their escorts like the Indian, whose blood is in his veins. The saints only can tell if he did not disgust this Captain Carroll into flight. He believes himself the sole custodian of the honor of our family — that he has a sacred mission from this Don Fulano of Koorotora to avert its fate. Without doubt he keeps up his delusions with aguardiente, and passes for a prophet among the silly peons and servants. He frightens the children with his ridiculous stories and teaches them to decorate that heathen mound as if it were a shrine of Our Lady of Sorrows. He was almost rude to Dr. West yesterday."

"But you have encouraged him in his confidential position here," said Maruja. "You forget, my mother, how you got him to 'dueña' Enriqueta with the Colonel Brown; how you let him frighten the young Englishman who was too attentive to Dorotea; how you set him even upon poor Raymond, and failed so dismally that I had to take him myself in hand."

"But if I choose to charge him with explanations that I cannot make myself without derogating from the time-honored hospitality of the casa, that is another thing. It is not," said Doña Maria, with a certain massive dignity, that, inconsistent as it was with the weakness of her argument, was not without impressiveness, "it is not yet, Blessed Santa Maria, that we are obliged to take notice ourself of the pretensions of every guest beneath our roof like the match-making, daughter-selling English and Americans. And *then* Pereo had tact and discrimination. Now he is mad! There are strangers and strangers. The whole valley is full of them — one can discriminate, since the old families year by year are growing less."

" Surely not," said Maruja innocently. " There is the excellent Ramierrez, who has lately almost taken him a wife from the singing-hall in San Francisco ; he may yet be snatched from the fire. There is the youthful José Castro, the sole padroño of our national bull-fight at Soquel, the famous horse-breaker, and the winner of I know not how many races. And have we not Vincente Peralta, who will run, it is said, for the American Congress. He can read and write — truly I have a letter from him here." She turned back the folded slip of Captain Carroll's note and discovered another below.

Mrs. Saltonstall tapped her daughter's hand with her fan. " You jest at them, yet you uphold Pereo ! Go, now, and sleep yourself into a better frame of mind. Stop ! I hear the Doctor's horse. Run and see that Pereo receives him properly."

Maruja had barely entered the dark corridor when she came upon the visitor, — a gray, hard-featured man of sixty, — who had evidently entered without ceremony. " I see you did not wait to be announced," she said sweetly. " My mother will be flattered by your impatience. You will find her in the patio."

" Pereo did not announce me, as he was probably still under the effect of the aguardiente he swallowed yesterday," said the Doctor dryly. " I met him outside the tienda on the highway the other night, talking to a pair of cut-throats that I would shoot on sight."

" The major-domo has many purchases to make, and must meet a great many people," said Maruja. " What would you ? We cannot select *his* acquaintances ; we can hardly choose our own," she added sweetly.

The Doctor hesitated, as if to reply, and then, with a grim " good-morning," passed on towards the patio. Maruja did not follow him. Her attention was suddenly absorbed by a hitherto unnoticed motionless figure, that

seemed to be hiding in the shadow of an angle of the passage, as if waiting for her to pass. The keen eyes of the
daughter of Joseph Saltonstall were not deceived. She
walked directly towards the figure, and said sharply,
" Pereo ! "

The figure came hesitatingly forward into the light of
the grated window. It was that of an old man, still tall
and erect, though the hair had disappeared from his temples, and hung in two or three straight, long dark elf-locks
on his neck. His face, over which one of the bars threw
a sinister shadow, was the yellow of a dried tobacco-leaf,
and veined as strongly. His garb was a strange mingling
of the vaquero and the ecclesiastic — velvet trousers, open
from the knee down, and fringed with bullion buttons ; a
broad red sash around his waist, partly hidden by a long,
straight chaqueta ; with a circular sacerdotal cape of black
broadcloth slipped over his head through a slitlike opening braided with gold. His restless yellow eyes fell before
the young girl's ; and the stiff, varnished, hard-brimmed
sombrero he held in his wrinkled hands trembled.

" You are spying again, Pereo," said Maruja in another
dialect than the one she had used to her mother. " It is
unworthy of my father's trusted servant."

" It is that man — that coyote, Doña Maruja, that is
unworthy of your father, of your mother, of *you !* " he
gesticulated in a fierce whisper. " I, Pereo, do not spy.
I follow, follow the track of the prowling, stealing brute
until I run him down. Yes, it was *I*, Pereo, who warned
your father he would not be content with the half of the
land he stole ! It was I, Pereo, who warned your mother
that each time he trod the soil of La Mision Perdida he
measured the land he could take away ! " He stopped
pantingly, with the insane abstraction of a fixed idea glittering in his eyes.

" And it was *you*, Pereo," she said caressingly, laying

her soft hand on his heaving breast, "*you* who carried me in your arms when I was a child. It was you, Pereo, who took me before you on your pinto horse to the rodeo, when no one knew it but ourselves, my Pereo, was it not?" He nodded his head violently. "It was you who showed me the gallant caballeros, the Pachecos, the Castros, the Alvarados, the Estudillos, the Peraltas, the Vallejos." His head kept time with each name as the fire dimmed in his wet eyes. "You made me promise I would not forget them for the Americanos who were here. Good! That was years ago! I am older now. I have seen many Americans. Well, I am still free!"

He caught her hand, and raised it to his lips with a gesture almost devotional. His eyes softened; as the exaltation of passion passed, his voice dropped into the querulousness of privileged age. "Ah, yes! — you, the first-born, the heiress — of a verity, yes! You were ever a Guitierrez. But the others? Eh, where are they now? And it was always: 'Eh, Pereo, what shall we do to-day? Pereo, good Pereo, we are asked to ride here and there; we are expected to visit the new people in the valley — what say you, Pereo? Who shall we dine to-day?' Or: 'Inquire me of this or that strange caballero — and if we may speak.' Ah, it is but yesterday that Amita would say: 'Lend me thine own horse, Pereo, that I may outstrip this swaggering Americano that clings ever to my side,' ha! ha! Or the grave Dorotea would whisper: 'Convey to this Señor Presumptuous Pomposo that the daughters of Guitierrez do not ride alone with strangers!' Or even the little Liseta would say, he! he! 'Why does the stranger press my foot in his great hand when he helps me into the saddle? Tell him that is not the way, Pereo.' Ha! ha!" He laughed childishly, and stopped. "And why does Señorita Amita now — look — complain that Pereo, old Pereo, comes between her and this Señor Raymond — the maquinista? Eh,

and why does *she*, the lady mother, the Castellaña, shut
Pereo from her councils ? " he went on, with rising excitement. " What are these secret meetings, eh ? — what these
appointments, alone with this Judas — without the family
— without *me !* "

" Hearken, Pereo," said the young girl, again laying her
hand on the old man's shoulder ; " you have spoken truly
— but you forget — the years pass. These are no longer
strangers ; old friends have gone — these have taken their
place. My father forgave the Doctor — why cannot you ?
For the rest, believe in me — me — Maruja "— she dra-
matically touched her heart over the international complications of the letters of Captain Carroll and Peralta. " I
will see that the family honor does not suffer. And now,
good Pereo, calm thyself. Not with aguardiente, but with
a bottle of old wine from the Mision refectory that I will
send to thee. It was given to me by thy friend, Padre
Miguel, and is from the old vines that were here. Courage,
Pereo ! And thou sayest that Amita complains that thou
comest between her and Raymond. So ! What matter ?
Let it cheer thy heart to know that I have summoned the
Peraltas, the Pachecos, the Estudillos, all thy old friends,
to dine here to-day. Thou wilt hear the old names, even
if the faces are young to thee. Courage ! Do thy duty,
old friend ; let them see that the hospitality of La Mision
Perdida does not grow old, if its major-domo does.
Faquita will bring thee the wine. No; not *that* way;
thou needest not pass the patio, nor meet that man again.
Here, give me thy hand, I will lead thee. It trembles,
Pereo ! These are not the sinews that only two years ago
pulled down the bull at Soquel with thy single lasso !
Why, look ! I can drag thee ; see ! " and with a light
laugh and a boyish gesture, she half pulled, half dragged
him along, until their voices were lost in the dark corridor.

Maruja kept her word. When the sun began to cast

long shadows along the veranda, not only the outer shell of La Mision Perdida, but the dark inner heart of the old casa, stirred with awakened life. Single horsemen and carriages began to arrive; and mingled with the modern turnouts of the home party and the neighboring Americans were a few of the cumbrous vehicles and chariots of fifty years ago, drawn by gayly trapped mules with bizarre postilions, and occasionally an outrider. Dark faces looked from the balcony of the patio, a light cloud of cigarette-smoke made the dark corridors the more obscure, and mingled with the forgotten incense. Bare-headed pretty women, with roses starring their dark hair, wandered with childish curiosity along the broad veranda and in and out of the French windows that opened upon the grand saloon. Scrupulously shaved men with olive complexion, stout men with accurately curving whiskers meeting at their dimpled chins, lounged about with a certain unconscious dignity that made them contentedly indifferent to any novelty of their surroundings. For a while the two races kept mechanically apart; but, through the tactful gallantry of Garnier, the cynical familiarity of Raymond, and the impulsive recklessness of Aladdin, who had forsaken his enchanted Palace on the slightest of invitations, and returned with the party in the hope of again seeing the Princess of China, an interchange of civilities, of gallantries, and even of confidences, at last took place. Jovita Castro had heard (who had not ?) of the wonders of Aladdin's Palace, and was it of actual truth that the ladies had a bouquet and a fan to match their dress presented to them every morning, and that the gentlemen had a champagne cocktail sent to their rooms before breakfast ? "Just you come, Miss, and bring your father and your brothers, and stay a week and you 'll see," responded Aladdin gallantly. "Hold on! What 's your father's first name ? I 'll send a team over there for you to-morrow." "And is it true that you frightened the handsome Captain

Carroll away from Amita ? " said Dolores Briones, over the edge of her fan to Raymond. " Perfectly," said Raymond, with ingenuous frankness. " I made it a matter of life or death. He was a soldier, and naturally preferred the former as giving him a better chance for promotion." " Ah ! we thought it was Maruja you liked best." " That was two years ago," said Raymond gravely. " And you Americanos can change in that time ? " " I have just experienced that it can be done in less," he responded, over the fan, with bewildering significance. Nor were these confidences confined to only one nationality. " I always thought you Spanish gentlemen were very dark, and wore long mustaches and a cloak," said pretty little Miss Walker, gazing frankly into the smooth round face of the eldest Pacheco — " why, you are as fair as I am." " Eaf I tink that, I am forever mizzarable," he replied, with grave melancholy. In the dead silence that followed he was enabled to make his decorous point. " Because I shall not ezcape ze fate of Narcissus." Mr. Buchanan, with the unrestrained and irresponsible enjoyment of a traveler, entered fully into the spirit of the scene. He even found words of praise for Aladdin, whose extravagance had at first seemed to him almost impious. " Eh, but I 'm not prepared to say he is a fool, either," he remarked to his friend, the San Francisco banker. " Those who try to pick him up for one," returned the banker, " will find themselves mistaken. His is the prodigality that loosens others' purse-strings besides his own. Everybody contents himself with criticising his way of spending money, but is ready to follow his way of making it."

The dinner was more formal, and when the mistress of the house, massive in black silk, velvet and gold embroidery, moved like a pageant to the head of her table, where she remained like a sacerdotal effigy, not even the presence of the practical Scotchman at her side could remove the prevailing sense of restraint. For a while the conversation of the relatives might have been brought with them in their antique vehicles of fifty years ago, so faded, so worn, and so springless it was. General Pico related the festivities at Monterey, on the occasion of the visit of Sir George Simpson early in the present century, of which he was an eye-witness, with great precision of detail. Don Juan Estudillo was comparatively frivolous, with anecdotes of Louis Philippe, whom he had seen in Paris. Far-seeing Pedro Guitierrez was gloomily impressed with a Mongolian invasion of California by the Chinese, in which the prevailing religion would be supplanted by heathen temples, and polygamy engrafted on the Constitution. Everybody agreed, however, that the vital question of the hour was the settlement of land titles — Americans who claimed under preemption and the native holders of Spanish grants were equally of the opinion. In the midst of this the musical voice of Maruja was heard asking, " What is a tramp ? "

Raymond, on her right, was ready but not conclusive. A tramp, if he could sing, would be a troubadour ; if he could pray, would be a pilgrim friar — in either case a natural object of womanly solicitude. But as he could do neither, he was simply a curse.

" And you think that is not an object of womanly solicitude ? But that does not tell me *what* he is."

A dozen gentlemen, swept in the radius of those softly inquiring eyes, here started to explain. From them it appeared that there was no such thing in California as a tramp, and there were also a dozen varieties of tramp in California.

" But is he always very uncivil ? " asked Maruja.

Again there were conflicting opinions. You might have to shoot him on sight, and you might have him invariably run from you. When the question was finally settled, Maruja was found to have become absorbed in conversation with some one else.

Amita, a taller copy of Maruja, and more regularly beautiful, had built up a little pile of bread crumbs between
herself and Raymond, and was listening to him with a certain shy, girlish interest that was as inconsistent with the
serene regularity of her face as Maruja's self-possessed,
subtle intelligence was incongruous with her youthful figure.
Raymond's voice, when he addressed Amita, was low and
earnest; not from any significance of matter, but from its
frank confidential quality.

"They are discussing the new railroad project, and your
relations are all opposed to it; to-morrow they will each
apply privately to Aladdin for the privilege of subscribing.
I have never seen a railroad," said Amita, slightly coloring; "but you are an engineer, and I know they must be
something very clever."

Notwithstanding the coolness of the night, a full moon
drew the guests to the veranda, where coffee was served,
and where, mysteriously muffled in cloaks and shawls, the
party took upon itself the appearance of groups of dominoed
masqueraders, scattered along the veranda and on the broad
steps of the porch in gypsy-like encampments, from whose
cloaked shadow the moonlight occasionally glittered upon a
varnished boot or peeping satin slipper. Two or three of
these groups had resolved themselves into detached couples,
who wandered down the acacia walk to the sound of a harp
in the grand saloon or the occasional uplifting of a thin
Spanish tenor. Two of these couples were Maruja and
Garnier, followed by Amita and Raymond.

"You are restless to-night, Maruja," said Amita, shyly
endeavoring to make a show of keeping up with her sister's
boyish stride, in spite of Raymond's reluctance. "You are
paying for your wakefulness to-day."

The same idea passed through the minds of both men.
She was missing the excitement of Captain Carroll's presence.

"The air is so refreshing away from the house," responded Maruja, with a bright energy that belied any suggestion of fatigue or moral disquietude. "I'm tired of running against those turtle-doves in the walks and bushes. Let us keep on to the lane. If you are tired, Mr. Raymond will give you his arm."

They kept on, led by the indomitable little figure, who, for once, did not seem to linger over the attentions, both piquant and tender, with which Garnier improved his opportunity. Given a shadowy lane, a lovers' moon, a pair of bright and not unkindly eyes, a charming and not distant figure — what more could he want? Yet he wished she had n't walked so fast. One might be vivacious, audacious, brilliant, at an Indian trot; but impassioned — never! The pace increased; they were actually hurrying. More than that, Maruja had struck into a little trot; her lithe body swaying from side to side, her little feet straight as an arrow before her; accompanying herself with a quaint musical chant, which she obligingly explained had been taught her as a child by Pereo. They stopped only at the hedge, where she had that morning encountered the tramp.

There is little doubt that the rest of the party was disconcerted: Amita, whose figure was not adapted to this Camilla-like exercise; Raymond, who was annoyed at the poor girl's discomfiture; and Garnier, who had lost a golden opportunity, with the faint suspicion of having looked ridiculous. Only Maruja's eyes, or rather the eyes of her lamented father, seemed to enjoy it.

"You are too effeminate," she said, leaning against the fence, and shading her eyes with her fan, as she glanced around in the staring moonlight. "Civilization has taken away your legs. A man ought to be able to trust to his feet all day, and to nothing else."

"In fact — a tramp," suggested Raymond.

"Possibly. I think I should like to have been a gypsy,

and to have wandered about, finding a new home every
night."

"And a change of linen on the early morning hedges,"
said Raymond. "But do you think seriously that you and
your sister are suitably clad to commence to-night? It is
bitterly cold," he added, turning up his collar. "Could
you begin by showing a pal the nearest haystack or hen-
roost?"

"Sybarite!" She cast a long look over the fields and
down the lane. Suddenly she started. "What is that?"

She pointed to a tall erect figure slowly disappearing on
the other side of the hedge.

"It's Pereo, only Pereo. I knew him by his long
serape," said Garnier, who was nearest the hedge, compla-
cently. "But what is surprising, he was not there when
we came, nor did he come out of that open field. He must
have been walking behind us on the other side of the
hedge."

The eyes of the two girls sought each other simultaneously, but not without Raymond's observant glance.
Amita's brow darkened as she moved to her sister's side,
and took her arm with a confidential pressure that was
returned. The two men, with a vague consciousness of
some *contretemps*, dropped a pace behind, and began to
talk to each other, leaving the sisters to exchange a few
words in a low tone as they slowly returned to the house.

Meanwhile, Pereo's tall figure had disappeared in the
shrubbery, to emerge again in the open area by the summer-house and the old pear-tree. The red sparks of two
or three cigarettes in the shadow of the summer-house, and
the crouching forms of two shawled women came forward
to greet him.

"And what hast thou heard, Pereo?" said one of the
women.

"Nothing," said Pereo impatiently. "I told thee I

would answer for this little primogenita with my life. She is but leading this Frenchman a dance, as she has led the others, and the Doña Amita and her Raymond are but wax in her hands. Besides, I have spoken with the little 'Ruja to-day, and spoke my mind, Pepita, and she says there is nothing."

"And whilst thou wert speaking to her, my poor Pereo, the devil of an American Doctor was speaking to her mother, thy mistress — our mistress, Pereo! Wouldst thou know what he said? Oh, it was nothing."

"Now, the curse of Koorotora on thee, Pepita!" said Pereo excitedly. "Speak, fool, if thou knowest any-thing!"

"Of a verity, no. Let Faquita, then, speak: she heard it." She reached out her hand, and dragged Maruja's maid, not unwilling, before the old man.

"Good! 'T is Faquita, daughter of Gomez, and a child of the land. Speak, little one. What said this coyote to the mother of thy mistress?"

"Truly, good Pereo, it was but accident that befriended me."

"Truly, for thy mistress's sake, I hoped it had been more. But let that go. Come, what said he, child?"

"I was hanging up a robe behind the curtain in the ora-tory when Pepita ushered in the Americano. I had no time to fly."

"Why shouldst thou fly from a dog like this?" said one of the cigarette-smokers who had drawn near.

"Peace!" said the old man.

"When the Doña Maria joined him they spoke of affairs. Yes, Pereo, she, thy mistress, spoke of affairs to this man —ay, as she might have talked to *thee*. And, could he advise this? and could he counsel that? and should the cattle be taken from the lower lands, and the fields turned to grain? and had he a purchaser for Los Osos?"

"Los Osos! It is the boundary land — the frontier — the line of the arroyo — older than the Mision," muttered Pereo.

"Ay, and he talked of the — the — I know not what it is! — the r-r-rail-r-road."

"The railroad," gasped the old man. "I will tell thee what it is! It is the cut of a burning knife through La Mision Perdida — as long as eternity, as dividing as death. On either side of that gash life is blasted; wherever that cruel steel is laid the track of it is livid and barren; it cuts down all barriers; leaps all boundaries, be they cañada or cañon; it is a torrent in the plain, a tornado in the forest; its very pathway is destruction to whoso crosses it — man or beast; it is the heathenish God of the Americanos; they build temples for it, and flock there and worship it whenever it stops, breathing fire and flame like a very Moloch."

"Eh! St. Anthony preserve us!" said Faquita, shuddering; "and yet they spoke of it as 'shares' and 'stocks,' and said it would double the price of corn."

"Now, Judas pursue thee and thy railroad, Pereo," said Pepita impatiently. "It is not such bagatela that Faquita is here to relate. Go on, child, and tell all that happened."

"And then," continued Faquita, with a slight affectation of maiden bashfulness, in the closer-drawing circle of cigarettes, "and then they talked of other things and of themselves; and, of a verity, this gray-bearded Doctor will play the goat and utter gallant speeches, and speak of a lifelong devotion and of the time he should have a right to protect" —

"The right, girl! Didst thou say the right? No, thou didst mistake. It was not *that* he meant?"

"Thy life to a quarter peso that the little Faquita does not mistake," said the evident satirist of the household. "Trust to Gomez' muchacha to understand a proposal."

When the laugh was over, and the sparks of the cigarette,

cleverly whipped out of the speaker's lips by Faquita's fan, had disappeared in the darkness, she resumed, pettishly, "I know not what you call it when he kissed her hand and held it to his heart."

"Judas!" gasped Pereo. "But," he added feverishly, "she, the Doña Maria, thy mistress, *she* summoned thee at once to call me to cast out this dust into the open air; thou didst fly to her assistance? What! thou sawest this, and did nothing — eh?" He stopped, and tried to peer into the girl's face. "No! Ah, I see; I am an old fool. Yes; it was Maruja's own mother that stood there. He! he! he!" he laughed piteously; "and she smiled and smiled and broke the coward's heart, as Maruja might. And when he was gone, she bade thee bring her water to wash the filthy Judas stain from her hand."

"Santa Ana!" said Faquita, shrugging her shoulders. "She did what the veriest muchacha would have done. When he had gone, she sat down and cried."

The old man drew back a step, and steadied himself by the table. Then, with a certain tremulous audacity, he began: "So! that is all you have to tell — nothing! Bah! A lazy slut sleeps at her duty, and dreams behind a curtain! Yes, dreams! — you understand — *dreams!* And for this she leaves her occupations, and comes to gossip here! Come," he continued, steadily working himself into a passion, "come, enough of this! Get you gone! — you, and Pepita, and Andreas, and Victor — all of you — back to your duty. Away! Am I not master here? Off! I say!"

There was no mistaking the rising anger of his voice. The cowed group rose in a frightened way and disappeared one by one silently through the labyrinth. Pereo waited until the last had vanished, and then, cramming his stiff sombrero over his eyes with an ejaculation, brushed his way through the shrubbery in the direction of the stables.

Later, when the full glory of the midnight moon had put

out every straggling light in the great house; when the long
veranda slept in massive bars of shadow, and even the trade-
winds were hushed to repose, Pereo silently issued from the
stable-yard in vaquero's dress, mounted and caparisoned.
Picking his way cautiously along the turf-bordered edge of
the gravel path, he noiselessly reached a gate that led to the
lane.   Walking his spirited mustang with difficulty until
the house had at last disappeared in the intervening foliage,
he turned with an easy canter into a border bridle-path that
seemed to lead to the cañada.   In a quarter of an hour he
had reached a low amphitheatre of meadows, shut in a half
circle of grassy treeless hills.

Here, putting spurs to his horse, he entered upon a
singular exercise.   Twice he made a circuit of the meadow
at a wild gallop, with flying serape and loosened rein, and
twice returned.   The third time his speed increased; the
ground seemed to stream from under him; in the distance
the limbs of his steed became invisible in their furious action,
and, lying low forward on his mustang's neck, man and horse
passed like an arrowy bolt around the circle.   Then something like a light ring of smoke up-curved from the saddle
before him, and slowly uncoiling itself in mid air, dropped
gently to the ground as he passed.   Again, and once again,
the shadowy coil sped upward and onward, slowly detaching
its snaky rings with a weird deliberation that was in strange
contrast to the impetuous onset of the rider, and yet seemed
a part of his fury.   And then turning, Pereo trotted gently
to the centre of the circle.

Here he divested himself of his serape, and, securing it in
a cylindrical roll, placed it upright on the ground and once
more sped away on his furious circuit.   But this time he
wheeled suddenly before it was half completed and bore
down directly upon the unconscious object.   Within a
hundred feet he swerved slightly; the long detaching rings
again writhed in mid air and softly descended as he thun-

dered past. But when he had reached the line of circuit again, he turned and made directly for the road he had entered. Fifty feet behind his horse's heels, at the end of a shadowy cord, the luckless serape was dragging and bounding after him !

"The old man is quiet enough this morning," said Andreas, as he groomed the sweat-dried skin of the mustang the next day. "It is easy to see, friend Pinto, that he has worked off his madness on thee."

CHAPTER IV

THE Rancho of San Antonio might have been a characteristic asylum for its blessed patron, offering as it did a secure
retreat from temptations for the carnal eye, and affording
every facility for uninterrupted contemplation of the sky
above, unbroken by tree or elevation. Unlike La Mision
Perdida, of which it had been part, it was a level plain of
rich adobe, half the year presenting a billowy sea of tossing
verdure breaking on the far-off horizon line, half the year
presenting a dry and dusty shore, from which the vernal
sea had ebbed, to the low sky that seemed to mock it with
a visionary sea beyond. A row of rough, irregular, and
severely practical sheds and buildings housed the machinery
and the fifty or sixty men employed in the cultivation of
the soil, but neither residential mansion nor farmhouse
offered any nucleus of rural comfort or civilization in the
midst of this wild expanse of earth and sky. The simplest
adjuncts of country life were unknown; milk and butter
were brought from the nearest town; weekly supplies of
fresh meat and vegetables came from the same place; in
the harvest season, the laborers and harvesters lodged and
boarded in the adjacent settlement and walked to their
work. No cultivated flower bloomed beside the unpainted
tenement, though the fields were starred in early spring with
poppies and daisies; the humblest garden plant or herb had
no place in that prolific soil. The serried ranks of wheat
pressed closely round the straggling sheds and barns, and
hid the lower windows. But the sheds were fitted with
the latest agricultural machinery; a telegraphic wire con-

nected the nearest town with an office in the wing of one of the buildings, where Dr. West sat, and in the midst of the wilderness severely checked his accounts with nature.

Whether this strict economy of domestic outlay arose from an ostentatious contempt of country life and the luxurious habits of the former landholders, or whether it was a purely business principle of Dr. West, did not appear. Those who knew him best declared that it was both. Certain it was that unqualified commercial success crowned and dignified his method. A few survivors of the old native families came to see his strange machinery, that did the work of so many idle men and horses. It is said that he offered to "run" the distant estate of Joaquin Padilla from his little office amidst the grain of San Antonio. Some shook their heads, and declared that he only sucked the juices of the land for a few brief years to throw it away again; that in his fierce haste he skimmed the fatness of ages of gentle cultivation on a soil that had been barely tickled with native oaken ploughshares.

His own personal tastes and habits were as severe and practical as his business : the little wing he inhabited contained only his office, his living room or library, his bedroom, and a bathroom. This last inconsistent luxury was due to a certain catlike cleanliness which was part of his nature. His iron-gray hair — a novelty in this country of young Americans — was always scrupulously brushed, and his linen spotless. A slightly professional and somewhat old-fashioned respectability in his black clothes was also characteristic. His one concession to the customs of his neighbors was the possession of two or three of the half-broken and spirited mustangs of the country, which he rode with the fearlessness, if not the perfect security and ease, of a native. Whether the subjection of this lawless and powerful survival of a wild and unfettered nature around him was part of his plan, or whether it was only a lingering

trait of some younger prowess, no one knew; but his grim
and decorous figure, contrasting with the picturesque and
flowing freedom of the horse he bestrode, was a frequent
spectacle in road and field.

It was the second day after his visit to La Mision Perdida. He was sitting by his desk, at sunset, in the faint
afterglow of the western sky, which flooded the floor through
the open door. He was writing, but presently lifted his
head, with an impatient air, and called out, "Harrison!"

The shadow of Dr. West's foreman appeared at the door.

"Who's that you're talking to?"

"Tramp, sir."

"Hire him, or send him about his business. Don't
stand gabbling there."

"That's just it, sir. He won't hire for a week or a
day. He says he'll do an odd job for his supper and a
shakedown, but no more."

"Pack him off! . . . Stay. . . . What's he like?"

"Like the rest of 'em, only a little lazier, I reckon."

"Umph! Fetch him in."

The foreman disappeared, and returned with the tramp
already known to the reader. He was a little dirtier and
grimier than on the morning he had addressed Maruja at
La Mision Perdida; but he wore the same air of sullen
indifference, occasionally broken by furtive observation.
His laziness — or weariness — if the term could describe
the lassitude of perfect physical condition, seemed to have
increased; and he leaned against the door as the Doctor
regarded him with slow contempt. The silence continuing,
he deliberately allowed himself to slip down into a sitting
position in the doorway, where he remained.

"You seem to have been born tired," said the Doctor
grimly.

"Yes."

"What have you got to say for yourself?"

"I told *him*," said the tramp, nodding his head towards the foreman, "what I'd do for a supper and a bed. I don't want anything but that."

"And if you don't get what you want on your own conditions, what'll you do?" asked the Doctor dryly.

"Go."

"Where did you come from?"

"States."

"Where are you going?"

"On."

"Leave him to me," said Dr. West to his foreman. The man smiled, and withdrew.

The Doctor bent his head again over his accounts. The tramp, sitting in the doorway, reached out his hand, pulled a young wheat-stalk that had sprung up near the doorstep, and slowly nibbled it. He did not raise his eyes to the Doctor, but sat, a familiar culprit awaiting sentence, without fear, without hope, yet not without a certain philosophical endurance of the situation.

"Go into that passage," said the Doctor, lifting his head as he turned a page of his ledger, "and on the shelf you'll find some clothing stores for the men. Pick out something to fit you."

The tramp arose, moved towards the passage, and stopped. "It's for the job only, you understand?" he said.

"For the job," answered the Doctor.

The tramp returned in a few moments with overalls and woolen shirt hanging on his arm and a pair of boots and socks in his hand. The Doctor had put aside his pen. "Now go into that room and change. Stop! First wash the dust from your feet in that bathroom."

The tramp obeyed, and entered the room. The Doctor walked to the door, and looked out reflectively on the paling sky. When he turned again he noticed that the

door of the bathroom was opened, and the tramp, who had
changed his clothes by the fading light, was drying his
feet. The Doctor approached, and stood for a moment
watching him.

"What's the matter with your foot?" [1] he asked,
after a pause.

"Born so."

The first and second toe were joined by a thin mem-
brane.

"Both alike?" asked the Doctor.

"Yes," said the young man, exhibiting the other foot.

"What did you say your name was?"

"I didn't say it. It's Henry Guest, same as my
father's."

"Where were you born?"

"Dentville, Pike County, Missouri."

"What was your mother's name?"

"Spalding, I reckon."

"Where are your parents now?"

"Mother got divorced from father, and married again
down South, somewhere. Father left home twenty years
ago. He's somewhere in California — if he ain't dead."

"He isn't dead."

"How do you know?"

"Because I am Henry Guest, of Dentville, and" — he
stopped, and shading his eyes with his hand as he deliberately examined the tramp, added coldly — "your father,
I reckon."

There was a slight pause. The young man put down
the boot he had taken up. "Then I am to stay here?"

"Certainly not. Here my name is only West, and I

---

[1] This apparent classical plagiarism is actually a fact of identification
on record in the California Law Reports. It is therefore unnecessary for
me to add that the attendant circumstances and characters are purely
fictitious. — B. H.

have no son. You 'll go on to San José, and stay there
until I look into this thing. You have n't got any money,
of course ? '' he asked, with a scarcely suppressed sneer.

" I 've got a little," returned the young man.

" How much ? "

The tramp put his hand into his breast, and drew out a
piece of folded paper containing a single gold coin.

" Five dollars. I 've kept it a month ; it does n't cost
much to live as I do," he added dryly.

" There 's fifty more. Go to some hotel in San José,
and let me know where you are. You 've got to live, and
you don't want to work. Well, you don't seem to be a
fool ; so I need n't tell you that if you expect anything
from me, you must leave this matter in my hands. I have
chosen to acknowledge you to-day of my own free will ;
I can as easily denounce you as an impostor to-morrow, if
I choose. Have you told your story to any one in the
valley ? "

" No."

" See that you don't, then. Before you go, you must
answer me a few more questions."

He drew a chair to his table, and dipped a pen in the ink,
as if to take down the answers. The young man, finding
the only chair thus occupied, moved the Doctor's books
aside, and sat down on the table beside him.

The questions were repetitions of those already asked,
but more in detail, and thoroughly practical in their nature.
The answers were given straightforwardly and unconcern-
edly, as if the subject was not worth the trouble of inven-
tion or evasion. It was difficult to say whether questioner
or answerer took least pleasure in the interrogation, which
might have referred to the concerns of a third party. Both,
however, spoke disrespectfully of their common family,
with almost an approach to sympathetic interest.

" You might as well be going now," said the Doctor,

finally rising. " You can stop at the fonda, about two
miles further on, and get your supper and bed, if you
like."

The young man slipped from the table, and lounged to
the door. The Doctor put his hands in his pockets and
followed him. The young man, as if in unconscious imitation, had put *his* hands in his pockets also, and looked at
him.

" I 'll hear from you, then, when you are in San José ? "
said Dr. West, looking past him into the grain, with a
slight approach to constraint in his indifference.

" Yes — if that 's agreed upon," returned the young
man, pausing on the threshold. A faint sense of some
purely conventional responsibility in their position affected
them both. They would have shaken hands if either had
offered the initiative. A sullen consciousness of gratuitous
rectitude in the selfish mind of the father, an equally
sullen conviction of twenty years of wrong in the son,
withheld them both. Unpleasantly observant of each
other's awkwardness, they parted with a feeling of relief.

Dr. West closed the door, lit his lamp, and going to his
desk, folded the paper containing the memoranda he had
just written and placed it in his pocket. Then he summoned his foreman. The man entered, and glanced around
the room as if expecting to see the Doctor's guest still
there.

" Tell one of the men to bring round ' Buckeye.' "

The foreman hesitated. " Going to ride to-night, sir ? "

" Certainly ; I may go as far as Saltonstall's. If I do,
you need n't expect me back till morning."

" Buckeye 's mighty fresh to-night, boss. Regularly
bucked his saddle clean off an hour ago, and there ain't a
man dare exercise him."

" I 'll bet he don't buck his saddle off with me on it,"
said the Doctor grimly. " Bring him along."

The man turned to go. " You found the tramp pow'ful
lazy, did n't ye ? "

" I found a heap more in him than in some that call
themselves smart," said Dr. West, unconsciously setting
up an irritable defense of the absent one. " Hurry up
that horse ! "

The foreman vanished. The Doctor put on a pair of
leather leggings, large silver spurs, and a broad soft-
brimmed hat, but made no other change in his usual half-
professional conventional garb. He then went to the
window and glanced in the direction of the highway.
Now that his son was gone, he felt a faint regret that he
had not prolonged the interview. Certain peculiarities in
his manner, certain suggestions of expression in his face,
speech, and gesture, came back to him now with unsatisfied
curiosity. " No matter," he said to himself ; " he 'll turn
up soon again — as soon as I want him, if not sooner. He
thinks he 's got a mighty soft thing here, and he is n't
going to let it go. And there 's that same d—d sullen
dirty pride of his mother, for all he does n't cotton to her.
Wonder I did n't recognize it at first. And hoarding up
that five dollars ! That 's Jane's brat, all over ! And, of
course," he added bitterly, " nothing of *me* in him. No ;
nothing ! Well, well, what 's the difference ? " He turned
towards the door, with a certain sullen defiance in his face
so like the man he believed he did not resemble, that his
foreman, coming upon him suddenly, might have been
startled at the likeness. Fortunately, however, Harrison
was too much engrossed with the antics of the irrepressible
Buckeye, which the hostler had just brought to the door, to
notice anything else. The arrival of the horse changed the
Doctor's expression to one of more practical and significant
resistance. With the assistance of two men at the head of
the restive brute, he managed to vault into the saddle. A
few wild plunges only seemed to settle him the firmer in

his seat — each plunge leaving its record in a thin red line on the animal's flanks, made by the cruel spurs of its rider. Any lingering desire of following his son's footsteps was quickly dissipated by Buckeye, who promptly bolted in the opposite direction, and before Dr. West could gain active control over him, they were half a mile on their way to La Mision Perdida.

Dr. West did not regret it. Twenty years ago he had voluntarily abandoned a legal union of mutual unfaithfulness and misconduct, and allowed his wife to get the divorce he might have obtained for equal cause. He had abandoned to her the issue of that union — an infant son. Whatever he chose to do now was purely gratuitous; the only hold which this young stranger had on his respect was that *he* also recognized that fact with a cold indifference equal to his own. At present the half-savage brute he bestrode occupied all his attention. Yet he could not help feeling his advancing years tell upon him more heavily that evening; fearless as he was, his strength was no longer equal when measured with the untiring youthful malevolence of his unbroken mustang. For a moment he dwelt regretfully on the lazy half-developed sinews of his son; for a briefer instant there flashed across him the thought that those sinews ought to replace his own; ought to be *his* to lean upon — that thus, and thus only, could he achieve the old miracle of restoring his lost youth by perpetuating his own power in his own blood; and he, whose profound belief in personality had rejected all hereditary principle, felt this with a sudden exquisite pain. But his horse, perhaps recognizing a relaxing grip, took that opportunity to "buck." Curving his back like a cat, and throwing himself into the air with an unexpected bound, he came down with four stiff, inflexible legs, and a shock that might have burst the saddle-girths, had not the wily old man as quickly brought the long rowels of his spurs together and fairly

locked his heels under Buckeye's collapsing barrel.   It was
the mustang's last rebellious struggle.   The discomfited
brute gave in, and darted meekly and apologetically forward, and, as it were, left all its rider's doubts and fears far
behind in the vanishing distance.

CHAPTER V

MEANWHILE, the subject of Dr. West's meditations was slowly making his way along the highroad towards the fonda. He walked more erect and with less of a shuffle in his gait; but whether this was owing to his having cast the old skin of garments adapted to his slouch, and because he was more securely shod, or whether it was from the sudden straightening of some warped moral quality, it would have been difficult to say. The expression of his face certainly gave no evidence of actual and prospective good fortune; if anything, the lines of discontent around his brow and mouth were more strongly drawn. Apparently, his interview with his father had only the effect of reviving and stirring into greater activity a certain dogged sentiment that, through long years, had become languidly mechanical. He was no longer a beaten animal, but one roused by a chance success into a dangerous knowledge of his power. In his honest workman's dress, he was infinitely more to be feared than in his rags; in the lifting of his downcast eye, there was the revelation of a baleful intelligence. In his changed condition, civilization only seemed to have armed him against itself.

The fonda, a long low building, with a red-tiled roof extending over a porch or whitewashed veranda, in which drunken vaqueros had been known to occasionally disport their mustangs, did not offer a very reputable appearance to the eye of young Guest as he approached it in the gathering shadows. One or two half-broken horses were securely fastened to the stout cross-beams of some heavy posts driven in the roadway before it, and a primitive trough of roughly excavated stone stood near it.   Through a broken gate at the side there was a glimpse of a grass-grown and deserted court-yard piled with the disused packing-cases and barrels of the tienda, or general country shop, which huddled under the same roof at the other end of the building.   The opened door of the fonda showed a low-studded room fitted up with a rude imitation of an American bar on one side, and containing a few small tables, at which half a dozen men were smoking, drinking, and playing cards.   The faded pictorial poster of the last bull-fight at Monterey and an American " Sheriff's notice " were hung on the wall and in the door-way.   A thick yellow atmosphere of cigarette smoke, through which the inmates appeared like brown shadows, pervaded the room.

The young man hesitated before this pestilential interior, and took a seat on a bench on the veranda.   After a moment's interval, the yellow landlord came to the door with a look of inquiry, which Guest answered by a demand for lodging and supper.   When the landlord had vanished again in the cigarette fog, the several other guests, one after the other, appeared at the doorway, with their cigarettes in their mouths and their cards still in their hands, and gazed upon him.

There may have been some excuse for their curiosity. As before hinted, Guest's appearance in his overalls and woolen shirt was somewhat incongruous, and for some inexplicable reason, the same face and figure which did not look inconsistent in rags and extreme poverty now at once suggested a higher social rank both of intellect and refine-ment than his workman's dress indicated.   This, added to his surliness of manner and expression, strengthened a growing suspicion in the mind of the party that he was a fugitive from justice — a forger, a derelict banker, or possi-bly a murderer.   It is only fair to say that the moral sense

of the spectators was not shocked at the suspicion, and that
a more active sympathy was only withheld by his reticence.
An unfortunate incident seemed to complete the evidence
against him.   In impatiently responding to the landlord's
curt demand for prepayment of his supper, he allowed three
or four pieces of gold to escape from his pocket on the veranda.   In the quick glances of the party, as he stooped to
pick them up, he read the danger of his carelessness.

His sullen self-possession did not seem to be shaken.
Calling to the keeper of the tienda, who had appeared at
his door in time to witness the Danaë-like shower, he bade
him approach, in English.

" What sort of knives have you got ? "

"Knives, Señor ? "

" Yes ; bowie-knives or dirks.   Knives like that," he
said, making an imaginary downward stroke at the table
before him.

The shopkeeper entered the tienda, and presently reappeared with three or four dirks in red leather sheaths.
Guest selected the heaviest, and tried its point on the
table.

" How much ? "

" Tres pesos."

The young man threw him one of his gold pieces, and
slipped the knife and its sheath in his boot.   When he had
received his change from the shopkeeper, he folded his
arms and leaned back against the wall in quiet indifference.

The simple act seemed to check aggressive, but not insinuating interference.   In a few moments one of the men
appeared at the doorway.

" It is fine weather for the road, little comrade ! "

Guest did not reply.

" Ah ! the night, it ess splendid," he repeated in broken
English, rubbing his hands, as if washing in the air.

Still no reply.

"You shall come from Sank Hosay?"

"I sha'n't."

The stranger muttered something in Spanish, but the landlord, who reappeared to place Guest's supper on a table on the veranda, here felt the obligation of interfering to protect a customer apparently so aggressive and so opulent. He pushed the inquisitor aside, with a few hasty words, and after Guest had finished his meal, offered to show him his room. It was a dark vaulted closet on the ground-floor, gaining light from the stable-yard through a barred iron grating. At the first glimpse it looked like a prison cell; looking more deliberately at the black tresseled bed, and the votive images hanging on the wall, it might have been a tomb.

"It is the best," said the landlord. "The Padre Vincento will have none other on his journey."

"I suppose God protects him," said Guest; "that door don't." He pointed to the worm-eaten door, without bolt or fastening.

"Ah, what matter! Are we not all friends?"

"Certainly," responded Guest, with his surliest manner, as he returned to the veranda. Nevertheless, he resolved not to occupy the cell of the reverend Padre; not from any personal fear of his disreputable neighbors, though he was fully alive to their peculiarities, but from the nomadic instinct which was still strong in his blood. He felt he could not yet bear the confinement of a close room or the propinquity of his fellow man. He would rest on the veranda until the moon was fairly up, and then he would again take to the road.

He was half reclining on the bench, with the slowly closing and opening lids of some tired but watchful animal, when the sound of wheels, voices, and clatter of hoofs on the highway arrested his attention, and he sat upright. The moon was slowly lifting itself over the limitless stretch

of grain-fields before him on the other side of the road, and
dazzling him with its level lustre. He could barely discern
a cavalcade of dark figures and a large vehicle rapidly
approaching, before it drew up tumultuously in front of the
fonda. It was a pleasure-party of ladies and gentlemen on
horseback and in a four-horsed char-à-bancs returning to La
Mision Perdida. Buchanan, Raymond, and Garnier were
there ; Amita and Dorotea in the body of the char-à-bancs,
and Maruja seated on the box. Much to his own astonishment and that of some others of the party, Captain Carroll
was among the riders. Only Maruja and her mother knew
that he was recalled to refute a repetition of the gossip already circulated regarding his sudden withdrawal; only
Maruja alone knew the subtle words which made that call
so potent yet so hopeless.

Maruja's quick eyes, observant of everything, even under
the double fire of Captain Carroll and Garnier, instantly
caught those of the erect figure on the bench in the veranda.
Surely that was the face of the tramp she had spoken to !
and yet there was a change not only in the dress but in
the general resemblance. After the first glance, Guest withdrew his eyes and gazed at the other figures in the char-à-
bancs without moving a muscle.

Maruja's whims and caprices were many and original ;
and when, after a sudden little cry and a declaration that
she could stand her cramped position no longer, she leaped
from the box into the road, no one was surprised. Garnier and Captain Carroll quickly followed.

" I should like to look into the fonda while the horses
are being watered," she said laughingly, " just to see what
it is that attracts Pereo there so often." Before any one
could restrain this new caprice, she was already upon the
veranda.

To reach the open door, she had to pass so near Guest
that her soft white flounces brushed his knees, and the

flowers in her girdle left their perfume in his face. But he neither moved nor raised his eyes. When she had passed, he rose quietly and stepped into the road.

On her nearer survey, Maruja was convinced it was the same man. She remained for an instant, with a little hand on the door-post. " What a horrid place, and what dreadful people ! " she said in audible English as she glanced quickly after Guest. " Really, Pereo ought to be warned against keeping such company. Come, let us go."

She contrived to pass Guest again in regaining the carriage ; but in the few moments' further delay he walked on down the road before them, and by the time they were ready to start, he was slowly sauntering some hundred yards ahead. They passed him at a rapid trot, but the next moment the char-à-bancs was suddenly pulled up.

" My fan ! " cried Maruja. " Blessed Santa Maria ! — my fan ! "

A small black object, seen distinctly in the moonlight, was lying on the road, directly in the track of the sauntering stranger. Garnier attempted to alight ; Carroll reined in his horse.

" Stop, all of you ! " said Maruja ; " that man will bring it to me."

It seemed as if he would. He stopped and picked it up, and approached the carriage. Maruja stood up in her seat, with her veil thrown back, her graceful hand extended, her eyes and mouth tremulous with an irresistible smile. The stranger came nearer, singled out Captain Carroll, tossed the fan to him with a slight nod, and passed on the other side.

" One moment," said Maruja, almost harshly, to the driver. " One moment," she continued, drawing her purse from her pocket brusquely. " Let me reward this civil gentleman of the road ! Here, sir ; " but before she could continue, Carroll wheeled to her side, and interposed. "Pray collect yourself, Miss Saltonstall, " he said hurriedly; "you cannot tell who this man may be. He does not seem to be one who would insult you, or whom *you* would insult gratuitously."

"Give me the fan, Captain Carroll," she said, with a soft and caressing smile. "Thank you." She took it, and breaking it through the middle between her gloved hands, tossed it into the highway. "You are right — it smells of the fonda — and the road. Thank you, again. You are so thoughtful for me, Captain Carroll," she murmured, raising her eyes gently to his, and then suddenly withdrawing them with a half sigh. "But I am keeping you all. Go on."

The carriage rolled away and Guest returned from the hedge to the middle of the road. San José lay in the opposite direction from the disappearing calvacade; but on leaving the fonda, he had determined to lead his inquisitors astray by doubling and making a circuit of the hostelry through the fields hidden in the tall grain. This he did, securely passing them within sound of their voices, and was soon well on his way again. He avoided the highway, and striking a trail through the meadows, diverged to the right, where the low towers and brown walls of a ruined mission church rose above the plain. This would enable him to escape any direct pursuit on the highroad, besides, from its slight elevation, giving him a more extended view of the plain. As he neared it, he was surprised to see that, although it was partly dismantled, and the roof had fallen in the central aisle, a part of it was still used as a chapel, and a light was burning behind a narrow opening, partly window and partly shrine. He was almost upon it, when the figure of a man who had been kneeling beneath, with his back towards him, rose, crossed himself devoutly, and stood upright. Before he could turn, Guest disappeared round the angle of the wall, and the tall erect figure of the solitary worshiper passed on without heeding him.

But if Guest had been successful in evading the observation of the man he had come so suddenly upon, he was utterly unconscious of another figure that had been tracking *him* for the last ten minutes through the tall grain, and had even succeeded in gaining the shadow of the wall behind him; and it was this figure, and not his own, that eventually attracted the attention of the tall stranger. The pursuing figure was rapidly approaching the unconscious Guest; in another moment it would have been upon him, when it was suddenly seized from behind by the tall devotee. There was a momentary struggle, and then it freed itself, with the exclamation, "Pereo!"

"Yes — Pereo!" said the old man, panting from his exertions. "And thou art Miguel. So thou wouldst murder a man for a few pesos!" he said, pointing to the knife which the desperado had hurriedly hid in his jacket, "and callest thyself a Californian!"

"'T is only an Americano — a runaway, with some ill-gotten gold," said Miguel sullenly, yet with unmistakable fear of the old man. "Besides, it was only to frighten him, the braggart. But since thou fearest to touch a hair of those interlopers" —

"Fearest!" said Pereo fiercely, clutching him by the throat, and forcing him against the wall. "Fearest! sayest thou. I, Pereo, fear? Dost thou think I would soil these hands, that might strike a higher quarry, with blood of thy game?"

"Forgive me, padroño," gasped Miguel, now thoroughly alarmed at the old man's awakened passion; "pardon; I meant that, since thou knowest him" —

"I know him?" repeated Pereo scornfully, contemptuously throwing Miguel aside, who at once took that opportunity to increase his distance from the old man's arm. "I know him? Thou shalt see. Come hither, child," he called, beckoning to Guest. "Come hither, thou hast nothing to fear now."

Guest, who had been attracted by the sound of alterca-
tion behind him, but who was utterly unconscious of its
origin or his own relation to it, came forward impatiently.
As he did so, Miguel took to his heels. The act did not
tend to mollify Guest's surly suspicions, and pausing a
few feet from the old man, he roughly demanded his business with him.

Pereo raised his head, with the dignity of years and
habits of command. The face of the young man confronting him was clearly illuminated by the moonlight. Pereo's
eyes suddenly dilated, his mouth stiffened, he staggered
back against the wall.

" Who are you ? " he gasped in uncertain English.

Believing himself the subject of some drunkard's pastime,
Guest replied savagely, " One who has enough of this
d—d nonsense, and will stand no more of it from any
one, young or old," and turned abruptly on his heel.

" Stay, one moment, Señor, for the love of God ! "

Some keen accent of agony in the old man's voice touched
even Guest's selfish nature. He halted.

" You are — a stranger here ? " faltered Pereo. " Yes ? "
" I am."

" You do not live here ? — you have no friends ? "

" I told you I am a stranger. I never was here before in
my life," said Guest impatiently.

" True ; I am a fool," said the old man, hurriedly, to himself. " I am mad — mad ! It is not *his* voice. No ! It
is not *his* look, now that his face changes. I am crazy."
He stopped, and passed his trembling hands across his eyes.
" Pardon, Señor," he continued, recalling himself with a
humility that was almost ironical in its extravagance.
" Pardon, pardon ! Yet, perhaps it is not too much to have
wanted to know who was the man one has saved."

" Saved ! " repeated Guest, with incredulous contempt.

" Ay ! " said Pereo haughtily, drawing his figure erect ;

" ay, saved! Señor." He stopped and shrugged his shoulders. "But let it pass — I say — let it pass. Take an old man's advice, friend: show not your gold hereafter to strangers lightly, no matter how lightly you have come by it. Good-night!"

Guest for a moment hesitated whether to resent the old man's speech, or to let it pass as the incoherent fancy of a brain maddened by drink. Then he ended the discussion by turning his back abruptly and continuing his way to the highroad.

"So!" said Pereo, looking after him with abstracted eyes, "so! it was only a fancy. And yet — even now, as he turned away, I saw the same cold insolence in his eye. Caramba! Am I mad — mad — that I must keep forever before my eyes, night and day, the image of that dog in every outcast, every ruffian, every wayside bully that I meet? No, no, good Pereo! Softly! this is mere madness, good Pereo," he murmured to himself; "thou wilt have none of it; none, good Pereo. Come, come!" He let his head fall slowly forward on his breast, and in that action, seeming to take up again the burden of a score more years upon his shoulders, he moved slowly away.

When he entered the fonda half an hour later, the awe in which he was held by the half-superstitious ruffians appeared to have increased. Whatever story the fugitive Miguel had told his companions regarding Pereo's protection of the young stranger, it was certain that it had its full effect. Obsequious to the last degree, the landlord was so profoundly touched, when Pereo, not displeased with this evidence of his power over his countrymen, condescendingly offered to click glasses with him, that he endeavored to placate him still further.

"It is a pity your worship was not here earlier," he began, with a significant glance at the others, "to have seen a gallant young stranger that was here. A spice of wickedness about him, truly — a kind of Don Cæsar — but bearing himself like a very caballero always. It would have pleased your worship, who likes not these canting Puritans such as our neighbor yonder."

"Ah," said Pereo reflectively, warming under the potent fires of flattery and aguardiente, "possibly I *have* seen him. He was like " —

"Like none of the dogs thou hast seen about San Antonio," interrupted the landlord. "Scarcely did he seem Americano, though he spoke no Spanish."

The old man chuckled to himself viciously. "And thou, thou old fool, Pereo, must needs see a likeness to thine enemy in this poor runaway child — this fugitive Don Juan! He! he!" Nevertheless, he still felt a vague terror of the condition of mind which had produced this fancy, and drank so deeply to dispel his nervousness that it was with difficulty he could mount his horse again. The exaltation of liquor, however, appeared only to intensify his characteristics: his face became more lugubrious and melancholy; his manner more ceremonious and dignified; and erect and stiff in his saddle from the waist upwards, but leaning from side to side with the motion of his horse, like the tall mast of some laboring sloop, he "loped" away towards the House of the Lost Mission. Once or twice he broke into sentimental song. Strangely enough, his ditty was a popular Spanish refrain of some matador's aristocratic inamorata :—

> Do you see my black eyes ?
> I am Manuel's Duchess, —

sang Pereo, with infinite gravity. His horse's hoofs seemed to keep time with the refrain, and he occasionally waved in the air the long leather thong of his bridle-rein.

It was quite late when he reached La Mision Perdida. Turning into the little lane that led to the stable-yard, he dismounted at a gate in the hedge which led to the summer-house of the old Mision garden, and throwing his reins on his mustang's neck, let the animal precede him to the stables. The moon shone full on the inclosure as he emerged from the labyrinth. With uncovered head he approached the Indian mound, and sank on his knees before it.

The next moment he rose, with an exclamation of terror, and his hat dropped from his trembling hand. Directly before him, a small, gray, wolfish-looking animal had stopped halfway down the mound on encountering his motionless figure. Frightened by his outcry, and unable to retreat, the shadowy depredator had fallen back on his slinking haunches with a snarl, and bared teeth that glittered in the moonlight.

In an instant the expression of terror on the old man's ashen face turned into a fixed look of insane exaltation. His white lips moved; he advanced a step further, and held out both hands towards the crouching animal.

"So! It is thou — at last! And comest thou here thy tardy Pereo to chide? Comest *thou*, too, to tell the poor old man his heart is cold, his limbs are feeble, his brain weak and dizzy? that he is no longer fit to do thy master's work? Ay, gnash thy teeth at him! Curse him! — curse him in thy throat! But listen! — listen, good friend — I will tell thee a secret — ay, good gray friar, a secret — such a secret! A plan, all mine — fresh from this old gray head; ha! ha! — all mine! To be wrought by these poor old arms; ha! ha! All mine! Listen!"

He stealthily made a step nearer the affrighted animal. With a sudden sidelong snap, it swiftly bounded by his side, and vanished in the thicket; and Pereo, turning wildly, with a moan sank down helplessly on the grave of his forefathers.

CHAPTER VI

To the open chagrin of most of the gentlemen and the unexpected relief of some of her own sex, Maruja, after an evening of more than usual caprice and willfulness, retired early to her chamber. Here she beguiled Enriquita, a younger sister, to share her solitude for an hour, and with a new and charming melancholy presented her with mature counsel and some younger trinkets and adornments.

"Thou wilt find them but folly, 'Riquita; but thou art young, and wilt outgrow them as I have. I am sick of the Indian beads, everybody wears them; but they seem to suit thy complexion. Thou art not yet quite old enough for jewelry; but take thy choice of these." "'Ruja," replied Enriquita eagerly, "surely thou wilt not give up this necklace of carved amber, that was brought thee from Manilla? — it becomes thee so! Everybody says it. All the caballeros, Raymond and Victor, swear that it sets off thy beauty like nothing else." "When thou knowest men better," responded Maruja in a deep voice, "thou wilt care less for what they say, and despise what they do. Besides, I wore it to-day — and — I hate it." "But what fan wilt thou keep thyself? The one of sandalwood thou hadst to-day?" continued Enriquita, timidly eying the pretty things upon the table. "None," responded Maruja didactically, "but the simplest, which I shall buy myself. Truly, it is time to set one's self against this extravagance. Girls think nothing of spending as much upon a fan as would buy a horse and saddle for a poor man." "But why so serious to-night, my sister?" said the little Enriquita, her eyes filling with ready tears. "It grieves me," responded Maruja promptly, "to find thee, like the rest, giving thy soul up to the mere glitter of the world. However, go, child, take the beads, but leave the amber; it would make thee yellower than thou art, which the Blessed Virgin forbid! Good-night!"

She kissed her affectionately, and pushed her from the room. Nevertheless, after a moment's survey of her lonely chamber, she hastily slipped on a pale satin dressing-gown, and darting across the passage, dashed into the bedroom of the youngest Miss Wilson, haled that sentimental brunette from her night toilet, dragged her into her own chamber, and enwrapping her in a huge mantle of silk and gray fur, fed her with chocolates and chestnuts, and reclining on her sympathetic shoulder, continued her arraignment of the world and its follies until nearly daybreak.

It was past noon when Maruja awoke, to find Faquita standing by her bedside with ill-concealed impatience.

"I ventured to awaken the Doña Maruja," she said, with vivacious alacrity, "for news! Terrible news! The American, Dr. West, is found dead this morning in the San José road!"

"Dr. West dead!" repeated Maruja thoughtfully, but without emotion.

"Surely dead — very dead. He was thrown from his horse and dragged by the stirrups — how far, the Blessed Virgin only knows. But he is found dead — this Dr. West — his foot in the broken stirrup, his hand holding a piece of the bridle! I thought I would waken the Doña Maruja, that no one else should break it to the Doña Maria."

"That no one else should break it to my mother?" repeated Maruja coldly. "What mean you, girl?"

"I mean that no stranger should tell her," stammered Faquita, lowering her bold eyes.

"You mean," said Maruja slowly, "that no silly, staring, tongue-wagging gossip should dare to break upon the morning devotions of the lady mother with open-mouthed tales of horror! You are wise, Faquita! I will tell her myself. Help me to dress."

But the news had already touched the outer shell of the great house, and little groups of the visitors were discussing it upon the veranda. For once, the idle badinage of a pleasure-seeking existence was suspended; stupid people with facts came to the fore; practical people with inquiring minds became interesting; servants were confidentially appealed to; the local expressman became a hero, and it was even noticed that he was intelligent and good looking.

"What makes it more distressing," said Raymond, joining one of the groups, "is, that it appears the Doctor visited Mrs. Saltonstall last evening, and left the casa at eleven. Sanchez, who was perhaps the last person who saw him alive, says that he noticed his horse was very violent, and the Doctor did not seem able to control him. The accident probably happened half an hour later, as he was picked up about three miles from here, and from appearances must have been dragged, with his foot in the stirrup, fully half a mile before the girth broke and freed the saddle and stirrup together. The mustang, with nothing on but his broken bridle, was found grazing at the rancho as early as four o'clock, an hour before the body of his master was discovered by the men sent from the rancho to look for him."

"Eh, but the man must have been clean daft to have trusted himself to one of those savage beasts of the country," said Mr. Buchanan. "And he was no so young either — about sixty, I should say. It didna look even respectable, I remember, when we met him the other day, careering over the country for all the world like one of those crazy Mexicans. And yet he seemed steady and sensible enough when he didna let his schemes of 'improve-

ments' run away with him like yon furious beastie. Eh
well, puir man — it was a sudden ending ! And his family
— eh ? "

" I don't think he has one — at least here," said Raymond. " You can't always tell in California. I believe
he was a widower."

" Ay, man, but the heirs; there must be considerable
property ? " said Buchanan impatiently.

" Oh, the heirs. If he's made no will, which does n't
look like so prudent and practical a man as he was — the
heirs will probably crop up some day."

" *Probably !* crop up some day," repeated Buchanan
aghast.

" Yes. You must remember that *we* don't take heirs
quite as much into account as you do in the old country.
The loss of the *man,* and how to replace *him,* is much
more to us than the disposal of his property. Now, Dr.
West was a power far beyond his actual possessions — and
we will know very soon how much those were dependent
upon him."

" What do you mean ? " asked Buchanan anxiously.

" I mean that five minutes after the news of the Doctor's
death was confirmed, your friend Mr. Stanton sent a messenger with a dispatch to the nearest telegraphic office, and
that he himself drove over to catch Aladdin before the
news could reach him."

Buchanan looked uneasy; so did one or two of the
native Californians who composed the group, and who had
been listening attentively. " And where is this same telegraphic office ? " asked Buchanan cautiously.

" I 'll drive you over there presently," responded Raymond grimly. " There 'll be nothing doing here to-day. As
Dr. West was a near neighbor of the family, his death sus-
pends our pleasure-seeking until after the funeral."

Mr. Buchanan moved away. Captain Carroll and Garnier drew nearer the speaker. "I trust it will not withdraw from us the society of Miss Saltonstall," said Garnier lightly — "at least, that she will not be inconsolable."

"She did not seem to be particularly sympathetic with Dr. West the other day," said Captain Carroll, coloring slightly with the recollection of the morning in the summer-house, yet willing, in his hopeless passion, even to share that recollection with his rival. "Did you not think so, Monsieur Garnier?"

"Very possibly; and as Miss Saltonstall is quite artless and childlike in the expression of her likes and dislikes," said Raymond, with the faintest touch of irony, "you can judge as well as I can."

Garnier parried the thrust lightly. "You are no kinder to our follies than you are to the grand passions of these gentlemen. Confess, you frightened them horribly. You are — what is called — a bear — eh? You depreciate in the interests of business."

Raymond did not at first appear to notice the sarcasm. "I only stated," he said gravely, "that which these gentlemen will find out for themselves before they are many hours older. Dr. West was the brain of the country, as Aladdin is its life-blood. It only remains to be seen how far the loss of that brain affects the county. The Stock Exchange market in San Francisco will indicate that to-day in the shares of the San Antonio and Soquel Railroad and the West Mills and Manufacturing Co. It is a matter that may affect even our friends here. Whatever West's social standing was in this house, lately he was in confidential business relations with Mrs. Saltonstall." He raised his eyes for the first time to Garnier as he added slowly, "It is to be hoped that if our hostess has no social reasons to deplore the loss of Dr. West, she at least will have no other."

With a lover's instinct, conscious only of some annoyance to Maruja, in all this, Carroll anxiously looked for her appearance among the others. He was doomed to disappointment, however. His half-timid inquiries only resulted in the information that Maruja was closeted with her mother. The penetralia of the casa was only accessible to the family; yet as he wandered uneasily about, he could not help passing once or twice before the quaint low archway, with its grated door, that opened from the central hall. His surprise may be imagined when he suddenly heard his name uttered in a low voice; and looking up, he beheld the soft eyes of Maruja at the grating.

She held the door partly open with one little hand, and made a sign for him to enter with the other. When he had done so, she said, " Come with me," and preceded him down the dim corridor. His heart beat thickly; the incense of this sacred inner life, with its faint suggestion of dead rose leaves, filled him with a voluptuous languor; his breath was lost, as if a soft kiss had taken it away; his senses swam in the light mist that seemed to suffuse everything. His step trembled as she suddenly turned aside, and, opening a door, ushered him into a small vaulted chamber.

In the first glance it seemed to be an oratory or chapel. A large gold and ebony crucifix hung on the wall. There was a priedieu of heavy dark mahogany in the centre of the tiled floor; there was a low ottoman or couch, covered with a mantle of dark violet velvet, like a pall; there were two quaintly carved stiff chairs; a religious, almost ascetic, air pervaded the apartment; but no dreamy Eastern seraglio could have affected him with an intoxication so profoundly and mysteriously sensuous.

Maruja pointed to a chair, and then, with a peculiarly feminine movement, placed herself sideways upon the ottoman, half reclining on her elbow on a high cushion, her deep billowy flounces partly veiling the funereal velvet be-

low. Her oval face was pale and melancholy, her eyes
moist as if with recent tears ; an expression as of troubled
passion lurked in their depths and in the corners of her
mouth. Scarcely knowing why, Carroll fancied that thus
she might appear if she were in love ; and the daring
thought made him tremble.

"I wanted to speak with you alone," she said gently,
as if in explanation ; "but don't look at me so. I have
had a bad night, and now this calamity," — she stopped,
and then added softly, "I want you to do a favor for —
my mother ? "

Captain Carroll, with an effort, at last found his voice.
"But *you* are in trouble ; *you* are suffering. I had no idea
this unfortunate affair came so near to you."

"Nor did I," said Maruja, closing her fan with a slight
snap. "I knew nothing of it until my mother told me
this morning. To be frank with you, it now appears that
Dr. West was her most intimate business adviser. All her
affairs were in his hands. I cannot explain how, or why,
or when ; but it is so."

"And is that all ? " said Carroll, with boyish openness
of relief. "And you have no other sorrow ? "

In spite of herself, a tender smile, such as she might
have bestowed on an impulsive boy, broke on her lips.
"And is that not enough ? What would you ? No —
sit where you are ! We are here to talk seriously. And
you do not ask what is this favor my mother wishes ? "

"No matter what it is, it shall be done," said Carroll
quickly. "I am your mother's slave if she will but let
me serve at your side. Only," he paused, "I wish it was
not business — I know nothing of business."

"If it were only business, Captain Carroll," said Maruja
slowly, "I would have spoken to Raymond or the Señor
Buchanan ; if it were only confidence, Pereo, our major-
domo, would have dragged himself from his sick-bed this

morning to do my mother's bidding. But it is more than that — it is the functions of a gentleman — and my mother, Captain Carroll, would like to say of — a friend."

He seized her hand and covered it with kisses. She withdrew it gently.

"What have I to do?" he asked eagerly.

She drew a note from her belt. "It is very simple. You must ride over to Aladdin with that note. You must give it to him *alone* — more than that, you must not let any one who may be there think you are making any but a social call. If he keeps you to dine — you must stay — you will bring back anything he may give you, and deliver it to me secretly for her."

"Is that all?" asked Carroll, with a slight touch of disappointment in his tone.

"No," said Maruja, rising impulsively. "No, Captain Carroll — it is *not* all! And you shall know all, if only to prove to you how we confide in you — and to leave you free, after you have heard it, to do as you please." She stood before him, quite white, opening and shutting her fan quickly, and tapping the tiled floor with her little foot. "I have told you Dr. West was my mother's business adviser. She looked upon him as more — as a friend. Do you know what a dangerous thing it is for a woman who has lost one protector to begin to rely upon another? Well, my mother is not yet old. Dr. West appreciated her — Dr. West did not depreciate himself — two things that go far with a woman, Captain Carroll, and my mother is a woman." She paused, and then, with a light toss of her fan, said: "Well, to make an end, but for this excellent horse and this too ambitious rider, one knows not how far the old story of my mother's first choice would have been repeated, and the curse of Koorotora again fallen on the land."

"And you tell me this — you, Maruja — you who warned me against my hopeless passion for you?"

"Could I foresee this ? " she said passionately; "and are you mad enough not to see that this very act would have made *your* suit intolerable to my relations ? "

"Then you did think of my suit, Maruja ? " he said, grasping her hand.

"Or any one's suit," she continued hurriedly, turning away with a slight increase of color in her cheeks. After a moment's pause, she added, in a gentler and half-reproachful voice, "Do you think I have confided my mother's story to you for this purpose only ? Is this the help you proffer ? "

"Forgive me, Maruja," said the young officer earnestly. "I am selfish, I know — for I love you. But you have not told me yet how I could help your mother by delivering this letter, which any one could do."

"Let me finish, then," said Maruja. "It is for you to judge what may be done. Letters have passed between my mother and Dr. West. My mother is imprudent; I know not what she may have written, or what she might not write, in confidence. But you understand, they are not letters to be made public nor to pass into any hands but hers. They are not to be left to be bandied about by his American friends ; to be commented upon by strangers ; to reach the ears of the Guitierrez. They belong to that grave which lies between the Past and my mother ; they must not rise from it to haunt her."

"I understand," said the young officer quietly. "This letter, then, is my authority to recover them ? "

"Partly, though it refers to other matters. This Mr. Prince, whom you Americans call Aladdin, was a friend of Dr. West; they were associated in business, and he will probably have access to his papers. The rest we must leave to you."

"I think you may," said Carroll simply.

Maruja stretched out her hand. The young man bent over it respectfully and moved towards the door.

She had expected him to make some protestation — perhaps even to claim some reward. But the instinct which made him forbear even in thought to take advantage of the duty laid upon him, which dominated even his miserable passion for her, and made it subservient to his exaltation of honor ; this epaulet of the officer, and blood of the gentleman, this simple possession of knighthood not laid on by perfunctory steel, but springing from within — all this, I grieve to say, was partly unintelligible to Maruja, and not entirely satisfactory. Since he had entered the room they seemed to have changed their situations ; he was no longer the pleading lover that trembled at her feet. For one base moment she thought it was the result of his knowledge of her mother's weakness ; but the next instant, meeting his clear glance, she colored with shame. Yet she detained him vaguely a moment before the grated door in the secure shadow of the arch. He might have kissed her there ! He did not.

In the gloomy stagnation of the great house, it was natural that he should escape from it for a while, and the saddling of his horse for a solitary ride attracted no attention. But it might have been noticed that his manner had lost much of that nervous susceptibility and anxiety which indicates a lover ; and it was with a return of his professional coolness and precision that he rode out of the patio as if on parade. Erect, observant, and self-possessed, he felt himself " on duty," and putting spurs to his horse, cantered along the highroad, finding an inexpressible relief in motion. He was doing something in the interest of helplessness and of *her*. He had no doubt of his right to interfere. He did not bother himself with the rights of others. Like all self-contained men, he had no plan of action, except what the occasion might suggest.

He was more than two miles from La Mision Perdida, when his quick eye was attracted by a saddle-blanket lying in the roadside ditch. A recollection of the calamity of the

previous night made him rein in his horse and examine it.
It was without doubt the saddle-blanket of Dr. West's
horse, lost when the saddle came off, after the Doctor's
body had been dragged by the runaway beast. But a second fact forced itself equally upon the young officer. It
was lying nearly a mile from the spot where the body had
been picked up. This certainly did not agree with the accepted theory that the accident had taken place further on,
and that the body had been dragged until the saddle came
off where it was found. His professional knowledge of
equitation and the technique of accoutrements exploded the
idea that the saddle could have slipped here, the saddle-
blanket fallen, and the horse have run nearly a mile ham-
pered by the saddle hanging under him. Consequently, the
saddle, blanket, and unfortunate rider must have been pre-
cipitated together, and at the same moment, on or near
this very spot. Captain Carroll was not a detective; he
had no theory to establish, no motive to discover, only as
an officer, he would have simply rejected any excuse offered
on those terms by one of his troopers to account for a similar accident. He troubled himself with no further deduction. Without dismounting, he gave a closer attention to
the marks of struggling hoofs near the edge of the ditch,
which had not yet been obliterated by the daily travel. In
doing so, his horse's hoof struck a small object partly hidden in the thick dust of the highway. It seemed to be a
leather letter or memorandum case adapted for the breast
pocket. Carroll instantly dismounted and picked it up.
The name and address of Dr. West were legibly written on
the inside. It contained a few papers and notes, but nothing more. The possibility that it might disclose the letters he was seeking was a hope quickly past. It was only
a corroborative fact that the accident had taken place on
the spot where he was standing. He was losing time; he
hurriedly put the book in his pocket, and once more
spurred forward on his road.

CHAPTER VII

THE exterior of Aladdin's Palace, familiar as it already was to Carroll, struck him that afternoon as looking more than usually unreal, ephemeral, and unsubstantial. The Moorish arches, of the thinnest white pine; the arabesque screens and lattices that looked as if made of pierced cardboard; the golden minarets that seemed to be glued to the shell-like towers, and the hollow battlements that visibly warped and cracked in the fierce sunlight, — all appeared more than ever like a theatrical scene that might sink through the ground, or vanish on either side to the sound of the prompter's whistle. Recalling Raymond's cynical insinuations, he could not help fancying that the house had been built by a conscientious genie with a view to the possibility of the lamp and the ring passing, with other effects, into the hands of the sheriff.

Nevertheless, the servant who took Captain Carroll's horse summoned another domestic, who preceded him into a small waiting-room off the gorgeous central hall, which looked not unlike the private bar-room of a first-class hotel, and presented him with a sherry cobbler. It was a peculiarity of Aladdin's Palace that the host seldom did the honors of his own house, but usually deputed the task to some friend, and generally the last newcomer. Carroll was consequently not surprised when he was presently joined by an utter stranger, who again pressed upon him the refreshment he had just declined. "You see," said the transitory host, "I 'm a stranger myself here, and have n't got the ways of the regular customers; but call for anything

you like, and I 'll see it got for you. Jim" (the actual
Christian name of Aladdin) " is headin' a party through the
stables. Would you like to join 'em — they ain't more than
half through now — or will you come right to the billiard-
room — the latest thing out in stained glass and iron — ez
pretty as fresh paint? or will you meander along to the
bridal suite, and see the bamboo and silver dressing-room,
and the white satin and crystal bed that cost fifteen thousand
dollars as it stands. Or," he added confidentially, " would
you like to cut the whole cussed thing, and I 'll get out
Jim's 2.32 trotter and his spider-legged buggy, and we 'll
take a spin over to the Springs afore dinner?" It was,
however, more convenient to Carroll's purpose to conceal
his familiarity with the Aladdin treasures, and to politely
offer to follow his guide through the house. " I reckon
Jim's pretty busy just now," continued the stranger; " what
with old Doc West going under so suddent, just ez he 'd got
things boomin' with that railroad and his manufactory company. The stocks went down to nothing this morning;
and 'twixt you and me, the boys say," he added, mysteriously sinking his voice, " it was jest the tightest squeeze
there whether there would n't be a general burst-up all
round. But Jim was over at San Antonio afore the Doctor's
body was laid out; just ran that telegraph himself for about
two hours; had a meeting of trustees and directors afore the
Coroner came; had the Doctor's books and papers brought
over here in a buggy, and another meeting before luncheon.
Why, by the time the other fellows began to drop in to
know if the Doctor was really dead, Jim Prince had discounted the whole affair two years ahead. Why, bless you,
nearly everybody is in it. That Spanish woman over there,
with the pretty daughter — that high-toned Greaser with
the big house — you know who I mean" . . .

"I don't think I do," said Carroll coldly. "I know a
lady named Saltonstall, with several daughters."

"That's her; thought I'd seen you there once. Well, the Doctor's got her into it, up to the eyes. I reckon she's mortgaged everything to him."

It required all Carroll's trained self-possession to prevent his garrulous guide from reading his emotion in his face. This, then, was the secret of Maruja's melancholy. Poor child! how bravely she had borne up under it; and *he*, in his utter selfishness, had never suspected it. Perhaps that letter was her delicate way of breaking the news to him, for he should certainly now hear it all from Aladdin's lips. And this man, who evidently had succeeded to the control of Dr. West's property, doubtless had possession of the letters too! Humph! He shut his lips firmly together, and strode along by the side of his innocent guide, erect and defiant.

He did not have long to wait. The sound of voices, the opening of doors, and the trampling of feet indicated that the other party were being "shown over" that part of the building Carroll and his companion were approaching.

"There's Jim and his gang now," said his cicerone; "I'll tell him you're here, and step out of this show business myself. So long! I reckon I'll see you at dinner." At this moment Prince and a number of ladies and gentlemen appeared at the further end of the hall; his late guide joined them, and apparently indicated Carroll's presence, as, with a certain lounging, off-duty, officer-like way, the young man sauntered on.

Aladdin, like others of his class, objected to the military, theoretically and practically; but he was not above recognizing their social importance in a country of no society, and of being fascinated by Carroll's quiet and secure self-possession and self-contentment in a community of restless ambition and aggressive assertion. He came forward to welcome him cordially; he introduced him with an air of satisfaction; he would have preferred if he had been in uniform, but he contented himself with the fact that Carroll, like all men of disciplined limbs, carried himself equally well in mufti.

"You have shown us everything," said Carroll, smiling, "except the secret chamber where you keep the magic lamp and ring. Are we not to see the spot where the incantation that produces these marvels is held, even if we are forbidden to witness the ceremony? The ladies are dying to see your sanctum — your study — your workshop — where you really live."

"You'll find it a mere den, as plain as my bedroom," said Prince, who prided himself on the Spartan simplicity of his own habits, and was not averse to the exhibition. "Come this way." He crossed the hall, and entered a small, plainly furnished room, containing a table piled with papers, some of which were dusty and worn-looking. Carroll instantly conceived the idea that these were Dr. West's property. He took his letter quietly from his pocket; and when the attention of the others was diverted, laid it on the table, with the remark, in an undertone, audible only to Prince, "From Mrs. Saltonstall."

Aladdin had that sublime audacity which so often fills the place of tact. Casting a rapid glance at Carroll, he cried, "Hallo!" and wheeling suddenly round on his following guests, with a bewildering extravagance of playful brusqueness, actually bundled them from the room. "The incantation is on!" he cried, waving his arms in the air; "the genie is at work. No admittance except on business! Follow Miss Wilson," he added, clapping both hands on the shoulders of the prettiest and shyest young lady of the party, with an irresistible paternal familiarity. "She's your hostess. I'll honor her drafts to any amount;" and before they were aware of his purpose, or that Carroll was no longer among them, Aladdin had closed the door, that shut with a spring-lock, and was alone with

the young man.   He walked quickly to his desk, took up
the letter, and opened it.

His face of dominant, self-satisfied good humor became
set and stern.   Without taking the least notice of Carroll,
he rose, and stepping to a telegraph instrument at a side
table, manipulated half a dozen ivory knobs with a sudden
energy.   Then he returned to the table, and began hurriedly to glance over the memoranda and indorsements of
the files of papers piled upon it.   Carroll's quick eye caught
sight of a small packet of letters in a writing of unmistakable feminine delicacy, and made certain they were the ones
he was in quest of.   Without raising his eyes, Mr. Prince
asked, almost rudely : —

"Who else has she told this to?"

"If you refer to the contents of that letter, it was written
and handed to me about three hours ago.   It has not been
out of my possession since then."

"Humph!   Who's at the casa?   There's Buchanan,
and Raymond, and Victor Guitierrez, eh?"

"I think I can say almost positively that Mrs. Saltonstall
has seen no one but her daughter since the news reached
her, if that is what you wish to know," said Carroll, still
following the particular package of letters with his eyes, as
Mr. Prince continued his examination.   Prince stopped.

"Are you sure?"

"Almost sure."

Prince rose, this time with a greater ease of manner, and
going to the table, ran his fingers over the knobs, as if mechanically.   "One would like to know at once all there is
to know about a transaction that changes the front of four
millions of capital in about four hours, eh, Captain?" he
said, for the first time really regarding his guest.   "Just
four hours ago, in this very room, we found out that the
widow Saltonstall owed Dr. West about a million, tied up
in investments, and we calculated to pull her through with

perhaps the loss of half. If she's got this assignment of
the Doctor's property that she speaks of in her letter, as
collateral security, and it's all regular, and she — so to
speak — steps into Dr. West's place, by G—d, sir, we owe
him about three millions, and we've got to settle with *her*
— and that's all about it. You've dropped a little bomb-
shell in here, Captain, and the splinters are flying around as
far as San Francisco, now. I confess it beats me regularly.
I always thought the old man was a little keen over there
at the casa — but she was a woman, and he was a man for
all his sixty years, and *that* combination I never thought
of. I only wonder she had n't gobbled him up before."

Captain Carroll's face betrayed no trace of the bewilderment and satisfaction at this news of which he had been
the unconscious bearer, nor of resentment at the coarseness
of its translation.

"There does not seem to be any memorandum of this
assignment," continued Prince, turning over the papers.

"Have you looked here?" said Carroll, taking up the
packet of letters.

"No — they seem to me some private letters she refers
to in this letter, and that she wants back again."

"Let us see," said Carroll, untying the packet. There
were three or four closely written notes in Spanish and
English.

"Love-letters, I reckon," said Prince — "that's why
the old girl wants 'em back. She don't care to have the
wheedling that fetched the Doctor trotted out to the
public."

"Let us look more carefully," said Carroll pleasantly,
opening each letter before Prince, yet so skillfully as to
frustrate any attempt of the latter to read them. "There
does not seem to be any memorandum here. They are
evidently only private letters."

"Quite so," said Prince.

Captain Carroll retied the packet and put it in his pocket. "Then I'll return them to her," he said quietly.

"Hullo! — here — I say," said Prince, starting to his feet.

"I said I would return them to her," repeated Carroll calmly.

"But I never gave them to you! I never consented to their withdrawal from the papers."

"I'm sorry you did not," said Carroll coldly; "it would have been more polite."

"Polite! D—n it, sir! I call this stealing."

"Stealing, Mr. Prince, is a word that might be used by the person who claims these letters to describe the act of any one who would keep them from *her*. It really cannot apply to you or me."

"Once for all, do you refuse to return them to me?" said Prince, pale with anger.

"Decidedly."

"Very well, sir! We shall see." He stepped to the corner and rang a bell. "I have summoned my manager, and will charge you with the theft in his presence."

"I think not."

"And why, sir?"

"Because the presence of a third party would enable me to throw this glove in your face, which, as a gentleman, I could n't do without witnesses." Steps were heard along the passage; Prince was no coward in a certain way; neither was he a fool. He knew that Carroll would keep his word; he knew that he should have to fight him; that, whatever the issue of the duel was, the cause of the quarrel would be known, and scarcely redound to his credit. At present there were no witnesses to the offered insult, and none would be wiser. The letters were not worth it. He stepped to the door, opened it, said, "No matter," and closed it again.

He returned with an affectation of carelessness. "You are right. I don't know that I'm called upon to make a scene here which the *law* can do for me as well elsewhere. It will settle pretty quick whether you've got the right to those letters, and whether you've taken the right way to get them, sir."

"I have no desire to evade any responsibility in this matter, legal or otherwise," said Carroll coldly, rising to his feet.

"Look here," said Prince suddenly, with a return of his brusque frankness; "you might have *asked* me for those letters, you know."

"And you wouldn't have given them to me," said Carroll.

Prince laughed. "That's so! I say, Captain. Did they teach you this sort of strategy at West Point?"

"They taught me that I could neither receive nor give an insult under a white flag," said Carroll pleasantly. "And they allowed me to make exchanges under the same rule. I picked up this pocket-book on the spot where the accident occurred to Dr. West. It is evidently his. I leave it with you, who are his executor."

The instinct of reticence before a man with whom he could never be confidential kept him from alluding to his other discovery.

Prince took the pocket-book, and opened it mechanically. After a moment's scrutiny of the memoranda it contained, his face assumed something of the same concentrated attention it wore at the beginning of the interview. Raising his eyes suddenly to Carroll, he said quickly : —

"You have examined it?"

"Only so far as to see that it contained nothing of importance to the person I represent," returned Carroll simply.

The capitalist looked at the young officer's clear eyes. Something of embarrassment came into his own as he turned them away.

"Certainly. Only memoranda of the Doctor's business. Quite important to us, you know. But nothing referring to *your* principal." He laughed. "Thank you for the exchange. I say — take a drink!"

"Thank you — no!" returned Carroll, going to the door.

"Well, good-by."

He held out his hand. Carroll, with his clear eyes still regarding him, passed quietly by the outstretched hand, opened the door, bowed and made his exit.

A slight flush came into Prince's cheek. Then, as the door closed, he burst into a half laugh. Had he been a dramatic villain, he would have added to it several lines of soliloquy, in which he would have rehearsed the fact that the opportunity for revenge had "come at last;" that the "haughty victor who had just left with his ill-gotten spoil had put into his hands the weapon of his friend's destruction;" that the "hour had come;" and possibly he might have said, "Ha! ha!" But being a practical, good-natured, selfish rascal, not much better or worse than his neighbors, he sat himself down at his desk and began to carefully consider how *he* could best make use of the memoranda jotted down by Dr. West of the proofs of the existence of his son, and the consequent discovery of a legal heir to his property

CHAPTER VIII

WHEN Faquita had made sure that her young mistress was so securely closeted with Doña Maria that morning as to be inaccessible to curious eyes and ears, she saw fit to bewail to her fellow servants this further evidence of the decay of the old feudal and patriarchal mutual family confidences. "Time was, thou rememberest, Pepita, when an affair of this kind was openly discussed at chocolate with everybody present and before us all. When Joaquin Padilla was shot at Monterey, it was the Doña herself who told us, who read aloud the letters describing it and the bullet-holes in his clothes, and made it quite a gala day — and he was a first cousin of Guitierrez. And now, when this American goat of a doctor is kicked to death by a mule, the family must shut themselves up, that never a question is asked or answered." "Ay," responded Pepita; "and as regards that, Sanchez there knows as much as they do, for it was he that almost saw the whole affair."

"How ? — sawest it ? " inquired Faquita eagerly.

"Why, was it not he that was bringing home Pereo, who had been lying in one of his trances or visions — blessed St. Antonio preserve us ! " said Pepita, hastily crossing herself — " on Koorotora's grave, when the Doctor's mustang charged down upon them like a wild bull, and the Doctor's foot half out of the stirrups, and he not yet fast in his seat ? And Pereo laughs a wild laugh and says: ' Watch if the coyote does not drag yet at his mustang's heels ; ' and Sanchez ran and watched the Doctor out of sight, careering and galloping to his death ! — ay, as Pereo prophesied.

For it was only half an hour afterwards that Sanchez again heard the tramp of his hoofs — as if it were here — and knowing it two miles away — thou understandest, he said to himself ' It is over.' "

The two women shuddered and crossed themselves.

"And what says Pereo of the fulfillment of his prophecy ? " asked Faquita, hugging herself in her shawl with a certain titillating shrug of fascinating horror.

"It is even possible he understands it not. Thou knowest how dazed and dumb he ever is after these visions — that he comes from them as one from the grave, remembering nothing. He has lain like a log all the morning."

"Ay; but this news should awaken him, if aught can. He loved not this sneaking Doctor. Let us seek him ; mayhap, Sanchez may be there. Come ! The mistress lacks us not just now ; the guests are provided for. Come ! "

She led the way to the eastern angle of the casa communicating by a low corridor with the corral and stables. This was the old "gate-keep" or quarters of the major-domo, who, among his functions, was supposed to exercise a supervision over the exits and entrances of the house. A large steward's room or office, beyond it a room of general assembly, half guard-room, half servants' hall, and Pereo's sleeping-room, constituted his domain. A few peons were gathered in the hall near the open door of the apartment where Pereo lay.

Stretched on a low pallet, his face yellow as wax, a light burning under a crucifix near his head, and a spray of blessed palm, popularly supposed to avert the attempts of evil spirits to gain possession of his suspended faculties, Pereo looked not unlike a corpse. Two muffled and shawled domestics, who sat by his side, might have been mourners, but for their voluble and incessant chattering.

"So thou art here, Faquita," said a stout virago. "It is a wonder thou couldst spare time from prayers for the repose of the American Doctor's soul to look after the health of thy superior, poor Pereo! Is it, then, true that Doña Maria said she would have naught more to do with the drunken brute of her major-domo ? "

The awful fascination of Pereo's upturned face did not prevent Faquita from tossing her head as she replied, pertly, that she was not there to defend her mistress from lazy gossip. " Nay, but *what* said she ? " asked the other attendant.

" She said Pereo was to want for nothing; but at present she could not see him."

A murmur of indignation and sympathy passed through the company. It was followed by a long sigh from the insensible man. " His lips move," said Faquita, still fascinated by curiosity. " Hush! he would speak."

" His lips move, but his soul is still asleep," said Sanchez oracularly. " Thus they have moved since early morning, when I came to speak with him, and found him lying here in a fit upon the floor. He was half dressed, thou seest, as if he had risen to go forth, and had been struck down so " —

" Hush! I tell thee he speaks," said Faquita.

The sick man was faintly articulating through a few tiny bubbles that broke upon his rigid lips. " He — dared — me ! He — said — I was old — too old."

" Who dared thee ? Who said thou wast too old ? " asked the eager Faquita, bending over him.

" He, Koorotora himself! in the shape of a coyote."

Faquita fell back with a little giggle, half of shame, half of awe.

" It is ever thus," said Sanchez sententiously; " it is what he said last night, when I picked him up on the mound. He will sleep now — thou shalt see. He will get no further than Koorotora and the coyote — and then he will sleep."

And to the awe of the group, and the increased respect
for Sanchez's wisdom, Pereo seemed to fall again into a
lethargic slumber. It was late in the evening when he
appeared to regain perfect consciousness. "Ah — what is
this?" he said roughly, sitting up in bed, and eying the
watchers around him, some of whom had succumbed to
sleep, and others were engaged in playing cards. "Caramba! are ye mad? Thou, Sanchez, here; who shouldst
be at thy work in the stables! Thou, Pepita, is thy mistress asleep or dead, that thou sittest here? Blessed San
Antonio! would ye drive me mad?" He lifted his hand
to his head, with a dull movement of pain, and attempted
to rise from the bed.

"Softly, good Pereo; lie still," said Sanchez, approaching him. "Thou hast been ill — so ill. These, thy
friends, have been waiting only for this moment to be
assured that thou art better. For this idleness there is no
blame — truly none. The Doña Maria has said that thou
shouldst lack no care; and, truly, since the terrible news
there has been little to do."

"The terrible news?" repeated Pereo.

Sanchez cast a meaning glance upon the others, as if to
indicate this confirmation of his diagnosis.

"Ay, terrible news! The Dr. West was found this
morning dead two miles from the casa."

"Dr. West dead!" repeated Pereo slowly, as if endeavoring to master the real meaning of the words. Then, seeing
the vacuity of his question reflected on the faces of those
around him, he added hurriedly, with a feeble smile, "O
— ay — dead! Yes! I remember. And he has been ill
— very ill, eh?"

"It was an accident. He was thrown from his horse,
and so killed," returned Sanchez gravely.

"Killed — by his horse! sayest thou?" said Pereo,
with a sudden fixed look in his eye.

"Ay, good Pereo. Dost thou not remember when the mustang bolted with him down upon us in the lane, and then thou didst say he would come to evil with the brute? He did — blessed San Antonio! — within half an hour!"

"How — thou sawest it?"

"Nay; for the mustang was running away and I did not follow. Bueno! it happened all the same. The Alcalde, Coroner, who knows all about it, has said so an hour ago. Juan brought the news from the rancho where the inquest was. There will be a funeral the day after to-morrow! and so it is that some of the family will go. Fancy, Pereo, a Guitierrez at the funeral of the Americano Doctor! Nay, I doubt not that the Doña Maria will ask thee to say a prayer over his bier."

"Peace, fool! and speak not of thy lady mistress," thundered the old man, sitting upright. "Begone to the stables. Dost thou hear me? Go!"

"Now, by the Mother of Miracles," said Sanchez, hastening from the room as the gaunt figure of the old man rose, like a sheeted spectre, from the bed, "that was his old self again! Blessed San Antonio! Pereo has recovered."

The next day he was at his usual duties, with perhaps a slight increase of sternness in his manner. The fulfillment of his prophecy related by Sanchez added to the superstitious reputation in which he was held, although Faquita voiced the opinions of a growing skeptical party in the statement that it was easy to prophesy the Doctor's accident, with the spectacle of the horse actually running away before the prophet's eyes. It was even said that Doña Maria's aversion to Pereo since the accident arose from a belief that some assistance might have been rendered by him. But it was pointed out by Sanchez that Pereo had, a few moments before, fallen under one of those singular, epileptic-like strokes to which he was subject, and not only was unfit, but even required the entire care of Sanchez at the time. He did not attend the funeral, nor did Mrs. Saltonstall; but the family was represented by Maruja and Amita, accompanied by one or two dark-faced cousins, Captain Carroll, and Raymond. A number of friends and business associates from the neighboring towns, Aladdin and a party from his house, the farm laborers, and a crowd of workingmen from his mills in the foot-hills, swelled the assemblage that met in and around the rude agricultural sheds and outhouses which formed the only pastoral habitation of the Rancho of San Antonio. It had been a characteristic injunction of the deceased that he should be buried in the midst of one of his most prolific grain-fields, as a grim return to that nature he was impoverishing, with neither mark nor monument to indicate the spot; and that even the temporary mound above him should, at the fitting season of the year, be leveled with the rest of the field by the obliterating ploughshares. A grave was accordingly dug about a quarter of a mile from his office, amidst a " volunteer " crop so dense that the large space mown around the narrow opening, to admit of the presence of the multitude, seemed like a golden amphitheatre.

A distinguished clergyman from San Francisco officiated. A man of tact and politic adaptation, he dwelt upon the blameless life of the deceased, on his practical benefit for civilization in the county, and even treated his grim Pantheism in the selection of his grave as a formal recognition of the text, "dust to dust." He paid a not ungrateful compliment to the business associates of the deceased, and, without actually claiming in the usual terms "a continuance of past favors" for their successors, managed to interpolate so strong a recommendation of the late Doctor's commercial projects as to elicit from Aladdin the expressive commendation that his sermon was "as good as five per cent. in the stock."

Maruja, who had been standing near the carriage, languidly silent and abstracted even under the tender attentions of Carroll, suddenly felt the consciousness of another pair of eyes fixed upon her. Looking up, she was surprised to find herself regarded by the man she had twice met, once as a tramp and once as a wayfarer at the fonda, who had quietly joined a group not far from her. At once impressed by the idea that this was the first time that he had really looked at her, she felt a singular shyness creeping over her, until, to her own astonishment and indignation, she was obliged to lower her eyes before his gaze. In vain she tried to lift them, with her old supreme power of fascination. If she had ever blushed, she felt she would have done so now. She knew that her face must betray her consciousness ; and at last she — Maruja, the self-poised and all-sufficient goddess — actually turned, in half-hysterical and girlish bashfulness, to Carroll for relief in an affected and exaggerated absorption of his attentions. She scarcely knew that the clergyman had finished speaking, when Raymond approached them softly from behind. "Pray don't believe," he said appealingly, "that all the human virtues are about to be buried — I should say sown — in that wheat-field. A few will still survive, and creep about above the Doctor's grave. Listen to a story just told me, and disbelieve — if you dare — in human gratitude. Do you see that picturesque young ruffian over there ? "

Maruja did not lift her eyes. She felt herself breathlessly hanging on the speaker's next words.

" Why, that 's the young man of the fonda, who picked up your fan," said Carroll, " is n't it ? "

" Perhaps," said Maruja indifferently. She would have given worlds to have been able to turn coldly and stare at him at that moment with the others, but she dared not. She contented herself with softly brushing some dust from

Captain Carroll's arm with her fan, and a feminine suggestion of tender care which thrilled that gentleman.

"Well," continued Raymond, "that Robert Macaire
over yonder came here some three or four days ago as a
tramp, in want of everything but honest labor. Our lamented friend consented to parley with him, which was
something remarkable in the Doctor; still more remarkable, he gave him a suit of clothes, and, it is said, some
money, and sent him on his way. Now, more remarkable
than all, our friend, on hearing of his benefactor's death,
actually tramps back here to attend his funeral. The Doctor being dead, his executors not of a kind to emulate the
Doctor's spasmodic generosity, and there being no chance
of future favors, the act must be recorded as purely and
simply gratitude. By Jove! I don't know but that he is
the only one here who can be called a real mourner. I'm
here because your sister is here; Carroll comes because
you do, and you come because your mother cannot."

"And who tells you these pretty stories?" asked Maruja, with her face still turned towards Carroll.

"The foreman, Harrison, who, with an extensive practical experience of tramps, was struck with this exception to
the general rule."

"Poor man; one ought to do something for him," said
Amita compassionately.

"What!" said Raymond, with affected terror, "and
spoil this perfect story? Never! If I should offer him
ten dollars, I'd expect him to kick me; if he took it, I'd
expect to kick *him*."

"He is not so bad-looking, is he, Maruja?" asked
Amita of her sister. But Maruja had already moved a few
paces off with Carroll, and seemed to be listening to him
only. Raymond smiled at the pretty perplexity of Amita's
eyebrows over this pronounced indiscretion.

"Don't mind them," he whispered; "you really cannot

expect to dueña your elder sister. Tell me, would you actually like me to see if I could assist the virtuous tramp? You have only to speak." But Amita's interest appeared to be so completely appeased with Raymond's simple offer that she only smiled, blushed, and said "No."

Maruja's quick ears had taken in every word of these asides, and for an instant she hated her sister for her aimless declination of Raymond's proposal. But becoming conscious — under her eyelids — that the stranger was moving away with the dispersing crowd, she rejoined Amita with her usual manner. The others had reëntered the carriage, but Maruja took it into her head to proceed on foot to the rude building whence the mourners had issued. The foreman, Harrison, flushed and startled by this apparition of inaccessible beauty at his threshold, came eagerly forward. "I shall not trouble you now, Mr. Har-r-r-rison," she said, with a polite exaggeration of the consonants; "but some day I shall ride over here, and ask you to show me your wonderful machines."

She smiled, and turned back to seek her carriage. But before she had gone many yards she found that she had completely lost it in the intervening billows of grain. She stopped, with an impatient little Spanish ejaculation. The next moment the stalks of wheat parted before her and a figure emerged. It was the stranger.

She fell back a step in utter helplessness.

He, on his side, retreated again into the wheat, holding it back with extended arms to let her pass. As she moved forward mechanically, without a word he moved backward, making a path for her until she was able to discern the coachman's whip above the bending heads of the grain just beyond her. He stopped here and drew to one side, his arms still extended, to give her free passage. She tried to speak, but could only bow her head, and slipped by him with a strange feeling — suggested by his attitude — that she was evading his embrace. But the next moment his arms were lowered, the grain closed around him, and he was lost to her view. She reached the carriage almost unperceived by the inmates, and pounced upon her sister with a laugh.

"Blessed Virgin!" said Amita, "where did you come from?"

"From there!" said Maruja, with a slight nervous shiver, pointing to the clustering grain.

"We were afraid you were lost."

"So was I," said Maruja, raising her pretty lashes heavenwards, as she drew a shawl tightly round her shoulders.

"Has anything happened? You look strange," said Carroll, drawing closer to her.

Her eyes were sparkling, but she was very pale.

"Nothing, nothing!" she said hastily, glancing at the grain again.

"If it were not that the haste would have been absolutely indecent, I should say that the late Doctor had made you a ghostly visit," said Raymond, looking at her curiously.

"He would have been polite enough not to have commented on my looks," said Maruja. "Am I really such a fright?"

Carroll thought he had never seen her so beautiful. Her eyelids were quivering over their fires as if they had been brushed by the passing wing of a strong passion.

"What are you thinking of?" said Carroll, as they drove on.

She was thinking that the stranger had looked at her admiringly, and that his eyes were blue. But she looked quietly into her lover's face, and said sweetly, "Nothing, I fear, that would interest you!"

CHAPTER IX

THE news of the assignment of Dr. West's property to
Mrs. Saltonstall was followed by the still more astonishing
discovery that the Doctor's will further bequeathed to her
his entire property, after payment of his debts and liabili-
ties. It was given in recognition of her talents and business integrity during their late association, and as an
evidence of the confidence and "undying affection" of the
testator. Nevertheless, after the first surprise, the fact
was accepted by the community as both natural and proper
under that singular instinct of humanity which acquiesces
without scruple in the union of two large fortunes, but
sharply questions the conjunction of poverty and affluence,
and looks only for interested motives where there is dis-
parity of wealth. Had Mrs. Saltonstall been a poor widow
instead of a rich one; had she been the Doctor's house-
keeper instead of his business friend, the bequest would
have been strongly criticised — if not legally tested. But
this combination, which placed the entire valley of San
Antonio in the control of a single individual, appeared to
be perfectly legitimate. More than that, some vague rumor
of the Doctor's past and his early entanglements only seemed
to make this eminently practical disposition of his property
the more respectable, and condoned for any moral irregulari-
ties of his youth.

The effect upon the collateral branches of the Guitierrez
family and the servants and retainers was even more impressive. For once, it seemed that the fortunes and traditions
of the family were changed ; the female Guitierrez, instead

of impoverishing the property, had augmented it; the foreigner and intruder had been despoiled; the fate of La Mision Perdida had been changed; the curse of Koorotora had proved a blessing; his prophet and descendant, Pereo, the major-domo, moved in an atmosphere of superstitious adulation and respect among the domestics and common people. This recognition of his power he received at times with a certain exaltation of grandiloquent pride beyond the conception of any but a Spanish servant, and at times with a certain dull, pained vacancy of perception and an expression of frightened bewilderment which also went far to establish his reputation as an unconscious seer and thaumaturgist. " Thou seest," said Sanchez to the partly skeptical Faquita, " he does not know more than an infant what is his power. That is the proof of it." The Doña Maria alone did not participate in this appreciation of Pereo, and when it was proposed that a feast or celebration of rejoicing should be given under the old pear-tree by the Indian's mound, her indignation was long remembered by those that witnessed it. " It is not enough that we have been made ridiculous in the past," she said to Maruja, " by the interference of this solemn fool, but that the memory of our friend is to be insulted by his generosity being made into a triumph of Pereo's idiotic ancestor. One would have thought those coyotes and Koorotora's bones had been buried with the cruel gossip of your relations " — (it had been the recent habit of Doña Maria to allude to " the family " as being particularly related to Maruja alone) — " over my poor friend. Let him beware that his ancestor's mound is not uprooted with the pear-tree, and his heathenish temple destroyed. If, as the engineer says, a branch of the new railroad can be established for La Mision Perdida, I agree with him that it can better pass at that point with less sacrifice to the domain. It is the one uncultivated part of the park, and lies at the proper angle."

" You surely would not consent to this, my mother ? " said Maruja, with a sudden impression of a newly found force in her mother's character.

"Why not, child ? " said the relict of Mr. Saltonstall and the mourner of Dr. West coldly. " I admit it was discreet of thee in old times to have thy sentimental passages there with caballeros who, like the guests of the hidalgo that kept a skeleton at his feast, were reminded of the mutability of their hopes by Koorotora's bones and the legend. But with the explosion of this idea of a primal curse, like Eve's, on the property," added the Doña Maria, with a slight bitterness, " thou mayst have thy citas — elsewhere. Thou canst scarcely keep this Captain Carroll any longer at a distance by rattling those bones of Koorotora in his face. And of a truth, child, since the affair of the letters, and his discreet and honorable conduct since, I see not why thou shouldst. He has thy mother's reputation in his hands."

" He is a gentleman, my mother," said Maruja quietly.

" And they are scarce, child, and should be rewarded and preserved. That is what I meant, silly one ; this Captain is not rich — but then, thou hast enough for both."

" But it was Amita that first brought him here," said Maruja, looking down with an air of embarrassed thoughtfulness, which Doña Maria chose to instantly accept as exaggerated coyness.

" Do not think to deceive me or thyself, child, with this folly. Thou art old enough to know a man's mind, if not thine own. Besides, I do not know that I shall object to her liking for Raymond. He is very clever, and would be a relief to some of thy relatives. He would be invaluable to us in the emergencies that may grow out of these mechanical affairs that I do not understand — such as the mill and the railroad."

" And you propose to take a few husbands as partners

in the business?" said Maruja, who had recovered her spirits. "I warn you that Captain Carroll is as stupid as a gentleman could be. I wonder that he has not blundered in other things as badly as he has in preferring me to Amita. He confided to me only last night, that he had picked up a pocket-book belonging to the Doctor and given it to Aladdin, without a witness or receipt, and evidently of his own accord."

"A pocket-book of the Doctor's?" repeated Doña Maria.

"Ay; but it contained nothing of thine," said Maruja. "The poor child had sense enough to think of that. But I am in no hurry to ask your consent and your blessing yet, little mother. I could even bear that Amita should precede me to the altar, if the exigencies of thy 'business' require it. It might also secure Captain Carroll for me. Nay, look not at me in that cheapening, commercial way — with compound interest in thine eyes. I am not so poor an investment, truly, of thy original capital."

"Thou art thy father's child," said her mother, suddenly kissing her; "and that is saying enough, the Blessed Virgin knows. Go now," she continued, gently pushing her from the room, "and send Amita hither." She watched the disappearance of Maruja's slightly rebellious shoulders, and added to herself, "And this is the child that Amita really believes is pining with lovesickness for Carroll, so that she can neither sleep nor eat. This is the girl that Faquita would have me think hath no longer any heart in her dress or in her finery! Soul of Joseph Saltonstall!" ejaculated the widow, lifting her shoulders and her eyes together, "thou hast much to account for."

Two weeks later she again astonished her daughter. "Why dost thou not join the party that drives over to see the wonders of Aladdin's Palace to-day? It would seem more proper that thou shouldst accompany thy guests than Raymond and Amita."

"I have never entered his doors since the day he was disrespectful to my mother's daughter," said Maruja, in surprise.

"Disrespectful!" repeated Doña Maria impatiently. "Thy father's daughter ought to know that such as he may be ignorant and vulgar, but cannot be disrespectful to her. And there are offenses, child, it is much more crushing to forget than to remember. As long as he has not the presumption to *apologize*, I see no reason why thou mayst not go. He has not been here since that affair of the letters. I shall not permit him to be uncivil over *that*— dost thou understand? He is of use to me in business. Thou mayst take Carroll with thee; he will understand that."

"But Carroll will not go," said Maruja. "He will not say what passed between them, but I suspect they quarreled."

"All the better, then, that thou goest alone. He need not be reminded of it. Fear not but that he will be only too proud of thy visit to think of aught else."

Maruja, who seemed relieved at this prospect of being unaccompanied by Captain Carroll, shrugged her shoulders and assented.

When the party that afternoon drove into the courtyard of Aladdin's Palace, the announcement that its hospitable proprietor was absent, and would not return until dinner, did not abate either their pleasure or their curiosity. As already intimated to the reader, Mr. Prince's functions as host were characteristically irregular; and the servant's suggestion, that Mr. Prince's private secretary would attend to do the honors, created little interest, and was laughingly waived by Maruja. "There really is not the slightest necessity to trouble the gentleman," she said politely. "I know the house thoroughly, and I think I have shown it once or twice before for your master. Indeed," she added, turning to her party, "I have been already complimented on my skill as a cicerone." After a pause, she continued, with a slight exaggeration of action and in her deepest contralto, "Ahem, ladies and gentlemen, the hall and court in which we are now standing is a perfect copy of the Court of Lions at the Alhambra, and was finished in fourteen days in white pine, gold, and plaster, at a cost of ten thousand dollars. A photograph of the original structure hangs on the wall; you will observe, ladies and gentlemen, that the reproduction is perfect. The Alhambra is in Granada, a province of Spain, which is said in some respects to resemble California, where you have probably observed the Spanish language is still spoken by the old settlers. We now cross the stable-yard on a bridge which is a facsimile in appearance and dimensions of the Bridge of Sighs at Venice, connecting the Doge's Palace with the State Prison. Here, on the contrary, instead of being ushered into a dreary dungeon, as in the great original, a fresh surprise awaits us. Allow me, ladies and gentlemen, to precede you for the surprise. We open a door thus — and — presto!" —

She stopped, speechless, on the threshold; the fan fell from her gesticulating hand.

In the centre of a brilliantly lit conservatory, with golden columns, a young man was standing. As her fan dropped on the tessellated pavement, he came forward, picked it up, and put it in her rigid and mechanical fingers. The party, who had applauded her apparently artistic climax, laughingly pushed by her into the conservatory, without noticing her agitation.

It was the same face and figure she remembered as last standing before her, holding back the crowding grain in the San Antonio field. But here he was appareled and appointed like a gentleman, and even seemed to be superior to the garish glitter of his new surroundings.

"I believe I have the pleasure of speaking to Miss Sal-tonstall," he said, with the faintest suggestion of his for-mer manner in his half-resentful sidelong glance. "I hear that you offered to dispense with my services, but I knew that Mr. Prince would scarcely be satisfied if I did not urge it once more upon you in person. I am his private secre-tary."

At the same moment, Amita and Raymond, attracted by the conversation, turned towards him. Their recognition of the man they had seen at Dr. West's was equally dis-tinct. The silence became embarrassing. Two pretty girls of the party pressed to Amita's side, with half-audible whispers. "What is it?" "Who's your handsome and wicked-looking friend?" "Is this the surprise?"

At the sound of their voices, Maruja recovered herself coldly. "Ladies," she said, with a slight wave of her fan, "this is Mr. Prince's private secretary. I believe it is hardly fair to take up his valuable time. Allow me to thank you, sir, FOR PICKING UP MY FAN!"

With a single subtle flash of the eye she swept by him, taking her companions to the other end of the conservatory. When she turned, he was gone.

"This was certainly an unexpected climax," said Ray-mond mischievously. "Did you really arrange it before-hand? We leave a picturesque tramp at the edge of a grave; we pass over six weeks and a Bridge of Sighs, and hey, presto! we find a private secretary in a conservatory! This is quite the regular Aladdin business."

"You may laugh," said Maruja, who had recovered her spirits, "but if you were really clever you'd find out what it all means. Don't you see that Amita is dying of curi-osity?"

"Let us fly at once and discover the secret, then," said Raymond, slipping Amita's arm through his. "We will consult the oracle in the stables. Come."

The others followed, leaving Maruja for an instant alone. She was about to rejoin them when she heard footsteps in the passage they had just crossed, and then perceived that the young stranger had merely withdrawn to allow the party to precede him before he returned to the other building through the conservatory, which he was just entering. In turning quickly to escape, the black lace of her overskirt caught in the spines of a snaky-looking cactus. She stopped to disengage herself with feverish haste in vain. She was about to sacrifice the delicate material, in her impatience, when the young man stepped quietly to her side.

"Allow me. Perhaps I have more patience, even if I have less time," he said, stooping down. Their ungloved hands touched. Maruja stopped in her efforts and stood up. He continued until he had freed the luckless flounce, conscious of the soft fire of her eyes on his head and neck.

"There," he said, rising, and encountering her glance. As she did not speak, he continued: "You are thinking, Miss Saltonstall, that you have seen me before, are you not? Well — you *have*; I asked you the road to San José one morning when I was tramping by your hedge."

"And as you probably were looking for something better — which you seem to have found — you didn't care to listen to *my* directions," said Maruja quickly.

"I found a man — almost the only one who ever offered me a gratuitous kindness — at whose grave I afterwards met you. I found another man who befriended me here — where I meet you again."

She was beginning to be hysterically nervous lest any one should return and find them together. She was conscious of a tingling of vague shame. Yet she lingered. The strange fascination of his half-savage melancholy, and a reproachfulness that seemed to arraign her, with the rest of the world, at the bar of his vague resentment, held the delicate fibres of her sensitive being as cruelly and relent-

lessly as the thorns of the cactus had gripped her silken
lace. Without knowing what she was saying, she stammered that she " was glad he connected her with his better fortune," and began to move away. He noticed it with
his sidelong lids, and added, with a slight bitterness: —

"I don't think I should have intruded here again, but I
thought you had gone. But I — I — am afraid you have
not seen the last of me. It was the intention of my
employer, Mr. Prince, to introduce me to you and your
mother. I suppose he considers it part of my duties here.
I must warn you that, if you are here when he returns, he
will insist upon it, and upon your meeting me with these
ladies at dinner."

"Perhaps so — he is my mother's friend," said Maruja;
" but you have the advantage of us — you can always take
to the road, you know."

The smile with which she had intended to accompany
this speech did not come as readily in execution as it had
in conception, and she would have given worlds to have
recalled her words. But he said, "That's so" quietly,
and turned away, as if to give her an opportunity to escape.
She moved hesitatingly towards the passage and stopped.
The sound of the returning voices gave her a sudden
courage.

" Mr." —

" Guest," said the young man.

" If we do conclude to stay to dinner, as Mr. Prince has
said nothing of introducing you to my sister, you must let
me have that pleasure."

He lifted his eyes to hers with a sudden flush. But
she had fled.

She reached her party, displaying her torn flounce as the
cause of her delay, and there was a slight quickness in her
breathing and her speech which was attributed to the same
grave reason. " But, only listen," said Amita, " we 've

got it all out of the butler and the grooms. It's such a romantic story ! "

" What is ? " said Maruja suddenly.

" Why, the private tramp's."

" The peripatetic secretary," suggested Raymond.

" Yes," continued Amita, " Mr. Prince was so struck with his gratitude to the old Doctor that he hunted him up in San José, and brought him here. Since then Prince has been so interested in him — it appears he was somebody in the States, or has rich relations — that he has been telegraphing and making all sorts of inquiries about him, and has even sent out his own lawyer to hunt up everything about him. Are you listening ? "

" Yes."

" You seem abstracted."

" I am hungry."

" Why not dine here; it 's an hour earlier than at home. Aladdin would fall at your feet for the honor. Do ! "

Maruja looked at them with innocent vagueness, as if the possibility were just beginning to dawn upon her.

" And Clara Wilson is just dying to see the mysterious unknown again. Say yes, little Maruja."

Little Maruja glanced at them with a large maternal compassion. " We shall see."

Mr. Prince, on his return an hour later, was unexpectedly delighted with Maruja's gracious acceptance of his invitation to dinner. He was thoroughly sensible of the significance which his neighbors had attached to the avoidance by the Saltonstall heiress of his various parties and gorgeous festivities ever since a certain act of indiscretion — now alleged to have been produced by the exaltation of wine — had placed him under ban. Whatever his feelings were towards her mother, he could not fail to appreciate fully this act of the daughter, which rehabilitated him. It was with more than his usual extravagance — shown even in a certain exaggeration of respect towards Maruja — that he welcomed the party, and made preparations for the dinner. The telegraph and mounted messengers were put into rapid requisition. The bridal suite was placed at the disposal of the young ladies for a dressing-room. The attendant genii surpassed themselves. The evening dresses of Maruja, Amita, and the Misses Wilson, summoned by electricity from La Mision Perdida, and dispatched by the fleetest conveyances, were placed in the arms of their maids, smothered with bouquets, an hour before dinner. An operatic concert troupe, passing through the nearest town, were diverted from their course by the slaves of the ring to discourse hidden music in the music-room during dinner. "Bite my finger, Sweetlips," said Miss Clara Wilson, who had a neat taste for apt quotation, to Maruja, "that I may see if I am awake. It's the Arabian Nights all over again!"

The dinner was a marvel, even in a land of gastronomic marvels; the dessert a miracle of fruits, even in a climate that bore the products of two zones. Maruja, from her seat beside her satisfied host, looked across a bank of yellow roses at her sister and Raymond, and was timidly conscious of the eyes of young Guest, who was seated at the other end of the table, between the two Misses Wilson. With a strange haunting of his appearance on the day she first met him, she stole glances of half-frightened curiosity at him while he was eating, and was relieved to find that he used his knife and fork like the others, and that his appetite was far from voracious. It was his employer who was the first to recall the experiences of his past life, with a certain enthusiasm and the air of a host anxious to contribute to the entertainment of his guests. "You'd hardly believe, Miss Saltonstall, that that young gentleman over there walked across the continent — and two thousand odd miles, wasn't it? — all alone, and with not much more in the way of traps than he's got on now. Tell 'em, Harry, how the Apaches nearly gobbled you up, and then let you go because they thought you as good an Injun as any one of them, and how you lived a week in the desert on two biscuits as big as that." A chorus of entreaty and delighted anticipation followed the suggestion. The old expression of being at bay returned for an instant to Guest's face, but, lifting his eyes, he caught a look of almost sympathetic anxiety from Maruja's, who had not spoken.

"It became necessary for me, some time ago," said Guest, half explanatorily, to Maruja, "to be rather explicit in the details of my journey here, and I told Mr. Prince some things which he seems to think interesting to others. That is all. To save my life on one occasion, I was obliged to show myself as good as an Indian, in his own way, and I lived among them and traveled with them for two weeks. I have been hungry, as I suppose others have on like occasions, but nothing more."

Nevertheless, in spite of his evident reticence, he was obliged to give way to their entreaties, and with a certain grim and uncompromising truthfulness of statement, recounted some episodes of his journey. It was none the less thrilling that he did it reluctantly, and in much the same manner as he had answered his father's questions, and as he had probably responded to the later cross-examination of Mr. Prince. He did not tell it emotionally, but rather with the dogged air of one who had been subjected to a personal grievance for which he neither asked nor expected sympathy. When he did not raise his eyes to Maruja's, he kept them fixed on his plate.

"Well," said Prince, when a long-drawn sigh of suspended emotion among the guests testified to his powers as a caterer to their amusement, "what do you say to some music with our coffee to follow the story?"

"It's more like a play," said Amita to Raymond.

"What a pity Captain Carroll, who knows all about Indians, is n't here to have enjoyed it. But I suppose Maruja,
who has n't lost a word, will tell it to him."

"I don't think she will," said Raymond dryly, glancing
at Maruja, who, lost in some intricate pattern of her Chinese
plate, was apparently unconscious that her host was waiting
her signal to withdraw. At last she raised her head, and
said, gently but audibly, to the waiting Prince : —

"It is positively a newer pattern ; the old one had not
that delicate straw line in the arabesque. You must have
had it made for you."

"I did," said the gratified Prince, taking up the plate.
"What eyes you have, Miss Saltonstall. They see everything."

"Except that I 'm keeping you all waiting," she returned, with a smile, letting the eyes in question fall with
a half-parting salutation on Guest as she rose. It was the
first exchange of a common instinct between them, and
left them as conscious as if they had pressed hands.

The music gave an opportunity for some desultory conversation, in which Mr. Prince and his young friend received
an invitation from Maruja to visit La Mision, and the party,
by common consent, turned into the conservatory, where
the genial host begged them each to select a flower from a
few especially rare exotics. When Maruja received hers,
she said, laughingly, to Prince, "Will you think me very
importunate if I ask for another?" "Take what you like
— you have only to name it," he replied gallantly. "But
that 's just what I can't do," responded the young girl,
"unless," she added, turning to Guest, "unless you can
assist me. It was the plant I was examining to-day." "I
think I can show it to you," said Guest, with a slight increase of color, as he preceded her towards the memorable
cactus near the door, "but I doubt if it has any flower."

Nevertheless, it had. A bright red blossom like a spot

of blood drawn by one of its thorns.   He plucked it for her, and she placed it in her belt.

"You are forgiving," he said admiringly.

"*You* ought to know that," she returned, looking down.

"*I?* — why ? "

"You were rude to me twice."

"Twice ! "

"Yes — once at the Mision of La Perdida ; once in the road at San Antonio."

His eyes became downcast and gloomy.   "At the Mision that morning, I, a wretched outcast, only saw in you a beautiful girl intent on overriding me with her merciless beauty.   At San Antonio I handed the fan I picked up to the man whose eyes told me he loved you."

She started impatiently.   "You might have been more gallant, and found more difficulty in the selection," she said pertly.   "But since when have you gentlemen become so observant and so punctilious ?   Would you expect him to be as considerate of others ? "

"I have few claims that any one seems bound to respect," he returned brusquely.   Then, in a softer voice, he added, looking at her gently : —

"You were in mourning when you came here this afternoon, Miss Saltonstall."

"Was I ?   It was for Dr. West — my mother's friend."

"It was very becoming to you."

"You are complimenting me.   But I warn you that Captain Carroll said something better than that ; he said mourning was not necessary for me.   I had only to 'put my eyelashes at half-mast.'   He is a soldier, you know."

"He seems to be as witty as he is fortunate," said Guest bitterly.

"Do you think he is fortunate ? " said Maruja, raising her eyes to his.   There was so much in this apparently simple question that Guest looked in her eyes for a suggestion. What he saw there for an instant made his heart stop beating. She apparently did not know it, for she began to tremble too.

" Is he not ? " said Guest in a low voice.

" Do you think he ought to be ? " she found herself whispering.

A sudden silence fell upon them. The voices of their companions seemed very far in the distance ; the warm breath of the flowers appeared to be drowning their senses ; they tried to speak, but could not ; they were so near to each other that the two long blades of a palm served to hide them. In the midst of this profound silence a voice that was like and yet unlike Maruja's said twice, " Go ! go ! " but each time seemed hushed in the stifling silence. The next moment the palms were pushed aside, the dark figure of a young man slipped like some lithe animal through the shrubbery, and Maruja found herself standing, pale and rigid, in the middle of the walk, in the full glare of the light, and looking down the corridor toward her approaching companions. She was furious and frightened ; she was triumphant and trembling ; without thought, sense, or reason, she had been kissed by Henry Guest, and — had returned it.

The fleetest horses of Aladdin's stud that night could not carry her far enough or fast enough to take her away from that moment, that scene, and that sensation. Wise and experienced, confident in her beauty, secure in her selfishness, strong over others' weaknesses, weighing accurately the deeds and words of men and women, recognizing all there was in position and tradition, seeing with her father's clear eyes the practical meaning of any divergence from that conventionality which as a woman of the world she valued, she returned again and again to the trembling joy of that intoxicating moment. She thought of her mother and sisters, of Raymond and Garnier, of Aladdin — she even forced herself to think of Carroll — only to shut her eyes, with a faint smile, and dream again the brief but thrilling dream of Guest that began and ended in their joined and parted lips. Small wonder that, hidden and silent in her enwrappings, as she lay back in the carriage, with her pale face against the cold starry sky, two other stars came out and glistened and trembled on her passion-fringed lashes.

CHAPTER X

THE rainy season had set in early. The last three weeks of summer drought had drained the great valley of its life-blood; the dead stalks of grain rustled like dry bones over Dr. West's grave. The desiccating wind and sun had wrought some disenchanting cracks and fissures in Aladdin's Palace, and otherwise disjoined it, so that it not only looked as if it were ready to be packed away, but had become finally untenable in the furious onset of the southwesterly rains. The gorgeous furniture of the reception-rooms was wrapped in mackintoshes, the conservatory was changed into an aquarium, the Bridge of Sighs crossed an actual canal in the stable-yard. Only the billiard-room and Mr. Prince's bedroom and office remained intact, and in the latter, one stormy afternoon, Mr. Prince himself sat busy over his books and papers. His station-wagon, splashed and streaked with mud, stood in the courtyard, just as it had been driven from the station, and the smell of the smoke of newly lit fires showed that the house had been opened only for this hurried visit of its owner.

The tramping of horse hoofs in the courtyard was soon followed by steps along the corridor, and the servant ushered Captain Carroll into the presence of his master. The Captain did not remove his military overcoat, but remained standing erect in the centre of the room, with his forage cap in his hand.

"I could have given you a lift from the station," said Prince, "if you had come that way. I've only just got in myself."

" I preferred to ride," said Carroll dryly.

" Sit down by the fire," said Prince, motioning to a chair, " and dry yourself."

"I must ask you first the purport of this interview," said Carroll curtly, " before I prolong it further. You have asked me to come here in reference to certain letters I returned to their rightful owner some months ago. If ·you seek to reclaim them again, or to refer to a subject which must remain forgotten, I decline to proceed further."

" It *does* refer to the letters, and it rests with you whether they shall be forgotten or not. It is not my fault if the subject has been dropped. You must remember that until yesterday you had been absent on a tour of inspection and could not be applied to before."

Carroll cast a cold glance at Prince, and then threw himself into a chair, with his overcoat still on and his long military boots crossed before the fire. Sitting there in profile, Prince could not but notice that he looked older and sterner than at their last interview, and his cheeks were thinned as if by something more than active service.

" When you were here last summer," began Prince, leaning forward over his desk, " you brought me a piece of news that astounded me, as it did many others. It was the assignment of Dr. West's property to Mrs. Saltonstall. That was something there was no gainsaying ; it was a purely business affair, and involved nobody's rights but the assignor. But this was followed, a day or two after, by the announcement of the Doctor's will, making the same lady the absolute and sole inheritor of the same property. That seemed all right too ; for there were, apparently, no legal heirs. Since then, however, it has been discovered that there is a legal heir — none other than the Doctor's only son. Now, as no allusion to the son's existence was made in that will — which was a great oversight of the Doctor's — it is a fiction of the law that such an omission is an act of forgetfulness, and therefore leaves the son the same rights as if there had been no will at all. In other words, if the Docter had seen fit to throw his scapegrace son a hundred dollar bill, it would have been legal evidence that he remembered him. As he did not, it's a fair legal presumption that he forgot him, or that the will is incomplete."

"This seems to be a question for Mrs. Saltonstall's lawyers — not for her friends," said Carroll coldly.

"Excuse me; that remains for you to decide — when you hear all. You understand at present, then, that Dr. West's property, both by assignment and will, was made over, in the event of his death, not to his legal heirs, but to a comparative stranger. It looked queer to a good many people, but the only explanation was, that the Doctor had fallen very much in love with the widow — that he would have probably married her — had he lived."

With an unpleasant recollection that this was almost exactly Maruja's explanation of her mother's relations to Dr. West, Carroll returned impatiently, "If you mean that their private relations may be made the subject of legal discussion, in the event of litigation in regard to the property, that again is a matter for Mrs. Saltonstall to decide — and not her friends. It is purely a matter of taste."

"It may be a matter of discretion, Captain Carroll."

"Of discretion!" repeated Carroll superciliously.

"Well," said Prince, leaving his desk and coming to the fireplace, with his hands in his pockets, "what would you call it, if it could be found that Dr. West, on leaving Mrs. Saltonstall's that night, did *not* meet with an accident, was *not* thrown from his horse, but was coolly and deliberately murdered!"

Captain Carroll's swift recollection of the discovery he himself had made in the road, and its inconsistency with the accepted theory of the accident, unmistakably showed itself in his face. It was a moment before he recovered himself.

"But even if it can be proved to have been a murder and not an accident, what has that to do with Mrs. Saltonstall or her claim to the property?"

"Only that she was the one person directly benefited by his death."

Captain Carroll looked at him steadily, and then rose to his feet. "Do I understand that you have called me here to listen to this infamous aspersion of a lady?"

"I have called you here, Captain Carroll, to listen to the arguments that may be used to set aside Dr. West's will, and return the property to the legal heir. You are to listen to them or not, as you choose; but I warn you that your opportunity to hear them in confidence and convey them to your friend will end here. *I* have no opinion in the case. *I* only tell you that it will be argued that Dr. West was unduly influenced to make a will in Mrs. Saltonstall's favor; that, after having done so, it will be shown that, just before his death, he became aware of the existence of his son and heir, and actually had an interview with him; that he visited Mrs. Saltonstall that evening, with the records of his son's identity and a memorandum of his interview in his pocket-book; and that, an hour after leaving the house, he was foully murdered. That is the theory which Mrs. Saltonstall has to consider. I told you I have no opinion. I only know that there are witnesses to the interview of the Doctor and his son; there is evidence of murder, and the murderer is suspected; there is the evidence of the pocket-book, with the memorandum picked up on the spot, which you handed me yourself."

"Do you mean to say that you will permit this pocket-book, handed you in confidence, to be used for such an infamous purpose?" said Carroll.

"I think you offered it to me in exchange for Dr. West's letters to Mrs. Saltonstall," returned Prince dryly. "The less said about that, the less is likely to be said about compromising letters written by the widow to the Doctor, which she got you to recover — letters which they may claim had a bearing on the case, and even lured him to his fate."

For an instant Captain Carroll recoiled before the gulf which seemed to open at the feet of the unhappy family. For an instant a terrible doubt possessed him, and in that doubt he found a new reason for a certain changed and altered tone in Maruja's later correspondence with him, and the vague hints she had thrown out of the impossibility of their union. "I beg you will not press me to greater candor," she had written, "and try to forget me before you learn to hate me." For an instant he believed — and even took a miserable comfort in the belief — that it was this hideous secret, and not some coquettish caprice, to which she vaguely alluded. But it was only for a moment; the next instant the monstrous doubt passed from the mind of the simple gentleman, with only a slight flush of shame at his momentary disloyalty.

Prince, however, had noticed it, not without a faint sense of sympathy. "Look here!" he said, with a certain brusqueness, which in a man of his character was less dangerous than his smoothness. "I know your feelings to that family, — at least to one of them, — and if I 've been playing it pretty rough on you, it 's only because you played it rather rough on *me* the last time you were here. Let 's understand each other. I 'll go so far as to say *I* don't believe that Mrs. Saltonstall had anything to do with that murder, but, as a business man, I 'm bound to say that these circumstances and her own indiscretion are quite enough to bring the biggest pressure down on her. I would n't want any better 'bear' on the market value of her rights than this. Take it at its best. Say that the Coroner's verdict is set aside, and a charge of murder against unknown parties is made " —

" One moment, Mr. Prince," said Carroll. " I shall be one of the first to insist that this is done, and I have confidence enough in Mrs. Saltonstall's honest friendship for the Doctor to know that she will lose no time in pursuing his murderers."

Prince looked at Carroll with a feeling of half envy and half pity. " I think not," he said dryly; " for all suspicion points to one man as the perpetrator, and that man was Mrs. Saltonstall's confidential servant — the major-domo, Pereo." He waited for a moment for the effect of this announcement on Carroll, and then went on : " You now understand that, even if Mrs. Saltonstall is acquitted of any connivance with or even knowledge of the deed, she will hardly enjoy the prosecution of her confidential servant for murder."

" But how can this be prevented ?   If, as you say, there are actual proofs, why have they not been acted upon before ? What can keep them from being acted upon now ? "

" The proofs have been collected by one man, have been in possession of one man, and will only pass out of his possession when it is for the benefit of the legal heir — who does not yet even know of their existence."

" And who is this one man ? "

" Myself."

" You ? — You ? " said Carroll, advancing towards him. " Then this is *your* work ! "

" Captain Carroll," said Prince, without moving, but drawing his lips tightly together and putting his head on one side, " I don't propose to have another scene like the one we had at our last meeting. If you try on anything of that kind, I shall put the whole matter into a lawyer's hands. I don't say that you won't regret it ; I don't say that *I* sha'n't be disappointed, too, for I have been managing this thing purely as a matter of business, with a view to profiting by it. It so happens that we can both work to the same end, even if our motives are not the same. I don't call myself an officer and a gentleman, but I reckon I've run this affair about as delicately as the best of them, and with a d—d sight more horse sense. I want this thing hushed up and compromised, to get some control of the property again, and to prevent it depreciating, as it would, in litigation ; you want it hushed up for the sake of the girl and your future mother-in-law. I don't know anything about your laws of honor, but I've laid my cards on the table for you to see, without asking what you've got in your hand. You can play the game or leave the board, as you choose." He turned and walked to the window — not without leaving on Carroll's mind a certain sense of firmness, truthfulness, and sincerity which commanded his respect.

"I withdraw any remark that might have seemed to reflect on your business integrity, Mr. Prince," said Carroll quietly. "I am willing to admit that you have managed this thing better than I could, and if I join you in an act to suppress these revelations, I have no right to judge of your intentions.   What do you propose to have me do ? "

"To state the whole case to Mrs. Saltonstall, and to ask her to acknowledge the young man's legal claim without litigation."

"But how do you know that she would not do this without — excuse me — without intimidation ? "

"I only reckon that a woman clever enough to get hold of a million, would be clever enough to keep it — against others."

"I hope to show you are mistaken.   But where is this heir ? "

"Here."

"Here ? "

"Yes.   For the last six months he has been my private secretary.   I know what you are thinking of, Captain Car-

roll.   You would consider it indelicate — eh ?   Well,
that 's just where we differ.   By this means I have kept
everything in my own hands — prevented him from getting
into the hands of outsiders — and I intend to dispose of
just as much of the facts to him as may be necessary for
him to prove his title.   What bargain I make with *him* —
is my affair."

"Does he suspect the murder ? "

"No.   I did not think it necessary for his good or mine.
He can be an ugly devil if he likes, and although there
was n't much love lost between him and the old man, it
would n't pay to have any revenge mixed up with business.
He knows nothing of it.   It was only by accident that,
looking after his movements while he was here, I ran across
the tracks of the murderer."

"But what has kept him from making known his claim
to the Saltonstalls ?   Are you sure he has not ? " said Carroll, with a sudden thought that it might account for Maruja's strangeness.

"Positive.   He 's too proud to make a claim unless he
could thoroughly prove it, and only a month ago he made
me promise to keep it dark.   He 's too lazy to trouble himself about it much anyway — as far as I can see.   D—d
if I don't think his being a tramp has made him lose his
taste for everything !   Don't worry yourself about *him*.
He is n't likely to make confidences with the Saltonstalls,
for he don't like 'em, and never went there but once.
Instinctively or not, the widow did n't cotton to him ; and
I fancy Miss Maruja has some old grudge against him for
that fan business on the road.   She is n't a girl to forgive
or forget anything, as I happen to know," he added, with
an uneasy laugh.

Carroll was too preoccupied with the danger that seemed
to threaten his friends from this surly pretender to resent
Prince's tactless allusion.   He was thinking of Maruja's

ominous agitation at his presence at Dr. West's grave.
" Do they suspect him at all ? " he asked hurriedly.

" How should they ? He goes by the name of Guest —
which was his father's real name until changed by an act of
legislation when he first came here. Nobody remembers it.
We only found it out from his papers. It was quite legal,
as all his property was acquired under the name of West."

Carroll rose and buttoned his overcoat. " I presume you
are able to offer conclusive proofs of everything you have
asserted ? "

" Perfectly."

" I am going to the Mision Perdida now," said Captain
Carroll quietly. " To-morrow I will bring you the answer
— Peace or War." He walked to the door, lifted his hand
to his cap, with a brief military salutation, and disappeared.

CHAPTER XI

As Captain Carroll urged his horse along the miry road to La Mision Perdida, he was struck with certain changes in the landscape before him other than those wrought by the winter rains. There were the usual deep gullies and trenches, half filled with water, in the fields and along the road, but there were ominous embankments and ridges of freshly turned soil, and a scattered fringe of timbers following a cruel, undeviating furrow on the broad grazing lands of the Mision. But it was not until he had crossed the arroyo that he felt the full extent of the late improvements. A quick rumbling in the distance, a light flash of steam above the willow copse, that drifted across the field on his right, and he knew that the railroad was already in operation. Captain Carroll reined in his frightened charger, and passed his hand across his brow with a dazed sense of loss. He had been gone only four months — yet he already felt strange and forgotten.

It was with a feeling of relief that he at last turned from the highroad into the lane. Here everything was unchanged, except that the ditches were more thickly strewn with the sodden leaves of fringing oaks and sycamores. Giving his horse to a servant in the courtyard, he did not enter the patio, but, crossing the lawn, stepped upon the long veranda. The rain was dripping from its eaves and striking a minute spray from the vines that clung to its columns; his footfall awoke a hollow echo as he passed, as if the outer shell of the house were deserted; the formal yews and hemlocks that in summer had relieved the daz-

zling glare of six months' sunshine had now taken gloomy
possession of the garden, and the evening shadows, thickened by rain, seemed to lie in wait at every corner. The
servant, who had, with old-fashioned courtesy, placed the
keys and the "disposition" of that wing of the house at
his service, said that Doña Maria would wait upon him in
the salon before dinner. Knowing the difficulty of breaking the usual rigid etiquette, and trusting to the happy intervention of Maruja, — though here, again, custom debarred
him from asking for her, — he allowed the servant to remove his wet overcoat, and followed him to the stately and
solemn chamber prepared for him. The silence and gloom
of the great house, so grateful and impressive in the ardent
summer, began to weigh upon him under this shadow of an
overcast sky. He walked to the window and gazed out on
the cloister-like veranda. A melancholy willow at an angle
of the stables seemed to be wringing its hands in the rising
wind. He turned for relief to the dim fire that flickered like
a votive taper in the vault-like hearth, and drew a chair
towards it. In spite of the impatience and preoccupation
of a lover, he found himself again and again recurring to the
story he had just heard, until the vengeful spirit of the
murdered Doctor seemed to darken and possess the house.
He was striving to shake off the feeling, when his attention was attracted to stealthy footsteps in the passage.
Could it be Maruja? He rose to his feet, with his eye
upon the door. The footsteps ceased — it remained closed.
But another door, which had escaped his attention in the
darkened corner, slowly swung on its hinges, and with a
stealthy step, Pereo, the major-domo, entered the room.

Courageous and self-possessed as Captain Carroll was by
nature and education, this malevolent vision, and incarnation of the thought uppermost in his mind, turned him
cold. He had half drawn a derringer from his breast, when
his eye fell on the grizzled locks and wrinkled face of the

old man, and his hand dropped to his side. But Pereo, with the quick observation of insanity, had noticed the weapon, and rubbed his hands together, with a malicious laugh.

"Good! good! good!" he whispered rapidly in a strange bodiless voice; "'twill serve! 'twill serve! And you are a soldier too — and know how to use it! Good, it is a Providence!" He lifted his hollow eyes to heaven, and then added, "Come! come!"

Carroll stepped towards him. He was alone and in the presence of an undoubted madman — one strong enough, in spite of his years, to inflict a deadly injury, and one whom he now began to realize might have done so once before. Nevertheless, he laid his hand on the old man's arm, and looking him calmly in the eye, said quietly, "Come? Where, Pereo? I have only just arrived."

"I know it," whispered the old man, nodding his head violently. "I was watching them, when you rode up. That is why I lost the scent; but together we can track them still — we can track them. Eh, Captain, eh! Come! come!" and he moved slowly backward, waving his hand towards the door.

"Track whom, Pereo?" said Carroll soothingly. "Whom do you seek?"

"Whom?" said the old man, startled for a moment and passing his hand over his wrinkled forehead. "Whom? Eh! Why, the Doña Maruja and the little black cat — her maid — Faquita!"

"Yes, but why seek them? Why track them?"

"Why?" said the old man, with a sudden burst of impotent passion. "*You* ask me why! Because they are going to the rendezvous again. They are going to seek him. Do you understand — to seek *him* — the Coyote!"

Carroll smiled a faint smile of relief. "So — the Coyote!"

"Ay," said the old man in a confidential whisper; "the Coyote! But not the *big* one — you understand — the little one. The big one is dead — dead — dead! But the little one lives yet. You shall do for *him* what I, Pereo — listen " he glanced around the room furtively — " what I — the good old Pereo, did for the big one! Good, it is a Providence. Come!"—

Of the terrible thoughts that crossed Carroll's mind at this unexpected climax one alone was uppermost. The trembling irresponsible wretch before him meditated some deep crime — and Maruja was in danger. He did not allow himself to dwell upon any other suspicion suggested by that speech; he quickly conceived a plan of action. To have rung the bell and given Pereo into the hands of the servants would have only exposed to them the lunatic's secret — if he had any — and he might either escape in his fury or relapse into useless imbecility. To humor him and follow him, and trust afterwards to his own quickness and courage to avert any calamity, seemed to be the only plan. Captain Carroll turned his clear glance on the restless eyes of Pereo, and said, without emotion, "Let us go, then, and quickly. You shall track them for me; but remember, good Pereo, you must leave the rest to me."

In spite of himself, some accidental significance in this ostentatious adjuration to lull Pereo's suspicions struck him with pain. But the old man's eyes glittered with gratified passion as he said, "Ay, good! I will keep my word. Thou shalt work thy will on the little one as I have said. Truly it is a Providence! Come!" Seeing Captain Carroll glance round for his overcoat, he seized a poncho from the wall, wrapped it round him, and grasped his hand. Carroll, who would have evaded this semblance of disguise, had no time to parley, and they turned together, through the door by which Pereo had entered, into a long dark passage, which seemed to be made through the outer shell of the building that flanked the park. Following his guide in the profound obscurity, perfectly conscious that any change in his madness might be followed by a struggle in the dark, where no help could reach them, they presently came to a door that opened upon the fresh smell of rain and leaves. They were standing at the bottom of a secluded alley, between two high hedges that hid it from the end of the garden. Its grass-grown walk and untrimmed hedges showed that it was seldom used. Carroll, still keeping close to Pereo's side, felt him suddenly stop and tremble. "Look!" he said, pointing to a shadowy figure some distance before them; "look, 'tis Maruja, and alone!"

With a dexterous movement, Carroll managed to slip his arm securely through the old man's, and even to throw himself before him, as if in his eagerness to discern the figure.

"'Tis Maruja — and alone!" said Pereo, trembling. "Alone! Eh! And the Coyote is not here!" He passed his hand over his staring eyes. "So." Suddenly he turned upon Carroll. "Ah, do you not see, it is a trick! The Coyote is escaping with Faquita! Come! Nay; thou wilt not? Then will I!" With an unexpected strength born of his madness, he freed his arm from Carroll and darted down the alley. The figure of Maruja, evidently alarmed at his approach, glided into the hedge, as Pereo passed swiftly by, intent only on his one wild fancy. Without a further thought of his companion or even the luckless Faquita, Carroll also plunged through the hedge, to intercept Maruja. But by that time she was already crossing the upper end of the lawn, hurrying towards the entrance to the patio. Carroll did not hesitate to follow. Keeping in view the lithe, dark, active little figure, now hidden by an intervening cluster of bushes, now fading in the gathering evening shadows, he nevertheless did not succeed in gaining upon her until she had nearly reached the patio. Here he lost ground, as, turning to the right, instead of entering the courtyard, she kept her way toward the stables. He was near enough, however, to speak. " One moment, Miss Saltonstall," he said hurriedly ; " there is no danger. I am alone. But I must speak with you."

The young girl seemed only to redouble her exertions. At last she stopped before a narrow door hidden in the wall, and fumbled in her pocket for a key. That moment Carroll was upon her.

" Forgive me, Miss Saltonstall — Maruja ; but you must hear me ! You are safe, but I fear for your maid, Faquita ! "

A little laugh followed his speech ; the door yielded and opened to her vanishing figure. For an instant the lace shawl muffling her face was lifted, as the door closed and locked behind her. Carroll drew back in consternation. It was the laughing eyes and saucy face of Faquita.

CHAPTER XII

WHEN Captain Carroll turned from the highroad into the lane, an hour before, Maruja and Faquita had already left the house by the same secret passage and garden-door that opened afterwards upon himself and Pereo. The young women had evidently changed dresses: Maruja was wearing the costume of her maid; Faquita was closely veiled and habited like her mistress; but it was characteristic that, while Faquita appeared awkward and overdressed in her borrowed plumes, Maruja's short saya and trim bodice, with the striped shawl that hid her fair hair, looked infinitely more coquettish and bewitching than on their legitimate owner.

They passed hurriedly down the long alley, and at its further end turned at right angles to a small gate half hidden in the shrubbery. It opened upon a venerable vineyard, that dated back to the occupation of the padres, but was now given over to the chance cultivation of peons and domestics. Its long, broken rows of low vines, knotted and overgrown with age, reached to the thicketed hillside of buckeye that marked the beginning of the cañada. Here Maruja parted from her maid, and muffling the shawl more closely round her head, hastily passed between the vine rows to a ruined adobe building near the hillside. It was originally part of the refectory of the old Mision, but had been more recently used as a viñadero's cottage. As she neared it, her steps grew slower, until, reaching its door, she hesitated, with her hand timidly on the latch. The next moment she opened it gently; it was closed quickly behind her, and with a little stifled cry, she found herself in the arms of Henry Guest.

It was only for an instant; the pleading of her white hands, disengaged from his neck, where at first they had found themselves, and uplifted before her face, touched him more than the petitioning eyes or the sweet voiceless mouth, whose breath even was forgotten. Letting her sink into the chair from which he had just risen, he drew back a step, with his hands clasped before him, and his dark half-savage eyes bent earnestly upon her. Well might he have gazed. It was no longer the conscious beauty, proud and regnant, seated before him; but a timid, frightened girl, struggling with her first deep passion.

All that was wise and gentle that she had intended to say, all that her clear intellect and experience had taught her, died upon her lips with that kiss. And all that she could do of womanly dignity and high-bred decorum was to tuck her small feet under her chair, in the desperate attempt to lengthen her short skirt, and beg him not to look at her.

"I have had to change dresses with Faquita, because we were watched," she said, leaning forward in her chair and drawing the striped shawl around her shoulders. "I have had to steal out of my mother's house and through the fields, as if I was a gypsy. If I only were a gypsy, Harry, and not" —

"And not the proudest heiress in the land," he interrupted, with something of his old bitterness. "True, I had forgot."

"But I never reminded *you* of it," she said, lifting her eyes to his. "I did not remind you of it on that day — in — in — in the conservatory, nor at the time you first spoke of — of — love to me — nor from the time I first consented to meet you here. It is *you*, Harry, who have spoken of the difference of our condition, *you* who have talked of my wealth, my family, my position — until I would gladly have changed places with Faquita as I have garments, if I had thought it would make you happier."

"Forgive me, darling!" he said, dropping on one knee before her and bending over the cold little hand he had taken, until his dark head almost rested in her lap. "Forgive me! You are too proud, Maruja, to admit, even to yourself, that you have given your heart where your hand and fortune could not follow. But others may not think so. I am proud, too, and will not have it said that I have won you before I was worthy of you."

"You have no right to be more proud than I, sir," she said, rising to her feet, with a touch of her old supreme assertion. "No — don't, Harry — please, Harry — there!" Nevertheless, she succumbed; and when she went on, it was with her head resting on his shoulder. "It's this deceit and secrecy that is so shameful, Harry. I think I could bear everything with you, if it were all known — if you came to woo me like — like — the others. Even if they abused you — if they spoke of your doubtful origin — of your poverty — of your hardships! When they aspersed you, I could fight them; when they spoke of your having no father that you could claim, I could even lie for you, I think, Harry, and say that you had; if they spoke of your poverty, I would speak of my wealth; if they talked of your hardships, I should only be proud of your endurance — if I could only keep the tears from my eyes!" They were there now. He kissed them away.

"But if they threatened you? If they drove me from the house?"

"I should fly with you," she said, hiding her head in his breast.

"What if I were to ask you to fly with me now?" he said gloomily.

"Now!" she repeated, lifting her frightened eyes to his.

His face darkened, with its old look of savage resentment. " Hear me, Maruja," he said, taking her hands tightly in his own. " When I forgot myself — when I was mad that day in the conservatory, the only expiation I could think of was to swear in my inmost soul that I would never take advantage of your forgiveness, that I would never tempt you to forget yourself, your friends, your family, for me, an unknown outcast. When I found you pitied me, and listened to my love — I was too weak to forego the one ray of sunshine in my wretched life — and thinking that I had a prospect before me in an idea I promised to reveal to you later, I swore never to beguile you or myself in that hope by any act that might bring you to repent it — or myself to dishonor. But I taxed myself too much, Maruja. I have asked too much of you. You are right, darling ; this secrecy — this deceit — is unworthy of us ! Every hour of it — blest as it has been to me — every moment — sweet as it is — blackens the purity of our only defense, makes you false and me a coward ! It must end here — to-day ! Maruja, darling, my precious one ! God knows what may be the success of my plans. We have but one chance now. I must leave here to-day, never to return, or I must take you with me. Do not start, Maruja — but hear me out. Dare you risk all ? Dare you fly with me now, to-night, to the old Padre at the ruined Mision, and let him bind us in those bonds that none dare break ? We can take Faquita with us — it is but a few miles — and we can return and throw ourselves at your mother's feet. She can only drive us forth together. Or we can fly from this cursed wealth, and all the misery it has entailed — forever."

She raised her head, and with her two hands on his shoulders, gazed at him with her father's searching eyes, as if to read his very soul.

" Are you mad, Harry ! — think what you propose ! Is

this not tempting me ?   Think again, dearest," she said,
half convulsively, seizing his arm when her grasp had
slipped from his shoulder.

There was a momentary silence as she stood with her
eyes fixed almost wildly on his set face.   But a sudden
shock against the bolted door and an inarticulate outcry
startled them.   With an instinctive movement, Guest
threw his arm round her.

"It's Pereo," she said in a hurried whisper, but once
more mistress of her strength and resolution.   "He is
seeking *you !*   Fly at once.   He is mad, Harry ; a raving
lunatic.   He watched us the last time.   He has tracked
us here.   He suspects you.   You must not meet him.
You can escape through the other door, that opens upon
the cañada.   If you love me — fly ! "

"And leave *you* exposed to his fury— are you mad !
No.   Fly yourself by the other door, lock it behind you,
and alarm the servants.   I will open this door to him,
secure him here, and then be gone.   Do not fear for me.
There is no danger — and if I mistake not," he added,
with a strange significance, " he will hardly attack me ! "

"But he may have already alarmed the household.
Hark ! "

There was the noise of a struggle outside the door, and
then the voice of Captain Carroll, calm and collected, rose
clearly for an instant.   " You are quite safe, Miss Saltonstall.   I think I have him secure, but perhaps you had
better not open the door until assistance comes."

They gazed at each other, without a word.   A grim
challenge played on Guest's lips.   Maruja lifted her little
hands deliberately, and clasped them round his defiant
neck.

"Listen, darling," she said softly and quietly, as if only
the security of silence and darkness encompassed them.
'You asked me just now if I would fly with you — if I

would marry you without the consent of my family —
against the protest of my friends — and at once ! I hesitated, Harry, for I was frightened and foolish. But I say
to you now that I will marry you when and where you like
— for I love you, Harry, and you alone."

"Then let us go at once," he said, passionately seizing her ; "we can reach the road by the cañada before
assistance comes — before we are discovered. Come !"

"And you will remember in the years to come, Harry,"
she said, still composedly, and with her arms still around
his neck, "that I never loved any but you — that I never
knew what love was before, and that since I have loved
you — I have never thought of any other. Will you
not ? "

"I will — and now" —

"And now," she said, with a superb gesture towards the
barrier which separated them from Carroll, "OPEN THE
DOOR !"

CHAPTER XIII

WITH a swift glance of admiration at Maruja, Guest
flung open the door. The hastily summoned servants were
already bearing away the madman, exhausted by his efforts.
Captain Carroll alone remained there, erect and motionless,
before the threshold.

At a sign from Maruja, he entered the room. In the
flash of light made by the opening door, he had been perfectly conscious of her companion, but not a motion of his
eye or the movement of a muscle of his face betrayed it.
The trained discipline of his youth stood him in good service, and for the moment left him master of the situation.

"I think no apology is needed for this intrusion," he
said, with cool composure. "Pereo seemed intent on mur-
dering somebody or something, and I followed him here.
I suppose I might have got him away more quietly, but I
was afraid you might have thoughtlessly opened the door."
He stopped, and added, "I see now how unfounded was the
supposition."

It was a fatal addition. In the next instant, the Maruja
who had been standing beside Guest, conscious-stricken and
remorseful in the presence of the man she had deceived,
and calmly awaiting her punishment, changed at this luckless exhibition of her own peculiar womanly weapons. The
old Maruja, supreme, ready, undaunted, and passionless,
returned to the fray.

"You were wrong, Captain," she said sweetly; "fortunately, Mr. Guest — whom I see you have forgotten in your
absence — was with me, and I think would have felt it his

duty to have protected me. But I thank you all the same, and I think even Mr. Guest will not allow his envy of your good fortune in coming so gallantly to my rescue to prevent his appreciating its full value. I am only sorry that on your return to La Mision Perdida you should have fallen into the arms of a madman before extending your hands to your friends."

Their eyes met. She saw that he hated her — and felt relieved.

"It may not have been so entirely unfortunate," he said, with a coldness strongly in contrast with his gradually blazing eyes, "for I was charged with a message to you, in which this madman is supposed by some to play an important part."

"Is it a matter of business?" said Maruja lightly, yet with a sudden instinctive premonition of coming evil in the relentless tones of his voice.

"It is business, Miss Saltonstall — purely and simply business," said Carroll dryly, "under whatever *other* name it may have been since presented to you."

"Perhaps you have no objection to tell it before Mr. Guest," said Maruja, with an inspiration of audacity; "it sounds so mysterious that it must be interesting. Otherwise, Captain Carroll, who abhors business, would not have undertaken it with more than his usual enthusiasm."

"As the business *does* interest Mr. Guest, or Mr. West, or whatever name he may have decided upon since I had the pleasure of meeting him," said Carroll — for the first time striking fire from the eyes of his rival — "I see no reason why I should not, even at the risk of telling you what you already know. Briefly, then, Mr. Prince charged me to advise you and your mother to avoid litigation with this gentleman, and admit his claim, as the son of Dr. West, to his share of the property."

The utter consternation and bewilderment shown in the

face of Maruja convinced Carroll of his fatal error. She *had* received the addresses of this man without knowing his real position! The wild theory that had seemed to justify his resentment — that she had sold herself to Guest to possess the property — now recoiled upon him in its utter baseness. She had loved Guest for himself alone; by this base revelation he had helped to throw her into his arms.

But he did not even yet know Maruja. Turning to Guest, with flashing eyes, she said, "Is it true — are you the son of Dr. West, and " — she hesitated — "kept out of your inheritance by *us?*"

"I *am* the son of Dr. West," he said earnestly, "though I alone had the right to tell you that at the proper time and occasion. Believe me that I have given no one the right — least of all any tool of Prince — to *trade* upon it."

"Then," said Carroll fiercely, forgetting everything in his anger, "perhaps you will disclaim before this young lady the charge made by your employer that Pereo was instigated to Dr. West's murder by her mother?"

Again he had overshot the mark. The horror and indignation depicted in Guest's face were too plainly visible to Maruja, as well as himself, to permit a doubt that the idea was as new as the accusation. Forgetting her bewilderment at these revelations, her wounded pride, a torturing doubt suggested by Guest's want of confidence in her — indeed everything but the outraged feelings of her lover, she flew to his side. "Not a word," she said proudly, lifting her little hand before his darkening face. "Do not insult me by replying to such an accusation in my presence. Captain Carroll," she continued, turning towards him, "I cannot forget that you were introduced into my mother's house as an officer and a gentleman. When you return to it as such, and not as a *man of business*, you will be welcome. Until then, farewell!"

She remained standing, erect and passionless, as Carroll, with a cold salutation, stepped back and disappeared in the darkness; and then she turned, and with tottering step and a little cry, fell upon Guest's breast. "O Harry — Harry! — why have you deceived me!"

"I thought it for the best, darling," he said, lifting her face to his. "You know now the prospect I spoke of — the hope that buoyed me up! I wanted to win you myself alone, without appealing to your sense of justice or even your sympathies! I did win you. God knows, if I had not, you would never have learned through me that a son of Dr. West had ever lived. But that was not enough. When I found that I could establish my right to my father's property, I wanted you to marry me before *you* knew it; so that it never could be said that you were influenced by anything but love for me. That was why I came here to-day. That was why I pressed you to fly with me!"

He ceased. She was fumbling with the buttons of his waistcoat. "Harry," she said softly, "did you think of the property when — when — you kissed me in the conservatory?"

"I thought of nothing but *you*," he answered tenderly.

Suddenly she started from his embrace. "But Pereo! — Harry — tell me quick — no one — nobody can think that this poor demented old man could — that Dr. West was — that — it's all a trick — is n't it? Harry — speak!"

He was silent for a moment, and then said gravely, "There were strange men at the fonda that night, and — my father was supposed to carry money with him. My own life was attempted at the Mision the same evening for the sake of some paltry gold pieces that I had imprudently shown. I was saved solely by the interference of one man. That man was Pereo, your major-domo!"

She seized his hand and raised it joyfully to her lips. "Thank you for those words! And you will come to him with me at once; and he will recognize you; and we will laugh at those lies; won't we, Harry ? "

He did not reply. Perhaps he was listening to a confused sound of voices rapidly approaching the cottage. Together they stepped out into the gathering night. A number of figures were coming towards them, among them Faquita, who ran a little ahead to meet her mistress.

" Oh, Doña Maruja, he has escaped ! "

" Who ?   Not Pereo ! "

" Truly.   And on his horse.   It was saddled and bridled in the stable all day.   One knew it not.   He was walking like a cat, when suddenly he parted the peons around him, like grain before a mad bull — and behold ! he was on the pinto's back and away.   And, alas ! there is no horse that can keep up with the pinto.   God grant he may not get in the way of the r-r-railroad, that, in his very madness, he will even despise."

" My own horse is in the thicket," whispered Guest, hurriedly, in Maruja's ear.   " I have measured him with the pinto before now.   Give me your blessing, and I will bring him back if he be alive."

She pressed his hand and said, " Go."   Before the astonished servants could identify the strange escort of their mistress, he was gone.

It was already quite dark.   To any but Guest, who had made the topography of La Mision Perdida a practical study, and who had known the habitual circuit of the major-domo in his efforts to avoid him, the search would have been hopeless.   But rightly conjecturing that he would in his demented condition follow the force of habit, he spurred his horse along the highroad until he reached the lane leading to the grassy amphitheatre already described, which was once his favorite resort.   Since then it had participated in the terrible transformation already wrought in the valley by the railroad.   A deep cutting through one of the grassy hills had been made for the line that now crossed the lower arc of the amphitheatre.

His conjecture was justified on entering it by the appearance of a shadowy horseman in full career round the circle, and he had no difficulty in recognizing Pereo. As there was no other exit than the one by which he came, the other being inaccessible by reason of the railroad track, he calmly watched him twice make the circuit of the arena, ready to ride towards him when he showed symptoms of slackening his speed.

Suddenly he became aware of some strange exercise on the part of the mysterious rider; and as the latter swept by on the nearer side of the circle, Guest saw that he was throwing a lasso! A horrible thought that he was witnessing an insane rehearsal of the murder of his father flashed across his mind.

A far-off whistle from the distant woods recalled him to his calmer senses at the same moment that it seemed also to check the evolutions of the furious rider. Guest felt confident that the wretched man could not escape him now. It was the approaching train, whose appearance would undoubtedly frighten Pereo toward the entrance of the little valley guarded by him. The hillside was already alive with the clattering echoes of the oncoming monster, when, to his horror, he saw the madman advancing rapidly towards the cutting. He put spurs to his horse, and started in pursuit; but the train was already emerging from the narrow passage, followed by the furious rider, who had wheeled abreast of the engine, and was, for a moment or two, madly keeping up with it. Guest shouted to him, but his voice was lost in the roar of the rushing caravan.

Something seemed to fly from Pereo's hand. The next moment the train had passed; rider and horse, crushed and battered out of all life, were rolling in the ditch, while the murderer's empty saddle dangled at the end of a lasso, caught on the smoke-stack of one of the murdered man's avenging improvements!

. . . .

The marriage of Maruja and the son of the late Dr. West was received in the valley of San Antonio as one of the most admirably conceived and skillfully matured plans of that lamented genius. There were many who were ready to state that the Doctor had confided it to them years before; and it was generally accepted that the widow Saltonstall had been simply made a trustee for the benefit of the prospective young couple. Only one person, perhaps, did not entirely accept these views; it was Mr. James Prince — otherwise known as Aladdin. In later years, he is said to have stated authoritatively "that the only combination in business that was uncertain — was man and woman."

SNOW-BOUND AT EAGLE'S

CHAPTER I

FOR some moments profound silence and darkness had accompanied a Sierran stagecoach towards the Summit. The huge, dim bulk of the vehicle, swaying noiselessly on its straps, glided onward and upward as if obeying some mysterious impulse from behind, so faint and indefinite appeared its relation to the viewless and silent horses ahead. The shadowy trunks of tall trees that seemed to approach the coach windows, look in, and then move hurriedly away, were the only distinguishable objects. Yet even these were so vague and unreal that they might have been the mere phantoms of some dream of the half-sleeping passengers; for the thickly strewn needles of the pine, that choked the way and deadened all sound, yielded under the silently crushing wheels a faint soporific odor that seemed to benumb their senses, already slipping back into unconsciousness during the long ascent. Suddenly the stage stopped.

Three of the four passengers inside struggled at once into upright wakefulness. The fourth passenger, John Hale, had not been sleeping, and turned impatiently towards the window. It seemed to him that two of the moving trees had suddenly become motionless outside. One of them moved again, and the door opened quickly but quietly, as of itself.

"Git down," said a voice in the darkness.

All the passengers except Hale started. The man next

to him moved his right hand suddenly behind him, but as quickly stopped. One of the motionless trees had apparently closed upon the vehicle, and what had seemed to be a bough projecting from it at right angles changed slowly into the faintly shining double-barrels of a gun at the window.

" Drop that ! " said the voice.

The man who had moved uttered a short laugh, and returned his hand empty to his knees. The two others perceptibly shrugged their shoulders as over a game that was lost. The remaining passenger, John Hale, fearless by nature, inexperienced by habit, awaking suddenly to the truth, conceived a desperate resistance. But without his making a gesture this was instinctively felt by the others; the muzzle of the gun turned spontaneously on him, and he was vaguely conscious of a certain contempt and impatience of him in his companions.

" Git down," repeated the voice imperatively.

The three passengers descended. Hale, furious, alert, but helpless of any opportunity, followed. He was surprised to find the stage-driver and express messenger standing beside him ; he had not heard them dismount. He instinctively looked toward the horses. He could see nothing.

" Hold up your hands ! "

One of the passengers had already lifted his, in a weary, perfunctory way. The others did the same reluctantly and awkwardly, but apparently more from the consciousness of the ludicrousness of their attitude than from any sense of danger. The rays of a bull's-eye lantern, deftly managed by invisible hands, while it left the intruders in shadow, completely illuminated the faces and figures of the passengers. In spite of the majestic obscurity and silence of surrounding nature, the group of humanity thus illuminated was more farcical than dramatic. A scrap of newspaper, part of a sandwich, and an orange peel that had fallen from the floor of the coach, brought into equal prominence by the searching light, completed the absurdity.

"There's a man here with a package of greenbacks," said the voice, with an official coolness that lent a certain suggestion of Custom House inspection to the transaction; "who is it?" The passengers looked at each other, and their glance finally settled on Hale.

"It's not *him*," continued the voice, with a slight tinge of contempt on the emphasis. "You'll save time and searching, gentlemen, if you'll tote it out. If we've got to go through every one of you we'll try to make it pay."

The significant threat was not unheeded. The passenger who had first moved when the stage stopped put his hand to his breast.

"T'other pocket first, if you please," said the voice.

The man laughed, drew a pistol from his hip pocket, and, under the strong light of the lantern, laid it on a spot in the road indicated by the voice. A thick envelope, taken from his breast pocket, was laid beside it. "I told the d—d fools that gave it to me, instead of sending it by express, it would be at their own risk," he said apologetically.

"As it's going with the express now, it's all the same," said the inevitable humorist of the occasion, pointing to the despoiled express treasure-box already in the road.

The intention and deliberation of the outrage was plain enough to Hale's inexperience now. Yet he could not understand the cool acquiescence of his fellow passengers, and was furious. His reflections were interrupted by a voice which seemed to come from a greater distance. He fancied it was even softer in tone, as if a certain austerity was relaxed.

"Step in as quick as you like, gentlemen. You've five minutes to wait, Bill."

The passengers reëntered the coach; the driver and express messenger hurriedly climbed to their places. Hale would have spoken, but an impatient gesture from his companions stopped him. They were evidently listening for something; he listened too.

Yet the silence remained unbroken. It seemed incredible that there should be no indication near or far of that forceful presence which a moment ago had been so dominant. No rustle in the wayside "brush," nor echo from the rocky cañon below, betrayed a sound of their flight. A faint breeze stirred the tall tips of the pines, a cone dropped on the stage roof, one of the invisible horses that seemed to be listening too moved slightly in his harness. But this only appeared to accentuate the profound stillness. The moments were growing interminable, when the voice, so near as to startle Hale, broke once more from the surrounding obscurity.

"Good-night!"

It was the signal that they were free. The driver's whip cracked like a pistol-shot, the horses sprang furiously forward, the huge vehicle lurched ahead, and then bounded violently after them. When Hale could make his voice heard in the confusion — a confusion which seemed greater from the colorless intensity of their last few moments' experience — he said hurriedly, "Then that fellow was there all the time?"

"I reckon," returned his companion, "he stopped five minutes to cover the driver with his double-barrel, until the two other men got off with the treasure."

"The *two* others!" gasped Hale. "Then there were only *three* men, and we *six*."

The man shrugged his shoulders. The passenger who had given up the greenbacks drawled, with a slow, irritating tolerance, "I reckon you 're a stranger here?"

"I am — to this sort of thing, certainly, though I live a

dozen miles from here, at Eagle's Court," returned Hale scornfully.

"Then you're the chap that's doin' that fancy ranchin' over at Eagle's?" continued the man lazily.

"Whatever I'm doing at Eagle's Court, I'm not ashamed of it," said Hale tartly; "and that's more than I can say of what I've done — or *have n't* done — to-night. I've been one of six men overawed and robbed by *three*."

"As to the over-awin', ez you call it — mebbe you know more about it than us. As to the robbin'— ez far as I kin remember, *you* have n't onloaded much. Ef you're talkin' about what *oughter* been done, I'll tell you what *could* have happened. P'r'aps ye noticed that when he pulled up I made a kind of grab for my wepping behind me?"

"I did; and you were n't quick enough," said Hale shortly.

"I was n't quick enough, and that saved *you*. For ef I got that pistol out and in sight o' that man that held the gun" —

"Well," said Hale impatiently, "he'd have hesitated."

"He'd hev blown *you* with both barrels outer the window, and that before I'd got a half-cock on my revolver."

"But that would have been only one man gone, and there would have been five of you left," said Hale haughtily.

"That might have been, ef you'd contracted to take the hull charge of two handfuls of buckshot and slugs; but ez one eighth o' that amount would have done your business, and yet left enough to have gone round, promiskiss, and satisfied the other passengers, it would n't do to kalkilate upon."

"But the express messenger and the driver were armed," continued Hale.

"They were armed, but not *fixed*; that makes all the difference."

" I don't understand."

" I reckon you know what a duel is ? "

" Yes."

" Well, the chances agin *us* was about the same as you 'd have ef you was put up agin another chap who was allowed to draw a bead on you, and the signal to fire was *your drawin' your weapon.* You may be a stranger to this sort o' thing, and p'r'aps you never fought a duel, but even then you would n't go foolin' your life away on any such chances."

Something in the man's manner, as in a certain sly amusement the other passengers appeared to extract from the conversation, impressed Hale, already beginning to be conscious of the ludicrous insufficiency of his own grievance beside that of his interlocutor.

" Then you mean to say this thing is inevitable," said he bitterly, but less aggressively.

" Ez long ez they hunt *you ;* when you hunt *them* you 've got the advantage, allus provided you know how to get at them ez well as they know how to get at you. This yer coach is bound to go regular, and on certain days. *They* ain't. By the time the sheriff gets out his posse they 've skedaddled, and the leader, like as not, is takin' his quiet cocktail at the Bank Exchange, or mebbe losin' his earnings to the sheriff over draw-poker, in Sacramento. You see, you can't prove anything agin them unless you take them ' on the fly.' It may be a part of Joaquim Murietta's band, though I would n't swear to it."

" The leader might have been Gentleman George, from up-country," interposed a passenger. " He seemed to throw in a few fancy touches, particlerly in that ' Good-night.' Sorter chucked a little sentiment in it. Did n't seem to be the same thing ez ' Git, yer d—d suckers ! ' on the other line."

" Whoever he was, he knew the road and the men who

traveled on it.   Like ez not, he went over the line beside
the driver on the box on the down trip, and took stock of
everything.   He even knew I had those greenbacks ; though
they were handed to me in the bank at Sacramento.   He
must have been hangin' round there."

For some moments Hale remained silent.   He was a
civic-bred man, with an intense love of law and order ; the
kind of man who is the first to take that law and order into
his own hands when he does not find it existing to please
him.   He had a Bostonian's respect for respectability, tradition, and propriety, but was willing to face irregularity
and impropriety to create order elsewhere.   He was fond
of Nature with these limitations, never quite trusting her
unguided instincts, and finding her as an instructress greatly
inferior to Harvard University, though possibly not to Cor-
nell.   With dauntless enterprise and energy he had built
and stocked a charming cottage farm in a nook in the
Sierras, whence he opposed, like the lesser Englishman that
he was, his own tastes to those of the alien West.   In the
present instance he felt it incumbent upon him not only to
assert his principles, but to act upon them with his usual
energy.   How far he was impelled by the half-contemptu-
ous passiveness of his companions it would be difficult to
say.

"What is to prevent the pursuit of them at once ? " he
asked suddenly.   "We are a few miles from the station,
where horses can be procured."

"Who's to do it ? " replied the other lazily.   "The
stage company will lodge the complaint with the authori-
ties, but it will take two days to get the county officers
out, and it's nobody else's funeral."

"I will go for one," said Hale quietly.   "I have a
horse waiting for me at the station, and can start at once."

There was an instant of silence.   The stagecoach had
left the obscurity of the forest, and by the stronger light

Hale could perceive that his companion was examining him with two colorless, lazy eyes. Presently he said, meeting Hale's clear glance, but rather as if yielding to a careless reflection : —

"It *might* be done with four men. We oughter raise one man at the station." He paused. "I don't know ez I'd mind taking a hand myself," he added, stretching out his legs with a slight yawn.

"Ye can count *me* in, if you're goin', Kernel. I reckon I'm talkin' to Kernel Clinch," said the passenger beside Hale with sudden alacrity. "I'm Rawlins, of 'Frisco. Heerd of ye afore, Kernel, and kinder spotted you jist now from your talk."

To Hale's surprise, the two men, after awkwardly and perfunctorily grasping each other's hand, entered at once into a languid conversation on the recent election at Fresno, without the slightest further reference to the pursuit of the robbers.   It was not until the remaining and undenominated passenger turned to Hale, and, regretting that he had immediate business at the Summit, offered to accompany the party if they would wait a couple of hours, that Colonel Clinch briefly returned to the subject.

"*Four* men will do, and ez we'll hev to take horses from the station we'll hev to take the fourth man from there."

With these words he resumed his uninteresting conversation with the equally uninterested Rawlins, and the undenominated passenger subsided into an admiring and dreamy contemplation of them both.   With all his principle and really high-minded purpose, Hale could not help feeling constrained and annoyed at the sudden subordinate and auxiliary position to which he, the projector of the enterprise, had been reduced.   It was true that he had never offered himself as their leader ; it was true that the principle he wished to uphold and the effect he sought to obtain

would be equally demonstrated under another; it was true
that the execution of his own conception gravitated by
some occult impulse to the man who had not sought it, and
whom he had always regarded as an incapable. But all
this was so unlike precedent or tradition that, after the
fashion of conservative men, he was suspicious of it, and
only that his honor was now involved he would have withdrawn from the enterprise. There was still a chance of
reasserting himself at the station, where he was known,
and where some authority might be deputed to him.

But even this prospect failed. The station, half stable,
contained only the landlord, who was also express agent,
and the new volunteer whom Clinch had suggested would
be found among the stable-men. The nearest justice of the
peace was ten miles away, and Hale had to abandon even
his hope of being sworn in as a deputy constable. This introduction of a common and illiterate hostler into the party
on equal terms with himself did not add to his satisfaction,
and a remark from Rawlins seemed to complete his embarrassment.

"Ye had a mighty narrer escape down there just now,"
said that gentleman confidentially, as Hale buckled his saddle-girths.

"I thought, as we were not supposed to defend ourselves, there was no danger," said Hale scornfully.

"Oh, I don't mean them road agents. But *him*."

"Who?"

"Kernel Clinch. You jist ez good as allowed he had n't
any grit."

"Whatever I said, I suppose I am responsible for it,"
answered Hale haughtily.

"That's what gits me," was the imperturbable reply.
"He's the best shot in Southern California, and hez let
daylight through a dozen chaps afore now for half what you
said."

" Indeed ! "

" Howsummever," continued Rawlins philosophically, " ez he 's concluded to go *with* ye instead of *for* ye, you 're likely to hev your ideas on this matter carried out up to the handle. He 'll make short work of it, you bet. Ef, ez I suspect, the leader is an airy young feller from 'Frisco, who hez took to the road lately, Clinch hez got a personal grudge agin him from a quarrel over draw-poker."

This was the last blow to Hale's ideal crusade. Here he was — an honest, respectable citizen — engaged as simple accessory to a lawless vendetta originating at a gambling-table ! When the first shock was over that grim philosophy which is the reaction of all imaginative and sensitive natures came to his aid. He felt better ; oddly enough he began to be conscious that he was thinking and acting like his companions. With this feeling a vague sympathy, before absent, faintly showed itself in their actions. The Sharpe's rifle put into his hands by the stableman was accompanied by a familiar word of suggestion as to an equal, which he was ashamed to find flattered him. He was able to continue the conversation with Rawlins more coolly.

" Then you suspect who is the leader ? "

" Only on giniral principles. There was a finer touch, so to speak, in this yer robbery that was n't in the old-fashioned style. Down in my country they hed crude ideas about them things — used to strip the passengers of everything, includin' their clothes. They say that at the station hotels, when the coach came in, the folks used to stand round with blankets to wrap up the passengers so ez not to skeer the wimen. Thar 's a story that the driver and express manager drove up one day with only a copy of the 'Alty Californy' wrapped around 'em ; but thin," added Rawlins grimly, "there *was* folks ez said the hull story was only an advertisement got up for the 'Alty.' "

"Time 's up."

"Are you ready, gentlemen?" said Colonel Clinch.

Hale started. He had forgotten his wife and family at Eagle's Court, ten miles away. They would be alarmed at his absence, would perhaps hear some exaggerated version of the stagecoach robbery, and fear the worst.

"Is there any way I could send a line to Eagle's Court before daybreak?" he asked eagerly.

The station was already drained of its spare men and horses. The undenominated passenger stepped forward and offered to take it himself when his business, which he would dispatch as quickly as possible, was concluded.

"That ain't a bad idea," said Clinch reflectively, "for ef yer hurry you 'll head 'em off in case they scent us, and try to double-back on the North Ridge. They 'll fight shy of the trail if they see anybody on it, and one man 's as good as a dozen."

Hale could not help thinking that he might have been that one man, and had his opportunity for independent action but for his rash proposal, but it was too late to withdraw now. He hastily scribbled a few lines to his wife on a sheet of the station paper, handed it to the man, and took his place in the little cavalcade as it filed silently down the road.

They had ridden in silence for nearly an hour, and had passed the scene of the robbery by a higher track. Morning had long ago advanced its colors on the cold white peaks to their right, and was taking possession of the spur where they rode.

"It looks like snow," said Rawlins quietly.

Hale turned towards him in astonishment. Nothing on earth or sky looked less likely. It had been cold, but that might have been only a current from the frozen peaks beyond, reaching the lower valley. The ridge on which they had halted was still thick with yellowish-green summeı foliage, mingled with the darker evergreen of pine and fir. Oven-like cañons in the long flanks of the mountain seemed still to glow with the heat of yesterday's noon; the breathless air yet trembled and quivered over stifling gorges and passes in the granite rocks, while far at their feet sixty miles of perpetual summer stretched away over the winding American River, now and then lost in a gossamer haze. It was scarcely ripe October where they stood; they could see the plenitude of August still lingering in the valleys.

"I 've seen Thomson's Pass choked up with fifteen feet o' snow earlier than this," said Rawlins, answering Hale's gaze; "and last September the passengers sledded over the road we came last night, and all the time Thomson, a mile lower down over the ridge in the hollow, smoking his pipes under roses in his piazzy! Mountains is mighty uncertain; they make their own weather ez they want it. I reckon you ain't wintered here yet?"

Hale was obliged to admit that he had only taken Eagle's Court in the early spring.

"Oh, you 're all right at Eagle's — when you 're there! But it 's like Thomson's — it 's the gettin' there that — Hall ›! What 's that?"

A shot, distant but distinct, had rung through the keen air. It was followed by another so alike as to seem an echo.

"That 's over yon, on the North Ridge," said the hostler, "about two miles as the crow flies and five by the trail. Somebody 's shootin' b'ar."

"Not with a shot-gun," said Clinch, quickly wheeling his horse with a gesture that electrified them. "It 's *them*, and they 've doubled on us! To the North Ridge, gentlemen, and ride all you know!"

It needed no second challenge to completely transform that quiet cavalcade. The wild man-hunting instinct, inseparable to most humanity, rose at their leader's look and word. With an incoherent and unintelligible cry, giving voice to the chase like the commonest hound of their fields, the order-loving Hale and the philosophical Rawlins wheeled with the others, and in another instant the little band swept out of sight in the forest.

An immense and immeasurable quiet succeeded. The sunlight glistened silently on cliff and scar, the vast distance below seemed to stretch out and broaden into repose. It might have been fancy, but over the sharp line of the North Ridge a light smoke lifted as of an escaping soul.

CHAPTER II

EAGLE'S COURT, one of the highest cañons of the Sierras, was in reality a plateau of table-land, embayed like a green lake in a semicircular sweep of granite, that, lifting itself three thousand feet higher, became a foundation for the eternal snows. The mountain genii of space and atmosphere jealously guarded its seclusion and surrounded it with illusions; it never looked to be exactly what it was: the traveler who saw it from the North Ridge apparently at his feet in descending found himself separated from it by a mile-long abyss and a rushing river; those who sought it by a seeming direct trail at the end of an hour lost sight of it completely, or, abandoning the quest and retracing their steps, suddenly came upon the gap through which it was entered. That which from the Ridge appeared to be a copse of bushes beside the tiny dwelling were trees three hundred feet high; the cultivated lawn before it, which might have been covered by the traveler's handkerchief, was a field of a thousand acres.

The house itself was a long, low, irregular structure, chiefly of roof and veranda, picturesquely upheld by rustic pillars of pine, with the bark still adhering, and covered with vines and trailing roses. Yet it was evident that the coolness produced by this vast extent of cover was more than the architect, who had planned it under the influence of a staring and bewildering sky, had trustfully conceived, for it had to be mitigated by blazing fires in open hearths when the thermometer marked a hundred degrees in the field beyond. The dry, restless wind that continually rocked the tall masts of the pines with a sound like the distant sea, while it stimulated outdoor physical exertion and defied fatigue, left the sedentary dwellers in these altitudes chilled in the shade they courted, or scorched them with heat when they ventured to bask supinely in the sun.   White muslin curtains at the French windows, and rugs, skins, and heavy furs dispersed in the interior, with certain other charming but incongruous details of furniture, marked the inconsistencies of the climate.

There was a coquettish indication of this in the costume of Miss Kate Scott as she stepped out on the veranda that morning.   A man's broad-brimmed Panama hat, partly unsexed by a twisted gayly colored scarf, but retaining enough character to give piquancy to the pretty curves of the face beneath, protected her from the sun ; a red flannel shirt — another spoil from the enemy — and a thick jacket shielded her from the austerities of the morning breeze.   But the next inconsistency was peculiarly her own.   Miss Kate always wore the freshest and lightest of white cambric skirts, without the least reference to the temperature.   To the practical sanatory remonstrances of her brother-in-law, and to the conventional criticism of her sister, she opposed the same defense : " How else is one to tell when it is summer in this ridiculous climate ?   And then, woolen is stuffy, color draws the sun, and one at least knows when one is clean or dirty."   Artistically the result was far from unsatisfactory.   It was a pretty figure under the sombre pines, against the gray granite and the steely sky, and seemed to lend the yellowing fields from which the flowers had already fled a floral relief of color.   I do not think the few masculine wayfarers of that locality objected to it ; indeed, some had betrayed an indiscreet admiration, and had curiously followed the invitation of Miss Kate's warmly colored figure until they had encountered the invincible indifference of Miss Kate's cold gray eyes.   With these manifestations her brother-in-law did not concern himself; he had perfect confidence in her unqualified disinterest in the neighboring humanity, and permitted her to wander in her solitary picturesqueness, or accompanied her when she rode in her dark green habit, with equal freedom from anxiety.

For Miss Scott, although only twenty, had already subjected most of her maidenly illusions to mature critical analyses. She had voluntarily accompanied her sister and mother to California, in the earnest hope that nature contained something worth saying to her, and was disappointed to find she had already discounted its value in the pages of books. She hoped to find a vague freedom in this unconventional life thus opened to her, or rather to show others that she knew how intelligently to appreciate it, but as yet she was only able to express it in the one detail of dress already alluded to. Some of the men, and nearly all the women, she had met thus far, she was amazed to find, valued the conventionalities she believed she despised, and were voluntarily assuming the chains she thought she had thrown off. Instead of learning anything from them, these children of nature had bored her with eager questionings regarding the civilization she had abandoned, or irritated her with crude imitations of it for her benefit. "Fancy," she had written to a friend in Boston, "my calling on Sue Murphy, who remembered the Donner tragedy, and who once shot a grizzly that was prowling round her cabin, and think of her begging me to lend her my sack for a pattern, and wanting to know if 'polonays' were still worn." She remembered more bitterly the romance that had tickled her earlier fancy, told of two college friends of her brother-in-law's who were living the "perfect life" in the mines, laboring in the ditches with a copy of Homer in their pockets, and writing letters of the purest philosophy under the free air of the pines. How, coming unexpectedly on them in their Arcadia, the party found them unpresentable through dirt, and thenceforth unknowable through domestic complications that had filled their Arcadian cabin with half-bred children.

Much of this disillusion she had kept within her own heart, from a feeling of pride, or only lightly touched upon it in her relations with her mother and sister. For Mrs. Hale and Mrs. Scott had no idols to shatter, no enthusiasm to subdue. Firmly and unalterably conscious of their own superiority to the life they led and the community that surrounded them, they accepted their duties cheerfully, and performed them conscientiously. Those duties were loyalty to Hale's interests and a vague missionary work among the neighbors, which, like most missionary work, consisted rather in making their own ideas understood than in understanding the ideas of their audience. Old Mrs. Scott's zeal was partly religious, an inheritance from her Puritan ancestry ; Mrs. Hale's was the affability of a gentlewoman and the obligation of her position. To this was added the slight langour of the cultivated American wife, whose health has been affected by the birth of her first child, and whose views of marriage and maternity were slightly tinged with gentle skepticism. She was sincerely attached to her husband, " who dominated the household " like the rest of his " women-folk," with the faint consciousness of that division of service which renders the position of the sultan of a seraglio at once so prominent and so precarious. The attitude of John Hale in his family circle was dominant because it had never been subjected to criticism or comparison ; and perilous for the same reason.

Mrs. Hale presently joined her sister in the veranda, and, shading her eyes with a narrow white hand, glanced on the prospect with a polite interest and ladylike urbanity. The searching sun, which, as Miss Kate once intimated, was " vulgarity itself," stared at her in return, but could not call a blush to her somewhat sallow cheek. Neither could

it detract, however, from the delicate prettiness of her refined face with its soft gray shadows, or the dark gentle
eyes, whose blue-veined lids were just then wrinkled into
coquettishly mischievous lines by the strong light.   She
was taller and thinner than Kate, and had at times a certain
shy, coy sinuosity of movement which gave her a more
virginal suggestion than her unmarried sister.   For Miss
Kate, from her earliest youth, had been distinguished by
that matronly sedateness of voice and step, and complete-
ness of figure, which indicates some members of the gal-
linaceous tribe from their callow infancy.

"I suppose John must have stopped at the Summit on
some business," said Mrs. Hale, "or he would have been
here already.   It's scarcely worth while waiting for him,
unless you choose to ride over and meet him.   You might
change your dress," she continued, looking doubtfully at
Kate's costume.   "Put on your riding-habit, and take
Manuel with you."

"And take the only man we have, and leave you alone?"
returned Kate slowly.   "No!"

"There are the Chinese field-hands," said Mrs. Hale;
"you must correct your ideas, and really allow them some
humanity, Kate.   John says they have a very good com-
pulsory school system in their own country, and can read
and write."

"That would be of little use to you here alone if — if"
— Kate hesitated.

"If what?" said Mrs. Hale, smiling.   "Are you thinking of Manuel's dreadful story of the grizzly tracks across
the fields this morning?   I promise you that neither I, nor
mother, nor Minnie shall stir out of the house until you
return, if you wish it."

"I wasn't thinking of that," said Kate; "though I
don't believe the beating of a gong and the using of strong
language is the best way to frighten a grizzly from the

house. Besides, the Chinese are going down the river to-day to a funeral, or a wedding, or a feast of stolen chickens — they're all the same — and won't be here."

"Then take Manuel," repeated Mrs. Hale. "We have the Chinese servants and Indian Molly in the house to protect us from Heaven knows what! I have the greatest confidence in Chy-Lee as a warrior, and in Chinese warfare generally. One has only to hear him pipe in time of peace to imagine what a terror he might become in war time. Indeed, anything more deadly and soul-harrowing than that love-song he sang for us last night I cannot conceive. But really, Kate, I am not afraid to stay alone. You know what John says : we ought to be always prepared for anything that might happen."

"My dear Josie," returned Kate, putting her arm around her sister's waist, "I am perfectly convinced that if three-fingered Jack, or two-toed Bill, or even Joaquim Murietta himself, should step, red-handed, on that veranda, you would gently invite him to take a cup of tea, inquire about the state of the road, and refrain delicately from any allusions to the sheriff. But I sha'n't take Manuel from you. I really cannot undertake to look after his morals at the station, and keep him from drinking aguardiente with suspicious characters at the bar. It is true he 'kisses my hand' in his speech, even when it is thickest, and offers his back to me for a horse-block, but I think I prefer the sober and honest familiarity of even that Pike County landlord who is satisfied to say, 'Jump, girl, and I'll ketch ye!'"

"I hope you did n't change your manner to either of them for that," said Mrs. Hale, with a faint sigh. "John wants to be good friends with them, and they are behaving quite decently lately, considering that they can't speak a grammatical sentence nor know the use of a fork."

"And now the man puts on gloves and a tall hat to

come here on Sundays, and the woman won't call until you've called first," retorted Kate; "perhaps you call that improvement. The fact is, Josephine," continued the young girl, folding her arms demurely, "we might as well admit it at once — these people don't like us."

"That's impossible!" said Mrs. Hale, with sublime simplicity. "You don't like them, you mean."

"I like them better than you do, Josie, and that's the reason why *I* feel it and *you* don't." She checked herself, and after a pause resumed in a lighter tone: "No; I sha'n't go to the station; I'll commune with nature to-day, and won't 'take any humanity in mine, thank you,' as Bill the driver says. Adios."

"I wish Kate would not use that dreadful slang, even in jest," said Mrs. Scott, in her rocking-chair at the French window, when Josephine reëntered the parlor as her sister walked briskly away. "I am afraid she is being infected by the people at the station. She ought to have a change."

"I was just thinking," said Josephine, looking abstractedly at her mother, "that I would try to get John to take her to San Francisco this winter. The Careys are expected, you know; she might visit them."

"I'm afraid, if she stays here much longer, she won't care to see them at all. She seems to care for nothing now that she ever liked before," returned the old lady ominously.

Meantime the subject of these criticisms was carrying away her own reflections tightly buttoned up in her short jacket. She had driven back her dog Spot — another one of her disillusions, who, giving way to his lower nature, had once killed a sheep — as she did not wish her Jacques-like contemplation of any wounded deer to be inconsistently interrupted by a fresh outrage from her companion. The air was really very chilly, and for the first time in her mountain experience the direct rays of the sun seemed to

be shorn of their power.   This compelled her to walk more
briskly than she was conscious of, for in less than an hour
she came suddenly and breathlessly upon the mouth of the
cañon, or natural gateway to Eagle's Court.

To her always a profound spectacle of mountain magnifi-
cence, it seemed to-day almost terrible in its cold, strong
grandeur.   The narrowing pass was choked for a moment
between two gigantic buttresses of granite, approaching each
other so closely at their towering summits that trees growing in opposite clefts of the rock intermingled their branches
and pointed the soaring Gothic arch of a stupendous gateway.   She raised her eyes with a quickly beating heart.
She knew that the interlacing trees above her were as large
as those she had just quitted ; she knew also that the point
where they met was only halfway up the cliff, for she had
once gazed down upon them, dwindled to shrubs from the
airy summit ; she knew that their shaken cones fell a thousand feet perpendicularly, or bounded like shot from the
scarred walls they bombarded.   She remembered that one
of these pines, dislodged from its high foundations, had once
dropped like a portcullis in the archway, blocking the pass,
and was only carried afterwards by assaults of steel and fire.
Bending her head mechanically, she ran swiftly through the
shadowy passage, and halted only at the beginning of the
ascent on the other side.

It was here that the actual position of the plateau, so indefinite of approach, began to be realized.   It now appeared
an independent elevation, surrounded on three sides by
gorges and watercourses, so narrow as to be overlooked from
the principal mountain range, with which it was connected
by a long cañon that led to the Ridge.   At the outlet of
this cañon — in bygone ages a mighty river — it had the
appearance of having been slowly raised by the diluvium
of that river, and the débris washed down from above — a
suggestion repeated in miniature by the artificial plateaus of

excavated soil raised before the mouths of mining tunnels in
the lower flanks of the mountain. It was the realization of a
fact — often forgotten by the dwellers in Eagle's Court —
that the valley below them, which was their connecting link
with the surrounding world, was only reached by ascending
the mountain, and the nearest road was over the higher
mountain ridge. Never before had this impressed itself so
strongly upon the young girl as when she turned that morning to look upon the plateau below her. It seemed to illus-
trate the conviction that had been slowly shaping itself out
of her reflections on the conversation of that morning. It
was possible that the perfect understanding of a higher life
was only reached from a height still greater, and that to
those halfway up the mountain the summit was never
as truthfully revealed as to the humbler dwellers in the
valley.

I do not know that these profound truths prevented her
from gathering some quaint ferns and berries, or from keeping her calm gray eyes open to certain practical changes
that were taking place around her. She had noticed a
singular thickening in the atmosphere that seemed to prevent the passage of the sun's rays, yet without diminishing
the transparent quality of the air. The distant snow-peaks
were as plainly seen, though they appeared as if in moonlight. This seemed due to no cloud or mist, but rather to
a fading of the sun itself. The occasional flurry of wings
overhead, the whirring of larger birds in the cover, and a
frequent rustling in the undergrowth, as of the passage of
some stealthy animal, began equally to attract her attention.
It was so different from the habitual silence of these sedate
solitudes. Kate had no vague fear of wild beasts; she
had been long enough a mountaineer to understand the
general immunity enjoyed by the unmolesting wayfarer,
and kept her way undismayed. She was descending an
abrupt trail when she was stopped by a sudden crash in

the bushes. It seemed to come from the opposite incline, directly in a line with her, and apparently on the very trail that she was pursuing. The crash was then repeated again and again lower down, as of a descending body. Expecting the apparition of some fallen tree, or detached boulder bursting through the thicket, in its way to the bottom of the gulch, she waited. The foliage was suddenly brushed aside, and a large grizzly bear half rolled, half waddled, into the trail on the opposite side of the hill. A few moments more would have brought them face to face at the foot of the gulch; when she stopped there were not fifty yards between them.

She did not scream; she did not faint; she was not even frightened. There did not seem to be anything terrifying in this huge, stupid beast, who, arrested by the rustle of a stone displaced by her descending feet, rose slowly on his haunches and gazed at her with small, wondering eyes. Nor did it seem strange to her, seeing that he was in her way, to pick up a stone, throw it in his direction, and say simply, "Sho! get away!" as she would have done to an intruding cow. Nor did it seem odd that he should actually "go away" as he did, scrambling back into the bushes again, and disappearing like some grotesque figure in a transformation scene. It was not until after he had gone that she was taken with a slight nervousness and giddiness, and retraced her steps somewhat hurriedly, shying a little at every rustle in the thicket. By the time she had reached the great gateway she was doubtful whether to be pleased or frightened at the incident, but she concluded to keep it to herself.

It was still intensely cold. The light of the midday sun had decreased still more, and on reaching the plateau again she saw that a dark cloud, not unlike the precursor of a thunder-storm, was brooding over the snowy peaks beyond. In spite of the cold this singular suggestion of

summer phenomena was still borne out by the distant smiling valley, and even in the soft grasses at her feet. It
seemed to her the crowning inconsistency of the climate,
and with a half-serious, half-playful protest on her lips she
hurried forward to seek the shelter of the house.

CHAPTER III

To Kate's surprise, the lower part of the house was deserted, but there was an unusual activity on the floor above, and the sound of heavy steps. There were alien marks of dusty feet on the scrupulously clean passage, and on the first step of the stairs a spot of blood. With a sudden genuine alarm that drove her previous adventure from her mind, she impatiently called her sister's name. There was a hasty yet subdued rustle of skirts on the staircase, and Mrs. Hale, with her finger on her lip, swept Kate unceremoniously into the sitting-room, closed the door, and leaned back against it, with a faint smile. She had a crumpled paper in her hand.

"Don't be alarmed, but read that first," she said, handing her sister the paper. "It was brought just now."

Kate instantly recognized her brother's distinct hand. She read hurriedly, "The coach was robbed last night; nobody hurt. I've lost nothing but a day's time, as this business will keep me here until to-morrow, when Manuel can join me with a fresh horse. No cause for alarm. As the bearer goes out of his way to bring you this, see that he wants for nothing."

"Well," said Kate expectantly.

"Well, the 'bearer' was fired upon by the robbers, who were lurking on the Ridge. He was wounded in the leg. Luckily he was picked up by his friend, who was coming to meet him, and brought here as the nearest place. He's upstairs in the spare bed in the spare room, with his friend, who won't leave his side. He won't even have mother in the room. They've stopped the bleeding with John's ambulance things, and now, Kate, here's a chance for you to show the value of your education in the ambulance class. The ball has got to be extracted. Here's your opportunity."

Kate looked at her sister curiously. There was a faint pink flush on her pale cheeks, and her eyes were gently sparkling. She had never seen her look so pretty before.

"Why not have sent Manuel for a doctor at once?" asked Kate.

"The nearest doctor is fifteen miles away, and Manuel is nowhere to be found. Perhaps he's gone to look after the stock. There's some talk of snow; imagine the absurdity of it!"

"But who are they?"

"They speak of themselves as 'friends,' as if it were a profession. The wounded one was a passenger, I suppose."

"But what are they like?" continued Kate. "I suppose they're like them all."

Mrs. Hale shrugged her shoulders.

"The wounded one, when he's not fainting away, is laughing. The other is a creature with a mustache, and gloomy beyond expression."

"What are you going to do with them?" said Kate.

"What should I do? Even without John's letter I could not refuse the shelter of my house to a wounded and helpless man. I shall keep him, of course, until John comes. Why, Kate, I really believe you are so prejudiced against these people you'd like to turn them out. But I forget! It's because you *like* them so well. Well, you need not fear to expose yourself to the fascinations of the wounded Christy Minstrel — I'm sure he's that — or to the unspeakable one, who is shyness itself, and would not dare to raise his eyes to you."

There was a timid, hesitating step in the passage. It

paused before the door, moved away, returned, and finally asserted its intentions in the gentlest of taps.

"It's him; I'm sure of it," said Mrs. Hale, with a suppressed smile.

Kate threw open the door smartly, to the extreme discomfiture of a tall, dark figure that already had slunk away from it. For all that, he was a good-looking enough fellow, with a mustache as long and almost as flexible as a ringlet. Kate could not help noticing also that his hand, which was nervously pulling the mustache, was white and thin.

"Excuse me," he stammered, without raising his eyes, "I was looking for — for — the old lady. I — I beg your pardon. I didn't know that you — the young ladies — company — were here. I intended — I only wanted to say that my friend" — He stopped at the slight smile that passed quickly over Mrs. Hale's mouth, and his pale face reddened with an angry flush.

"I hope he is not worse," said Mrs. Hale, with more than her usual languid gentleness. "My mother is not here at present. Can I — can *we* — this is my sister — do as well?"

Without looking up he made a constrained recognition of Kate's presence, that, embarrassed and curt as it was, had none of the awkwardness of rusticity.

"Thank you; you're very kind. But my friend is a little stronger, and if you can lend me an extra horse I'll try to get him on the Summit to-night."

"But you surely will not take him away from us so soon?" said Mrs. Hale, with a languid look of alarm, in which Kate, however, detected a certain real feeling. "Wait at least until my husband returns to-morrow."

"He won't be here to-morrow," said the stranger hastily. He stopped, and as quickly corrected himself. "That is, his business is so very uncertain, my friend says."

Only Kate noticed the slip; but she noticed also that her

sister was apparently unconscious of it. "You think," she said, "that Mr. Hale may be delayed?"

He turned upon her almost brusquely. "I mean that it is already snowing up there;" he pointed through the window to the cloud Kate had noticed; "if it comes down lower in the pass the roads will be blocked up. That is why it would be better for us to try and get on at once."

"But if Mr. Hale is likely to be stopped by snow, so are you," said Mrs. Hale playfully; "and you had better let us try to make your friend comfortable here rather than expose him to that uncertainty in his weak condition. We will do our best for him. My sister is dying for an opportunity to show her skill in surgery," she continued, with an unexpected mischievousness that only added to Kate's surprised embarrassment. "Are n't you, Kate?"

Equivocal as the young girl knew her silence appeared, she was unable to utter the simplest polite evasion. Some unaccountable impulse kept her constrained and speechless. The stranger did not, however, wait for her reply, but, casting a swift, hurried glance around the room, said, "It's impossible; we must go. In fact, I've already taken the liberty to order the horses round. They are at the door now. You may be certain," he added, with quick earnestness, suddenly lifting his dark eyes to Mrs. Hale, and as rapidly withdrawing them, "that your horse will be returned at once, and — and — we won't forget your kindness." He stopped and turned towards the hall. "I — I have brought my friend downstairs. He wants to thank you before he goes."

As he remained standing in the hall the two women stepped to the door. To their surprise, half reclining on a cane sofa was the wounded man, and what could be seen of his slight figure was wrapped in a dark serape. His beardless face gave him a quaint boyishness quite inconsistent with the mature lines of his temples and forehead. Pale, and in pain, as he evidently was, his blue eyes twinkled with intense amusement. Not only did his manner offer a marked contrast to the sombre uneasiness of his companion, but he seemed to be the only one perfectly at his ease in the group around him.

"It's rather rough making you come out here to see me off," he said, with a not unmusical laugh that was very infectious, "but Ned there, who carried me downstairs, wanted to tote me round the house in his arms like a baby to say ta-ta to you all. Excuse my not rising, but I feel as uncertain below as a mermaid, and as out of my element," he added, with a mischievous glance at his friend. "Ned concluded I must go on. But I must say good-by to the old lady first. Ah! here she is."

To Kate's complete bewilderment, not only did the utter familiarity of this speech pass unnoticed and unrebuked by her sister, but actually her own mother advanced quickly with every expression of lively sympathy, and with the authority of her years and an almost maternal anxiety endeavored to dissuade the invalid from going. "This is not my house," she said, looking at her daughter, "but if it were I should not hear of your leaving, not only to-night, but until you were out of danger. Josephine! Kate! What are you thinking of to permit it? Well, then, *I* forbid it — there!"

Had they become suddenly insane, or were they bewitched by this morose intruder and his insufferably familiar confidant? The man was wounded, it was true; they might have to put him up in common humanity; but here was her austere mother, who would n't come in the room when Whiskey Dick called on business, actually pressing both of the invalid's hands, while her sister, who never extended a finger to the ordinary visiting humanity of the neighborhood, looked on with evident complacency.

The wounded man suddenly raised Mrs. Scott's hand to

his lips, kissed it gently, and, with his smile quite vanished, endeavored to rise to his feet. "It's of no use — we must go. Give me your arm, Ned. Quick! Are the horses there?"

"Dear me," said Mrs. Scott quickly, "I forgot to say the horse cannot be found anywhere. Manuel must have taken him this morning to look up the stock. But he will be back to-night certainly, and if to-morrow" —

The wounded man sank back to a sitting position. "Is Manuel your man?" he asked grimly.

"Yes."

The two men exchanged glances.

"Marked on his left cheek and drinks a good deal?"

"Yes," said Kate, finding her voice. "Why?"

The amused look came back to the man's eyes. "That kind of man isn't safe to wait for. We must take our own horse, Ned. Are you ready?"

"Yes."

The wounded man again attempted to rise. He fell back, but this time quite heavily. He had fainted.

Involuntarily and simultaneously the three women rushed to his side. "He cannot go," said Kate suddenly.

"He will be better in a moment."

"But only for a moment. Will nothing induce you to change your mind?"

As if in reply a sudden gust of wind brought a volley of rain against the window.

"*That* will," said the stranger bitterly.

"The rain?"

"A mile from here it is *snow;* and before we could reach the Summit with these horses the road would be impassable."

He made a slight gesture to himself, as if accepting an inevitable defeat, and turned to his companion, who was slowly reviving under the active ministration of the two women.

The wounded man looked around with a weak smile. " This is one way of going off," he said faintly, " but I could do this sort of thing as well on the road."

" You can do nothing now," said his friend decidedly. " Before we get to the Gate the road will be impassable for our horses."

" For *any* horses ? " asked Kate.

" For any horses. For any man or beast I might say. Where we cannot get out, no one can get in," he added, as if answering her thoughts. " I am afraid that you won't see your brother to-morrow morning. But I 'll reconnoitre as soon as I can do so without torturing *him*," he said, looking anxiously at the helpless man ; " he 's got about his share of pain, I reckon, and the first thing is to get him easier." It was the longest speech he had made to her ; it was the first time he had fairly looked her in the face. His shy restlessness had suddenly given way to dogged resignation, less abstracted, but scarcely more flattering to his entertainers. Lifting his companion gently in his arms, as if he had been a child, he reascended the staircase, Mrs. Scott and the hastily summoned Molly following with overflowing solicitude. As soon as they were alone in the parlor Mrs. Hale turned to her sister : " Only that our guests seemed to be as anxious to go just now as you were to pack them off, I should have been shocked at your inhospitality. What has come over you, Kate ? These are the very people you have reproached me so often with not being civil enough to."

" But *who* are they ? "

" How do I know ? There is *your brother's* letter."

She usually spoke of her husband as " John." This slight shifting of relationship and responsibility to the feminine mind was significant. Kate was a little frightened and remorseful.

" I only meant you don't even know their names."

"That was n't necessary for giving them a bed and band-ages. Do you suppose the good Samaritan ever asked the wounded Jew's name, and that the Levite did not excuse himself because the thieves had taken the poor man's card-case ? Do the directions, 'In case of accident,' in your ambulance rules, read, 'First lay the sufferer on his back and inquire his name and family connections' ? Besides, you can call one 'Ned' and the other 'George,' if you like."

"Oh, you know what I mean," said Kate irrelevantly. "Which is George ? "

"George is the wounded man," said Mrs. Hale ; "*not* the one who talked to you more than he did to any one else. I suppose the poor man was frightened and read dismissal in your eyes."

"I wish John were here."

"I don't think we have anything to fear in his absence from men whose only wish is to get away from us. If it is a question of propriety, my dear Kate, surely there is the presence of mother to prevent any scandal — although really her own conduct with the wounded one is not above suspicion," she added, with that novel mischievousness that seemed a return of her lost girlhood. "We must try to do the best we can with them and for them," she said decidedly, "and meantime I 'll see if I can't arrange John's room for them."

"John's room ? "

"Oh, mother is perfectly satisfied ; indeed, suggested it. It 's larger and will hold two beds, for 'Ned,' the friend, must attend to him at night. And, Kate, don't you think, if you 're not going out again, you might change your cos-tume ? It does very well while we are alone " —

"Well," said Kate indignantly, "as I am not going into his room " —

"I 'm not so sure about that, if we can't get a regular

doctor. But he is very restless, and wanders all over the house like a timid and apologetic spaniel."

" Who ? "

" Why 'Ned.' But I must go and look after the patient. I suppose they 've got him safe in his bed again," and with a nod to her sister she tripped upstairs.

Uncomfortable and embarrassed, she knew not why, Kate sought her mother. But that good lady was already in attendance on the patient, and Kate hurried past that baleful centre of attraction with a feeling of loneliness and strangeness she had never experienced before. Entering her own room she went to the window — that first and last refuge of the troubled mind — and gazed out. Turning her eyes in the direction of her morning's walk, she started back with a sense of being dazzled. She rubbed first her eyes and then the rain-dimmed pane. It was no illusion ! The whole landscape, so familiar to her, was one vast field of dead, colorless white ! Trees, rocks, even distance itself, had vanished in those few hours. An even, shadowless, motionless white sea filled the horizon. On either side a vast wall of snow seemed to shut out the world like a shroud. Only the green plateau before her, with its sloping meadows and fringe of pines and cotton-wood, lay alone like a summer island in this frozen sea.

A sudden desire to view this phenomenon more closely, and to learn for herself the limits of this new tethered life, completely possessed her, and, accustomed to act upon her independent impulses, she seized a hooded waterproof cloak, and slipped out of the house unperceived. The rain was falling steadily along the descending trail where she walked, but beyond, scarcely a mile across the chasm, the wintry distance began to confuse her brain with the inextricable swarming of snow. Hurrying down with feverish excitement, she at last came in sight of the arching granite portals of their domain. But her first glance through the

gateway showed it closed as if with a white portcullis.   Kate
remembered that the trail began to ascend beyond the arch,
and knew that what she saw was only the mountain side
she had partly climbed this morning.   But the snow had
already crept down its flank, and the exit by trail was
practically closed.   Breathlessly making her way back to
the highest part of the plateau — the cliff behind the house
that here descended abruptly to the rain-dimmed valley —
she gazed at the dizzy depths in vain for some undiscovered
or forgotten trail along its face.   But a single glance convinced her of its inaccessibility.   The gateway was indeed
their only outlet to the plain below.   She looked back at
the falling snow beyond, until she fancied she could see in
the crossing and recrossing lines the moving meshes of a
fateful web woven around them by viewless but inexorable
fingers.

Half frightened, she was turning away, when she perceived, a few paces distant, the figure of the stranger,
"Ned," also apparently absorbed in the gloomy prospect.
He was wrapped in the clinging folds of a black serape
braided with silver; the broad flap of a slouched hat
beaten back by the wind exposed the dark, glistening curls
on his white forehead.   He was certainly very handsome
and picturesque, and that apparently without effort or consciousness.   Neither was there anything in his costume or
appearance inconsistent with his surroundings, or even with
what Kate could judge were his habits or position.   Nevertheless, she instantly decided that he was *too* handsome and
too picturesque, without suspecting that her ideas of the
limits of masculine beauty were merely personal experience.

As he turned away from the cliff they were brought face
to face.   "It does n't look very encouraging over there,"
he said quietly, as if the inevitableness of the situation had
relieved him of his previous shyness and effort; "it's even

worse than I expected. The snow must have begun there last night, and it looks as if it meant to stay." He stopped for a moment, and then, lifting his eyes to her, said, "I suppose you know what this means?"

"I don't understand you."

"I thought not. Well! it means that you are absolutely cut off here from any communication or intercourse with any one outside of that cañon. By this time the snow is five feet deep over the only trail by which one can pass in and out of that gateway. I am not alarming you, I hope, for there is no real physical danger; a place like this ought to be well garrisoned, and certainly is self-supporting so far as the mere necessities and even comforts are concerned. You have wood, water, cattle, and game at your command, but for two weeks at least you are completely isolated."

"For two weeks!" said Kate, growing pale — "and my brother!"

"He knows all by this time, and is probably as assured as I am of the safety of his family."

"For two weeks!" continued Kate; "impossible! You don't know my brother! He will find some way to get to us."

"I hope so," returned the stranger gravely, "for what is possible for him is possible for us."

"Then you are anxious to get away?" Kate could not help saying.

"Very."

The reply was not discourteous in manner, but was so far from gallant that Kate felt a new and inconsistent resentment. Before she could say anything he added, "And I hope you will remember, whatever may happen, that I did my best to avoid staying here longer than was necessary to keep my friend from bleeding to death in the road."

"Certainly," said Kate; then added awkwardly, "I

hope he 'll be better soon." She was silent, and then, quickening her pace, said hurriedly, " I must tell my sister this dreadful news."

" I think she is prepared for it. If there is anything I can do to help you I hope you will let me know. Perhaps I may be of some service. I shall begin by exploring the trails to-morrow, for the best service we can do you possibly is to take ourselves off ; but I can carry a gun, and the woods are full of game driven down from the mountains. Let me show you something you may not have noticed." He stopped, and pointed to a small knoll of sheltered shrubbery and granite on the opposite mountain, which still remained black against the surrounding snow. It seemed to be thickly covered with moving objects. " They are wild animals driven out of the snow," said the stranger. " That larger one is a grizzly ; there is a panther, wolves, wildcats, a fox, and some mountain goats."

" An ill-assorted party," said the young girl.

" Ill luck makes them companions. They are too frightened to hurt one another now."

" But they will eat each other later on," said Kate, stealing a glance at her companion.

He lifted his long lashes and met her eyes. " Not on a haven of refuge."

CHAPTER IV

KATE found her sister, as the stranger had intimated, fully prepared. A hasty inventory of provisions and means of subsistence showed that they had ample resources for a much longer isolation.

"They tell me it is by no means an uncommon case, Kate; somebody over at somebody's place was snowed in for four weeks, and now it appears that even the Summit House is not always accessible. John ought to have known it when he bought the place; in fact, I was ashamed to admit that he did not. But that is like John to prefer his own theories to the experience of others. However, I don't suppose we should even notice the privation except for the mails. It will be a lesson to John, though. As Mr. Lee says, he is on the outside, and can probably go wherever he likes from the Summit except to come here."

"Mr. Lee?" echoed Kate.

"Yes, the wounded one; and the other's name is Falkner. I asked them in order that you might be properly introduced. There were very respectable Falkners in Charlestown, you remember; I thought you might warm to the name, and perhaps trace the connection, now that you are such good friends. It's providential they are here, as we have n't got a horse or a man in the place since Manuel disappeared, though Mr. Falkner says he can't be far away, or they would have met him on the trail if he had gone towards the Summit."

"Did they say anything more of Manuel?"

"Nothing; though I am inclined to agree with you that

he is n't trustworthy. But that again is the result of John's idea of employing native skill at the expense of retaining native habits."

The evening closed early, and with no diminution in the falling rain and rising wind. Falkner kept his word, and unostentatiously performed the outdoor work in the barn and stables, assisted by the only Chinese servant remaining, and under the advice and supervision of Kate. Although he seemed to understand horses, she was surprised to find that he betrayed a civic ignorance of the ordinary details of the farm and rustic household. It was quite impossible that she should retain her distrustful attitude, or he his reserve in their enforced companionship. They talked freely of subjects suggested by the situation, Falkner exhibiting a general knowledge and intuition of things without parade or dogmatism. Doubtful of all versatility as Kate was, she could not help admitting to herself that his truths were none the less true for their quantity or that he got at them without ostentatious processes. His talk certainly was more picturesque than her brother's, and less subduing to her faculties. John had always crushed her.

When they returned to the house he did not linger in the parlor or sitting-room, but at once rejoined his friend. When dinner was ready in the dining-room, a little more deliberately arranged and ornamented than usual, the two women were somewhat surprised to receive an excuse from Falkner, begging them to allow him for the present to take his meals with the patient, and thus save the necessity of another attendant.

"It is all shyness, Kate," said Mrs. Hale confidently, "and must not be permitted for a moment."

"I 'm sure I should be quite willing to stay with the poor boy myself," said Mrs. Scott simply, "and take Mr. Falkner's place while he dines."

"You are too willing, mother," said Mrs. Hale pertly,

"and your ' poor boy,' as you call him, will never see thirty-five again."

"He will never see any other birthday," retorted her mother, "unless you keep him more quiet. He only talks when you 're in the room."

"He wants some relief to his friend's long face and mustaches that make him look prematurely in mourning," said Mrs. Hale, with a slight increase of animation. "I don't propose to leave them too much together. After dinner we 'll adjourn to their room and lighten it up a little. You must come, Kate, to look at the patient, and counteract the baleful effects of my frivolity."

Mrs. Hale's instincts were truer than her mother's experience; not only that the wounded man's eyes became brighter under the provocation of her presence, but it was evident that his naturally exuberant spirits were a part of his vital strength, and were absolutely essential to his quick recovery. Encouraged by Falkner's grave and practical assistance, which she could not ignore, Kate ventured to make an examination of Lee's wound. Even to her unpracticed eye it was less serious than at first appeared. The great loss of blood had been due to the laceration of certain small vessels below the knee, but neither artery nor bone was injured. A recurrence of the hemorrhage or fever was the only thing to be feared, and these could be averted by bandaging, repose, and simple nursing.

The unfailing good humor of the patient under this manipulation, the quaint originality of his speech, the freedom of his fancy, which was, however, always controlled by a certain instinctive tact, began to affect Kate nearly as it had the others. She found herself laughing over the work she had undertaken in a pure sense of duty ; she joined in the hilarity produced by Lee's affected terror of her surgical mania, and offered to undo the bandages in search of the thimble he declared she had left in the wound with a view to further experiments.

"You ought to broaden your practice," he suggested. "A good deal might be made out of Ned and a piece of soap left carelessly on the first step of the staircase, while mountains of surgical opportunities lie in a humble orange peel judiciously exposed. Only I warn you that you would n't find him as docile as I am. Decoyed into a snowdrift and frozen, you might get some valuable experiences in resuscitation by thawing him."

"I fancied you had done that already, Kate," whispered Mrs. Hale.

"Freezing is the new suggestion for painless surgery," said Lee, coming to Kate's relief with ready tact, "only the knowledge should be more generally spread. There was a man up at Strawberry fell under a sledge-load of wood in the snow. Stunned by the shock, he was slowly freezing to death, when, with a tremendous effort, he succeeded in freeing himself all but his right leg, pinned down by a small log. His axe happened to have fallen within reach, and a few blows on the log freed him."

"And saved the poor fellow's life," said Mrs. Scott, who was listening with sympathizing intensity.

"At the expense of his *left leg*, which he had unknowingly cut off under the pleasing supposition that it was a log," returned Lee demurely.

Nevertheless, in a few moments he managed to divert the slightly shocked susceptibilities of the old lady with some raillery of himself, and did not again interrupt the even good-humored communion of the party. The rain beating against the windows and the fire sparkling on the hearth seemed to lend a charm to their peculiar isolation, and it was not until Mrs. Scott rose with a warning that they were trespassing upon the rest of their patient that they discovered that the evening had slipped by unnoticed. When the door at last closed on the bright, sympathetic eyes of the two young women and the motherly benedic-

tion of the elder, Falkner walked to the window, and remained silent, looking into the darkness. Suddenly he
turned bitterly to his companion.

"This is just h—ll, George."

George Lee, with a smile still on his boyish face, lazily
moved his head.

"I don't know! If it was n't for the old woman, who is
the one solid chunk of absolute goodness here, expecting
nothing, wanting nothing, it would be good fun enough!
These two women, cooped up in this house, wanted excitement. They 've got it! That man Hale wanted to show
off by going for us; he 's had his chance, and will have it
again before I 've done with him. That d—d fool of a
messenger wanted to go out of his way to exchange shots
with me; I reckon he 's the most satisfied of the lot! I
don't know why *you* should growl. You did your level
best to get away from here, and the result is, that little
Puritan is ready to worship you."

"Yes — but this playing it on them — George —
this " —

"Who 's playing it? Not you; I see you 've given
away our names already."

"I could n't lie, and they know nothing by that."

"Do you think they would be happier by knowing it?
Do you think that soft little creature would be as happy as
she was to-night if she knew that her husband had been in-
directly the means of laying me by the heels here? Where
is the swindle? This hole in my leg? If you had been
five minutes under that girl's d—d sympathetic fingers
you 'd have thought it was genuine. Is it in our trying to
get away? Do you call that ten-feet drift in the pass a
swindle? Is it in the chance of Hale getting back while
we 're here? That 's real enough, is n't it? I say, Ned,
did you ever give your unfettered intellect to the contemplation of *that*?"

Falkner did not reply. There was an interval of silence, but he could see from the movement of George's shoulders that he was shaking with suppressed laughter.

"Fancy Mrs. Hale archly introducing her husband! My offering him a chair, but being all the time obliged to cover him with a derringer under the bedclothes. Your rushing in from your peaceful pastoral pursuits in the barn, with a pitchfork in one hand and the girl in the other, and dear old mammy sympathizing all round and trying to make everything comfortable."

"I should not be alive to see it, George," said Falkner gloomily.

"You'd manage to pitchfork me and those two women on Hale's horse and ride away; that's what you'd do, or I don't know you! Look here, Ned," he added more seriously, "the only swindling was our bringing that note here. That was *your* idea. You thought it would remove suspicion, and as you believed I was bleeding to death you played that game for all it was worth to save me. You might have done what I asked you to do — propped me up in the bushes, and got away yourself. I was good for a couple of shots yet, and after that — what mattered? That night, the next day, the next time I take the road, or a year hence? It will come when it will come, all the same!"

He did not speak bitterly, nor relax his smile. Falkner, without speaking, slid his hand along the coverlet. Lee grasped it, and their hands remained clasped together for a few moments in silence.

"How is this to end? We cannot go on here in this way," said Falkner suddenly.

"If we cannot get away it must go on. Look here, Ned. I don't reckon to take anything out of this house that I didn't bring in it, or isn't freely offered to me; yet I don't otherwise, you understand, intend making myself

out a d—d bit better than I am.   That's the only excuse
I have for not making myself out *just what* I am.   I don't
know the fellow who's obliged to tell every one the last
company he was in, or the last thing he did!   Do you
suppose even these pretty little women tell *us* their whole
story ?   Do you fancy that this St. John in the wilderness
is canonized in his family ?   Perhaps, when I take the
liberty to intrude in his affairs, as he has in mine, he'd see
he isn't.   I don't blame you for being sensitive, Ned.
It's natural.   When a man lives outside the revised stat-
utes of his own State he is apt to be awfully fine on points
of etiquette in his own household.   As for me, I find it
rather comfortable here.   The beds of other people's making strike me as being more satisfactory than my own.
Good-night."

In a few moments he was sleeping the peaceful sleep of
that youth which seemed to be his own dominant quality.
Falkner stood for a little space and watched him, following
the boyish lines of his cheek on the pillow, from the shadow
of the light brown lashes under his closed lids to the lifting
of his short upper lip over his white teeth, with his regular
respiration.   Only a sharp accenting of the line of nostril
and jaw and a faint depression of the temple betrayed his
already tried manhood.

The house had long sunk to repose when Falkner returned
to the window, and remained looking out upon the storm.
Suddenly he extinguished the light, and passing quickly to
the bed laid his hand upon the sleeper.   Lee opened his
eyes instantly.

" Are you awake ? "

" Perfectly."

" Somebody is trying to get into the house ! "

" Not *him*, eh ? " said Lee gayly.

" No ; two men.   Mexicans, I think.   One looks like
Manuel."

"Ah," said Lee, drawing himself up to a sitting posture. "Well?"

"Don't you see? He believes the women are alone."

"The dog — d—d hound!"

"Speak respectfully of one of my people, if you please, and hand me my derringer. Light the candle again, and open the door. Let them get in quietly. They'll come here first. It's *his* room, you understand, and if there's any money it's here. Anyway, they must pass here to get to the women's rooms. Leave Manuel to me, and you take care of the other."

"I see."

"Manuel knows the house, and will come first. When he's fairly in the room shut the door and go for the other. But no noise. This is just one of the *sw-eetest* things out — if it's done properly."

"But *you*, George?"

"If I couldn't manage that fellow without turning down the bedclothes I'd kick myself. Hush. Steady now."

He lay down and shut his eyes as if in natural repose. Only his right hand, carelessly placed under his pillow, closed on the handle of his pistol. Falkner quietly slipped into the passage. The light of the candle faintly illuminated the floor and opposite wall, but left it on either side in pitchy obscurity.

For some moments the silence was broken only by the sound of the rain without. The recumbent figure in bed seemed to have actually succumbed to sleep. The multitudinous small noises of a house in repose might have been misinterpreted by ears less keen than the sleeper's; but when the apparent creaking of a far-off shutter was followed by the sliding apparition of a dark head of tangled hair at the door, Lee had not been deceived, and was as prepared as if he had seen it. Another step, and the figure entered the room. The door closed instantly behind it. The sound

of a heavy body struggling against the partition outside
followed, and then suddenly ceased.

The intruder turned, and violently grasped the handle of
the door, but recoiled at a quiet voice from the bed.

"Drop that, and come here."

He started back with an exclamation. The sleeper's
eyes were wide open; the sleeper's extended arm and pistol covered him.

"Silence! or I 'll let that candle shine through you."

"Yes, captain!" growled the astounded and frightened
half-breed. "I did n't know you were here."

Lee raised himself, and grasped the long whip in his
left hand and whirled it round his head.

"*Will you* dry up?"

The man sank back against the wall in silent terror.

"Open that door now — softly."

Manuel obeyed with trembling fingers.

"Ned," said Lee in a low voice, "bring him in here —
quick."

There was a slight rustle, and Falkner appeared, back-
ing in another gasping figure, whose eyes were starting
under the strong grasp of the captor at his throat.

"Silence," said Lee, "all of you."

There was a breathless pause. The sound of a door
hesitatingly opened in the passage broke the stillness, followed by the gentle voice of Mrs. Scott.

"Is anything the matter?"

Lee made a slight gesture of warning to Falkner, of
menace to the others. "Everything 's the matter," he
called out cheerily. "Ned 's managed to half pull down
the house trying to get at something from my saddle-bags."

"I hope he has not hurt himself," broke in another voice
mischievously.

"Answer, you clumsy villain," whispered Lee, with
twinkling eyes.

"I'm all right, thank you," responded Falkner, with unaffected awkwardness.

There was a slight murmuring of voices, and then the door was heard to close. Lee turned to Falkner.

"Disarm that hound and turn him loose outside, and make no noise. And you, Manuel! tell him what his and your chances are if he shows his black face here again."

Manuel cast a single, terrified, supplicating glance, more suggestive than words, at his confederate, as Falkner shoved him before him from the room. The next moment they were silently descending the stairs.

"May I go too, captain?" entreated Manuel. "I swear to God" —

"Shut the door!" The man obeyed.

"Now, then," said Lee, with a broad, gratified smile, laying down his whip and pistol within reach, and comfortably settling the pillows behind his back, "we'll have a quiet confab. A sort of old-fashioned talk, eh? You're not looking well, Manuel. You're drinking too much again. It spoils your complexion."

"Let me go, captain," pleaded the man, emboldened by the good-humored voice, but not near enough to notice a peculiar light in the speaker's eye.

"You've only just come, Manuel; and at considerable trouble, too. Well, what have you got to say? What's all this about? What are you doing here?"

The captured man shuffled his feet nervously, and only uttered an uneasy laugh of coarse discomfiture.

"I see. You're bashful. Well, I'll help you along. Come! You knew that Hale was away and these women were here without a man to help them. You thought you'd find some money here, and have your own way generally, eh?"

The tone of Lee's voice inspired him to confidence; unfortunately, it inspired him with familiarity also.

"I reckoned I had the right to a little fun on my own account, cap. I reckoned ez one gentleman in the profession would n't interfere with another gentleman's little game," he continued coarsely.

"Stand up."

"Wot for?"

"Up, I say!"

Manuel stood up and glanced at him.

"Utter a cry that might frighten these women, and by the living God they 'll rush in here only to find you lying dead on the floor of the house you 'd have polluted."

He grasped the whip and laid the lash of it heavily twice over the ruffian's shoulders. Writhing in suppressed agony, the man fell imploringly on his knees.

"Now, listen!" said Lee, softly twirling the whip in the air. "I want to refresh your memory. Did you ever learn, when you were with me — before I was obliged to kick you out of gentlemen's company — to break into a private house? Answer!"

"No," stammered the wretch.

"Did you ever learn to rob a woman, a child, or any but a man, and that face to face?"

"No," repeated Manuel.

"Did you ever learn from me to lay a finger upon a woman, old or young, in anger or kindness?"

"No."

"Then, my poor Manuel, it 's as I feared; civilization has ruined you. Farming and a simple, bucolic life have perverted your morals. So you were running off with the stock and that mustang, when you got stuck in the snow; and the luminous idea of this little game struck you? Eh? That was another mistake, Manuel; I never allowed you to think when you were with me."

"No, captain."

"Who 's your friend?"

"A d—d cowardly nigger from the Summit."

"I agree with you for once; but he has n't had a very brilliant example. Where's he gone now?"

"To h—ll, for all I care!"

"Then I want you to go with him. Listen. If there's a way out of the place, you know it or can find it. I give you two days to do it — you and he. At the end of that time the order will be to shoot you on sight. Now take off your boots."

The man's dark face visibly whitened, his teeth chattered in superstitious terror.

"I'm not going to shoot you now," said Lee, smiling, "so you will have a chance to die with your boots on,[1] if you are superstitious. I only want you to exchange them for that pair of Hale's in the corner. The fact is I have taken a fancy to yours. That fashion of wearing the stockings outside strikes me as one of the neatest things out."

Manuel sullenly drew off his boots with their muffled covering, and put on the ones designated.

"Now open the door."

He did so. Falkner was already waiting at the threshold. "Turn Manuel loose with the other, Ned, but disarm him first. They might quarrel. The habit of carrying arms, Manuel," added Lee, as Falkner took a pistol and bowie-knife from the half-breed, "is of itself provocative of violence, and inconsistent with a bucolic and pastoral life."

When Falkner returned he said hurriedly to his companion, "Do you think it wise, George, to let those hell-hounds loose? Good God! I could scarcely let my grip of his throat go, when I thought of what they were hunting."

"My dear Ned," said Lee, luxuriously ensconcing him-

[1] "To die with one's boots on." A synonym for death by violence, popular among Southwestern desperadoes, and the subject of superstitious dread.

self under the bedclothes again with a slight shiver of delicious warmth, "I must warn you against allowing the natural pride of a higher walk to prejudice you against the
general level of our profession.   Indeed, I was quite struck
with the justice of Manuel's protest that I was interfering
with certain rude processes of his own towards results aimed
at by others."

"George!" interrupted Falkner, almost savagely.

"Well.   I admit it's getting rather late in the evening
for pure philosophical inquiry, and you are tired.   Practically, then, it *was* wise to let them get away before they
discovered two things.   One, our exact relations here with
these women; and the other, *how many* of us were here.
At present they think we are three or four in possession
and with the consent of the women."

"The dogs!"

"They are paying us the highest compliment they can conceive of by supposing us cleverer scoundrels than themselves.
You are very unjust, Ned."

"If they escape and tell their story?"

"We shall have the rare pleasure of knowing we are better than people believe us.   And now put those boots away
somewhere where we can produce them if necessary, as evidence of Manuel's evening call.   At present we'll keep the
thing quiet, and in the early morning you can find out where
they got in and remove any traces they have left.   It is
no use to frighten the women.   There's no fear of their
returning."

"And if they get away?"

"We can follow in their tracks."

"If Manuel gives the alarm?"

"With his burglarious boots left behind in the house?
Not much!   Good-night, Ned.   Go to bed."

With these words Lee turned on his side and quietly resumed his interrupted slumber.   Falkner did not, however,

follow this sensible advice. When he was satisfied that his friend was sleeping he opened the door softly and looked out. He did not appear to be listening, for his eyes were fixed upon a small pencil of light that stole across the passage from the foot of Kate's door. He watched it until it suddenly disappeared, when, leaving the door partly open, he threw himself on his couch without removing his clothes. The slight movement awakened the sleeper, who was beginning to feel the accession of fever. He moved restlessly.

"George," said Falkner softly.

"Yes."

"Where was it we passed that old Mission Church on the road one dark night, and saw the light burning before the figure of the Virgin through the window?"

There was a moment of crushing silence. "Does that mean you 're wanting to light the candle again?"

"No."

"Then don't lie there inventing sacrilegious conundrums, but go to sleep."

Nevertheless, in the morning his fever was slightly worse. Mrs. Hale, offering her condolence, said, "I know that you have not been resting well, for even after your friend met with that mishap in the hall, I heard your voices, and Kate says your door was open all night. You have a little fever too, Mr. Falkner."

George looked curiously at Falkner's pale face — it was burning.

CHAPTER V

THE speed and fury with which Clinch's cavalcade swept on in the direction of the mysterious shot left Hale no chance for reflection. He was conscious of shouting incoherently with the others, of urging his horse irresistibly forward, of momentarily expecting to meet or overtake something, but without any further thought. The figures of Clinch and Rawlins immediately before him shut out the prospect of the narrowing trail. Once only, taking advantage of a sudden halt that threw them confusedly together, he managed to ask a question.

"Lost their track — found it again!" shouted the hostler, as Clinch, with a cry like the baying of a hound, again darted forward. Their horses were panting and trembling under them, the ascent seemed to be growing steeper, a singular darkness, which even the density of the wood did not sufficiently account for, surrounded them, but still their leader madly urged them on. To Hale's returning senses they did not seem in a condition to engage a single resolute man, who might have ambushed in the woods or beaten them in detail in the narrow gorge, but in another instant the reason of their furious haste was manifest. Spurring his horse ahead, Clinch dashed out into the open with a cheering shout — a shout that as quickly changed to a yell of imprecation. They were on the Ridge in a blinding snowstorm! The road had already vanished under their feet, and with it the fresh trail they had so closely followed! They stood helplessly on the shore of a trackless white sea, blank and spotless of any trace or sign of the fugitives.

" 'Pears to me, boys," said the hostler, suddenly ranging before them, " ef you 're not kalkilatin' on gittin' another party to dig ye out, ye 'd better be huntin' fodder and cover instead of road agents. 'Skuse me, gentlemen, but I 'm responsible for the hosses, and this ain't no time for circus-ridin'. We 're a matter o' six miles from the station in a bee-line."

"Back to the trail, then," said Clinch, wheeling his horse towards the road they had just quitted.

" 'Skuse me, Kernel," said the hostler, laying his hand on Clinch's rein, " but that way only brings us back the road we kem — the stage road — three miles further from home. That three miles is on the divide, and by the time we get there it will be snowed up worse nor this. The shortest cut is along the Ridge. If we hump ourselves we ken cross the divide afore the road is blocked. And that, 'skuse me, gentlemen, is *my* road."

There was no time for discussion. The road was already palpably thickening under their feet. Hale's arm was stiffened to his side by a wet, clinging snow-wreath. The figures of the others were almost obliterated and shapeless. It was not snowing — it was snow-balling ! The huge flakes, shaken like enormous feathers out of a vast blue-black cloud, commingled and fell in sprays and patches.

All idea of their former pursuit was forgotten ; the blind rage and enthusiasm that had possessed them was gone. They dashed after their new leader with only an instinct for shelter and succor.

They had not ridden long when fortunately, as it seemed to Hale, the character of the storm changed. The snow no longer fell in such large flakes, nor as heavily. A bitter wind succeeded ; the soft snow began to stiffen and crackle under the horses' hoofs ; they were no longer weighted and encumbered by the drifts upon their bodies ; the smaller flakes now rustled and rasped against them like sand, or bounded from them like hail.   They seemed to be moving more easily and rapidly, their spirits were rising with the stimulus of cold and motion, when suddenly their leader halted.

"It's no use, boys.   It can't be done!   This is no blizzard, but a regular two days' snifter!   It's no longer meltin', but packin' and driftin' now.   Even if we get over the divide, we're sure to be blocked up in the pass."

It was true!   To their bitter disappointment they could now see that the snow had not really diminished in quantity, but that the now finely powdered particles were rapidly filling all inequalities of the surface, packing closely against projections, and swirling in long furrows across the levels.   They looked with anxiety at their self-constituted leader.

"We must make a break to get down in the woods again before it's too late," he said briefly.

But they had already drifted away from the fringe of larches and dwarf pines that marked the sides of the Ridge, and lower down merged into the dense forest that clothed the flank of the mountain they had lately climbed, and it was with the greatest difficulty that they again reached it, only to find that at that point it was too precipitous for the descent of their horses.   Benumbed and speechless, they continued to toil on, opposed to the full fury of the stinging snow, and at times obliged to turn their horses to the blast to keep from being blown over the Ridge.   At the end of half an hour the hostler dismounted, and, beckoning to the others, took his horse by the bridle, and began the descent.   When it came to Hale's turn to dismount he could not help at first recoiling from the prospect before him.   The trail — if it could be so called — was merely the track or furrow of some fallen tree dragged, by accident or design, diagonally across the sides of the mountain.   At times it appeared scarcely a foot in width; at other times a mere crumbling gully, or a narrow shelf made by the projections of dead boughs and collected débris. It seemed perilous for a foot passenger, it appeared impossible for a horse. Nevertheless, he had taken a step forward when Clinch laid his hand on his arm.

"You'll bring up the rear," he said not unkindly, "ez you're a stranger here. Wait until we sing out to you."

"But if I prefer to take the same risks as you all?" said Hale stiffly.

"You kin," said Clinch grimly. "But I reckoned, as you were n't familiar with this sort o' thing, you would n't keer, by any foolishness o' yours, to stampede the rocks ahead of us, and break down the trail, or send down an avalanche on top of us. But just ez you like."

"I will wait, then," said Hale hastily.

The rebuke, however, did him good service. It preoccupied his mind, so that it remained unaffected by the dizzy depths, and enabled him to abandon himself mechanically to the sagacity of his horse, who was contented simply to follow the hoof-prints of the preceding animal, and in a few moments they reached the broader trail below without a mishap. A discussion regarding their future movements was already taking place. The impossibility of regaining the station at the Summit was admitted; the way down the mountain to the next settlement was still left to them, or the adjacent woods, if they wished for an encampment. The hostler once more assumed authority.

"'Skuse me, gentlemen, but them horses don't take no pasear down the mountain to-night. The stage road ain't a mile off, and I kalkilate to wait here till the up stage comes. She's bound to stop on account of the snow; and I've done my dooty when I hand the horses over to the driver."

"But if she hears of the block up yer, and waits at the lower station?" said Rawlins.

"Then I've done my dooty all the same. 'Skuse me, gentlemen, but them ez hez their own horses kin do ez they like."

As this clearly pointed to Hale, he briefly assured his companions that he had no intention of deserting them. "If I cannot reach Eagle's Court, I shall at least keep as near it as possible. I suppose any messenger from my house to the Summit will learn where I am and why I am delayed?"

"Messenger from your house!" gasped Rawlins. "Are you crazy, stranger? Only a bird would get outer Eagle's now; and it would hev to be an eagle at that! Between your house and the Summit the snow must be ten feet by this time, to say nothing of the drift in the pass."

Hale felt it was the truth. At any other time he would have worried over this unexpected situation, and utter violation of all his traditions. He was past that now, and even felt a certain relief. He knew his family were safe; it was enough. That they were locked up securely, and incapable of interfering with *him*, seemed to enhance his new, half-conscious, half-shy enjoyment of an adventurous existence.

The hostler, who had been apparently lost in contemplation of the steep trail he had just descended, suddenly clapped his hand to his leg with an ejaculation of gratified astonishment.

"Waal, darn my skin ef that ain't Hennicker's 'slide' all the time! I heard it was somewhat about here."

Rawlins briefly explained to Hale that a slide was a rude incline for the transit of heavy goods that could not be carried down a trail.

"And Hennicker's," continued the man, "ain't more nor a mile away. Ye might try Hennicker's at a push, eh?"

By a common instinct the whole party looked dubiously at Hale. "Who's Hennicker?" he felt compelled to ask.

The hostler hesitated, and glanced at the others to reply.

"There *are* folks," he said lazily, at last, " ez beleeves that Hennicker ain't much better nor the crowd we're hunting; but they don't say it *to* Hennicker. We need n't let on what we're after."

"I for one," said Hale stoutly, " decidedly object to any concealment of our purpose."

"It don't follow," said Rawlins carelessly, "that Hennicker even knows of this yer robbery. It's his gineral gait we refer to. Ef yer think it more polite, and it makes it more sociable to discuss this matter afore him, I'm agreed."

"Hale means," said Clinch, "that it would n't be on the square to take and make use of any points we might pick up there agin the road agents."

"Certainly," said Hale. It was not at all what he had meant, but he felt singularly relieved at the compromise.

"And ez I reckon Hennicker ain't such a fool ez not to know who we are and what we're out for," continued Clinch, "I reckon there ain't any concealment."

"Then it's Hennicker's?" said the hostler, with swift deduction.

"Hennicker it is! Lead on."

The hostler remounted his horse, and the others followed. The trail presently turned into a broader track, that bore some signs of approaching habitations, and at the end of five minutes they came upon a clearing. It was part of one of the fragmentary mountain terraces, and formed by itself a vast niche, or bracketed shelf, in the hollow flank of the mountain that, to Hale's first glance, bore a rude resemblance to Eagle's Court. But there was neither meadow nor open field; the few acres of ground had been wrested from the forest by axe and fire, and unsightly stumps everywhere marked the rude and difficult attempts at cultivation. Two or three rough buildings of unplaned and unpainted boards, connected by rambling sheds, stood in the centre of the amphitheatre. Far from being protected by the encircling rampart, it seemed to be the selected arena for the combating elements. A whirlwind from the outer abyss continually filled this cave of Æolus with driving snow, which, however, melted as it fell, or was quickly whirled away again.

A few dogs barked and ran out to meet the cavalcade, but there was no other sign of any life disturbed or concerned at their approach.

"I reckon Hennicker ain't home, or he'd hev been on the lookout afore this," said the hostler, dismounting and rapping at the door.

After a silence, a female voice, unintelligible to the others, apparently had some colloquy with the hostler, who returned to the party.

"Must go in through the kitchin — can't open the door for the wind."

Leaving their horses in the shed, they entered the kitchen, which communicated, and presently came upon a square room filled with smoke from a fire of green pine logs. The doors and windows were tightly fastened; the only air came in through the large-throated chimney in voluminous gusts, which seemed to make the hollow shell of the apartment swell and expand to the point of bursting. Despite the stinging of the resinous smoke, the temperature was grateful to the benumbed travelers. Several cushionless armchairs, such as were used in bar-rooms, two tables, a sideboard, half bar and half cupboard, and a rocking-chair comprised the furniture, and a few bear and buffalo skins covered the floor. Hale sank into one of the armchairs, and, with a lazy satisfaction, partly born of his fatigue and partly from some newly discovered appreciative faculty, gazed around the room, and then at the mistress of the house, with whom the others were talking.

She was tall, gaunt, and withered; in spite of her evident years, her twisted hair was still dark and full, and her eyes bright and piercing; her complexion and teeth had

long since succumbed to the vitiating effects of frontier
cookery, and her lips were stained with the yellow juice of
a brier-wood pipe she held in her mouth.   The hostler had
explained their intrusion, and veiled their character under
the vague epithet of a "hunting party," and was now
evidently describing them personally.   In his new-found
philosophy the fact that the interest of his hostess seemed
to be excited only by the names of his companions, that he
himself was carelessly, and even deprecatingly, alluded to as
the "stranger from Eagle's" by the hostler, and completely
overlooked by the old woman, gave him no concern.

"You'll have to talk to Zenobia yourself.   Dod rot ef
I'm gine to interfere.   She knows Hennicker's ways, and
if she chooses to take in transients it ain't no funeral o'
mine.   Zeenie!   You, Zeenie!   Look yer!"

A tall, lazy-looking, handsome girl appeared on the threshold of the next room, and with a hand on each door-post
slowly swung herself backwards and forwards, without entering.   "Well, maw?"

The old woman briefly and unalluringly pictured the condition of the travelers.

"Paw ain't here," began the girl doubtfully, "and —
Howdy, Dick! is that you?"   The interruption was
caused by her recognition of the hostler, and she lounged
into the room.   In spite of a skimp, slatternly gown, whose
straight skirt clung to her lower limbs, there was a quaint,
nymph-like contour to her figure.   Whether from languor,
ill health, or more probably from a morbid consciousness of
her own height, she moved with a slightly affected stoop
that had become a habit.   It did not seem ungraceful to
Hale, already attracted by her delicate profile, her large
dark eyes, and a certain weird resemblance she had to some
half-domesticated dryad.

"That'll do, maw," she said, dismissing her parent with
a nod.   "I'll talk to Dick."

As the door closed on the old woman, Zenobia leaned her hands on the back of a chair, and confronted the admiring eyes of Dick with a goddess-like indifference.

"Now wot's the use of your playin' this yer game on me, Dick? Wot's the good of your ladlin' out that hogwash about huntin'? *Huntin'!* I'll tell yer the huntin' you-uns hev been at! You've been huntin' George Lee and his boys since an hour before sun-up. You've been followin' a blind trail up to the Ridge, until the snow got up and hunted *you* right here! You've been whoopin' and yellin' and circus-ridin' on the roads like ez yer wos Comanches, and frightening all the women-folk within miles — that's your huntin'! You've been climbin' down paw's old slide at last, and makin' tracks for here to save the skins of them condemned government horses of the Kempany! And *that's* your huntin'!"

To Hale's surprise, a burst of laughter from the party followed this speech. He tried to join in, but this ridiculous summary of the result of his enthusiastic sense of duty left him — the only earnest believer — mortified and embarrassed. Nor was he the less concerned as he found the girl's dark eyes had rested once or twice upon him curiously.

Zenobia laughed too, and, lazily turning the chair around, dropped into it. "And by this time George Lee's loungin' back in his chyar and smokin' his cigyar somewhar in Sacramento," she added, stretching her feet out to the fire, and suiting the action to the word with an imaginary cigar between the long fingers of a thin and not over-clean hand.

"We cave, Zeenie!" said Rawlins, when their hilarity had subsided to a more subdued and scarcely less flattering admiration of the unconcerned goddess before them. "That's about the size of it. You kin rake down the pile. I forgot you're an old friend of George's."

"He's a white man!" said the girl decidedly.

"Ye used to know him?" continued Rawlins.

" Once.   Paw ain't in that line now," she said simply.

There was such a sublime unconsciousness of any moral degradation involved in this allusion that even Hale accepted it without a shock.   She rose presently, and, going to the little sideboard, brought out a number of glasses; these she handed to each of the party, and then, producing a demijohn of whiskey, slung it dexterously and gracefully over her arm, so that it rested on her elbow like a cradle, and, going to each one in succession, filled their glasses. It obliged each one to rise to accept the libation, and as Hale did so in his turn he met the dark eyes of the girl full on his own.   There was a pleased curiosity in her glance that made this married man of thirty-five color as awkwardly as a boy.

The tender of refreshment being understood as a tacit recognition of their claims to a larger hospitality, all further restraint was removed.   Zenobia resumed her seat, and placing her elbow on the arm of her chair, and her small round chin in her hand, looked thoughtfully in the fire.   " When I say George Lee's a white man, it ain't because I know him.   It's his general gait.   Wot's he ever done that's underhanded or mean ?   Nothin' !   You can't show the poor man he's ever took a picayune from.   When he's helped himself to a pile it's been outer them banks or them express companies, that think it mighty fine to bust up themselves, and swindle the poor folks o' their last cent, and nobody talks o' huntin' *them !*   And does he keep their money ?   No ; he passes it round among the boys that help him, and they put it in circulation.   *He* don't keep it for himself ; he ain't got fine houses in 'Frisco ; he don't keep fast horses for show.   Like ez not the critter he did that job with — ef it was him — none of you boys would have rid !   And he takes all the risks himself ; you ken bet your life that every man with him was safe and away afore he turned his back on you-uns."

"He certainly drops a little of his money at draw-poker, Zeenie," said Clinch, laughing. "He lost five thousand dollars to Sheriff Kelly last week."

"Well, I don't hear of the sheriff huntin' him to give it back, nor do I reckon Kelly handed it over to the Express it was taken from. I heard *you* won suthin' from him a spell ago. I reckon you've been huntin' him to find out whar you should return it." The laugh was clearly against Clinch. He was about to make some rallying rejoinder when the young girl suddenly interrupted him. "Ef you're wantin' to hunt somebody, why don't you take higher game? Thar's that Jim Harkins: go for him, and I'll join you."

"Harkins!" exclaimed Clinch and Hale simultaneously.

"Yes, Jim Harkins; do you know him?" she said, glancing from the one to the other.

"One of my friends does," said Clinch, laughing; "but don't let that stop you."

"And *you* — over there," continued Zenobia, bending her head and eyes towards Hale.

"The fact is — I believe he was my banker," said Hale, with a smile. "I don't know him personally."

"Then you'd better hunt him before he does you."

"What's *he* done, Zeenie?" asked Rawlins, keenly enjoying the discomfiture of the others.

"What?" She stopped, threw her long black braids over her shoulder, clasped her knee with her hands, and rocking backwards and forwards, sublimely unconscious of the apparition of a slim ankle and half-dropped-off slipper from under her shortened gown, continued, "It might n't please *him*," she said slyly, nodding towards Hale.

"Pray don't mind me," said Hale, with unnecessary eagerness.

"Well," said Zenobia, "I reckon you all know Ned Falkner and the Excelsior Ditch?"

"Yes, Falkner's the superintendent of it," said Rawlins. "And a square man too. Thar ain't anything mean about him."

"Shake," said Zenobia, extending her hand. Rawlins shook the proffered hand with eager spontaneousness, and the girl resumed : "He's about ez good ez they make 'em — you bet. Well, you know Ned has put all his money, and all his strength, and all his sabe, and" —

"His good looks," added Clinch mischievously.

"Into that Ditch," continued Zenobia, ignoring the interruption. "It's his mother, it's his sweetheart, it's his everything! When other chaps of his age was cavortin' round 'Frisco, and havin' high jinks, Ned was in his Ditch. ' Wait till the Ditch is done,' he used to say. ' Wait till she begins to boom, and then you just stand round.' Mor'n that, he got all the boys to put in their last cent — for they loved Ned, and love him now, like ez ef he wos a woman."

"That's so," said Clinch and Rawlins simultaneously, "and he's worth it."

"Well," continued Zenobia, "the Ditch did n't boom ez soon ez they kalkilated. And then the boys kept gettin' poorer and poorer, and Ned he kept gettin' poorer and poorer in everything but his hopefulness and grit. Then he looks around for more capital. And about this time, that coyote Harkins smelt suthin' nice up there, and he gits Ned to give him control of it, and he 'll lend him his name and fix up a company. Soon ez he gets control, the first thing he does is to say that it wants half a million o' money to make it pay, and levies an assessment of two hundred dollars a share. That's nothin' for them rich fellows to pay, or pretend to pay, but for boys on grub wages it meant only ruin. They could n't pay, and had to forfeit their shares for next to nothing. And Ned made one more desperate attempt to save them and himself by borrowing money on his shares; when that hound Harkins got wind of it, and let it be buzzed around that the Ditch is a failure, and that he was goin' out of it; that brought the shares down to nothing. As Ned could n't raise a dollar, the new company swooped down on his shares for the debts *they* had put up, and left him and the boys to help themselves. Ned could n't bear to face the boys that he 'd helped to ruin, and put out, and ain't been heard from since. After Harkins had got rid of Ned and the boys he manages to pay off that wonderful debt, and sells out for a hundred thousand dollars. That money — Ned's money — he sends to Sacramento, for he don't dare to travel with it himself, and is kalkilatin' to leave the kentry, for some of the boys allow to kill him on sight. So ef you 're wantin' to hunt suthin', thar 's yer chance, and you need n't go inter the snow to do it."

"But surely the law can recover this money?" said Hale indignantly. "It is as infamous a robbery as " — He stopped as he caught Zenobia's eye.

"Ez last night's, you were goin' to say. I 'll call it *more*. Them road agents don't pretend to be your friend — but take yer money and run their risks. For ez to the law — that can't help yer."

"It 's a skin game, and you might ez well expect to recover a gambling debt from a short card sharp," explained Clinch; "Falkner oughter shot him on sight."

"Or the boys lynched him," suggested Rawlins.

"I think," said Hale, more reflectively, "that in the absence of legal remedy a man of that kind should have been forced under strong physical menace to give up his ill-gotten gains. The money was the primary object, and if that could be got without bloodshed — which seems to me a useless crime — it would be quite as effective. Of course, if there was resistance or retaliation, it might be necessary to kill him."

He had unconsciously fallen into his old didactic and dogmatic habit of speech, and perhaps, under the spur of Zenobia's eyes, he had given it some natural emphasis.   A dead silence followed, in which the others regarded him with amused and gratified surprise, and it was broken only by Zenobia rising and holding out her hand.   " Shake ! "

Hale raised it gallantly, and pressed his lips on the one spotless finger.

" That 's gospel truth.   And you ain't the first white man to say it."

" Indeed," laughed Hale.   " Who was the other ? "

" George Lee ! "

CHAPTER VI

THE laughter that followed was interrupted by a sudden barking of the dogs in the outer clearing. Zenobia rose lazily and strode to the window. It relieved Hale of certain embarrassing reflections suggested by her comment.

"Ef it ain't that God-forsaken fool Dick bringing up passengers from the snow-bound up stage in the road! I reckon *I've* got suthin' to say to that!" But the later appearance of the apologetic Dick, with the assurance that the party carried a permission from her father, granted at the lower station in view of such an emergency, checked her active opposition. "That's like paw," she soliloquized aggrievedly; "shuttin' us up and settin' dogs on everybody for a week, and then lettin' the whole stage service pass through one door and out at another. Well, it's *his* house and *his* whiskey, and they kin take it, but they don't get me to help 'em."

They certainly were not a prepossessing or good-natured acquisition to the party. Apart from the natural antagonism which, on such occasions, those in possession always feel towards the newcomer, they were strongly inclined to resist the dissatisfied querulousness and aggressive attitude of these fresh applicants for hospitality. The most offensive one was a person who appeared to exercise some authority over the others. He was loud, assuming, and dressed with vulgar pretension. He quickly disposed himself in the chair vacated by Zenobia, and called for some liquor.

"I reckon you 'll hev to help yourself," said Rawlins

dryly, as the summons met with no response. "There are only two women in the house, and I reckon their hands are full already."

"I call it d—d uncivil treatment," said the man, raising his voice; "and Hennicker had better sing smaller if he don't want his old den pulled down some day. He ain't any better than men that hev been picked up afore now."

"You oughter told him that, and mebbe he'd hev come over with yer," returned Rawlins. "He's a mild, soft, easy-going man, is Hennicker! Ain't he Colonel Clinch?"

The casual mention of Clinch's name produced the effect which the speaker probably intended. The stranger stared at Clinch, who, apparently oblivious of the conversation, was blinking his cold gray eyes at the fire. Dropping his aggressive tone to mere querulousness, the man sought the whiskey demijohn, and helped himself and his companions. Fortified by liquor he returned to the fire.

"I reckon you've heard about this yer robbery, Colonel," he said, addressing Clinch, with an attempt at easy familiarity.

Without raising his eyes from the fire, Clinch briefly assented, "I reckon."

"I'm up yer, examining into it, for the Express."

"Lost much?" asked Rawlins.

"Not so much ez they might hev. That fool Harkins had a hundred thousand dollars in greenbacks sealed up like an ordinary package of a thousand dollars, and gave it to a friend, Bill Guthrie, in the bank to pick out some unlikely chap among the passengers to take charge of it to Reno. He wouldn't trust the Express. Ha! ha!"

The dead, oppressive silence that followed his empty laughter made it seem almost artificial. Rawlins held his breath, and looked at Clinch. Hale, with the instincts of a refined, sensitive man, turned hot with the embarrassment Clinch should have shown. For that gentleman, without lifting his eyes from the fire, and with no apparent change in his demeanor, lazily asked : —

"Ye did n't ketch the name o' that passenger ? "

"Naturally, no ! For when Guthrie hears what was said agin him he would n't give his name until he heard from him."

"And *what* was said agin him ? " asked Clinch musingly.

"What would be said agin a man that give up that sum o' money, like a chaw of tobacco, for the asking ! Why, there were but three men, as far ez we kin hear, that did the job. And there were four passengers inside, armed, and the driver and express messenger on the box. Six were robbed by *three !* — they were a sweet-scented lot ! Reckon they must hev felt mighty small, for I hear they got up and skedaddled from the station under the pretext of lookin' for the robbers." He laughed again, and the laugh was noisily repeated by his five companions at the other end of the room.

Hale, who had forgotten that the stranger was only echoing a part of his own criticism of eight hours before, was on the point of rising with burning cheeks and angry indignation, when the lazily uplifted eye of Clinch caught his, and absolutely held him down with its paralyzing and deadly significance. Murder itself seemed to look from those cruelly quiet and remorseless gray pupils. For a moment he forgot his own rage in this glimpse of Clinch's implacable resentment ; for a moment he felt a thrill of pity for the wretch who had provoked it. He remained motionless and fascinated in his chair as the lazy lids closed like a sheath over Clinch's eyes again. Rawlins, who had probably received the same glance of warning, remained equally still.

"They have n't heard the last of it yet, you bet," continued the infatuated stranger. "I 've got a little statement here for the newspaper," he added, drawing some papers from his pocket; "suthin' I just run off in the coach as I came along. I reckon it'll show things up in a new light. It's time there should be some change. All the cussin' that's been usually done hez been by the passengers agin the express and stage companies. I propose that the Company should do a little cussin' themselves. See? P'r'aps you don't mind my readin' it to ye? It's just spicy enough to suit them newspaper chaps."

"Go on," said Colonel Clinch quietly.

The man cleared his throat, with the preliminary pose of authorship, and his five friends, to whom the composition was evidently not unfamiliar, assumed anticipatory smiles.

"I call it 'Prize Pusillanimous Passengers.' Sort of runs easy off the tongue, you know.

"'It now appears that the success of the late stage-coach robbery near the Summit was largely due to the pusillanimity — not to use a more serious word'" — He stopped, and looked explanatorily towards Clinch: "Ye'll see in a minit what I'm gettin' at by that pusillanimity of the passengers themselves. 'It now transpires that there were only three robbers who attacked the coach, and that although passengers, driver, and express messenger were fully armed, and were double the number of their assailants, not a shot was fired. We mean no reflections upon the well-known courage of Yuba Bill, nor the experience and coolness of Bracy Tibbetts, the courteous express messenger, both of whom have since confessed to have been more than astonished at the Christian and lamb-like submission of the insiders. Amusing stories of some laughable yet sickening incidents of the occasion — such as grown men kneeling in the road, and offering to strip themselves completely, if their lives were only spared; of one of the passengers hiding under the seat, and only being dislodged by pulling his coat-tails; of incredible sums promised, and even offers of menial service, for the preservation of their wretched carcases — are received with the greatest gusto; but we are in possession of facts which may lead to more serious accusations. Although one of the passengers is said to have lost a large sum of money intrusted to him, while attempting with barefaced effrontery to establish a rival "carrying" business in one of the Express Company's own coaches' — I call that a good point." He interrupted himself to allow the unrestrained applause of his own party. "Don't you?"

"It's just h—ll," said Clinch musingly.

"'Yet the affair,'" resumed the stranger, from his manuscript, "'is locked up in great and suspicious mystery. The presence of Jackson N. Stanner, Esq.' (that's me), 'special detective agent to the Company, and his staff in town, is a guaranty that the mystery will be thoroughly probed.' Hed to put that in to please the Company," he again deprecatingly explained. "'We are indebted to this gentleman for the facts.'"

"The pint you want to make in that article," said Clinch, rising, but still directing his face and his conversation to the fire, "ez far ez I ken see ez that no three men kin back down six unless they be cowards, or are willing to be backed down."

"That's the point what I start from," rejoined Stanner, "and work up. I leave it to you ef it ain't so."

"I can't say ez I agree with you," said the Colonel dryly. He turned, and still without lifting his eyes walked towards the door of the room which Zenobia had entered. The key was on the inside, but Clinch gently opened the door, removed the key, and closing the door again locked it from his side. Hale and Rawlins felt their hearts beat quickly; the others followed Clinch's slow movements and downcast mien with amused curiosity. After locking the other outlet from the room, and putting the keys in his pocket, Clinch returned to the fire. For the first time he lifted his eyes; the man nearest him shrank back in terror.

"I am the man," he said slowly, taking deliberate breath between his sentences, "who gave up those greenbacks to the robbers. I am one of the three passengers you have lampooned in that paper, and these gentlemen beside me are the other two." He stopped and looked around him. "You don't believe that three men can back down six! Well, I'll show you how it can be done. More than that, I'll show you how ONE man can do it; for, by the living G—d, if you don't hand over that paper I'll kill you where you sit! I'll give you until I count ten; if one of you moves he and you are dead men — but *you* first!"

Before he had finished speaking Hale and Rawlins had both risen, as if in concert, with their weapons drawn. Hale could not tell how or why he had done so, but he was equally conscious, without knowing why, of fixing his eye on one of the other party, and that he should, in the event of an affray, try to kill him. He did not attempt to reason; he only knew that he should do his best to kill that man and perhaps others.

"One," said Clinch, lifting his derringer, "two — three " —

"Look here, Colonel — I swear I didn't know it was you. Come — d—n it! I say — see here," stammered Stanner, with white cheeks, not daring to glance for aid to his stupefied party.

"Four — five — six " —

"Wait! Here!" He produced the paper and threw it on the floor.

"Pick it up and hand it to me. Seven — eight " —

Stanner hastily scrambled to his feet, picked up the paper, and handed it to the Colonel. "I was only joking, Colonel," he said, with a forced laugh.

"I'm glad to hear it. But as this joke is in black and white, you wouldn't mind saying so in the same fashion. Take that pen and ink and write as I dictate. 'I certify that I am satisfied that the above statement is a base calumny against the characters of Ringwood Clinch, Robert Rawlins, and John Hale, passengers, and that I do hereby apologize to the same.' Sign it. That'll do. Now let the rest of your party sign as witnesses."

They complied without hesitation; some, seizing the opportunity of treating the affair as a joke, suggested a drink.

"Excuse me," said Clinch quietly, "but ez this house ain't big enough for me and that man, and ez I've got business at Wild Cat Station with this paper, I think I'll go without drinkin'." He took the keys from his pocket, unlocked the doors, and taking up his overcoat and rifle turned as if to go.

Rawlins rose to follow him; Hale alone hesitated. The rapid occurrences of the last half hour gave him no time for reflection. But he was by no means satisfied of the legality of the last act he had aided and abetted, although he admitted its rude justice, and felt he would have done so again. A fear of this, and an instinct that he might be led into further complications if he continued to identify himself with Clinch and Rawlins; the fact that they had professedly abandoned their quest, and that it was really supplanted by the presence of an authorized party whom they had already come in conflict with — all this urged him to remain behind. On the other hand, the apparent desertion of his comrades at the last moment was opposed both to his sense of honor and the liking he had taken to them. But he reflected that he had already shown his active partisanship, that he could be of little service to them at Wild Cat Station, and would be only increasing the distance from his home; and above all, an impatient longing

for independent action finally decided him. "I think I
will stay here," he said to Clinch, "unless you want me."

Clinch cast a swift and meaning glance at the enemy, but
looked approval. "Keep your eyes skinned, and you're
good for a dozen of 'em," he said, *sotto voce*, and then
turned to Stanner. "I'm going to take this paper to Wild
Cat. If you want to communicate with me hereafter, you
know where I am to be found, unless" — he smiled grimly
— "you'd like to see me outside for a few minutes before
I go?"

"It is a matter that concerns the Stage Company, not
me," said Stanner, with an attempt to appear at his ease.

Hale accompanied Clinch and Rawlins through the kitchen
to the stables. The hostler, Dick, had already returned to
the rescue of the snow-bound coach.

"I shouldn't like to leave many men alone with that
crowd," said Clinch, pressing Hale's hand; "and I wouldn't
have allowed your staying behind ef I didn't know I could
bet my pile on you. Your offerin' to stay just puts a clean
finish on it. Look yer, Hale, I didn't cotton much to you
at first; but ef you ever want a friend, call on Ringwood
Clinch."

"The same here, old man," said Rawlins, extending his
hand as he appeared from a hurried conference with the
old woman at the woodshed, "and trust to Zeenie to give
you a hint ef there's anythin' underhanded goin' on. So
long."

Half inclined to resent this implied suggestion of protection, yet half pleased at the idea of a confidence with the
handsome girl he had seen, Hale returned to the room. A
whispered discussion among the party ceased on his entering, and an awkward silence followed, which Hale did not
attempt to break as he quietly took his seat again by the
fire. He was presently confronted by Stanner, who with
an affectation of easy familiarity crossed over to the hearth.

"The old Kernel's d——d peppery and high-toned when he's got a little more than his reg'lar three fingers o' corn juice, eh?"

"I must beg you to understand distinctly, Mr. Stanner," said Hale, with a return of his habitual precision of statement, "that I regard any slighting allusion to the gentleman who has just left not only as in exceedingly bad taste coming from *you*, but very offensive to myself. If you mean to imply that he was under the influence of liquor, it is my duty to undeceive you; he was so perfectly in possession of his faculties as to express not only his own but *my* opinion of your conduct. You must also admit that he was discriminating enough to show his objection to your company by leaving it. I regret that circumstances do not make it convenient for me to exercise that privilege; but if I am obliged to put up with your presence in this room, I strongly insist that it is not made unendurable with the addition of your conversation."

The effect of this deliberate and passionless declaration was more discomposing to the party than Clinch's fury. Utterly unaccustomed to the ideas and language suddenly confronting them, they were unable to determine whether it was the real expression of the speaker, or whether it was a vague badinage or affectation to which any reply would involve them in ridicule. In a country terrorized by practical joking, they did not doubt that this was a new form of hoaxing calculated to provoke some response that would constitute them as victims. The immediate effect upon them was that complete silence in regard to himself that Hale desired. They drew together again and conversed in whispers, while Hale, with his eyes fixed on the fire, gave himself up to somewhat late and useless reflection.

He could scarcely realize his position. For however he might look at it, within a space of twelve hours he had not only changed some of his most cherished opinions, but he

had acted in accordance with that change in a way that
made it seem almost impossible for him ever to recant.   In
the interests of law and order he had engaged in an unlaw-
ful and disorderly pursuit of criminals, and had actually
come in conflict not with the criminals, but with the only
party apparently authorized to pursue them.   More than
that, he was finding himself committed to a certain sympathy with the criminals.   Twenty-four hours ago, if any one
had told him that he would have condoned an illegal act for
its abstract justice, or assisted to commit an illegal act for
the same purpose, he would have felt himself insulted.
That he knew he would not now feel it as an insult perplexed him still more.   In these circumstances the fact that
he was separated from his family, and as it were from
all his past life and traditions, by a chance accident, did not
disturb him greatly; indeed, he was for the first time a
little doubtful of their probable criticism on his inconsistency, and was by no means in a hurry to subject himself
to it.

Lifting his eyes, he was suddenly aware that the door
leading to the kitchen was slowly opening.   He had thought
he heard it creak once or twice during his deliberate reply
to Stanner.   It was evidently moving now so as to attract
his attention, without disturbing the others.   It presently
opened sufficiently wide to show the face of Zeenie, who,
with a gesture of caution towards his companions, beckoned
him to join her.   He rose carelessly as if going out, and,
putting on his hat, entered the kitchen as the retreating
figure of the young girl glided lightly towards the stables.
She ascended a few open steps as if to a hay-loft, but stopped
before a low door.   Pushing it open, she preceded him into
a small room, apparently under the roof, which scarcely
allowed her to stand upright.   By the light of a stable
lantern hanging from a beam he saw that, though poorly
furnished, it bore some evidence of feminine taste and hab-

itation. Motioning to the only chair, she seated herself
on the edge of the bed, with her hands clasping her knees in
her familiar attitude. Her face bore traces of recent agitation, and her eyes were shining with tears. By the closer
light of the lantern he was surprised to find it was from
laughter.

"I reckoned you'd be right lonely down there with
that Stanner crowd, particklerly after that little speech o'
yourn, so I sez to maw I'd get you up yer for a spell.
Maw and I heerd you exhort 'em! Maw allowed you
woz talkin' a furrin' tongue all along, but I — sakes alive!
— I hed to hump myself to keep from bustin' into a yell
when yer jist drawed them Webster-unabridged sentences
on 'em." She stopped and rocked backwards and forwards
with a laugh that, subdued by the proximity of the roof
and the fear of being overheard, was by no means unmusical. "I'll tell ye whot got me, though! That part
commencing, 'Suckamstances over which I've no con-
troul.'"

"Oh, come! I didn't say that," interrupted Hale,
laughing.

"'Don't make it convenient for me to exercise the privilege of kickin' yer out to that extent,'" she continued;
"'but if I cannot dispense with your room, the least I can
say is that it's a d—d sight better than your company' —
or suthin' like that! And then the way you minded your
stops, and let your voice rise and fall just ez easy ez if you
wos a First Reader in large type. Why, the Kernel wasn't
nowhere. *His* cussin' didn't come within a mile o' yourn.
That Stanner jist turned yaller."

"I'm afraid you are laughing at me," said Hale, not
knowing whether to be pleased or vexed at the girl's
amusement.

"I reckon I'm the only one that dare do it, then," said
the girl simply. "The Kernel sez the way you turned

round after he'd done his cussin', and said yer believed you'd stay and take the responsibility of the whole thing — and did in that kam, soft, did-anybody-speak-to-me style — was the neatest thing he'd seen yet! No! Maw says I ain't much on manners, but I know a man when I see him."

For an instant Hale gave himself up to the delicious flattery of unexpected, unintended, and apparently uninterested compliment. Becoming at last a little embarrassed under the frank curiosity of the girl's dark eyes, he changed the subject.

"Do you always come up here through the stables?" he asked, glancing round the room, which was evidently her own.

"I reckon," she answered half abstractedly. "There's a ladder down thar to maw's room" — pointing to a trap-door beside the broad chimney that served as a wall — "but it's handier the other way, and nearer the hosses ef you want to get away quick."

This palpable suggestion — borne out by what he remembered of the other domestic details — that the house had been planned with reference to sudden foray or escape reawakened his former uneasy reflections. Zeenie, who had been watching his face, added, "It's no slouch, when b'ar or painters hang round nights and stampede the stock, to be able to swing yourself on to a hoss whenever you hear a row goin' on outside."

"Do you mean that *you*" —

"Paw *used*, and I do *now*, sense I've come into the room." She pointed to a nondescript garment, half cloak, half habit, hanging on the wall. "I've been outer bed and on Pitchpine's back as far ez the trail five minutes arter I heard the first bellow."

Hale regarded her with undisguised astonishment. There was nothing at all Amazonian or horsey in her manners,

nor was there even the robust physical contour that might
have been developed through such experiences.   On the
contrary, she seemed to be lazily effeminate in body and
mind.   Heedless of his critical survey of her, she beckoned
him to draw his chair nearer, and, looking into his eyes,
said : —

"Whatever possessed *you* to take to huntin' men ? "

Hale was staggered by the question, but nevertheless
endeavored to explain.   But he was surprised to find that
his explanation appeared stilted even to himself, and, he
could not doubt, was utterly incomprehensible to the girl.
She nodded her head, however, and continued : —

"Then you haven't anythin' agin George ? "

"I don't know George," said Hale, smiling.   "My proceeding was against the highwayman."

"Well, *he* was the highwayman."

"I mean, it was the principle I objected to — a principle
that I consider highly dangerous."

"Well, *he* is the principal, for the others only *helped*, I
reckon," said Zeenie, with a sigh, "and I reckon he *is*
dangerous."

Hale saw it was useless to explain.   The girl continued : —

"What made you stay here instead of going on with the
Kernel ?   There was suthin' else besides your wanting to
make that Stanner take water.   What is it ? "

A light sense of the propinquity of beauty, of her confidence, of their isolation, of the eloquence of her dark
eyes, at first tempted Hale to a reply of simple gallantry ;
a graver consideration of the same circumstances froze it
upon his lips.

"I don't know," he returned awkwardly.

"Well, I 'll tell you," she said.   "You did n't cotton
to the Kernel and Rawlins much more than you did to
Stanner.   They ain't your kind."

In his embarrassment Hale blundered upon the thought he had honorably avoided.

"Suppose," he said, with a constrained laugh, "I had stayed to see you?"

"I reckon *I* ain't your kind, neither," she replied promptly. There was a momentary pause when she rose and walked to the chimney. "It's very quiet down there," she said, stooping and listening over the roughly boarded floor that formed the ceiling of the room below. "I wonder what's going on?"

In the belief that this was a delicate hint for his return to the party he had left, Hale rose, but the girl passed him hurriedly, and, opening the door, cast a quick glance into the stable beyond.

"Just as I reckoned — the horses are gone too. They've skedaddled," she said blankly.

Hale did not reply. In his embarrassment a moment ago the idea of taking an equally sudden departure had flashed upon him. Should he take this as a justification of that impulse, or how? He stood irresolutely gazing at the girl, who turned and began to descend the stairs silently. He followed. When they reached the lower room they found it as they had expected — deserted.

"I hope I didn't drive them away," said Hale, with an uneasy look at the troubled face of the girl. "For I really had an idea of going myself a moment ago."

She remained silent, gazing out of the window. Then, turning with a slight shrug of her shoulders, said half defiantly: "What's the use now? Oh, maw! the Stanner crowd has vamosed the ranch, and this yer stranger kalkilates to stay!"

CHAPTER VII

A WEEK had passed at Eagle's Court — a week of mingled clouds and sunshine by day, of rain over the green plateau and snow on the mountain by night. Each morning had brought its fresh greenness to the winter-girt domain, and a fresh coat of dazzling white to the barrier that separated its dwellers from the world beyond. There was little change in the encompassing wall of their prison; if anything, the snowy circle round them seemed to have drawn its lines nearer day by day. The immediate result of this restricted limit had been to confine the range of cattle to the meadows nearer the house, and at a safe distance from the fringe of wilderness now invaded by the prowling tread of predatory animals.

Nevertheless, the two figures lounging on the slope at sunset gave very little indication of any serious quality in the situation. Indeed, so far as appearances were concerned, Kate, who was returning from an afternoon stroll with Falkner, exhibited, with feminine inconsistency, a decided return to the world of fashion and conventionality apparently just as she was effectually excluded from it. She had not only discarded her white dress as a concession to the practical evidence of the surrounding winter, but she had also brought out a feather hat and sable muff which had once graced a fashionable suburb of Boston. Even Falkner had exchanged his slouch hat and picturesque serape for a beaver overcoat and fur cap of Hale's which had been pressed upon him by Kate, under the excuse of the exigencies of the season. Within a stone's throw of the thicket, turbulent with the savage forces of nature, they walked with the abstraction of people hearing only their own voices; in the face of the solemn peaks clothed with white austerity they talked gravely of dress.

"I don't mean to say," said Kate demurely, "that you 're to give up the serape entirely; you can wear it on rainy nights and when you ride over here from your friend's house to spend the evening — for the sake of old times," she added, with an unconscious air of referring to an already antiquated friendship; "but you must admit it 's a little too gorgeous and theatrical for the sunlight of day and the public highway."

"But why should that make it wrong, if the experience of a people has shown it to be a garment best fitted for their wants and requirements?" said Falkner argumentatively.

"But you are not one of those people," said Kate, "and that makes all the difference. You look differently and act differently, so that there is something irreconcilable between your clothes and you that makes you look odd."

"And to look odd, according to your civilized prejudices, is to be wrong," said Falkner bitterly.

"It is to seem different from what one really is — which is wrong. Now, you are a mining superintendent, you tell me. Then you don't want to look like a Spanish brigand, as you do in that serape. I am sure if you had ridden up to a stagecoach while I was in it, I 'd have handed you my watch and purse without a word. There! you are not offended?" she added, with a laugh, which did not, however, conceal a certain earnestness. "I suppose I ought to have said I would have given it gladly to such a romantic figure, and perhaps have got out and danced a saraband or bolero with you — if that is the thing to do nowadays. Well!" she said, after a dangerous pause, "consider that I 've said it."

He had been walking a little before her, with his face

turned towards the distant mountain.   Suddenly he stopped
and faced her.   "You would have given enough of your
time to the highwayman, Miss Scott, as would have enabled
you to identify him for the police — and no more.   Like
your brother, you would have been willing to sacrifice yourself
for the benefit of the laws of civilization and good order."

If a denial to this assertion could have been expressed
without the use of speech, it was certainly transparent in the
face and eyes of the young girl at that moment.   If Falkner
had been less self-conscious he would have seen it plainly.
But Kate only buried her face in her lifted muff, slightly
raised her pretty shoulders, and, dropping her tremulous
eyelids, walked on.   "It seems a pity," she said, after a
pause, "that we cannot preserve our own miserable existence
without taking something from others — sometimes even a
life!"   He started.   "And it's horrid to have to remind
you that you have yet to kill something for the invalid's
supper," she continued.   "I saw a hare in the field yonder."

"You mean that jackass-rabbit?" he said abstractedly.

"What you please.   It's a pity you did n't take your
gun instead of your rifle."

"I brought the rifle for protection."

"And a shot-gun is only aggressive, I suppose?"

Falkner looked at her for a moment, and then, as the
hare suddenly started across the open a hundred yards
away, brought the rifle to his shoulder.   A long interval —
as it seemed to Kate — elapsed ; the animal appeared to be
already safely out of range, when the rifle suddenly cracked ;
the hare bounded in the air like a ball, and dropped motionless.   The girl looked at the marksman in undisguised
admiration.   "Is it quite dead?" she said timidly.

"It never knew what struck it."

"It certainly looks less brutal than shooting it with a
shot-gun, as John does, and then not killing it outright,"
said Kate.   "I hate what is called sport and sportsmen, but
a rifle seems" —

" What ? " said Falkner.

" More — gentlemanly."

She had raised her pretty head in the air, and, with her hand shading her eyes, was looking around the clear ether, and said meditatively, " I wonder — no matter."

" What is it ? "

" Oh, nothing."

" It is something," said Falkner, with an amused smile, reloading his rifle.

" Well, you once promised me an eagle's feather for my hat. Is n't that thing an eagle ? "

" I am afraid it is only a hawk."

" Well, that will do. Shoot that ! "

Her eyes were sparkling. Falkner withdrew his own with a slight smile, and raised his rifle with provoking deliberation.

" Are you quite sure it 's what you want ? " he asked demurely.

" Yes — quick ! "

Nevertheless, it was some minutes before the rifle cracked again. The wheeling bird suddenly struck the wind with its wings aslant, and then fell like a plummet at a distance which showed the difficulty of the feat. Falkner started from her side before the bird reached the ground. He returned to her after a lapse of a few moments, bearing a trailing wing in his hand. " You shall make your choice," he said gayly.

" Are you sure it was killed outright ? "

" Head shot off," said Falkner briefly.

" And besides, the fall would have killed it," said Kate conclusively. " It 's lovely. I suppose they call you a very good shot ? "

" They — who ? "

" Oh ! the people you know — your friends, and their sisters."

"George shoots better than I do, and has had more experience. I've seen him do that with a pistol. Of course not such a long shot, but a more difficult one."

Kate did not reply, but her face showed a conviction that as an artistic and gentlemanly performance it was probably inferior to the one she had witnessed. Falkner, who had picked up the hare also, again took his place by her side, as they turned towards the house.

"Do you remember the day you came, when we were walking here, you pointed out that rock on the mountain where the poor animals had taken refuge from the snow?" said Kate suddenly.

"Yes," answered Falkner; "they seem to have diminished. I am afraid you were right; they have either eaten each other or escaped. Let us hope the latter."

"I looked at them with a glass every day," said Kate, "and they've got down to only four. There's a bear and that shabby, overgrown cat you call a California lion, and a wolf, and a creature like a fox or a squirrel."

"It's a pity they're not all of a kind," said Falkner.

"Why?"

"There'd be nothing to keep them from being comfortable together."

"On the contrary. *I* should think it would be simply awful to be shut up entirely with one's own kind."

"Then you believe it is possible for them, with their different natures and habits, to be happy together?" said Falkner, with sudden earnestness.

"I believe," said Kate hurriedly, "that the bear and the lion find the fox and the wolf very amusing, and that the fox and the wolf"—

"Well?" said Falkner, stopping short.

"Well, the fox and the wolf will carry away a much better opinion of the lion and bear than they had before."

They had reached the house by this time, and for some

Is n't that thing an eagle

occult reason Kate did not immediately enter the parlor, where she had left her sister and the invalid, who had already been promoted to a sofa and a cushion by the window, but proceeded directly to her own room. As a manœuvre to avoid meeting Mrs. Hale, it was scarcely necessary, for that lady was already in advance of her on the staircase, as if she had left the parlor a moment before they entered the house. Falkner, too, would have preferred the company of his own thoughts, but Lee, apparently the only unpreoccupied, all-pervading, and boyishly alert spirit in the party, hailed him from within, and obliged him to present himself on the threshold of the parlor with the hare and hawk's wing he was still carrying. Eying the latter with affected concern, Lee said gravely : " Of course, I *can* eat it, Ned, and I dare say it 's the best part of the fowl, and the hare is n't more than enough for the women, but I had no idea we were so reduced. Three hours and a half gunning, and only one hare and a hawk's wing. It 's terrible."

Perceiving that his friend was alone, Falkner dropped his burden in the hall and strode rapidly to his side. "Look here, George, we must, *I* must, leave this place at once. It 's no use talking ; I can stand this sort of thing no longer."

"Nor can I, with the door open. Shut it, and say what you want quick, before Mrs. Hale comes back. Have you found a trail ? "

"No, no ; that 's not what I mean."

"Well, it strikes me it ought to be, if you expect to get away. Have you proposed to Beacon Street, and she thinks it rather premature on a week's acquaintance ? "

"No ; but " —

"But you *will*, you mean ? *Don't*, just yet."

"But I cannot live this perpetual lie."

"That depends. I don't know *how* you 're lying when

I 'm not with you. If you 're walking round with that
girl, singing hymns and talking of your class in Sunday-
school, or if you 're insinuating that you 're a millionaire,
and think of buying the place for a summer hotel, I should
say you 'd better quit that kind of lying. But, on the
other hand, I don't see the necessity of your dancing round
here with a shot-gun, and yelling for Harkins's blood, or
counting that package of greenbacks in the lap of Miss
Scott, to be truthful. It seems to me there ought to be
something between the two."

"But, George, don't you think — you are on such good
terms with Mrs. Hale and her mother — that you might
tell them the whole story? That is, tell it in your own
way; they will hear anything from you, and believe it."

"Thank you; but suppose I don't believe in lying,
either?"

"You know what I mean! You have a way, d—n it,
of making everything seem like a matter of course, and the
most natural thing going."

"Well, suppose I did. Are you prepared for the
worst?"

Falkner was silent for a moment, and then replied,
"Yes, anything would be better than this suspense."

"I don't agree with you. Then you would be willing
to have them forgive us?"

"I don't understand you."

"I mean that their forgiveness would be the worst thing
that could happen. Look here, Ned. Stop a moment;
listen at that door. Mrs. Hale has the tread of an angel,
with the pervading capacity of a cat. Now listen! *I* don't
pretend to be in love with anybody here, but if I were I
should hardly take advantage of a woman's helplessness and
solitude with a sensational story about myself. It 's not
giving her a fair show. You know she won't turn you out
of the house."

"No," said Falkner, reddening; "but I should expect to go at once, and that would be my only excuse for telling her."

"Go! where? In your preoccupation with that girl you have n't even found the trail by which Manuel escaped. Do you intend to camp outside the house, and make eyes at her when she comes to the window?"

"Because you think nothing of flirting with Mrs. Hale," said Falkner bitterly, "you care little" —

"My dear Ned," said Lee, "the fact that Mrs. Hale has a husband, and knows that she can't marry me, puts us on equal terms. Nothing that she could learn about me hereafter would make a flirtation with me any less wrong than it would be now, or make her seem more a victim. Can you say the same of yourself and that Puritan girl?"

"But you did not advise me to keep aloof from her; on the contrary, you" —

"I thought you might make the best of the situation, and pay her some attention, *because* you could not go any further."

"You thought I was utterly heartless and selfish like" —

"Ned!"

Falkner walked rapidly to the fireplace, and returned.

"Forgive me, George — I 'm a fool — and an ungrateful one."

Lee did not reply at once, although he took and retained the hand Falkner had impulsively extended. "Promise me," he said slowly, after a pause, "that you will say nothing yet to either of these women. I ask it for your own sake, and this girl's, not for mine. If, on the contrary, you are tempted to do so from any Quixotic idea of honor, remember that you will only precipitate something that will oblige you, from that same sense of honor, to separate from the girl forever."

"I don't understand."

"Enough!" said he, with a quick return of his old reckless gayety. "Shoot-Off-His-Mouth — the Beardless Boy Chief of the Sierras — has spoken! Let the Pale Face with the black mustache ponder and beware how he talks hereafter to the Rippling Cochituate Water! Go!"

Nevertheless, as soon as the door had closed upon Falkner, Lee's smile vanished. With his colorless face turned to the fading light at the window, the hollows in his temples and the lines in the corners of his eyes seemed to have grown more profound. He remained motionless and absorbed in thought so deep that the light rustle of a skirt, that would at other times have thrilled his sensitive ear, passed unheeded. At last, throwing off his reverie with the full and unrestrained sigh of a man who believes himself alone, he was startled by the soft laugh of Mrs. Hale, who had entered the room unperceived.

"Dear me! How portentous! Really, I almost feel as if I were interrupting a *tête-à-tête* between yourself and some old flame. I have n't heard anything so old-fashioned and conservative as that sigh since I have been in California. I thought you never had any Past out here?"

Fortunately his face was between her and the light, and the unmistakable expression of annoyance and impatience which passed over it was spared her. There was, however, still enough dissonance in his manner to affect her quick feminine sense, and when she drew nearer to him it was with a certain maiden-like timidity.

"You are not worse, Mr. Lee, I hope? You have not over-exerted yourself?"

"There's little chance of that with one leg — if not in the grave at least mummified with bandages," he replied, with a bitterness new to him.

"Shall I loosen them? Perhaps they are too tight. There is nothing so irritating to one as the sensation of being tightly bound."

The light touch of her hand upon the rug that covered his knees, the thoughtful tenderness of the blue-veined lids, and the delicate atmosphere that seemed to surround her like a perfume cleared his face of its shadow and brought back the reckless fire into his blue eyes.

"I suppose I'm intolerant of all bonds," he said, looking at her intently, "in others as well as myself!"

Whether or not she detected any double meaning in his words, she was obliged to accept the challenge of his direct gaze, and, raising her eyes to his, drew back a little from him with a slight increase of color. "I was afraid you had heard bad news just now."

"What would you call bad news?" asked Lee, clasping his hands behind his head, and leaning back on the sofa, but without withdrawing his eyes from her face.

"Oh, any news that would interrupt your convalescence, or break up our little family party," said Mrs. Hale. "You have been getting on so well that really it would seem cruel to have anything interfere with our life of forgetting and being forgotten. But," she added, with apprehensive quickness, "has anything happened? Is there really any news from — from the trails? Yesterday Mr. Falkner said the snow had recommenced in the pass. Has he seen anything, noticed anything different?"

She looked so very pretty, with the rare, genuine, and youthful excitement that transfigured her wearied and wearying regularity of feature, that Lee contented himself with drinking in her prettiness as he would have inhaled the perfume of some flower.

"Why do you look at me so, Mr. Lee?" she asked, with a slight smile. "I believe something *has* happened. Mr. Falkner *has* brought you some intelligence."

"He has certainly found out something I did not foresee."

"And that troubles you?"

" It does."

" Is it a secret ? "

" No."

" Then I suppose you will tell it to me at dinner," she said, with a little tone of relief.

" I am afraid, if I tell it at all, I must tell it now," he said, glancing at the door.

" You must do as you think best," she said coldly, " as it seems to be a secret, after all." She hesitated. " Kate is dressing, and will not be down for some time."

" So much the better. For I 'm afraid that Ned has made a poor return to your hospitality by falling in love with her."

" Impossible ! He has known her for scarcely a week."

" I am afraid we won't agree as to the length of time necessary to appreciate and love a woman. I think it can be done in seven days and four hours, the exact time we have been here."

" Yes ; but as Kate was not in when you arrived, and did not come until later, you must take off at least one hour," said Mrs. Hale gayly.

" Ned can. *I* shall not abate a second."

" But are you not mistaken in his feelings ? " she continued hurriedly. " He certainly has not said anything to her."

" That is his last hold on honor and reason. And to preserve that little intact he wants to run away at once."

" But that would be very silly."

" Do you think so ? " he said, looking at her fixedly.

" Why not ? " she asked in her turn, but rather faintly.

" I 'll tell you why," he said, lowering his voice with a certain intensity of passion unlike his usual boyish light-heartedness. " Think of a man whose life has been one of alternate hardness and aggression, of savage disappointment and equally savage successes, who has known no other

relaxation than dissipation or extravagance ; a man to whom
the idea of the domestic hearth and family ties only meant
weakness, effeminacy, or — worse ; who had looked for
loyalty and devotion only in the man who battled for him
at his right hand in danger, or shared his privations and
sufferings.   Think of such a man, and imagine that an accident has suddenly placed him in an atmosphere of purity,
gentleness, and peace, surrounded him by the refinements
of a higher life than he had ever known, and that he found
himself as in a dream, on terms of equality with a pure
woman who had never known any other life, and yet would
understand and pity his.   Imagine his loving her !   Imagine
that the first effect of that love was to show him his own
inferiority and the immeasurable gulf that lay between his
life and hers !   Would he not fly rather than brave the
disgrace of her awakening to the truth ?   Would he not fly
rather than accept even the pity that might tempt her to a
sacrifice ? "

" But — is Mr. Falkner all that ? "

" Nothing of the kind, I assure you ! " said he demurely.
" But that 's the way a man in love feels."

" Really !   Mr. Falkner should get you to plead his
cause with Kate," said Mrs. Hale, with a faint laugh.

" I need all my persuasive powers in that way for myself," said Lee boldly.

Mrs. Hale rose.   " I think I hear Kate coming," she
said.   Nevertheless, she did not move away.   " It *is* Kate
coming," she added hurriedly, stopping to pick up her
work-basket, which had slipped with Lee's hand from her
own.

It was Kate, who at once flew to her sister's assistance,
Lee deploring from the sofa his own utter inability to aid
her.   " It 's all my fault, too," he said to Kate, but looking at Mrs. Hale.   " It seems I have a faculty for upsetting
existing arrangements without the power of improving

them, or even putting them back in their places. What shall I do ? I am willing to hold any number of skeins or re-wind any quantity of spools. I am even willing to forgive Ned for spending the whole day with you, and only bringing me the wing of a hawk for supper."

"That was all my folly, Mr. Lee," said Kate, with swift mendacity ; " he was all the time looking after something for you, when I begged him to shoot a bird to get a feather for my hat. And that wing is *so* pretty."

"It is a pity that mere beauty is not edible," said Lee gravely, " and that if the worst comes to the worst here you would probably prefer me to Ned and his mustaches, merely because I 've been tied by the leg to this sofa and slowly fattened like a Strasbourg goose."

Nevertheless, his badinage failed somehow to amuse Kate, and she presently excused herself to rejoin her sister, who had already slipped from the room. For the first time during their enforced seclusion a sense of restraint and uneasiness affected Mrs. Hale, her sister, and Falkner at dinner. The latter addressed himself to Mrs. Scott, almost entirely. Mrs. Hale was fain to bestow an exceptional and marked tenderness on her little daughter Minnie, who, however, by some occult childish instinct, insisted upon sharing it with Lee — her great friend — to Mrs. Hale's uneasy consciousness. Nor was Lee slow to profit by the child's suggestion, but responded with certain vicarious caresses that increased the mother's embarrassment. That evening they retired early, but in the intervals of a restless night Kate was aware, from the sound of voices in the opposite room, that the friends were equally wakeful.

A morning of bright sunshine and soft warm air did not, however, bring any change to their new and constrained relations. It only seemed to offer a reason for Falkner to leave the house very early for his daily rounds, and gave Lee that occasion for unaided exercise with an extempore crutch on the veranda which allowed Mrs. Hale to pursue her manifold duties without the necessity of keeping him company. Kate also, as if to avoid an accidental meeting with Falkner, had remained at home with her sister. With one exception, they did not make their guests the subject of their usual playful comments, nor, after the fashion of their sex, quote their ideas and opinions. That exception was made by Mrs. Hale.

"You have had no difference with Mr. Falkner?" she said carelessly.

"No," said Kate quickly. "Why?"

"I only thought he seemed rather put out at dinner last night, and you did n't propose to go and meet him to-day."

"He must be bored with my company at times, I dare say," said Kate, with an indifference quite inconsistent with her rising color. "I should n't wonder if he was a little vexed with Mr. Lee's chaffing him about his sport yesterday, and probably intends to go further to-day, and bring home larger game. I think Mr. Lee very amusing always, but I sometimes fancy he lacks feeling."

"Feeling! You don't know him, Kate," said Mrs. Hale quickly. She stopped herself, but with a half-smiling recollection in her dropped eyelids.

"Well, he does n't look very amiable now, stamping up and down the veranda. Perhaps you 'd better go and soothe him."

"I 'm really *so* busy just now," said Mrs. Hale, with sudden and inconsequent energy; "things have got dreadfully behind in the last week. You had better go, Kate, and make him sit down, or he 'll be overdoing it. These men never know any medium — in anything."

Contrary to Kate's expectation, Falkner returned earlier than usual, and, taking the invalid's arm, supported him in a more ambitious walk along the terrace before the house. They were apparently absorbed in conversation, but the two

women who observed them from the window could not help
noticing the almost feminine tenderness of Falkner's manner towards his wounded friend, and the thoughtful tenderness of his ministering care.

"I wonder," said Mrs. Hale, following them with softly
appreciative eyes, "if women are capable of as disinterested
friendship as men? I never saw anything like the devotion of these two creatures. Look! if Mr. Falkner has n't
got his arm round Mr. Lee's waist, and Lee, with his own
arm over Falkner's neck, is looking up in his eyes. I de-
clare Kate, it almost seems an indiscretion to look at
them."

Kate, however, to Mrs. Hale's indignation, threw her
pretty head back and sniffed the air contemptuously. "I
really don't see anything but some absurd sentimentalism
of their own, or some mannish wickedness they 're concoct-
ing by themselves. I am by no means certain, Josephine,
that Lee's influence over that young man is the best thing
for him."

"On the contrary! Lee's influence seems the only
thing that checks his waywardness," said Mrs. Hale quickly.
"I 'm sure, if any one makes sacrifices, it is Lee; I should n't
wonder that even now he is making some concession to
Falkner, and all those caressing ways of your friend are for
a purpose. They 're not much different from us, dear."

"Well, I would n't stand there and let them see me
looking at them as if I could n't bear them out of my sight
for a moment," said Kate, whisking herself out of the
room. "They 're conceited enough, Heaven knows, already."

That evening, at dinner, however, the two men exhibited
no trace of the restraint or uneasiness of the previous day.
If they were less impulsive and exuberant, they were still
frank and interested, and if the term could be used in
connection with men apparently trained to neither self-con-

trol nor repose, there was a certain gentle dignity in their
manner which for the time had the effect of lifting them a
little above the social level of their entertainers.   For even
with all their predisposition to the strangers, Kate and Mrs.
Hale had always retained a conscious attitude of gentle con-
descension and superiority towards them — an attitude not
inconsistent with a stronger feeling, nor altogether unprovo-
cative of it; yet this evening they found themselves impressed with something more than an equality in the men
who had amused and interested them, and they were perhaps a little more critical and doubtful of their own power.
Mrs. Hale's little girl, who had appreciated only the seriousness of the situation, had made her own application of it.
" Are you dow'in' away from aunt Kate and mamma ? "
she asked in an interval of silence.

" How else can I get you the red snow we saw at sunset, the other day, on the peak yonder ? " said Lee gayly.
" I 'll have to get up some morning very early, and catch it
when it comes at sunrise."

" What is this wonderful snow, Minnie, that you are
tormenting Mr. Lee for ? " asked Mrs. Hale.

" Oh ! it 's a fairy snow that he told me all about ; it only
comes when the sun comes up and goes down, and if you
catch ever so little of it in your hand it makes all you fink
you want come true !   Would n't that be nice ? "   But to
the child's astonishment her little circle of auditors, even
while assenting, sighed.

The red snow was there plain enough the next morning
before the valley was warm with light, and while Minnie,
her mother, and aunt Kate were still peacefully sleeping.
And Mr. Lee had kept his word, and was evidently seeking
it, for he and Falkner were already urging their horses
through the pass, with their faces towards and lit up by its
glow.

CHAPTER VIII

KATE was stirring early, but not as early as her sister, who met her on the threshold of her room. Her face was quite pale, and she held a letter in her hand. "What does this mean, Kate?"

"What is the matter?" asked Kate, her own color fading from her cheek.

"They are gone — with their horses. Left before day, and left this."

She handed Kate an open letter. The girl took it hurriedly, and read : —

When you get this we shall be no more; perhaps not even as much. Ned found the trail yesterday, and we are taking the first advantage of it before day. We dared not trust ourselves to say "Good-by!" last evening; we were too cowardly to face you this morning; we must go as we came, without warning, but not without regret. We leave a package and a letter for your husband. It is not only our poor return for your gentleness and hospitality, but, since it was accidentally the means of giving us the pleasure of your society, we beg you to keep it in safety until his return. We kiss your mother's hands. Ned wants to say something more, but time presses, and I only allow him to send his love to Minnie, and to tell her that he is trying to find the red snow.

GEORGE LEE.

"But he is not fit to travel," said Mrs. Hale. "And the trail — it may not be passable."

"It was passable the day before yesterday," said Kate drearily, "for I discovered it, and went as far as the buck-eyes."

"Then it was you who told them about it," said Mrs. Hale reproachfully.

"No," said Kate indignantly. "Of course I did n't." She stopped, and, reading the significance of her speech in the glistening eyes of her sister, she blushed. Josephine kissed her, and said : —

"It *was* treating us like children, Kate, but we must make them pay for it hereafter. For that package and letter to John means something, and we shall probably see them before long. I wonder what the letter is about, and what is in the package ? "

"Probably one of Mr. Lee's jokes. He is quite capable of turning the whole thing into ridicule. I dare say he considers his visit here a prolonged jest."

"With his poor leg, Kate ? You are as unfair to him as you were to Falkner when they first came."

Kate, however, kept her dark eyebrows knitted in a piquant frown.

"To think of his intimating *what* he would allow Falkner to say ! And yet you believe he has no evil influence over the young man."

Mrs. Hale laughed. "Where are you going so fast, Kate ? " she called mischievously, as the young lady flounced out of the room.

"Where ? Why, to tidy John's room. He may be coming at any moment now. Or do you want to do it yourself ? "

"No, no," returned Mrs. Hale hurriedly ; "you do it. I 'll look in a little later on."

She turned away with a sigh. The sun was shining brilliantly outside. Through the half-open blinds its long shafts seemed to be searching the house for the lost guests, and making the hollow shell appear doubly empty. What a contrast to the dear dark days of mysterious seclusion and delicious security, lit by Lee's laughter and the sparkling hearth, which had passed so quickly! The forgotten outer world seemed to have returned to the house through those open windows and awakened its dwellers from a dream.

The morning seemed interminable, and it was past noon, while they were deep in a sympathetic conference with Mrs. Scott, who had drawn a pathetic word-picture of the two friends perishing in the snow-drift, without flannels, brandy, smelling-salts, or jelly, which they had forgotten, when they were startled by the loud barking of Spot on the lawn before the house. The women looked hurriedly at each other.

"They have returned," said Mrs. Hale.

Kate ran to the window. A horseman was approaching the house. A single glance showed her that it was neither Falkner, Lee, nor Hale, but a stranger.

"Perhaps he brings some news of them," said Mrs. Scott quickly. So complete had been their preoccupation with the loss of their guests that they could not yet conceive of anything that did not pertain to it.

The stranger, who was at once ushered into the parlor, was evidently disconcerted by the presence of the three women.

"I reckoned to see John Hale yer," he began awkwardly.

A slight look of disappointment passed over their faces. "He has not yet returned," said Mrs. Hale briefly.

"Sho! I wanter know. He's hed time to do it, I reckon," said the stranger.

"I suppose he has n't been able to get over from the Summit," returned Mrs. Hale. "The trail is closed."

"It ain't now, for I kem over it this mornin' myself."

"You did n't — meet — any one?" asked Mrs. Hale timidly, with a glance at the others.

" No."

A long silence ensued. The unfortunate visitor plainly perceived an evident abatement of interest in himself, yet he still struggled politely to say something. "Then I reckon you know what kept Hale away?" he said dubiously.

"Oh, certainly — the stage robbery."

" I wish I 'd known that," said the stranger reflectively, " for I ez good ez rode over jist to tell it to ye. Ye see, John Hale, he sent a note to ye 'splainin' matters by a gentleman ; but the road agents tackled that man, and left him for dead in the road."

" Yes," said Mrs. Hale impatiently.

" Luckily he did n't die, but kem to, and managed to crawl inter the brush, whar I found him when I was lookin' for stock, and brought him to my house " —

"*You* found him ?   *Your* house ? " interrupted Mrs. Hale.

" Inter *my* house," continued the man doggedly. " I 'm Thompson of Thompson's Pass over yon ; mebbe it ain't much of a house ; but I brought him thar. Well, ez he could n't find the note that Hale had guv him, and like ez not the road agents had gone through him and got it, ez soon ez the weather let up I made a break over yer to tell ye."

" You say Mr. Lee came to your house," repeated Mrs. Hale, " and is there now ? "

"Not much," said the man grimly ; " and I never said *Lee* was thar. I mean that Bilson waz shot by Lee and kem " —

" Certainly, Josephine ! " said Kate, suddenly stepping between her sister and Thompson, and turning upon her a white face and eyes of silencing significance ; " certainly — don't you remember ? — that's the story we got from the Chinaman, you know, only muddled. Go on, sir," she continued, turning to Thompson calmly; "you say that the man who brought the note from my brother was shot by Lee?"

"And another fellow they call Falkner. Yes, that's about the size of it."

"Thank you; it's nearly the same story that we heard. But you have had a long ride, Mr. Thompson; let me offer you a glass of whiskey in the dining-room. This way, please."

The door closed upon them none too soon. For Mrs. Hale already felt the room whirling around her, and sank back into her chair with a hysterical laugh. Old Mrs. Scott did not move from her seat, but, with her eyes fixed on the door, impatiently waited Kate's return. Neither spoke, but each felt that the young, untried girl was equal to the emergency, and would get at the truth.

The sound of Thompson's feet in the hall and the closing of the front door was followed by Kate's reappearance. Her face was still pale, but calm.

"Well?" said the two women in a breath.

"Well," returned Kate slowly; "Mr. Lee and Mr. Falkner were undoubtedly the two men who took the paper from John's messenger and brought it here."

"You are sure?" said Mrs. Scott.

"There can be no mistake, mother."

"*Then*," said Mrs. Scott, with triumphant feminine logic, "I don't want anything more to satisfy me that they are *perfectly innocent!*"

More convincing than the most perfect masculine deduction, this single expression of their common nature sent a thrill of sympathy and understanding through each. They cried for a few moments on each other's shoulders. "To think," said Mrs. Scott, "what that poor boy must have suffered to have been obliged to do — that to — to — Bilson — is n't that the creature's name? I suppose we ought to send over there and inquire after him, with some chicken and jelly, Kate. It's only common humanity, and we must be just, my dear; for even if he shot Mr. Lee and provoked the poor boy to shoot him, he may have thought it his duty. And then, it will avert suspicions."

"To think," murmured Mrs. Hale, "what they must have gone through while they were here — momentarily expecting John to come, and yet keeping up such a light heart."

"I believe, if they had stayed longer, they would have told us everything," said Mrs. Scott.

Both the younger women were silent. Kate was thinking of Falkner's significant speech as they neared the house on their last walk; Josephine was recalling the remorseful picture drawn by Lee, which she knew was his own portrait. Suddenly she started.

"But John will be here soon; what are we to tell him? And then that package and that letter."

"Don't be in a hurry to tell him anything at present, my child," said Mrs. Scott gently. "It is unfortunate this Mr. Thompson called here, but we are not obliged to understand what he says now about John's message, or to connect our visitors with his story. I 'm sure, Kate, I should have treated them exactly as we did if they had come without any message from John; so I do not know why we should lay any stress on that, or even speak of it. The simple fact is that we have opened our house to the strangers in distress. Your husband," continued Mr. Hale's mother-in-law, "does not require to know more. As to the letter and package, we will keep that for further consideration. It cannot be of much importance, or they would have spoken of it before; it is probably some trifling present as a return for your hospitality. I should use no *indecorous* haste in having it opened."

The two women kissed Mrs. Scott with a feeling of relief, and fell back into the monotony of their household duties. It is to be feared, however, that the absence of their outlawed guests was nearly as dangerous as their presence in the opportunity it afforded for uninterrupted and imaginative reflection. Both Kate and Josephine were at first shocked and wounded by the discovery of the real character of the two men with whom they had associated so familiarly, but it was no disparagement to their sense of propriety to say that the shock did not last long, and was accompanied with the fascination of danger. This was succeeded by a consciousness of the delicate flattery implied in their indirect influence over the men who had undoubtedly risked their lives for the sake of remaining with them. The best woman is not above being touched by the effect of her power over the worst man, and Kate at first allowed herself to think of Falkner in that light. But if in her later reflections he suffered as a heroic experience to be forgotten, he gained something as an actual man to be remembered. Now that the proposed rides from " his friend's house " were a part of the illusion, would he ever dare to visit them again? Would she dare to see him? She held her breath with a sudden pain of parting that was new to her; she tried to think of something else, to pick up the scattered threads of her life before that eventful day. But in vain; that one week had filled the place with implacable memories, or more terrible, as it seemed to her and her sister, they had both lost their feeble, alien hold upon Eagle's Court in the sudden presence of the real genii of these solitudes, and henceforth they alone would be strangers there. They scarcely dared to confess it to each other, but this return to the dazzling sunlight and cloudless skies of the past appeared to them to be the one unreal experience; they had never known the true wild flavor of their home, except in that week of delicious isolation. Without breathing it aloud, they longed for some vague dénouement to this experience that should take them from Eagle's Court forever.

It was noon the next day when the little household beheld the last shred of their illusion vanish like the melting snow in the strong sunlight of John Hale's return. He was accompanied by Colonel Clinch and Rawlins, two strangers to the women. Was it fancy, or the avenging spirit of their absent companions? but *he* too looked a stranger, and as the little cavalcade wound its way up the slope he appeared to sit his horse and wear his hat with a certain slouch and absence of his usual restraint that strangely shocked them. Even the old half-condescending, half-punctilious gallantry of his greeting of his wife and family was changed, as he introduced his companions with a mingling of familiarity and shyness that was new to him. Did Mrs. Hale regret it, or feel a sense of relief in the absence of his usual seignorial formality? She only knew that she was grateful for the presence of the strangers, which for the moment postponed a matrimonial confidence from which she shrunk.

"Proud to know you," said Colonel Clinch, with a sudden outbreak of the antique gallantry of some remote Huguenot ancestor. "My friend, Judge Hale, must be a regular Roman citizen to leave such a family and such a house at the call of public duty. Eh, Rawlins?"

"You bet," said Rawlins, looking from Kate to her sister in undisguised admiration.

"And I suppose the duty could not have been a very pleasant one," said Mrs. Hale timidly, without looking at her husband.

"Gad, madam, that's just it," said the gallant Colonel, seating himself with a comfortable air, and an easy, though by no means disrespectful familiarity. "We went into this fight a little more than a week ago. The only scrimmage we've had has been with the detectives that were on

the robbers' track.   Ha! ha!   The best people we've met
have been the friends of the men we were huntin', and
we've generally come to the conclusion to vote the other
ticket!   Ez Judge Hale and me agreed ez we came along,
the two men ez we'd most like to see just now and shake
hands with are George Lee and Ned Falkner."

"The two leaders of the party who robbed the coach,"
explained Mr. Hale, with a slight return of his usual precision of statement.

The three women looked at each other with a blaze of
thanksgiving in their grateful eyes.   Without comprehend-
ing all that Colonel Clinch had said, they understood enough
to know that their late guests were safe from the pursuit
of that party, and that their own conduct was spared criticism.   I hardly dare write it, but they instantly assumed
the appearance of aggrieved martyrs, and felt as if they
were!

"Yes, ladies!" continued the Colonel, inspired by the
bright eyes fixed upon him.   "We haven't taken the road
ourselves yet, but — pohn honor — we wouldn't mind
doing it in a case like this."   Then with the fluent, but
somewhat exaggerated phraseology of a man trained to
"stump" speaking, he gave an account of the robbery and
his own connection with it.   He spoke of the swindling
and treachery which had undoubtedly provoked Falkner to
obtain restitution of his property by an overt act of violence
under the leadership of Lee.   He added that he had learned
since at Wild Cat Station that Harkins had fled the country, that a suit had been commenced by the Excelsior
Ditch Company, and that all available property of Harkins
had been seized by the sheriff.

"Of course it can't be proved yet, but there's no doubt
in my mind that Lee, who is an old friend of Ned Falkner's, got up that job to help him, and that Ned's off with
the money by this time — and I'm right glad of it.   I

can't say ez we've done much towards it, except to keep tumbling in the way of that detective party of Stanner's, and so throw them off the trail — ha, ha ! The Judge here, I reckon, has had his share of fun, for while he was at Hennicker's trying to get some facts from Hennicker's pretty daughter, Stanner tried to get up some sort of vigilance committee of the stage passengers to burn down Hennicker's ranch out of spite, but the Judge here stepped in and stopped that."

" It was really a high-handed proceeding, Josephine, but I managed to check it," said Hale, meeting somewhat consciously the first direct look his wife had cast upon him, and falling back for support on his old manner. " In its way, I think it was worse than the robbery by Lee and Falkner, for it was done in the name of law and order ; while, as far as I can judge from the facts, the affair that we were following up was simply a rude and irregular restitution of property that had been morally stolen."

" I have no doubt you did quite right, though I don't understand it," said Mrs. Hale languidly ; " but I trust these gentlemen will stay to luncheon, and in the mean time excuse us for running away, as we are short of servants, and Manuel seems to have followed the example of the head of the house and left us, in pursuit of somebody or something."

When the three women had gained the vantage-ground of the drawing-room, Kate said earnestly, " As it's all right, had n't we better tell him now ? "

" Decidedly not, child," said Mrs. Scott imperatively. " Do you suppose they are in a hurry to tell us *their* whole story ? Who are those Hennicker people ? and they were there a week ago ! "

" And did you notice John's hat when he came in, and the vulgar familiarity of calling him ' Judge ' ? " said Mrs. Hale.

"Well, certainly anything like the familiarity of this man Clinch *I* never saw," said Kate. "Contrast his manner with Mr. Falkner's."

At luncheon the three suffering martyrs finally succeeded in reducing Hale and his two friends to an attitude of vague apology. But their triumph was short-lived. At the end of the meal they were startled by the trampling of hoofs without, followed by loud knocking. In another moment the door was opened, and Mr. Stanner strode into the room. Hale rose with a look of indignation.

"I thought, as Mr. Stanner understood that I had no desire for his company elsewhere, he would hardly venture to intrude upon me in my house, and certainly not after " —

"Ef you 're alluding to the Vigilantes shakin' you and Zeenie up at Hennicker's, you can't make *me* responsible for that. I 'm here now on business — you understand — reg'lar business. Ef you want to see the papers yer ken. I suppose you know what a warrant is ? "

"I know what *you* are," said Hale hotly; "and if you don't leave my house" —

"Steady, boys," interrupted Stanner, as his five henchmen filed into the hall. "There 's no backin' down here, Colonel Clinch, unless you and Hale kalkilate to back down the State of Californy ! The matter stands like this. There 's a half-breed Mexican, called Manuel, arrested over at the Summit, who swears he saw George Lee and Edward Falkner in this house the night after the robbery. He says that they were makin' themselves at home here, as if they were among friends, and considerin' the kind of help we 've had from Mr. John Hale, it looks ez if it might be true."

"It 's an infamous lie !" said Hale.

"It may be true, John," said Mrs. Scott, suddenly stepping in front of her pale-cheeked daughters. "A wounded man was brought here out of the storm by his friend, who claimed the shelter of your roof. As your mother I should have been unworthy to stay beneath it and have denied that shelter or withheld it until I knew his name and what he was. He stayed here until he could be removed. He left a letter for you. It will probably tell you if he was the man this person is seeking."

"Thank you, mother," said Hale, lifting her hand to his lips quietly ; "and perhaps you will kindly tell these gen‌tlemen that, as your son does not care to know who or what the stranger was, there is no necessity for opening the letter, or keeping Mr. Stanner a moment longer."

"But you will oblige *me*, John, by opening it before these gentlemen," said Mrs. Hale, recovering her voice and color. "Please to follow me," she said, preceding them to the staircase.

They entered Mr. Hale's room, now restored to its original condition. On the table lay a letter and a small package. The eyes of Mr. Stanner, a little abashed by the attitude of the two women, fastened upon it and glistened.

Josephine handed her husband the letter. He opened it in breathless silence and read : —

JOHN HALE, — We owe you no return for voluntarily making yourself a champion of justice and pursuing us, except it was to offer you a fair field and no favor. We did n't get that much from you, but accident brought us into your house and into your family, where we *did* get it, and were fairly vanquished. To the victors belong the spoils. We leave the package of greenbacks which we took from Colonel Clinch in the Sierra coach, but which was first stolen by Harkins from forty-four shareholders of the Excelsior Ditch. We have no right to say what *you* should do with it, but if you are n't tired of following the same line of justice that induced you to run after *us*, you will try to restore it to its rightful owners.

We leave you another trifle as an evidence that our intrusion into your affairs was not without some service to you, even if the service was as accidental as the intrusion. You will find a pair of boots in the corner of your closet. They were taken from the burglarious feet of Manuel, your peon, who, believing the three ladies were alone and at his mercy, entered your house with an accomplice at two o'clock on the morning of the 21st, and was kicked out by

Your obedient servants,

GEORGE LEE & EDWARD FALKNER.

Hale's voice and color changed on reading this last paragraph. He turned quickly towards his wife; Kate flew to the closet, where the muffled boots of Manuel confronted them. "We never knew it. I always suspected something that night," said Mrs. Hale and Mrs. Scott in the same breath.

"That's all very well, and like George Lee's highfalutin'," said Stanner, approaching the table, "but as long ez the greenbacks are here he can make what capital he likes outer Manuel. I'll trouble you to pass over that package."

"Excuse me," said Hale, "but I believe this is the package taken from Colonel Clinch. Is it not?" he added, appealing to the Colonel.

"It is," said Clinch.

"Then take it," said Hale, handing him the package. "The first restitution is to you, but I believe you will fulfill Lee's instructions as well as myself."

"But," said Stanner, furiously interposing, "I've a warrant to seize that wherever found, and I dare you to disobey the law."

"Mr. Stanner," said Clinch slowly, "there are ladies present. If you insist upon having that package I must ask them to withdraw, and I'm afraid you'll find me better prepared to resist a *second* robbery than I was the first.

Your warrant, which was taken out by the Express Company, is supplanted by civil proceedings taken the day before yesterday against the property of the fugitive swindler Harkins! You should have consulted the sheriff before you came here."

Stanner saw his mistake. But in the faces of his grinning followers he was obliged to keep up his bluster. "You shall hear from me again, sir," he said, turning on his heel.

"I beg your pardon," said Clinch grimly, "but do I understand that at last I am to have the honor" —

"You shall hear from the Company's lawyers, sir," said Stanner, turning red, and noisily leaving the room.

"And so, my dear ladies," said Colonel Clinch, "you have spent a week with a highwayman. I say *a* highwayman, for it would be hard to call my young friend Falkner by that name for his first offense, committed under great provocation, and undoubtedly instigated by Lee, who was an old friend of his, and to whom he came, no doubt, in desperation."

Kate stole a triumphant glance at her sister, who dropped her lids over her glistening eyes. "And this Mr. Lee," she continued more gently, "is he really a highwayman?"

"George Lee," said Clinch, settling himself back oratorically in his chair, "my dear young lady, *is* a highwayman, but not of the common sort. He is a gentleman born, madam, comes from one of the oldest families of the Eastern Shore of Maryland. He never mixes himself up with anything but some of the biggest strikes, and he's an educated man. He is very popular with ladies and children; he was never known to do or say anything that could bring a blush to the cheek of beauty or a tear to the eye of innocence. I think I may say I'm sure you found him so."

"I shall never believe him anything but a gentleman," said Mrs. Scott firmly.

"If he has a defect, it is perhaps a too reckless indul-
gence in draw-poker," said the Colonel musingly; "not
unbecoming a gentleman, understand me, Mrs. Scott, but
perhaps too reckless for his own good. George played a
grand game, a glittering game, but pardon me if I say an
uncertain game. I've told him so; it's the only point on
which we ever differed."

"Then you know him?" said Mrs. Hale, lifting her soft
eyes to the Colonel.

"I have that honor."

"Did his appearance, Josephine," broke in Hale, somewhat ostentatiously, " appear to — er — er — correspond
with these qualities? You know what I mean."

"He certainly seemed very simple and natural," said
Mrs. Hale, slightly drawing her pretty lips together. "He
did not wear his trousers rolled up over his boots in the
company of ladies, as you're doing now, nor did he make
his first appearance in this house with such a hat as you
wore this morning, or I should not have admitted him."

There were a few moments of embarrassing silence.

"Do you intend to give that package to Mr. Falkner
yourself, Colonel?" asked Mrs. Scott.

"I shall hand it over to the Excelsior Company," said
the Colonel, "but I shall inform Ned of what I have done."

"Then," said Mrs. Scott "will you kindly take a message from us to him?"

"If you wish it."

"You will be doing *me* a great favor, Colonel," said
Hale politely.

Whatever the message was, six months later it brought
Edward Falkner, the reëstablished superintendent of the
Excelsior Ditch, to Eagle's Court. As he and Kate stood
again on the plateau, looking towards the distant slopes
once more green with verdure, Falkner said : —

" Everything here looks as it did the first day I saw it, except your sister."

" The place does not agree with her," said Kate hurriedly.   " That is why my brother thinks of leaving it before the winter sets in."

" It seems so sad," said Falkner, " for the last words poor George said to me, as he left to join his cousin's corps at Richmond, were : ' If I 'm not killed, Ned, I hope some day to stand again beside Mrs. Hale, at the window in Eagle's Court, and watch you and Kate coming home ! ' "

A MILLIONAIRE OF ROUGH-AND-READY

PROLOGUE

THERE was no mistake this time : he had struck gold at last !

It had lain there before him a moment ago — a misshapen piece of brown-stained quartz, interspersed with dull yellow metal ; yielding enough to have allowed the points of his pick to penetrate its honeycombed recesses, yet heavy enough to drop from the point of his pick as he endeavored to lift it from the red earth.

He was seeing all this plainly, although he found himself, he knew not why, at some distance from the scene of his discovery, his heart foolishly beating, his breath impotently hurried. Yet he was walking slowly and vaguely ; conscious of stopping and staring at the landscape, which no longer looked familiar to him. He was hoping for some instinct or force of habit to recall him to himself ; yet when he saw a neighbor at work in an adjacent claim, he hesitated, and then turned his back upon him. Yet only a moment before he had thought of running to him, saying, "By Jingo ! I 've struck it," or " D—n it, old man, I 've got it ; " but that moment had passed, and now it seemed to him that he could scarce raise his voice, or, if he did, the ejaculation would appear forced and artificial. Neither could he go over to him coolly and tell his good fortune ; and, partly from this strange shyness, and partly with a hope that another survey of the treasure might restore him to natural expression, he walked back to his tunnel.

Yes; it was there! No mere "pocket" or "deposit," but a part of the actual vein he had been so long seeking. It was there, sure enough, lying beside the pick and the débris of the "face" of the vein that he had exposed sufficiently, after the first shock of discovery, to assure himself of the fact and the permanence of his fortune. It was there, and with it the refutation of his enemies' sneers, the corroboration of his friends' belief, the practical demonstration of his own theories, the reward of his patient labors. It was there, sure enough. But, somehow, he not only failed to recall the first joy of discovery, but was conscious of a vague sense of responsibility and unrest. It was, no doubt, an enormous fortune to a man in his circumstances : perhaps it meant a couple of hundred thousand dollars, or more, judging from the value of the old Martin lead, which was not as rich as this, but it required to be worked constantly and judiciously. It was with a decided sense of uneasiness that he again sought the open sunlight of the hillside. His neighbor was still visible on the adjacent claim ; but he had apparently stopped working, and was contemplatively smoking a pipe under a large pine-tree. For an instant he envied him his apparent contentment. He had a sudden fierce and inexplicable desire to go over to him and exasperate his easy poverty by a revelation of his own new-found treasure. But even that sensation quickly passed, and left him staring blankly at the landscape again.

As soon as he had made his discovery known, and settled its value, he would send for his wife and her children in the States. He would build a fine house on the opposite hillside, if she would consent to it, unless she preferred, for the children's sake, to live in San Francisco. A sense of a loss of independence — of a change of circumstances that left him no longer his own master — began to perplex him, in the midst of his brightest projects. Certain other rela-

tions with other members of his family, which had lapsed
by absence and insignificance, must now be taken up anew.
He must do something for his sister Jane, for his brother
William, for his wife's poor connections.   It would be unfair to him to say that he contemplated those things with
any other instinct than that of generosity ; yet he was conscious of being already perplexed and puzzled.

Meantime, however, the neighbor had apparently finished
his pipe, and, knocking the ashes out of it, rose suddenly,
and ended any further uncertainty of their meeting by walking over directly towards him.   The treasure-finder advanced a few steps on his side, and then stopped irresolutely.

"Hollo, Slinn!" said the neighbor confidently.

"Hollo, Masters," responded Slinn faintly.   From the
sound of the two voices a stranger might have mistaken
their relative condition.   "What in thunder are you moon-
ing about for ?   What's up ? "   Then, catching sight of
Slinn's pale and anxious face, he added abruptly, "Are you
sick ? "

Slinn was on the point of telling him his good fortune,
but stopped.   The unlucky question confirmed his consciousness of his physical and mental disturbance, and he
dreaded the ready ridicule of his companion.   He would
tell him later; Masters need not know *when* he had made
the strike.   Besides, in his present vagueness, he shrank
from the brusque, practical questioning that would be sure
to follow the revelation to a man of Masters's tempera-
ment.

"I'm a little giddy here," he answered, putting his hand
to his head, "and I thought I'd knock off until I was better."

Masters examined him with two very critical gray eyes.
"Tell ye what, old man ! — if you don't quit this dog-
goned foolin' of yours in that God-forsaken tunnel you'll

get loony! Times you get so tangled up in follerin' that blind lead o' yours you ain't sensible!"

Here was the opportunity to tell him all, and vindicate the justice of his theories! But he shrank from it again; and now, adding to the confusion, was a singular sense of dread at the mental labor of explanation. He only smiled painfully, and began to move away. "Look you!" said Masters peremptorily, "ye want about three fingers of straight whiskey to set you right, and you've got to take it with me. D—n it, man, it may be the last drink we take together! Don't look so skeered! I mean — I made up my mind about ten minutes ago to cut the whole d—d thing, and light out for fresh diggings. I'm sick of getting only grub wages out o' this hill. So that's what I mean by saying it's the last drink you and me'll take together. You know my ways: sayin' and doin' with me's the same thing."

It was true. Slinn had often envied Masters's promptness of decision and resolution. But he only looked at the grim face of his interlocutor with a feeble sense of relief. He was *going*. And he, Slinn, would not have to explain anything!

He murmured something about having to go over to the settlement on business. He dreaded lest Masters should insist upon going into the tunnel.

"I suppose you want to mail that letter," said Masters dryly. "The mail don't go till to-morrow, so you've got time to finish it, and put it in an envelope."

Following the direction of Masters's eyes, Slinn looked down and saw, to his utter surprise, that he was holding an unfinished penciled note in his hand. How it came there, when he had written it, he could not tell; he dimly remembered that one of his first impulses was to write to his wife, but that he had already done so he had forgotten. He hastily concealed the note in his breast-pocket, with a vacant smile. Masters eyed him half contemptuously, half compassionately.

"Don't forget yourself and drop it in some hollow tree for a letter-box," he said. "Well — so long! — since you won't drink. Take care of yourself," and, turning on his heel, Masters walked away.

Slinn watched him as he crossed over to his abandoned claim, saw him gather his few mining utensils, strap his blanket over his back, lift his hat on his long-handled shovel as a token of farewell, and then stride light-heartedly over the ridge.

He was alone now with his secret and his treasure. The only man in the world who knew of the exact position of his tunnel had gone away forever. It was not likely that this chance companion of a few weeks would ever remember him or the locality again; he would now leave his treasure alone — for even a day perhaps — until he had thought out some plan and sought out some friend in whom to confide. His secluded life, the singular habits of concentration which had at last proved so successful, had, at the same time, left him few acquaintances and no associates. And in all his well-laid plans and patiently digested theories for finding the treasure, the means and methods of working it and disposing of it had never entered.

And now, at the hour when he most needed his faculties, what was the meaning of this strange benumbing of them!

Patience! He only wanted a little rest — a little time to recover himself. There was a large boulder under a tree in the highway to the settlement — a sheltered spot where he had often waited for the coming of the stagecoach. He would go there, and when he was sufficiently rested and composed he would go on.

Nevertheless, on his way he diverged and turned into the woods, for no other apparent purpose than to find a hollow tree. "A hollow tree." Yes! that was what Masters had

said; he remembered it distinctly; and something was to
be done there, but what it was, or why it should be done,
he could not tell.   However, it was done, and very luckily,
for his limbs could scarcely support him further, and reaching that boulder he dropped upon it like another stone.

And now, strange to say, the uneasiness and perplexity
which had possessed him ever since he had stood before his
revealed wealth dropped from him like a burden laid upon
the wayside.   A measureless peace stole over him, in which
visions of his new-found fortune, no longer a trouble and
perplexity, but crowned with happiness and blessing to all
around him, assumed proportions far beyond his own weak,
selfish plans.   In its even-handed benefaction, his wife and
children, his friends and relations, even his late poor
companion of the hillside, met and moved harmoniously
together; in its far-reaching consequences there was only
the influence of good.   It was not strange that this poor
finite mind should never have conceived the meaning of the
wealth extended to him; or that conceiving it he should
faint and falter under the revelation.   Enough that for a
few minutes he must have tasted a joy of perfect anticipation
that years of actual possession might never bring.

The sun seemed to go down in a rosy dream of his own
happiness, as he still sat there.   Later, the shadows of the
trees thickened and surrounded him, and still later fell the
calm of a quiet evening sky with far-spaced passionless
stars, that seemed as little troubled by what they looked
upon as he was by the stealthy creeping life in the grasses
and underbrush at his feet.   The dull patter of soft little
feet in the soft dust of the road, the gentle gleam of moist
and wondering little eyes on the branches and in the mossy
edges of the boulder, did not disturb him.   He sat patiently through it all, as if he had not yet made up his
mind.

But when the stage came with the flashing sun the next

morning, and the irresistible clamor of life and action, the driver suddenly laid his four spirited horses on their haunches before the quiet spot. The express messenger clambered down from the box, and approached what seemed to be a heap of cast-off clothes upon the boulder.

"He don't seem to be drunk," he said, in reply to a querulous interrogation from the passengers. "I can't make him out. His eyes are open, but he cannot speak or move. Take a look at him, Doc."

A rough, unprofessional-looking man here descended from the inside of the coach, and, carelessly thrusting aside the other curious passengers, suddenly leant over the heap of clothes in a professional attitude.

"He is dead," said one of the passengers.

The rough man let the passive head sink softly down again. "No such luck for him," he said curtly, but not unkindly. "It's a stroke of paralysis — and about as big as they make 'em. It's a toss-up if he ever speaks or moves again as long as he lives."

CHAPTER I

WHEN Alvin Mulrady announced his intention of growing potatoes and garden "truck" on the green slopes of Los Gatos, the mining community of that region, and the adjacent hamlet of Rough-and-Ready, regarded it with the contemptuous indifference usually shown by those adventurers towards all bucolic pursuits. There was certainly no active objection to the occupation of two hillsides, which gave so little promise to the prospector for gold that it was currently reported that a single prospector, called " Slinn," had once gone mad or imbecile through repeated failures. The only opposition came, incongruously enough, from the original pastoral owner of the soil, one Don Ramon Alvarado, whose claim for seven leagues of hill and valley, including the now prosperous towns of Rough-and-Ready and Red Dog, was met with simple derision from the squatters and miners. " Looks ez ef we woz goin' to travel three thousand miles to open up his d—d old wilderness, and then pay for the increased valoo we give it — don't it? Oh, yes, certainly!" was their ironical commentary. Mulrady might have been pardoned for adopting this popular opinion ; but by an equally incongruous sentiment, peculiar, however, to the man, he called upon Don Ramon, and actually offered to purchase the land, or "go shares" with him in the agricultural profits. It was alleged that the don was so struck with this concession he not only granted the land, but struck up a quaint reserved friendship for the simple-minded agriculturist and his family. It is scarcely necessary to add that this intimacy was viewed by the miners with the contempt that it deserved.   They would have been more contemptuous, however, had they known the opinion that Don Ramon entertained of their particular vocation, and which he early confided to Mulrady.

"They are savages, who expect to reap where they have not sown; to take out of the earth without returning anything to it but their precious carcasses; heathens, who worship the mere stones they dig up."   "And was there no Spaniard who ever dug gold?" asked Mulrady simply. "Ah, there are Spaniards and Moors," responded Don Ramon sententiously.   "Gold has been dug, and by caballeros; but no good ever came of it.   There were Alvarados in Sonora, look you, who had mines of *silver*, and worked them with peons and mules, and lost their money — a gold mine to work a silver one — like gentlemen! But this grubbing in the dirt with one's fingers, that a little gold may stick to them, is not for caballeros.   And then, one says nothing of the curse."

"The curse!" echoed Mary Mulrady, with youthful feminine superstition.   "What is that?"

"You knew not, friend Mulrady, that when these lands were given to my ancestors by Charles V., the Bishop of Monterey laid a curse upon any who should desecrate them. Good!   Let us see!   Of the three Americanos who founded yonder town, one was shot, another died of a fever, — poisoned, you understand, by the soil, — and the last got himself crazy of aguardiente.   Even the scientifico,[1] who came here years ago and spied into the trees and the herbs — he was afterwards punished for his profanation, and died of an accident in other lands.   But," added Don Ramon, with grave courtesy, "this touches not yourself.   Through me, *you* are of the soil."

---

[1] Don Ramon probably alluded to the eminent naturalist Douglas, who visited California before the gold excitement, and died of an accident in the Sandwich Islands.

Indeed, it would seem as if a secure if not a rapid prosperity was the result of Don Ramon's manorial patronage. The potato patch and market garden flourished exceedingly; the rich soil responded with magnificent vagaries of growth; the even sunshine set the seasons at defiance with extraordinary and premature crops. The salt pork and biscuit consuming settlers did not allow their contempt of Mulrady's occupation to prevent their profiting by this opportunity for changing their diet. The gold they had taken from the soil presently began to flow into his pockets in exchange for his more modest treasures. The little cabin, which barely sheltered his family, — a wife, son, and daughter, — was enlarged, extended, and refitted, but in turn abandoned for a more pretentious house on the opposite hill. A whitewashed fence replaced the rudely split rails, which had kept out the wilderness. By degrees, the first evidences of cultivation — the gashes of red soil, the piles of brush and undergrowth, the bared boulders, and heaps of stone — melted away, and were lost under a carpet of lighter green, which made an oasis in the tawny desert of wild oats on the hillside. Water was the only free boon denied this Garden of Eden; what was necessary for irrigation had to be brought from a mining ditch at great expense, and was of insufficient quantity. In this emergency Mulrady thought of sinking an artesian well on the sunny slope beside his house; not, however, without serious consultation and much objection from his Spanish patron. With great austerity Don Ramon pointed out that trifling with the entrails of the earth was not only an indignity to Nature almost equal to shaft-sinking and tunneling, but was a disturbance of vested interests. "I and my fathers — San Diego rest them!" said Don Ramon, crossing himself — "were content with wells and cisterns, filled by Heaven at its appointed seasons; the cattle, dumb brutes though they were, knew where to find water when they wanted it. But thou sayest truly," he added with a sigh, " that was before streams and rain were choked with hellish engines, and poisoned with their spume.   Go on, friend Mulrady, dig and bore if thou wilt, but in a seemly fashion, and not with impious earth-quakes of devilish gunpowder."

With this concession Alvin Mulrady began to sink his first artesian shaft.   Being debarred the auxiliaries of steam and gunpowder, the work went on slowly.   The market garden did not suffer meantime, as Mulrady had employed two Chinamen to take charge of the ruder tillage, while he superintended the engineering work of the well.   This trifling incident marked an epoch in the social condition of the family.   Mrs. Mulrady at once assumed a conscious importance among her neighbors.   She spoke of her hus-band's " men ; " she alluded to the well as " the works ; " she checked the easy frontier familiarity of her customers with pretty Mary Mulrady, her seventeen-year-old daughter. Simple Alvin Mulrady looked with astonishment at this sudden development of the germ planted in all feminine nature to expand in the slightest sunshine of prosperity. " Look yer, Malviny ; ain't ye rather puttin' on airs with the boys that want to be civil to Mamie ?   Like as not one of 'em may be makin' up to her already."   " You don't mean to say, Alvin Mulrady," responded Mrs. Mulrady, with sudden severity, " that you ever thought of givin' your daughter to a common miner, or that I 'm goin' to allow her to marry out of our own set ? "   " Our own set ! " echoed Mulrady feebly, blinking at her in astonishment, and then glancing hurriedly across at his freckle-faced son and the two Chinamen at work in the cabbages.   " Oh, you know what I mean," said Mrs. Mulrady sharply ; " the set that we move in.   The Alvarados and their friends ! Does n't the old don come here every day, and ain't his son the right age for Mamie ?   And ain't they the real first families here — all the same as if they were noblemen ?

No, leave Mamie to me, and keep to your shaft; there never was a man yet had the least sabe about these things, or knew what was due to his family." Like most of his larger-minded, but feebler-equipped sex, Mulrady was too glad to accept the truth of the latter proposition, which left the meannesses of life to feminine manipulation, and went off to his shaft on the hillside. But during that after- noon he was perplexed and troubled. He was too loyal a husband not to be pleased with this proof of an unexpected and superior foresight in his wife, although he was, like all husbands, a little startled by it. He tried to dismiss it from his mind. But looking down from the hillside upon his little venture, where gradual increase and prosperity had not been beyond his faculties to control and understand, he found himself haunted by the more ambitious projects of his helpmate. From his own knowledge of men, he doubted if Don Ramon, any more than himself, had ever thought of the possibility of a matrimonial connection between the families. He doubted if he would consent to it. And unfortunately it was this very doubt that, touch- ing his own pride as a self-made man, made him first seri- ously consider his wife's proposition. He was as good as Don Ramon, any day! With this subtle feminine poison instilled in his veins, carried completely away by the logic of his wife's illogical premises, he almost hated his old benefactor. He looked down upon the little Garden of Eden, where his Eve had just tempted him with the fatal fruit, and felt a curious consciousness that he was losing its simple and innocent enjoyment forever.

Happily, about this time Don Ramon died. It is not probable that he ever knew the amiable intentions of Mrs. Mulrady in regard to his son, who now succeeded to the paternal estate, sadly partitioned by relatives and lawsuits. The feminine Mulradys attended the funeral, in expensive mourning from Sacramento; even the gentle Alvin was forced into ready-made broadcloth, which accented his good-natured but unmistakably common presence. Mrs. Mulrady spoke openly of her "loss;" declared that the old families were dying out; and impressed the wives of a few new arrivals at Red Dog with the belief that her own family was contemporary with the Alvarados, and that her husband's health was far from perfect. She extended a motherly sympathy to the orphaned Don Cæsar. Reserved, like his father, in natural disposition, he was still more gravely ceremonious from his loss; and, perhaps from the shyness of an evident partiality for Mamie Mulrady, he rarely availed himself of her mother's sympathizing hospitality. But he carried out the intentions of his father by consenting to sell to Mulrady, for a small sum, the property he had leased. The idea of purchasing had originated with Mrs. Mulrady.

"It 'll be all in the family," had observed that astute lady, "and it's better for the looks of the things that we should n't be his tenants."

It was only a few weeks later that she was startled by hearing her husband's voice calling her from the hillside as he rapidly approached the house. Mamie was in her room putting on a new pink cotton gown, in honor of an expected visit from young Don Cæsar, and Mrs. Mulrady was tidying the house in view of the same event. Something in the tone of her good man's voice, and the unusual circumstance of his return to the house before work was done, caused her, however, to drop her dusting cloth, and run to the kitchen door to meet him. She saw him running through the rows of cabbages, his face shining with perspiration and excitement, a light in his eyes which she had not seen for years. She recalled, without sentiment, that he looked like that when she had called him — a poor farm hand of her father's — out of the brush heap at the back of their former home, in Illinois, to learn the consent of her parents. The recollection was the more embarrassing as he threw his arms around her, and pressed a resounding kiss upon her sallow cheek.

"Sakes alive, Mulrady!" she said, exorcising the ghost of a blush that had also been recalled from the past with her housewife's apron, "what are you doin', and company expected every minit?"

"Malviny, I've struck it; and struck it rich!"

She disengaged herself from his arms, without excitement, and looked at him with bright but shrewdly observant eyes.

"I've struck it in the well — the regular vein that the boys have been looking fer. There's a fortin' fer you and Mamie — thousands and tens of thousands!"

"Wait a minit."

She left him quickly, and went to the foot of the stairs. He could hear her wonderingly and distinctly. "Ye can take off that new frock, Mamie," she called out.

There was a sound of undisguised expostulation from Mamie.

"I'm speaking," said Mrs. Mulrady emphatically.

The murmuring ceased. Mrs. Mulrady returned to her husband. The interruption seemed to have taken off the keen edge of his enjoyment. He at once abdicated his momentary elevation as a discoverer, and waited for her to speak.

"Ye have n't told any one yet?" she asked.

"No. I was alone, down in the shaft. Ye see, Malviny, I was n't expectin' of anything." He began, with an attempt at fresh enjoyment, "I was just clearin' out, and had n't reckoned on anythin'."

"You see, I was right when I advised your taking the land," she said, without heeding him.

Mulrady's face fell. "I hope Don Cæsar won't think" — he began hesitatingly. "I reckon, perhaps, I oughter make some sorter compensation — you know."

"Stuff!" said Mrs Mulrady decidedly. "Don't be a fool. Any gold discovery, anyhow, would have been yours — that's the law. And you bought the land without any restrictions. Besides, you never had any idea of this!" — she stopped, and looked him suddenly in the face, — "had you?"

Mulrady opened his honest, pale gray eyes widely.

"Why, Malviny! You know I had n't. I could swear!"

"Don't swear, and don't let on to anybody but what you *did* know it was there. Now, Alvin Mulrady, listen to me." Her voice here took the strident form of action. "Knock off work at the shaft, and send your man away at once. Put on your things, catch the next stage to Sacramento at four o'clock, and take Mamie with you."

"Mamie!" echoed Mulrady feebly.

"You want to see Lawyer Cole and my brother Jim at once," she went on, without heeding him, "and Mamie wants change and some proper clothes. Leave the rest to me and Abner. I 'll break it to Mamie, and get her ready."

Mulrady passed his hands through his tangled hair, wet with perspiration. He was proud of his wife's energy and action; he did not dream of opposing her, but somehow he was disappointed. The charming glamour and joy of his discovery had vanished before he could fairly dazzle her with it; or, rather, she was not dazzled with it at all. It had become like business, and the expression "breaking it" to Mamie jarred upon him. He would have preferred to tell her himself; to watch the color come into her delicate oval face, to have seen her soft eyes light with an innocent joy he had not seen in his wife's; and he felt a sinking conviction that his wife was the last one to awaken it.

"You ain't got any time to lose," she said impatiently, as he hesitated.

Perhaps it was her impatience that struck harshly upon him ; perhaps, if she had not accepted her good fortune so confidently, he would not have spoken what was in his mind at the time ; but he said gravely, " Wait a minit, Malviny ; I 've suthin' to tell you 'bout this find of mine that 's sing'lar."

" Go on," she said quickly.

" Lyin' among the rotten quartz of the vein was a pick," he said constrainedly ; " and the face of the vein sorter looked ez if it had been worked at.   Follering the line outside to the base of the hill there was signs of there having been an old tunnel ; but it had fallen in, and was blocked up."

" Well ? " said Mrs. Mulrady contemptuously.

" Well," returned her husband somewhat disconnectedly, " it kinder looked as if some feller might have discovered it before."

" And went away, and left it for others !   That 's likely, ain't it ? " interrupted his wife, with ill-disguised intolerance.   " Everybody knows the hill was n't worth that for prospectin' ; and it was abandoned when we came here. It 's your property and you 've paid for it.   Are you goin' to wait to advertise for the owner, Alvin Mulrady, or are you going to Sacramento at four o'clock to-day ? "

Mulrady started.   He had never seriously believed in the possibility of a previous discovery ; but his conscientious nature had prompted him to give it a fair consideration. She was probably right.   What he might have thought had she treated it with equal conscientiousness he did not consider.   " All right," he said simply.   " I reckon we 'll go at once."

" And when you talk to Lawyer Cole and Jim, keep that silly stuff about the pick to yourself.   There 's no use of putting queer ideas into other people's heads because you happen to have 'em yourself."

When the hurried arrangements were at last completed, and Mr. Mulrady and Mamie, accompanied by a taciturn and discreet Chinaman, carrying their scant luggage, were on their way to the highroad to meet the up stage, the father gazed somewhat anxiously and wistfully into his daughter's face. He had looked forward to those few moments to enjoy the freshness and *naïveté* of Mamie's youthful delight and enthusiasm as a relief to his wife's practical, far-sighted realism. There was a pretty pink suffusion in her delicate cheek, the breathless happiness of a child in her half-opened little mouth, and a beautiful absorption in her large gray eyes that augured well for him.

"Well, Mamie, how do we like bein' an heiress? How do we like layin' over all the gals between this and 'Frisco?"

"Eh?"

She had not heard him. The tender beautiful eyes were engaged in an anticipatory examination of the remembered shelves in the Fancy Emporium at Sacramento; in reading the admiration of the clerks; in glancing down a little criticisingly at the broad cowhide brogues that strode at her side; in looking up the road for the stagecoach; in regarding the fit of her new gloves — everywhere but in the loving eyes of the man beside her.

He, however, repeated the question, touched with her charming preoccupation, and passing his arm around her little waist.

"I like it well enough, pa, you know," she said, slightly disengaging his arm, but adding a perfunctory little squeeze to his elbow to soften the separation. "I always had an idea *something* would happen. I suppose I 'm looking like a fright," she added; "but ma made me hurry to get away before Don Cæsar came."

"And you did n't want to go without seeing him?" he added archly.

"I did n't want him to see me in this frock," said Mamie simply. "I reckon that 's why ma made me change," she added, with a slight laugh.

"Well, I reckon you 're allus good enough for him in any dress," said Mulrady, watching her attentively; "and more than a match for him *now*," he added triumphantly.

"I don't know about that," said Mamie. "He 's been rich all the time, and his father and grandfather before him ; while we 've been poor and his tenants."

His face changed ; the look of bewilderment, with which he had followed her words, gave way to one of pain, and then of anger. "Did he get off such stuff as that ?" he asked quickly.

"No. I 'd like to catch him at it," responded Mamie promptly. "There 's better nor him to be had for the asking now."

They had walked on a few moments in aggrieved silence, and the Chinaman might have imagined some misfortune had just befallen them. But Mamie's teeth shone again between her parted lips. "La, pa ! it ain't that ! He cares everything for me, and I do for him ; and if ma had n't got new ideas" — She stopped suddenly.

"What new ideas ?" queried her father anxiously.

"Oh, nothing ! I wish, pa, you 'd put on your other boots ! Everybody can see these are made for the farrows. And you ain't a market gardener any more."

"What am I, then ?" asked Mulrady, with a half-pleased, half-uneasy laugh.

"You 're a capitalist, *I* say ; but ma says a landed proprietor." Nevertheless, the landed proprietor, when he reached the boulder on the Red Dog highway, sat down in somewhat moody contemplation, with his head bowed over the broad cowhide brogues, that seemed to have already gathered enough of the soil to indicate his right to that title. Mamie, who had recovered her spirits, but had not lost her preoccupation, wandered off by herself in the meadow, or ascended the hillside, as her occasional impatience at the delay of the coach, or the following of some ambitious fancy, alternately prompted her. She was so far away at one time that the stagecoach, which finally drew up before Mulrady, was obliged to wait for her.

When she was deposited safely inside, and Mulrady had climbed to the box beside the driver, the latter remarked curtly : —

"Ye gave me a right smart skeer, a minit ago, stranger."

"Ez how ? "

"Well, about three years ago, I was comin' down this yer grade, at just this time, and sittin' right on that stone, in just your attitude, was a man about your build and years. I pulled up to let him in, when, darn my skin ! if he ever moved, but sorter looked at me without speakin'. I called to him, and he never answered, 'cept with that idiotic stare. I then let him have my opinion of him, in mighty strong English, and drove off, leavin' him there. The next morning, when I came by on the up trip, darn my skin ! if he was n't thar, but lyin' all of a heap on the boulder. Jim drops down and picks him up. Dr. Duchesne, ez was along, allowst it was a played-out prospector, with a big case of paralysis, and we expressed him through to the County Hospital, like so much dead freight. I 've allus been kinder superstitious about passin' that rock, and when I saw you jist now, sittin' thar, dazed like, with your head down like the other chap, it rather threw me off my centre."

In the inexplicable and half-superstitious uneasiness that this coincidence awakened in Mulrady's unimaginative mind, he was almost on the point of disclosing his good fortune to the driver, in order to prove how preposterous was the parallel, but checked himself in time.

"Did you find out who he was ? " broke in a rash passenger. "Did you ever get over it?" added another unfortunate.

With a pause of insulting scorn at the interruption, the driver resumed, pointedly, to Mulrady : " The pint of the whole thing was my cussin' a helpless man, ez could neither cuss back nor shoot; and then afterwards takin' you for his ghost layin' for me to get even." He paused again, and then added carelessly, " They say he never kem to enuff to let on who he was or whar he kem from ; and he was eventooally taken to a 'Sylum for Doddering Idjits and Gin'ral and Permiskus Imbeciles at Sacramento.   I 've heerd it 's considered a first-class institooshun, not only for them ez is paralyzed and can't talk, as for them ez is the reverse and is too chipper.   Now," he added, languidly turning for the first time to his miserable questioners, " how did *you* find it ?"

CHAPTER II

WHEN the news of the discovery of gold in Mulrady's shaft was finally made public, it created an excitement hitherto unknown in the history of the country. Half of Red Dog and all Rough-and-Ready were emptied upon the yellow hills surrounding Mulrady's, until their circling camp-fires looked like a besieging army that had invested his peaceful pastoral home, preparatory to carrying it by assault. Unfortunately for them, they found the various points of vantage already garrisoned with notices of " preëmption " for mining purposes in the name of the various members of the Alvarado family. This stroke of business was due to Mrs. Mulrady, as a means of mollifying the conscientious scruples of her husband and of her placating the Alvarados, in view of some remote contingency. It is but fair to say that this degradation of his father's Castilian principles was opposed by Don Cæsar. " You need n't work them your-self, but sell out to them that will ; it 's the only way to keep the prospectors from taking it without paying for it at all," argued Mrs. Mulrady. Don Cæsar finally assented ; perhaps less to the business arguments of Mulrady's wife than to the simple suggestion of Mamie's mother. Enough that he realized a sum in money for a few acres that ex-ceeded the last ten years' income of Don Ramon's seven leagues.

Equally unprecedented and extravagant was the realiza-tion of the discovery in Mulrady's shaft. It was alleged that a company hastily formed in Sacramento paid him a million of dollars down, leaving him still a controlling two-thirds interest in the mine.   With an obstinacy, however, that amounted almost to a moral conviction, he refused to include the house and potato-patch in the property.   When the company had yielded the point, he declined, with equal tenacity, to part with it to outside speculators on even the most extravagant offers.   In vain Mrs. Mulrady protested; in vain she pointed out to him that the retention of the evidence of his former humble occupation was a green blot upon their social escutcheon.

"If you will keep the land, build on it, and root up the garden."   But Mulrady was adamant.

"It 's the only thing I ever made myself, and got out of the soil with my own hands; it 's the beginning of my fortune, and it may be the end of it.   Mebbe I 'll be glad enough to have it to come back to some day, and be thankful for the square meal I can dig out of it."

By repeated pressure, however, Mulrady yielded the compromise that a portion of it should be made into a vineyard and flower garden, and by a suitable coloring of ornament and luxury obliterate its vulgar part.   Less successful, however, was that energetic woman in another effort to mitigate the austerities of their earlier state.   It occurred to her to utilize the softer accents of Don Cæsar in the pronunciation of their family name, and privately had " Mulrade " take the place of Mulrady on her visiting-card. "It might be Spanish," she argued with her husband. " Lawyer Cole says most American names are corrupted, and how do you know that yours ain't ? "   Mulrady, who would not swear that his ancestors came from Ireland to the Carolinas in '98, was helpless to refute the assertion.   But the terrible Nemesis of an un-Spanish, American provincial speech avenged the orthographical outrage at once.   When Mrs. Mulrady began to be addressed orally, as well as by letter, as " Mrs. Mulraid," and when simple amatory effusions to her daughter rhymed with " lovely maid," she promptly restored the original vowel. But she fondly clung to the Spanish courtesy which transformed her husband's baptismal name, and usually spoke of him — in his absence — as " Don Alvino." But in the presence of his short, square figure, his orange tawny hair, his twinkling gray eyes, and *retroussé* nose, even that dominant woman withheld his title. It was currently reported at Red Dog that a distinguished foreigner had one day approached Mulrady with the formula, " I believe I have the honor of addressing Don Alvino Mulrady ? " " You kin bet your boots, stranger, that 's me," had returned that simple hidalgo.

Although Mrs. Mulrady would have preferred that Mamie should remain at Sacramento until she should join her, preparatory to a trip to " the States " and Europe, she yielded to her daughter's desire to astonish Rough - and - Ready, before she left, with her new wardrobe, and unfold in the parent nest the delicate and painted wings with which she was to fly from them forever. "I don't want them to remember me afterwards in those spotted prints, ma, and like as not say I never had a decent frock until I went away." There was something so like the daughter of her mother in this delicate foresight that the touched and gratified parent kissed her, and assented. The result was gratifying beyond her expectation. In that few weeks' sojourn at Sacramento, the young girl seemed to have adapted and assimilated herself to the latest modes of fashion with even more than the usual American girl's pliancy and taste. Equal to all emergencies of style and material, she seemed to supply, from some hitherto unknown quality she possessed, the grace and manner peculiar to each. Untrammeled by tradition, education, or precedent, she had the Western girl's confidence in all things being possible, which made them so often probable. Mr. Mulrady looked at his daughter with mingled sentiments of pride and awe. Was it possible that this delicate crea-

ture, so superior to him that he seemed like a degenerate
scion of her remoter race, was his own flesh and blood ?
Was she the daughter of her mother, who even in her remembered youth was never equipped like this ?   If the
thought brought no pleasure to his simple, loving nature, it
at least spared him the pain of what might have seemed
ingratitude in one more akin to himself.   " The fact is, we
ain't quite up to her style," was his explanation and
apology.   A vague belief that in another and a better
world than this he might approximate and understand this
perfection somewhat soothed and sustained him.

It was quite consistent, therefore, that the embroidered
cambric dress which Mamie Mulrady wore one summer
afternoon on the hillside at Los Gatos, while to the critical
feminine eye at once artistic and expensive, should not
seem incongruous to her surroundings or to herself in the
eyes of a general audience.   It certainly did not seem so to
one pair of frank, humorous ones that glanced at her from
time to time, as their owner, a young fellow of five-and-
twenty, walked at her side.   He was the new editor of the
" Rough-and-Ready Record," and, having been her fellow
passenger from Sacramento, had already once or twice
availed himself of her father's invitation to call upon them.
Mrs. Mulrady had not discouraged this mild flirtation.
Whether she wished to disconcert Don Cæsar for some
occult purpose, or whether, like the rest of her sex, she had
an overweening confidence in the unheroic, unseductive,
and purely platonic character of masculine humor, did not
appear.

" When I say I'm sorry you are going to leave us, Miss
Mulrady," said the young fellow lightly, " you will comprehend my unselfishness, since I frankly admit your departure would be a positive relief to me as an editor and a
man.   The pressure in the Poet's Corner of the ' Record,'
since it was unmistakingly discovered that a person of your

name might be induced to seek the ' glade' and ' shade'
without being ' afraid,' ' dismayed,' or ' betrayed,' has been
something enormous, and, unfortunately, I am debarred
from rejecting anything, on the just ground that I am myself an interested admirer."

" It is dreadful to be placarded around the country by
one's own full name, is n't it ? " said Mamie, without, however, expressing much horror in her face.

" They think it much more respectful than to call you
' Mamie,' " he responded lightly ; " and many of your
admirers are middle-aged men, with a mediæval style of
compliment.   I 've discovered that amatory versifying
was n't entirely a youthful passion.   Colonel Cash is about
as fatal with a couplet as with a double-barreled gun, and
scatters as terribly.   Judge Butts and Dr. Wilson have
both discerned the resemblance of your gifts to those of
Venus, and their own to Apollo.   But don't undervalue
those tributes, Miss Mulrady," he added more seriously.
" You 'll have thousands of admirers where you are going ;
but you 'll be willing to admit in the end, I think, that
none were more honest and respectful than your subjects at
Rough-and-Ready and Red Dog."   He stopped, and added
in a graver tone, " Does Don Cæsar write poetry ? "

" He has something better to do," said the young lady
pertly.

" I can easily imagine that," he returned mischievously ;
" it must be a pallid substitute for other opportunities."

" What did you come here for ? " she asked suddenly.

" To see you."

" Nonsense !   You know what I mean.   Why did you
ever leave Sacramento to come here ?   I should think it
would suit you so much better than this place."

" I suppose I was fired by your father's example, and
wished to find a gold mine."

" Men like you never do," she said simply.

" Is that a compliment, Miss Mulrady ? "

" I don't know. But I think that you think that it is."

He gave her the pleased look of one who had unexpectedly found a sympathetic intelligence. " Do I ? This is
interesting. Let's sit down." In their desultory rambling they had reached, quite unconsciously, the large boulder at the roadside.   Mamie hesitated a moment, looked up
and down the road, and then, with an already opulent indifference to the damaging of her spotless skirt, sat herself
upon it, with her furled parasol held by her two little
hands thrown over her half-drawn-up knee. The young
editor, half sitting, half leaning, against the stone, began to
draw figures in the sand with his cane.

" On the contrary, Miss Mulrady, I hope to make some
money here. You are leaving Rough-and-Ready because
you are rich. We are coming to it because we are poor."

" We ? " echoed Mamie lazily, looking up the road.

" Yes. My father and two sisters."

" I am sorry. I might have known them if I had n't
been going away." At the same moment, it flashed across
her mind that, if they were like the man before her, they
might prove disagreeably independent and critical. " Is
your father in business ? " she asked.

He shook his head. After a pause, he said, punctuating
his sentences with the point of his stick in the soft dust,
" He is paralyzed, and out of his mind, Miss Mulrady. I
came to California to seek him, as all news of him ceased
three years since; and I found him only two weeks ago,
alone, friendless — an unrecognized pauper in the county
hospital."

" Two weeks ago ? That was when I went to Sacramento."

" Very probably."

" It must have been very shocking to you ? "

" It was."

" I should think you 'd feel real bad ? "

" I do, at times." He smiled, and laid his stick on the stone. " You now see, Miss Mulrady, how necessary to me is this good fortune that you don't think me worthy of. Meantime I must try to make a home for them at Rough-and-Ready."

Miss Mulrady put down her knee and her parasol. " We must n't stay here much longer, you know."

" Why ? "

" Why, the stagecoach comes by at about this time."

" And you think the passengers will observe us sitting here ? "

" Of course they will."

" Miss Mulrady, I implore you to stay."

He was leaning over her with such apparent earnestness of voice and gesture that the color came into her cheek. For a moment she scarcely dared to lift her conscious eyes to his. When she did so, she suddenly glanced her own aside with a flash of anger. He was laughing.

" If you have any pity for me, do not leave me now," he repeated. " Stay a moment longer, and my fortune is made. The passengers will report us all over Red Dog as engaged. I shall be supposed to be in your father's secrets, and shall be sought after as a director of all the new companies. The 'Record' will double its circula-tion ; poetry will drop out of its columns, advertising rush to fill its place, and I shall receive five dollars a week more salary, if not seven and a half. Never mind the con-sequences to yourself at such a moment. I assure you there will be none. You can deny it the next day — *I* will deny it — nay, more, the 'Record' itself will deny it in an extra edition of one thousand copies, at ten cents each. Linger a moment longer, Miss Mulrady. Fly, oh, fly not yet. They 're coming — hark ! ho ! By Jove, it 's only Don Cæsar ! "

It was, indeed, only the young scion of the house of Alvarado, blue-eyed, sallow-skinned, and high-shouldered, coming towards them on a fiery, half-broken mustang, whose very spontaneous lawlessness seemed to accentuate and bring out the grave and decorous ease of his rider. Even in his burlesque preoccupation the editor of the "Record" did not withhold his admiration of this perfect horsemanship. Mamie, who, in her wounded *amour propre*, would like to have made much of it to annoy her companion, was thus estopped any ostentatious compliment.

Don Cæsar lifted his hat with sweet seriousness to the lady, with grave courtesy to the gentleman. While the lower half of this Centaur was apparently quivering with fury, and stamping the ground in his evident desire to charge upon the pair, the upper half, with natural dignity, looked from the one to the other, as if to leave the privilege of an explanation with them. But Mamie was too wise, and her companion too indifferent, to offer one. A slight shade passed over Don Cæsar's face. To complicate the situation at that moment, the expected stagecoach came rattling by. With quick feminine intuition, Mamie caught in the faces of the driver and the expressman, and reflected in the mischievous eyes of her companion, a peculiar interpretation of their meeting, that was not removed by the whispered assurance of the editor that the passengers were anxiously looking back "to see the shooting."

The young Spaniard, equally oblivious of humor or curiosity, remained impassive.

"You know Mr. Slinn, of the 'Record,'" said Mamie, "don't you?"

Don Cæsar had never before met the Señor Esslinn. He was under the impression that it was a Señor Robinson that was of the "Record."

"Oh! *he* was shot," said Slinn. "I'm taking his place."

"Bueno ! To be shot too ? I trust not."

Slinn looked quickly and sharply into Don Cæsar's grave face. He seemed to be incapable of any double meaning. However, as he had no serious reason for awakening Don Cæsar's jealousy, and very little desire to become an embarrassing third in this conversation, and possibly a burden to the young lady, he proceeded to take his leave of her.

From a sudden feminine revulsion of sympathy, or from some unintelligible instinct of diplomacy, Mamie said, as she extended her hand, "I hope you'll find a home for your family near here. Mamma wants pa to let our old house. Perhaps it might suit you, if not too far from your work. You might speak to ma about it."

"Thank you ; I will," responded the young man, pressing her hand with unaffected cordiality.

Don Cæsar watched him until he had disappeared behind the wayside buckeyes.

"He is a man of family — this one — your countryman ? "

It seemed strange to her to have a mere acquaintance spoken of as " her countryman " — not the first time nor the last time in her career. As there appeared no trace or sign of jealousy in her questioner's manner, she answered briefly but vaguely.

"Yes ; it 's a shocking story. His father disappeared some years ago, and he has just found him — a helpless paralytic — in the Sacramento Hospital. He'll have to support him — and they 're very poor."

"So, then, they are not independent of each other always — these fathers and children of Americans ! "

"No," said Mamie shortly. Without knowing why, she felt inclined to resent Don Cæsar's manner. His serious gravity — gentle and high-bred as it was, undoubtedly — was somewhat trying to her at times, and seemed even more so after Slinn's irreverent humor. She picked up her parasol a little impatiently, as if to go.

But Don Cæsar had already dismounted, and tied his horse to a tree with a strong lariat that hung at his saddle-bow.

"Let us walk through the woods towards your home. I can return alone for the horse when you shall dismiss me."

They turned in among the pines that, overcrowding the hollow, crept partly up the side of the hill of Mulrady's shaft. A disused trail, almost hidden by the waxen-hued yerba buena, led from the highway, and finally lost itself in the undergrowth. It was a lovers' walk; they were lovers, evidently, and yet the man was too self-poised in his grav-ity, the young woman too conscious and critical, to suggest an absorbing or oblivious passion.

"I should not have made myself so obtrusive to-day be-fore your friend," said Don Cæsar, with proud humility, "but I could not understand from your mother whether you were alone or whether my company was desirable. It is of this I have now to speak, Mamie. Lately your mother has seemed strange to me; avoiding any reference to our affection; treating it lightly, and even as to-day, I fancy, putting obstacles in the way of our meeting alone. She was disappointed at your return from Sacramento, where, I have been told, she intended you to remain until you left the country; and since your return I have seen you but twice. I may be wrong. Perhaps I do not comprehend the American mother; I have — who knows? — perhaps offended in some point of etiquette, omitted some ceremony that was her due. But when you told me, Mamie, that it was not necessary to speak to *her* first, that it was not the American fashion " —

Mamie started, and blushed slightly.

"Yes," she said hurriedly, "certainly; but ma has been

quite queer of late, and she may think — you know — that
since — since there has been so much property to dispose
of, she ought to have been consulted."

"Then let us consult her at once, dear child! And as
to the property, in Heaven's name, let her dispose of it as
she will. Saints forbid that an Alvarado should ever interfere. And what is it to us, my little one ? Enough that
Doña Mameta Alvarado will never have less state than the
richest bride that ever came to Los Gatos."

Mamie had not forgotten that scarcely a month ago, even
had she loved the man before her no more than she did at
present, she would still have been thrilled with delight at
these words ! Even now she was moved — conscious as
she had become that the "state" of a bride of the Alvarados was not all she had imagined, and that the bare adobe
court of Los Gatos was open to the sky and the free criticism of Sacramento capitalists!

"Yes, dear," she murmured, with a half-childlike pleasure, that lit up her face and eyes so innocently that it
stopped any minute investigation into its origin and real
meaning. "Yes, dear; but we need not have a fuss made
about it at present, and perhaps put ma against us. She
would n't hear of our marrying now; and she might forbid
our engagement."

"But you are going away."

"I should have to go to New York or Europe *first*, you
know," she answered naïvely, "even if it were all settled.
I should have to get things ! One could n't be decent
here."

With the recollection of the pink cotton gown, in which
she had first pledged her troth to him, before his eyes he
said, "But you are charming now. You cannot be more
so to me. If I am satisfied, little one, with you as you are,
let us go together, and then you can get dresses to please
others."

She had not expected this importunity. Really, if it came to this, she might have engaged herself to some one like Slinn; he at least would have understood her. He was much cleverer, and certainly more of a man of the world. When Slinn had treated her like a child, it was with the humorous tolerance of an admiring superior, and not the didactic impulse of a guardian. She did not say this, nor did her pretty eyes indicate it, as in the instance of her brief anger with Slinn. She only said gently: —

"I should have thought you, of all men, would have been particular about your wife doing the proper thing. But never mind! Don't let us talk any more about it. Perhaps, as it seems such a great thing to you, and so much trouble, there may be no necessity for it at all."

I do not think that the young lady deliberately planned this charmingly illogical deduction from Don Cæsar's speech, or that she calculated its effect upon him; but it was part of her nature to say it, and profit by it. Under the unjust lash of it his pride gave way.

"Ah, do you not see why I wish to go with you?" he said, with sudden and unexpected passion. "You are beautiful; you are good; it has pleased Heaven to make you rich also; but you are a child in experience, and know not your own heart. With your beauty, your goodness, and your wealth, you will attract all to you — as you do here — because you cannot help it. But you will be equally helpless, little one, if *they* should attract *you*, and you had no tie to fall back upon."

It was an unfortunate speech. The words were Don Cæsar's; but the thought she had heard before from her mother, although the deduction had been of a very different kind. Mamie followed the speaker with bright but visionary eyes. There must be some truth in all this. Her mother had said it; Mr. Slinn had laughingly admitted it. She *had* a brilliant future before her! Was she right in making it impossible by a rash and foolish tie ?   He himself had said she was inexperienced.   She knew it ; and yet, what was he doing now but taking advantage of that inexperience ? If he really loved her, he would be willing to submit to the test.   She did not ask a similar one from him ; and was willing, if she came out of it free, to marry him just the same.   There was something so noble in this thought that she felt for a moment carried away by an impulse of compassionate unselfishness, and smiled tenderly as she looked up in his face.

"Then you consent, Mamie ?" he said eagerly, passing his arm around her waist.

"Not now, Cæsar," she said, gently disengaging herself. "I must think it over ; we are both too young to act upon it rashly ; it would be unfair to you, who are so quiet and have seen so few girls — I mean Americans — to tie yourself to the first one you have known.   When I am gone you will go more into the world.   There are Mr. Slinn's two sisters coming here, — I should n't wonder if they were far cleverer and talked far better than I do, — and think how I should feel if I knew that only a wretched pledge to me kept you from loving them !"   She stopped, and cast down her eyes.

It was her first attempt at coquetry ; for, in her usual charming selfishness she was perfectly frank and open ; and it might not have been her last, but she had gone too far at first, and was not prepared for a recoil of her own argument.

"If you admit that it is possible — that it is possible to you !" he said quickly.

She saw her mistake.   "We may not have many opportunities to meet alone," she answered quietly ; "and I am sure we would be happier when we meet not to accuse each other of impossibilities.   Let us rather see how we can communicate together, if anything should prevent our meeting.   Remember, it was only by chance that you were able to see me now. If ma has believed that she ought to have been consulted, our meeting together in this secret way will only make matters worse. She is even now wondering where I am, and may be suspicious. I must go back at once. At any moment some one may come here looking for me."

"But I have so much to say," he pleaded. "Our time has been so short."

"You can write."

"But what will your mother think of that?" he said in grave astonishment.

She colored again as she returned quickly: "Of course, you must not write to the house. You can leave a letter somewhere for me — say, somewhere about here. Stop!" she added, with a sudden girlish gayety, "see, here's the very place. Look there!"

She pointed to the decayed trunk of a blasted sycamore, a few feet from the trail. A cavity, breast high, half filled with skeleton leaves and pine-nuts, showed that it had formerly been a squirrel's hoard, but for some reason had been deserted.

"Look! it's a regular letter-box," she continued gayly, rising on tiptoe to peep into its recesses. Don Cæsar looked at her admiringly; it seemed like a return to their first idyllic love-making in the old days, when she used to steal out of the cabbage rows in her brown linen apron and sun-bonnet to walk with him in the woods. He recalled the fact to her with the fatality of a lover already seeking to restore in past recollections something that was wanting in the present. She received it with the impatience of youth, to whom the present is all sufficient.

"I wonder how you could ever have cared for me in that holland apron," she said, looking down upon her new dress.

"Shall I tell you why?" he said fondly, passing his arm around her waist, and drawing her pretty head nearer his shoulder.

"No — not now!" she said laughingly, but struggling to free herself. "There's not time. Write it, and put it in the box. There," she added hastily, "listen! — what's that?"

"It's only a squirrel," he whispered reassuringly in her ear.

"No; it's somebody coming! I must go! Please! Cæsar, dear! There, then" —

She met his kiss halfway, released herself with a lithe movement of her wrist and shoulder, and the next moment seemed to slip into the woods, and was gone.

Don Cæsar listened with a sigh as the last rustling ceased, cast a look at the decayed tree as if to fix it in his memory, and then slowly retraced his steps towards his tethered mustang.

He was right, however, in his surmise of the cause of that interruption. A pair of bright eyes had been watching them from the bough of an adjacent tree. It was a squirrel, who, having had serious and prior intentions of making use of the cavity they had discovered, had only withheld examination by an apparent courteous discretion towards the intruding pair. Now that they were gone he slipped down the tree and ran towards the decayed stump.

CHAPTER III

APPARENTLY dissatisfied with the result of an investigation, which proved that the cavity was unfit as a treasure
hoard for a discreet squirrel, whatever its value as a receptacle for the love-tokens of incautious humanity, the little
animal at once set about to put things in order. He began
by whisking out an immense quantity of dead leaves, disturbed a family of tree-spiders, dissipated a drove of patient
aphides browsing in the bark, as well as their attendant
dairymen, the ants, and otherwise ruled it with the high
hand of dispossession and a contemptuous opinion of the
previous incumbents. It must not be supposed, however,
that his proceedings were altogether free from contempo-
raneous criticism; a venerable crow sitting on a branch
above him displayed great interest in his occupation, and,
hopping down a few moments afterwards, disposed of some
worm-eaten nuts, a few larvæ, and an insect or two, with
languid dignity and without prejudice. Certain incum-
brances, however, still resisted the squirrel's general evic-
tion; among them a folded square of paper with sharply
defined edges, that declined investigation, and, owing to a
nauseous smell of tobacco, escaped nibbling as it had apparently escaped insect ravages. This, owing to its sharp
angles, which persisted in catching in the soft decaying
wood in his whirlwind of house-cleaning, he allowed to remain. Having thus, in a general way, prepared for the
coming winter, the self-satisfied little rodent dismissed the
subject from his active mind.

His rage and indignation a few days later may be readily

conceived, when he found, on returning to his new-made home, another square of paper, folded like the first, but much fresher and whiter, lying within the cavity, on top of some moss which had evidently been placed there for the purpose. This he felt was really more than he could bear; but as it was smaller, with a few energetic kicks and whisks of his tail he managed to finally dislodge it through the opening, where it fell ignominiously to the earth. The eager eyes of the ever attendant crow, however, instantly detected it; he flew to the ground, and, turning it over, examined it gravely. It was certainly not edible, but it was exceedingly rare, and, as an old collector of curios, he felt he could not pass it by. He lifted it in his beak, and, with a desperate struggle against the superincumbent weight, regained the branch with his prize. Here, by one of those delicious vagaries of animal nature, he apparently at once discharged his mind of the whole affair, became utterly oblivious of it, allowed it to drop without the least concern, and eventually flew away with an abstracted air, as if he had been another bird entirely. The paper got into a manzanita bush, where it remained suspended until the evening, when, being dislodged by a passing wildcat on its way to Mulrady's hen-roost, it gave that delicately sensitive marauder such a turn that she fled into the adjacent county.

But the troubles of the squirrel were not yet over. On the following day the young man who had accompanied the young woman returned to the trunk, and the squirrel had barely time to make his escape before the impatient visitor approached the opening of the cavity, peered into it, and even passed his hand through its recesses. The delight visible upon his anxious and serious face at the disappearance of the letter, and the apparent proof that it had been called for, showed him to have been its original depositor, and probably awakened a remorseful recollection in the dark bosom of the omnipresent crow, who uttered a conscience-stricken croak from the bough above him. But the young man quickly disappeared again, and the squirrel was once more left in undisputed possession.

A week passed. A weary, anxious interval to Don Cæsar, who had neither seen nor heard from Mamie since their last meeting. Too conscious of his own self-respect to call at the house after the equivocal conduct of Mrs. Mulrady, and too proud to haunt the lanes and approaches in the hope of meeting her daughter, like an ordinary lover, he hid his gloomy thoughts in the monastic shadows of the courtyard at Los Gatos, or found relief in furious riding at night and early morning on the highway. Once or twice the up stage had been overtaken and passed by a rushing figure as shadowy as a phantom horseman, with only the star-like point of a cigarette to indicate its humanity. It was in one of these fierce recreations that he was obliged to stop in early morning at the blacksmith's shop at Rough-and-Ready, to have a loosened horseshoe replaced, and while waiting picked up a newspaper. Don Cæsar seldom read the papers; but noticing that this was the " Record," he glanced at its columns. A familiar name suddenly flashed out of the dark type like a spark from the anvil. With a brain and heart that seemed to be beating in unison with the blacksmith's sledge, he read as follows : —

" Our distinguished fellow townsman, Alvin Mulrady, Esq., left town day before yesterday to attend an important meeting of directors of the Red Dog Ditch Company, in San Francisco. Society will regret to hear that Mrs. Mulrady and her beautiful and accomplished daughter, who were expecting to depart for Europe at the end of the month, anticipated the event nearly a fortnight, by taking this opportunity of accompanying Mr. Mulrady as far as San Francisco, on their way to the East. Mrs. and Miss Mulrady intend to visit London, Paris, and Berlin, and will be absent three years. It is possible that Mr. Mulrady may join them later at one or other of those capitals. Considerable disappointment is felt that a more extended leave-taking was not possible, and that, under the circumstances, no opportunity was offered for a 'send-off' suitable to the condition of the parties and the esteem in which they are held in Rough-and-Ready."

The paper dropped from his hands. Gone! and without a word! No, that was impossible! There must be some mistake; she had written; the letter had miscarried; she must have sent word to Los Gatos, and the stupid messenger had blundered; she had probably appointed another meeting, or expected him to follow to San Francisco. "The day before yesterday!" It was the morning's paper — she had been gone scarcely two days — it was not too late yet to receive a delayed message by post, by some forgetful hand — by — ah — the tree!

Of course it was in the tree, and he had not been there for a week! Why had he not thought of it before? The fault was his, not hers. Perhaps she had gone away, believing him faithless, or a country boor.

"In the name of the Devil, will you keep me here till eternity!"

The blacksmith stared at him. Don Cæsar suddenly remembered that he was speaking, as he was thinking — in Spanish.

"Ten dollars, my friend, if you have done in five minutes!"

The man laughed. "That's good enough American," he said, beginning to quicken his efforts. Don Cæsar again took up the paper. There was another paragraph that recalled his last interview with Mamie : —

"Mr. Harry Slinn, Jr., the editor of this paper, has just moved into the pioneer house formerly occupied by Alvin Mulrady, Esq., which has already become historic in the annals of the county. Mr. Slinn brings with him his father — H. J. Slinn, Esq. — and his two sisters. Mr. Slinn, Sr., who has been suffering for many years from complete paralysis, we understand is slowly improving; and it is by the advice of his physicians that he has chosen the invigorating air of the foot-hills as a change to the debilitating heat of Sacramento."

The affair had been quickly settled, certainly, reflected Don Cæsar, with a slight chill of jealousy, as he thought of Mamie's interest in the young editor. But the next moment he dismissed it from his mind; all except a dull consciousness that, if she really loved him — Don Cæsar — as he loved her, she could not have assisted in throwing into his society the two young sisters of the editor, whom she expected might be so attractive.

Within the five minutes the horse was ready, and Don Cæsar in the saddle again. In less than half an hour he was at the wayside boulder. Here he picketed his horse, and took the narrow foot-trail through the hollow. It did not take him long to reach their old trysting-place. With a beating heart he approached the decaying trunk and looked into the cavity. There was no letter there!

A few blackened nuts and some of the dry moss he had put there were lying on the ground at its roots. He could not remember whether they were there when he had last visited the spot. He began to grope in the cavity with both hands. His fingers struck against the sharp angles of a flat paper packet; a thrill of joy ran through them and stopped his beating heart; he drew out the hidden object, and was chilled with disappointment.

It was an ordinary-sized envelope of yellowish-brown paper, bearing, besides the usual government stamp, the official legend of an express company, and showing its age as much by this record of a now obsolete carrying service as by the discoloration of time and atmosphere. Its weight, which was heavier than that of an ordinary letter of the same size and thickness, was evidently due to some loose inclosures, that slightly rustled and could be felt by the fingers, like minute pieces of metal or grains of gravel. It was within Don Cæsar's experience that gold specimens were often sent in that manner. It was in a state of singular preservation, except the address, which, being written in pencil, was scarcely discernible, and even when deciphered appeared to be incoherent and unfinished. The unknown correspondent had written "dear Mary," and then "Mrs. Mary Slinn," with an unintelligible scrawl following for the direction. If Don Cæsar's mind had not been lately preoccupied with the name of the editor, he would hardly have guessed the superscription.

In his cruel disappointment and fully aroused indignation, he at once began to suspect a connection of circumstances which at any other moment he would have thought purely accidental, or perhaps not have considered at all. The cavity in the tree had evidently been used as a secret receptacle for letters before; did Mamie know it at the time, and how did she know it? The apparent age of the letter made it preposterous to suppose that it pointed to any secret correspondence of hers with young Mr. Slinn; and the address was not in her handwriting. Was there any secret previous intimacy between the families? There was but one way in which he could connect this letter with Mamie's faithlessness. It was an infamous, a grotesquely horrible idea, a thought which sprang as much from his inexperience of the world and his habitual suspiciousness of all humor as anything else! It was that the letter was a brutal joke of Slinn's — a joke perhaps concocted by Mamie and himself — a parting insult that should at the last moment proclaim their treachery and his own credulity. Doubtless it contained a declaration of their shame, and the reason why she had fled from him without a word of explanation. And the inclosure, of course, was some significant and degrading illustration. Those Americans were full of those low conceits; it was their national vulgarity.

He held the letter in his angry hand. He could break it open if he wished, and satisfy himself; but it was not addressed to *him*, and the instinct of honor, strong even in his rage, was the instinct of an adversary as well. No; Slinn should open the letter before him. Slinn should explain everything, and answer for it. If it was nothing — a mere accident — it would lead to some general explanation, and perhaps even news of Mamie. But he would arraign Slinn, and at once. He put the letter in his pocket, quickly retraced his steps to his horse, and, putting spurs to the animal, followed the highroad to the gate of Mulrady's pioneer cabin.

He remembered it well enough. To a cultivated taste, it was superior to the more pretentious "new house." During the first year of Mulrady's tenancy, the plain square log-cabin had received those additions and attractions which only a tenant can conceive and actual experience suggest; and in this way the hideous right angles were broken with sheds, "lean-to" extensions, until a certain picturesqueness was given to the irregularity of outline, and a home-like security and companionship to the congregated buildings. It typified the former life of the great capitalist, as the tall new house illustrated the loneliness and isolation that wealth had given him. But the real points of vantage were the years of cultivation and habitation that had warmed and enriched the soil, and evoked the climbing vines and roses that already hid its unpainted boards, rounded its hard outlines, and gave projection and shadow from the pitiless glare of a summer's long sun, or broke the steady beating of the winter rains. It was true that pea and bean poles surrounded it on one side, and the only access to the house was through the cabbage rows that once were the pride and sustenance of the Mulradys. It was this fact, more than any other, that had impelled Mrs. Mulrady to abandon its site ; she did not like to read the history of their humble origin reflected in the faces of their visitors as they entered.

Don Cæsar tied his horse to the fence, and hurriedly approached the house. The door, however, hospitably opened when he was a few paces from it, and when he reached the threshold he found himself unexpectedly in the presence of two pretty girls. They were evidently Slinn's sisters, whom he had neither thought of nor included in the meeting he had prepared. In spite of his preoccupation, he felt himself suddenly embarrassed, not only by the actual distinction of their beauty, but by a kind of likeness that they seemed to bear to Mamie.

"We saw you coming," said the elder unaffectedly. "You are Don Cæsar Alvarado. My brother has spoken of you."

The words recalled Don Cæsar to himself and a sense of courtesy. He was not here to quarrel with these fair strangers at their first meeting ; he must seek Slinn elsewhere, and at another time. The frankness of his reception and the allusion to their brother made it appear impossible that they should be either a party to his disappointment, or even aware of it. His excitement melted away before a certain lazy ease which the consciousness of their beauty seemed to give them. He was able to put a few courteous inquiries, and, thanks to the paragraph in the "Record," to congratulate them upon their father's improvement.

"Oh, pa is a great deal better in his health, and has picked up even in the last few days, so that he is able to walk round with crutches," said the elder sister. "The air here seems to invigorate him wonderfully."

"And you know, Esther," said the younger, "I think

he begins to take more notice of things, especially when he is out of doors. He looks around on the scenery, and his eye brightens, as if he knew all about it; and sometimes he knits his brows, and looks down so, as if he was trying to remember."

"You know, I suppose," explained Esther, "that since his seizure his memory has been a blank — that is, three or four years of his life seem to have been dropped out of his recollection."

"It might be a mercy sometimes, señora," said Don Cæsar, with a grave sigh, as he looked at the delicate features before him, which recalled the face of the absent Mamie.

"That's not very complimentary," said the younger girl laughingly; "for pa did n't recognize us, and only remembered us as little girls."

"Vashti!" interrupted Esther rebukingly; then, turning to Don Cæsar, she added, "My sister, Vashti, means that father remembers more what happened before he came to California, when we were quite young, than he does of the interval that elapsed. Dr. Duchesne says it's a singular case. He thinks that, with his present progress, he will recover the perfect use of his limbs; though his memory may never come back again."

"Unless — You forget what the doctor told us this morning," interrupted Vashti again briskly.

"I was going to say it," said Esther a little curtly. "*Unless* he has another stroke. Then he will either die or recover his mind entirely."

Don Cæsar glanced at the bright faces, a trifle heightened in color by their eager recital and the slight rivalry of narration, and looked grave. He was a little shocked at a certain lack of sympathy and tenderness towards their unhappy parent. They seemed to him not only to have caught that dry, curious toleration of helplessness which characterizes even relationship in its attendance upon chronic suffering and weakness, but to have acquired an unconscious habit of turning it to account. In his present sensitive condition, he even fancied that they flirted mildly over their parent's infirmity.

"My brother Harry has gone to Red Dog," continued Esther; "he'll be right sorry to have missed you. Mrs. Mulrady spoke to him about you; you seem to have been great friends. I s'pose you knew her daughter, Mamie; I hear she is very pretty."

Although Don Cæsar was now satisfied that the Slinns knew nothing of Mamie's singular behavior to him, he felt embarrassed by this conversation. "Miss Mulrady is very pretty," he said, with grave courtesy; "it is a custom of her race. She left suddenly," he added, with affected calmness.

"I reckon she *did* calculate to stay here longer — so her mother said; but the whole thing was settled a week ago. I know my brother was quite surprised to hear from Mr. Mulrady that if we were going to decide about this house we must do it at once; he had an idea himself about moving out of the big one into this when they left."

"Mamie Mulrady had n't much to keep her here, considerin' the money and the good looks she has, I reckon," said Vashti. "She is n't the sort of girl to throw herself away in the wilderness, when she can pick and choose elsewhere. I only wonder she ever come back from Sacramento. They talk about papa Mulrady having *business* at San Francisco, and *that* hurrying them off! Depend upon it that 'business' was Mamie herself. Her wish is gospel to them. If she'd wanted to stay and have a farewell party, old Mulrady's business would have been nowhere."

"Ain't you a little rough on Mamie," said Esther, who had been quietly watching the young man's face with her large, languid eyes, "considering that we don't know her, and have n't even the right of friends to criticise?"

"I don't call it rough," returned Vashti frankly, "for
I'd do the same if I were in her shoes — and they're four-
and-a-halves, for Harry told me so.   Give me her money
and her looks, and you wouldn't catch me hanging round
these diggings — goin' to choir meetings Saturdays, church
Sundays, and buggy-riding once a month — for society!
No — Mamie's head was level — you bet!"

Don Cæsar rose hurriedly.   They would present his
compliments to their father, and he would endeavor to find
their brother at Red Dog.   He, alas! had neither father,
mother, nor sister; but if they would receive his aunt, the
Doña Inez Sepulvida, the next Sunday, when she came from
mass, she should be honored and he would be delighted.   It
required all his self-possession to deliver himself of this
formal courtesy before he could take his leave, and on the
back of his mustang give way to the rage, disgust, and hatred
of everything connected with Mamie that filled his heart.
Conscious of his disturbance, but not entirely appreciating
their own share in it, the two girls somewhat wickedly prolonged the interview by following him into the garden.

"Well, if you *must* leave now," said Esther at last,
languidly, "it ain't much out of your way to go down
through the garden and take a look at pa as you go.   He's
somewhere down there, near the woods, and we don't like
to leave him alone too long.   You might pass the time of
day with him; see if he's right side up.   Vashti and I have
got a heap of things to fix here yet; but if anything's wrong
with him, you can call us.   So long."

Don Cæsar was about to excuse himself hurriedly; but
that sudden and acute perception of all kindred sorrow,
which belongs to refined suffering, checked his speech.
The loneliness of the helpless old man in this atmosphere
of active and youthful selfishness touched him.   He bowed
assent, and turned aside into one of the long perspectives of
bean-poles.   The girls watched him until out of sight.

"Well," said Vashti, "don't tell *me*. But if there was n't something between him and that Mamie Mulrady, I don't know a jilted man when I see him."

"Well, you need n't have let him *see* that you knew it, so that any civility of ours would look as if we were ready to take up with her leavings," responded Esther astutely, as the girls reëntered the house.

Meantime, the unconscious object of their criticism walked sadly down the old market-garden, whose rude outlines and homely details he once clothed with the poetry of a sensitive man's first love. Well, it was a common cabbage field and potato patch after all. In his disgust he felt conscious of even the loss of that sense of patronage and superiority which had invested his affection for a girl of meaner condition. His self-respect was humiliated with his love. The soil and dirt of those wretched cabbages had clung to him, but not to her. It was she who had gone higher; it was he who was left in the vulgar ruins of his misplaced passion.

He reached the bottom of the garden without observing any sign of the lonely invalid. He looked up and down the cabbage rows, and through the long perspective of pea-vines, without result. There was a newer trail leading from a gap in the pines to the wooded hollow, which undoubtedly intersected the little path that he and Mamie had once followed from the highroad. If the old man had taken this trail he had possibly overtasked his strength, and there was the more reason why he should continue his search, and render any assistance if required. There was another idea that occurred to him, which eventually decided him to go on. It was that both these trails led to the decayed sycamore stump, and that the older Slinn might have something to do with the mysterious letter. Quickening his steps through the field, he entered the hollow, and reached the intersecting trail as he expected. To the right it lost itself in the dense woods in the direction of the

ominous stump ; to the left it descended in nearly a straight
line to the highway, now plainly visible, as was equally
the boulder on which he had last discovered Mamie sitting
with young Slinn.   If he was not mistaken, there was a
figure sitting there now ; it was surely a man.   And by
that half-bowed, helpless attitude, the object of his search !

It did not take him long to descend the track to the
highway and approach the stranger.   He was seated with
his hands upon his knee, gazing in a vague, absorbed fashion upon the hillside, now crowned with the engine-house
and chimney that marked the site of Mulrady's shaft.   He
started slightly, and looked up, as Don Cæsar paused before
him.   The young man was surprised to see that the unfortunate man was not as old as he had expected, and that his
expression was one of quiet and beatified contentment.

" Your daughters told me you were here," said Don
Cæsar, with gentle respect.   " I am Cæsar Alvarado, your
not very far neighbor ; very happy to pay his respects to
you as he has to them."

" My daughters ? " said the old man vaguely.   " Oh
yes ! nice little girls.   And my boy Harry.   Did you see
Harry ?   Fine little fellow, Harry."

" I am glad to hear that you are better," said Don
Cæsar hastily, " and that the air of our country does you
no harm.   God benefit you, señor," he added, with a profoundly reverential gesture, dropping unconsciously into
the religious habit of his youth.   " May He protect you,
and bring you back to health and happiness ! "

" Happiness ? " said Slinn amazedly.   " I am happy —
very happy !   I have everything I want : good air, good
food, good clothes, pretty little children, kind friends " —
He smiled benignantly at Don Cæsar.   " God is very good
to me ! "

Indeed, he seemed very happy ; and his face, albeit
crowned with white hair, unmarked by care and any dis-

turbing impression, had so much of satisfied youth in it that the grave features of his questioner made him appear the elder. Nevertheless, Don Cæsar noticed that his eyes, when withdrawn from him, sought the hillside with the same visionary abstraction.

"It is a fine view, Señor Esslinn," said Don Cæsar.

"It is a beautiful view, sir," said Slinn, turning his happy eyes upon him for a moment, only to rest them again on the green slope opposite.

"Beyond that hill which you are looking at — not far, Señor Esslinn — I live. You shall come and see me there — you and your family."

"You — you — live there?" stammered the invalid, with a troubled expression — the first and only change to the complete happiness that had hitherto suffused his face. "You — and your name is — is Ma " —

"Alvarado," said Don Cæsar gently. "Cæsar Alvarado."

"You said Masters," said the old man, with sudden querulousness.

"No, good friend. I said Alvarado," returned Don Cæsar gravely.

"If you did n't say Masters, how could *I* say it? I don't know any Masters."

Don Cæsar was silent. In another moment the happy tranquillity returned to Slinn's face; and Don Cæsar continued : —

"It is not a long walk over the hill, though it is far by the road. When you are better you shall try it. Yonder little trail leads to the top of the hill, and then " —

He stopped, for the invalid's face had again assumed its troubled expression. Partly to change his thoughts, and partly for some inexplicable idea that had suddenly seized him, Don Cæsar continued : —

"There is a strange old stump near the trail, and in it

a hole. In the hole I found this letter." He stopped
again — this time in alarm. Slinn had staggered to his
feet with ashen and distorted features, and was glancing at
the letter which Don Cæsar had drawn from his pocket.
The muscles of his throat swelled as if he was swallowing ;
his lips moved, but no sound issued from them. At last,
with a convulsive effort, he regained a disjointed speech,
in a voice scarcely audible.

"My letter ! my letter ! It 's mine ! Give it me ! It 's
my fortune — all mine ! In the tunnel — hill ! Masters
stole it — stole my fortune ! Stole it all ! See, see ! "

He seized the letter from Don Cæsar with trembling
hands, and tore it open forcibly : a few dull yellow grains
fell from it heavily, like shot, to the ground.

"See, it 's true ! My letter ! My gold ! My strike !
My — my — my God ! "

A tremor passed over his face. The hand that held the
letter suddenly dropped sheer and heavy as the gold had
fallen. The whole side of his face and body nearest Don
Cæsar seemed to drop and sink into itself as suddenly. At
the same moment, and without a word, he slipped through
Don Cæsar's outstretched hands to the ground. Don
Cæsar bent quickly over him, but not longer than to satisfy
himself that he lived and breathed, although helpless. He
then caught up the fallen letter, and, glancing over it with
flashing eyes, thrust it and the few specimens in his pocket.
He then sprang to his feet, so transformed with energy
and intelligence that he seemed to have added the lost
vitality of the man before him to his own. He glanced
quickly up and down the highway. Every moment to him
was precious now ; but he could not leave the stricken
man in the dust of the road ; nor could he carry him to
the house ; nor, having alarmed his daughters, could he
abandon his helplessness to their feeble arms. He remembered that his horse was still tied to the garden fence. He

would fetch it, and carry the unfortunate man across the
saddle to the gate.   He lifted him with difficulty to the
boulder, and ran rapidly up the road in the direction of his
tethered steed.   He had not proceeded far when he heard
the noise of wheels behind him.   It was the up stage coming furiously along.   He would have called to the driver
for assistance, but even through that fast-sweeping cloud of
dust and motion he could see that the man was utterly
oblivious of anything but the speed of his rushing chariot,
and had even risen in his box to lash the infuriated and
frightened animals forward.

An hour later, when the coach drew up at the Red Dog
Hotel, the driver descended from the box, white, but taciturn.   When he had swallowed a glass of whiskey at a
single gulp, he turned to the astonished express agent, who
had followed him in.

"One of two things, Jim, hez got to happen," he said
huskily.   "Either that there rock hez got to get off the
road, or _I_ have.   I 've seed _him_ on it agin!"

CHAPTER IV

No further particulars of the invalid's second attack were known than those furnished by Don Cæsar's brief statement, that he had found him lying insensible on the boulder. This seemed perfectly consistent with the theory of Dr. Duchesne; and as the young Spaniard left Los Gatos the next day, he escaped not only the active report of the "Record," but the perusal of a grateful paragraph in the next day's paper recording his prompt kindness and courtesy. Dr. Duchesne's prognosis, however, seemed at fault; the elder Slinn did not succumb to the second stroke, nor did he recover his reason. He apparently only relapsed into his former physical weakness, losing the little ground he had gained during the last month, and exhibiting no change in his mental condition, unless the fact that he remembered nothing of his seizure and the presence of Don Cæsar could be considered as favorable. Dr. Duchesne's gravity seemed to give that significance to this symptom, and his cross-questioning of the patient was characterized by more than his usual curtness.

"You are sure you don't remember walking in the garden before you were ill?" he said. "Come, think again. You must remember that." The old man's eyes wandered restlessly around the room, but he answered by a negative shake of his head. "And you don't remember sitting down on a stone by the road?"

The old man kept his eyes resolutely fixed on the bedclothes before him. "No!" he said, with a certain sharp decision that was new to him.

The doctor's eye brightened.   "All right, old man ; then don't."

On his way out he took the eldest Miss Slinn aside. " He 'll do," he said grimly : " he 's beginning to lie."

" Why, he only said he did n't remember," responded Esther.

" That was because he did n't want to remember," said the doctor authoritatively.   " The brain is acting on some impression that is either painful and unpleasant, or so vague that he can't formulate it; he is conscious of it, and won't attempt it yet.   It 's a heap better than his old self-satisfied incoherency."

A few days later, when the fact of Slinn's identification with the paralytic of three years ago by the stage-driver became generally known, the doctor came in quite jubilant.

" It 's all plain now," he said decidedly.   " That second stroke was caused by the nervous shock of his coming suddenly upon the very spot where he had the first one.   It proved that his brain still retained old impressions, but as this first act of his memory was a painful one, the strain was too great.   It was mighty unlucky ; but it was a good sign."

" And you think, then " — hesitated Harry Slinn.

" I think," said Dr. Duchesne, " that this activity still exists, and the proof of it, as I said before, is that he is now trying to forget it, and avoid thinking of it.   You will find that he will fight shy of any allusion to it, and will be cunning enough to dodge it every time."

He certainly did.   Whether the doctor's hypothesis was fairly based or not, it was a fact that, when he was first taken out to drive with his watchful physician, he apparently took no notice of the boulder — which still remained on the roadside, thanks to the later practical explanation of the stage-driver's vision — and curtly refused to talk about it.   But, more significant to Duchesne, and perhaps more perplexing, was a certain morose abstraction, which took the place of his former vacuity of contentment, and an intolerance of his attendants, which supplanted his old habitual trustfulness to their care, that had been varied only by the occasional querulousness of an invalid. His daughters sometimes found him regarding them with an attention little short of suspicion, and even his son detected a half-suppressed aversion in his interviews with him.

Referring this among themselves to his unfortunate malady, his children perhaps justified this estrangement by paying very little attention to it. They were more pleasantly occupied. The two girls succeeded to the position held by Mamie Mulrady in the society of the neighborhood, and divided the attentions of Rough-and-Ready. The young editor of the "Record" had really achieved, through his supposed intimacy with the Mulradys, the good fortune he had jestingly prophesied. The disappearance of Don Cæsar was regarded as a virtual abandonment of the field to his rival; and the general opinion was that he was engaged to the millionaire's daughter on a certain probation of work and influence in his prospective father-in-law's interests. He became successful in one or two speculations, the magic of the lucky Mulrady's name befriending him. In the superstition of the mining community, much of this luck was due to his having secured the old cabin.

"To think," remarked one of the augurs of Red Dog, French Pete, a polyglot jester, "that while every d—d fool went to taking up claims where the gold had already been found, no one thought of stepping into the old man's old *choux* in the cabbage garden!" Any doubt, however, of the alliance of the families was dissipated by the intimacy that sprang up between the elder Slinn and the millioniare after the latter's return from San Francisco.

It began in a strange kind of pity for the physical weakness of the man, which enlisted the sympathies of Mulrady, whose great strength had never been deteriorated by the luxuries of wealth, and who was still able to set his work-men an example of hard labor; it was sustained by a sin-gular and superstitious reverence for his mental condition, which, to the paternal Mulrady, seemed to possess that spiritual quality with which popular ignorance invests demented people.

"Then you mean to say that during these three years the vein o' your mind, so to speak, was a lost lead, and sorter dropped out o' sight or follerin'?" queried Mulrady, with infinite seriousness.

"Yes," returned Slinn, with less impatience than he usually showed to questions.

"And durin' that time, when you was dried up and waitin' for rain, I reckon you kinder had visions?"

A cloud passed over Slinn's face.

"Of course, of course!" said Mulrady, a little frightened at his tenacity in questioning the oracle. "Nat'rally, this was private, and not to be talked about. I meant, you had plenty of room for 'em without crowdin'; you kin tell me some day when you're better, and kin sorter select what's points and what ain't."

"Perhaps I may some day," said the invalid gloomily, glancing in the direction of his preoccupied daughters; "when we're alone."

When his physical strength had improved, and his left arm and side had regained a feeble but slowly gathering vitality, Alvin Mulrady one day surprised the family by bringing the convalescent a pile of letters and accounts, and spreading them on a board before Slinn's invalid chair, with the suggestion that he should look over, arrange, and docket them. The idea seemed preposterous, until it was found that the old man was actually able to perform this service, and exhibited a degree of intellectual activity and capacity for this kind of work that was unsuspected. Dr. Duchesne was delighted, and divided with admiration between his patient's progress and the millionaire's sagacity. " And there are envious people," said the enthusiastic doctor, " who believe that a man like him, who could conceive of such a plan for occupying a weak intellect without taxing its memory or judgment, is merely a lucky fool! Look here. Maybe it did n't require much brains to stumble on a gold mine, and it is a gift of Providence. But in my experience, Providence don't go round buyin' up d—d fools, or investin' in dead-beats."

When Mr. Slinn, finally, with the aid of crutches, was able to hobble every day to the imposing counting-house and office of Mr. Mulrady, which now occupied the lower part of the new house, and contained some of its gorgeous furniture, he was installed at a rosewood desk behind Mr. Mulrady's chair, as his confidential clerk and private secretary. The astonishment of Red Dog and Rough-and-Ready at this singular innovation knew no bounds; but the boldness and novelty of the idea carried everything before it. Judge Butts, the oracle of Rough-and-Ready, delivered its decision : " He 's got a man who 's physically incapable of running off with his money, and has no memory to run off with his ideas. How could he do better ? " Even his own son, Harry, coming upon his father thus installed, was for a moment struck with a certain filial respect, and for a day or two patronized him.

In this capacity Slinn became the confidant, not only of Mulrady's business secrets, but of his domestic affairs. He knew that young Mulrady, from a freckle-faced, slow country boy, had developed into a freckle-faced fast city man, with coarse habits of drink and gambling. It was through the old man's hands that extravagant bills and shameful claims passed on their way to be cashed by Mulrady; it was he that at last laid before the father one day his signature perfectly forged by the son.

"Your eyes are not ez good ez mine, you know, Slinn," said Mulrady gravely. "It's all right. I sometimes make my *y*'s like that. I'd clean forgot to cash that check. You must not think you've got the monoply of dis-remembering," he added, with a faint laugh.

Equally through Slinn's hands passed the record of the lavish expenditure of Mrs. Mulrady and the fair Mamie, as well as the chronicle of their movements and fashionable triumphs. As Mulrady had already noticed that Slinn had no confidence with his own family, he did not try to with-hold from him these domestic details, possibly as an offset to the dreary catalogue of his son's misdeeds, but more often in the hope of gaining from the taciturn old man some comment that might satisfy his innocent vanity as father and husband, and perhaps dissipate some doubts that were haunting him.

"Twelve hundred dollars looks to be a good figger for a dress, ain't it? But Malviny knows, I reckon, what ought to be worn at the Tooilleries, and she don't want our Mamie to take a back seat before them furrin princesses and gran' dukes. It's a slap-up affair, I kalkilate. Let's see. I disremember whether it's an emperor or a king that's rulin' over thar now. It must be suthin' first-class and A 1, for Malviny ain't the woman to throw away twelve hundred dollars on any of them small-potato despots! She says Mamie speaks French already like them French Petes. I don't quite make out what she means here. She met Don Cæsar in Paris, and she says, 'I think Mamie is nearly off with Don Cæsar, who has followed her here. I don't care about her dropping him *too* suddenly; the reason I'll tell you hereafter. I think the man might be a dangerous enemy.' Now, what do you make of this? I allus thought Mamie rather cottoned to him, and it was the old woman who fought shy, thinkin' Mamie would do better. Now, I am agreeable that my gal should marry any one she likes, whether it's a dook or a poor man, as long as he's on the square. I was ready to take Don Cæsar; but now things seem to have shifted round. As to Don Cæsar's being a dangerous enemy if Mamie won't have him, that's a little too high and mighty for me, and I wonder the old woman don't make him climb down. What do you think?"

"Who is Don Cæsar?" asked Slinn.

"The man what picked you up that day. I mean," continued Mulrady, seeing the marks of evident ignorance on the old man's face, — "I mean a sort of grave, genteel chap, suthin' between a parson and a circus-rider. You might have seen him round the house talkin' to your gals."

But Slinn's entire forgetfulness of Don Cæsar was evidently unfeigned. Whatever sudden accession of memory he had at the time of his attack, the incident that caused it had no part in his recollection. With the exception of these rare intervals of domestic confidences with his crippled private secretary, Mulrady gave himself up to money-getting. Without any especial faculty for it — an easy prey often to unscrupulous financiers — his unfailing luck, however, carried him safely through, until his very mistakes seemed to be simply insignificant means to a large significant end and a part of his original plan. He sank another shaft, at a great expense, with a view to following the lead he had formerly found, against the opinions of the best mining engineers, and struck the artesian spring he did *not* find at that time, with a volume of water that enabled him not only to work his own mine, but to furnish supplies to his less fortunate neighbors at a vast profit. A league of tangled forest and cañon behind Rough-and-Ready, for which he had paid Don Ramon's heirs an extravagant price in the presumption that it was auriferous, furnished the most accessible timber to build the town, at prices which amply remunerated him. The practical schemes of experienced men, the wildest visions of daring dreams delayed or abortive for want of capital, eventually fell into his hands. Men sneered at his methods, but bought his shares. Some who affected to regard him simply as a man of money were content to get only his name to any enterprise. Courted by his superiors, quoted by his equals, and admired by his inferiors, he bore his elevation equally without ostentation or dignity. Bidden to banquets, and forced by his position as director or president into the usual gastronomic feats of that civilization and period, he partook of simple food, and continued his old habit of taking a cup of coffee with milk and sugar, at dinner. Without professing temperance, he drank sparingly in a community where alcoholic stimulation was a custom. With neither refinement nor an extended vocabulary, he was seldom profane, and never indelicate. With nothing of the Puritan in his manner or conversation, he seemed to be as strange to the vices of civilization as he was to its virtues. That such a man should offer little to and receive little from the companionship of women of any kind was a foregone conclusion. Without the dignity of solitude, he was pathetically alone.

Meantime, the days passed; the first six months of his opulence were drawing to a close, and in that interval he had more than doubled the amount of his discovered fortune. The rainy season set in early. Although it dissipated the clouds of dust under which Nature and Art seemed to be slowly disappearing, it brought little beauty to the landscape at first, and only appeared to lay bare the crudenesses of civilization. The unpainted wooden buildings of Rough-and-Ready, soaked and dripping with rain, took upon themselves a sleek and shining ugliness, as of second-hand garments; the absence of cornices or projections to break the monotony of the long straight lines of down-

pour made the town appear as if it had been recently submerged, every vestige of ornamentation swept away, and
only the bare outlines left.   Mud was everywhere; the
outer soil seemed to have risen and invaded the houses even
to their most secret recesses, as if outraged Nature was trying to revenge herself.   Mud was brought into the saloons and
bar-rooms and express offices on boots, on clothes, on bag-
gage, and sometimes appeared mysteriously in splashes of
red color on the walls, without visible conveyance.   The
dust of six months, closely packed in cornice and carving,
yielded under the steady rain a thin yellow paint, that
dropped on wayfarers or unexpectedly oozed out of ceilings
and walls on the wretched inhabitants within.   The outskirts of Rough-and-Ready and the dried hills round Los
Gatos did not appear to fare much better; the new vegeta-
tion had not yet made much headway against the dead
grasses of the summer; the pines in the hollow wept lugu-
briously into a small rivulet that had sprung suddenly into
life near the old trail; everywhere was the sound of dropping, splashing, gurgling, or rushing waters.

More hideous than ever, the new Mulrady house lifted
itself against the leaden sky, and stared with all its large-
framed, shutterless windows blankly on the prospect, until
they seemed to the wayfarer to become mere mirrors set in
the walls, reflecting only the watery landscape, and unable
to give the least indication of light or heat within.   Nevertheless, there was a fire in Mulrady's private office that
December afternoon, of a smoky, intermittent variety, that
sufficed more to record the defects of hasty architecture
than to comfort the millionaire and his private secretary,
who had lingered after the early withdrawal of the clerks.
For the next day was Christmas, and, out of deference to
the near approach of this festivity, a half holiday had been
given to the employees.   "They'll want, some of them, to
spend their money before to-morrow; and others would

like to be able to rise up comfortably drunk Christmas morning," the superintendent had suggested. Mr. Mulrady had just signed a number of checks indicating his largess to those devoted adherents with the same unostentatious, undemonstrative, matter-of-fact manner that distinguished his ordinary business. The men had received it with something of the same manner. A half-humorous "Thank you, sir " — as if to show that, with their patron, they tolerated this deference to a popular custom, but were a little ashamed of giving way to it — expressed their gratitude and their independence.

"I reckon that the old lady and Mamie are having a high old time in some of them gilded pallises in St. Petersburg or Berlin about this time. Them diamonds that I ordered at Tiffany ought to have reached 'em about now, so that Mamie could cut a swell at Christmas with her warpaint. I suppose it's the style to give presents in furrin countries ez it is here, and I allowed to the old lady that whatever she orders in that way she is to do in Californy style — no dollar-jewelry and galvanized-watches business. If she wants to make a present to any of them nobles ez has been purlite to her, it's got to be something that Rough-and-Ready ain't ashamed of. I showed you that pin Mamie bought me in Paris, did n't I ? It's just come for my Christmas present. No! I reckon I put it in the safe, for them kind o' things don't suit my style: but s'pose I orter sport it to-morrow. It was mighty thoughtful in Mamie, and it must cost a lump ; it's got no slouch of a pearl in it. I wonder what Mamie gave for it ? "

"You can easily tell; the bill is here. You paid it yesterday," said Slinn. There was no satire in the man's voice, nor was there the least perception of irony in Mulrady's manner, as he returned quietly : —

"That's so ; it was suthin' like a thousand francs; but French money, when you pan it out as dollars and cents, don't make so much, after all." There was a few moments' silence, when he continued, in the same tone of voice: "Talkin' o' them things, Slinn, I've got suthin' for you." He stopped suddenly. Ever watchful of any undue excitement in the invalid, he had noticed a slight flush of disturbance pass over his face, and continued carelessly, "But we'll talk it over to-morrow; a day or two don't make much difference to you and me in such things, you know. P'r'aps I'll drop in and see you. We'll be shut up here."

"Then you're going out somewhere?" asked Slinn mechanically.

"No," said Mulrady hesitatingly. It had suddenly occurred to him that he had nowhere to go, if he wanted to, and he continued, half in explanation, "I ain't reckoned much on Christmas myself. Abner's at the Springs; it wouldn't pay him to come here for a day — even if there was anybody here he cared to see. I reckon I'll hang round the shanty, and look after things generally. I haven't been over the house upstairs to put things to rights since the folks left. But *you* needn't come here, you know."

He helped the old man to rise, assisted him in putting on his overcoat, and then handed him the cane which had lately replaced his crutches.

"Good-by, old man! You mustn't trouble yourself to say 'Merry Christmas' now, but wait until you see me again. Take care of yourself."

He slapped him lightly on the shoulder, and went back into his private office. He worked for some time at his desk, and then laid his pen aside, put away his papers methodically, placing a large envelope on his private secretary's vacant table. He then opened the office door and ascended the staircase. He stopped on the first landing to listen to the sound of rain on the glass skylight, that

seemed to echo through the empty hall like the gloomy roll
of a drum.   It was evident that the searching water had
found out the secret sins of the house's construction, for
there were great fissures of discoloration in the white and
gold paper in the corners of the wall.   There was a strange
odor of the dank forest in the mirrored drawing-room, as if
the rain had brought out the sap again from the unseasoned
timbers ; the blue and white satin furniture looked cold,
and the marble mantels and centre-tables had taken upon
themselves the clamminess of tombstones.   Mr. Mulrady,
who had always retained his old farmer-like habit of taking
off his coat with his hat on entering his own house, and
appearing in his shirt-sleeves, to indicate domestic ease and
security, was obliged to replace it, on account of the chill.
He had never felt at home in this room.   Its strangeness
had lately been heightened by Mrs. Mulrady's purchase of
a family portrait of some one she did n't know, but who,
she had alleged, resembled her " Uncle Bob," which hung
on the wall beside some paintings in massive frames.   Mr.
Mulrady cast a hurried glance at the portrait that, on the
strength of a high coat-collar and high top curl, — both
rolled with equal precision and singular sameness of color, —
had always glared at Mulrady as if *he* was the intruder,
and, passing through his wife's gorgeous bedroom, entered
the little dressing-room, where he still slept on the smallest
of cots, with hastily improvised surroundings, as if he was a
bailiff in " possession."   He did n't linger here long, but,
taking a key from a drawer, continued up the staircase, to
the ominous funeral marches of the beating rain on the
skylight, and paused on the landing to glance into his son's
and daughter's bedrooms, duplicates of the bizarre extravagance below.   If he were seeking some characteristic traces
of his absent family, they certainly were not here in the
painted and still damp blazoning of their later successes.
He ascended another staircase, and, passing to the wing of

the house, paused before a small door, which was locked. Already the ostentatious decorations of wall and passages were left behind, and the plain lath-and-plaster partition of the attic lay before him.   He unlocked the door, and threw it open.

CHAPTER V

THE apartment he entered was really only a lumber-room or loft over the wing of the house, which had been left bare and unfinished, and which revealed in its meagre skeleton of beams and joints the hollow sham of the whole structure. But in more violent contrast to the fresher glories of the other part of the house were its contents, which were the heterogeneous collection of old furniture, old luggage, and cast-off clothing, left over from the past life in the old cabin. It was a much plainer record of the simple beginnings of the family than Mrs. Mulrady cared to have remain in evidence, and for that reason it had been relegated to the hidden recesses of the new house, in the hope that it might absorb or digest it. There were old cribs, in which the infant limbs of Mamie and Abner had been tucked up; old looking-glasses, that had reflected their shining, soapy faces, and Mamie's best chip Sunday hat; an old sewing-machine, that had been worn out in active service; old patchwork quilts; an old accordion, to whose long-drawn inspirations Mamie had sung hymns; old pictures, books, and old toys. There were one or two old chromos, and, stuck in an old frame, a colored print from the "Illustrated London News" of a Christmas gathering in an old English country house. He stopped and picked up this print, which he had often seen before, gazing at it with a new and singular interest. He wondered if Mamie had seen anything of this kind in England, and why could n't he have had something like it here, in their own fine house, with themselves and a few friends?

He remembered a past Christmas, when he had bought Mamie that now headless doll with the few coins that were left him after buying their frugal Christmas dinner. There was an old spotted hobby-horse that another Christmas had brought to Abner — Abner, who would be driving a fast trotter to-morrow at the Springs! How everything had changed! How they all had got up in the world, and how far beyond this kind of thing — and yet — yet it would have been rather comfortable to have all been to-gether again here. Would *they* have been more comfort-able? No! Yet then he might have had something to do, and been less lonely to-morrow. What of that? He *had* something to do : to look after this immense fortune. What more could a man want, or should he want? It was rather mean in him, able to give his wife and children everything they wanted, to be wanting anything more. He laid down the print gently, after dusting its glass and frame with his silk handkerchief, and slowly left the room.

The drum-beat of the rain followed him down the stair-case, but he shut it out with his other thoughts, when he again closed the door of his office. He sat diligently to work by the declining winter light, until he was interrupted by the entrance of his Chinese waiter to tell him that supper — which was the meal that Mulrady religiously ad-hered to in place of the late dinner of civilization — was ready in the dining-room. Mulrady mechanically obeyed the summons ; but on entering the room, the oasis of a few plates in a desert of white table-cloth which awaited him made him hesitate. In its best aspect, the high dark Gothic mahogany ecclesiastical sideboard and chairs of this room, which looked like the appointments of a mortuary chapel, were not exhilarating ; and to-day, in the light of the rain-filmed windows and the feeble rays of a lamp half obscured by the dark, shining walls, it was most depress-ing.

" You kin take up supper into my office," said Mulrady, with a sudden inspiration. " I 'll eat it there."

He ate it there, with his usual healthy appetite, which did not require even the stimulation of company. He had just finished, when his Irish cook — the one female servant of the house — came to ask permission to be absent that evening and the next day.

" I suppose the likes of your honor won't be at home on the Christmas Day ? And it 's me cousins from the old counthry at Rough-and-Ready that are invitin' me."

" Why don't you ask them over here ? " said Mulrady, with another vague inspiration. " I 'll stand treat."

" Lord preserve you for a jinerous gintleman ! But it 's the likes of them and myself that would n't be at home here on such a day."

There was so much truth in this that Mulrady checked a sigh as he gave the required permission, without saying that he had intended to remain. He could cook his own breakfast : he had done it before ; and it would be something to occupy him. As to his dinner, perhaps he could go to the hotel at Rough-and-Ready. He worked on until the night had well advanced. Then, overcome with a certain restlessness that disturbed him, he was forced to put his books and papers away. It had begun to blow in fitful gusts, and occasionally the rain was driven softly across the panes like the passing of childish fingers. This disturbed him more than the monotony of silence, for he was not a nervous man. He seldom read a book, and the county paper furnished him only the financial and mercantile news which was part of his business. He knew he could not sleep if he went to bed. At last he rose, opened the window, and looked out from pure idleness of occupation. A splash of wheels in the distant muddy road and fragments of a drunken song showed signs of an early wandering reveler. There were no lights to be seen at the closed works; a profound darkness encompassed the house, as if the distant pines in the hollow·had moved up and round it.   The silence was broken now only by the occasional sighing of wind and rain.   It was not an inviting night for a perfunctory walk; but an idea struck him — he would call upon the Slinns, and anticipate his next day's visit!   They would probably have company, and be glad to see him : he could tell the girls of Mamie and her success.   That he had not thought of this before was a proof of his usual self-contained isolation ; that he thought of it now was an equal proof that he was becoming at last accessible to loneliness.   He was angry with himself for what seemed to him a selfish weakness.

He returned to his office, and, putting the envelope that had been lying on Slinn's desk in his pocket, threw a serape over his shoulders, and locked the front door of the house behind him.   It was well that the way was a familiar one to him, and that his feet instinctively found the trail, for the night was very dark.   At times he was warned only by the gurgling of water of little rivulets that descended the hill and crossed his path.   Without the slightest fear, and with neither imagination nor sensitiveness, he recalled how, the winter before, one of Don Cæsar's vaqueros, crossing this hill at night, had fallen down the chasm of a landslip caused by the rain, and was found the next morning with his neck broken in the gully.   Don Cæsar had to take care of the man's family.   Suppose such an accident should happen to him ?   Well, he had made his will.   His wife and children would be provided for, and the work of the mine would go on all the same ; he had arranged for that. Would anybody miss him ?   Would his wife, or his son, or his daughter ?   No.   He felt such a sudden and overwhelming conviction of the truth of this, that he stopped as suddenly as if the chasm had opened before him.   No ! It was the truth.   If he were to disappear forever in the

darkness of the Christmas night, there was none to feel
his loss. His wife would take care of Mamie; his son
would take care of himself, as he had before — relieved of
even the scant paternal authority he rebelled against. A
more imaginative man than Mulrady would have combated
or have followed out this idea, and then dismissed it; to
the millionaire's matter-of-fact mind it was a deduction
that, having once presented itself to his perception, was
already a recognized fact. For the first time in his life he
felt a sudden instinct of something like aversion towards
his family, a feeling that even his son's dissipation and
criminality had never provoked. He hurried on angrily
through the darkness.

It was very strange; the old house should be almost
before him now, across the hollow, yet there were no indications of light! It was not until he actually reached the
garden-fence, and the black bulk of shadow rose out against
the sky, that he saw a faint ray of light from one of the
lean-to windows. He went to the front door and knocked.
After waiting in vain for a reply, he knocked again. The
second knock proving equally futile, he tried the door; it
was unlocked, and, pushing it open, he walked in. The
narrow passage was quite dark; but from his knowledge of
the house he knew the " lean-to " was next to the kitchen,
and, passing through the dining-room into it, he opened
the door of the little room from which the light proceeded.
It came from a single candle on a small table; and beside it,
with his eyes moodily fixed on the dying embers of the fire,
sat old Slinn. There was no other light nor another human
being in the whole house.

For the instant Mulrady, forgetting his own feelings in
the mute picture of the utter desolation of the helpless
man, remained speechless on the threshold. Then, recalling
himself, he stepped forward and laid his hand gayly on the
bowed shoulders.

"Rouse up out o' this, old man! Come! this won't do. Look! I 've run over here in the rain, jist to have a sociable time with you all."

"I knew it," said the old man, without looking up; "I knew you 'd come."

"You knew I 'd come?" echoed Mulrady, with an uneasy return of the strange feeling of awe with which he regarded Slinn's abstraction.

"Yes; you were alone — like myself — all alone!"

"Then, why in thunder did n't you open the door or sing out just now?" he said, with an affected *brusquerie* to cover his uneasiness. "Where 's your daughters?"

"Gone to Rough-and-Ready to a party."

"And your son?"

"He never comes here when he can amuse himself else-where."

"Your children might have stayed home on Christmas Eve."

"So might yours."

He did n't say this impatiently, but with a certain abstracted conviction far beyond any suggestion of its being a retort. Mulrady did not appear to notice it.

"Well, I don't see why us old folks can't enjoy ourselves without them," said Mulrady, with affected cheerfulness. "Let 's have a good time, you and me. Let 's see — you have n't any one you can send to my house, hev you?"

"They took the servant with them," said Slinn briefly. "There is no one here."

"All right," said the millionaire briskly. "I 'll go myself. Do you think you could manage to light up a little more, and build a fire in the kitchen while I 'm gone? It used to be mighty comfortable in the old times."

He helped the old man to rise from his chair, and seemed to have infused into him some of his own energy. He then added, "Now, don't you get yourself down again into that chair until I come back," and darted out into the night once more.

In a quarter of an hour he returned with a bag on his broad shoulders which one of his porters would have shrunk from lifting, and laid it before the blazing hearth of the now-lighted kitchen. "It's something the old woman got for her party, that did n't come off," he said apologetically. "I reckon we can pick out enough for a spread. That darned Chinaman would n't come with me," he added, with a laugh, "because, he said, he'd knocked off work 'allee same, Mellican man!' Look here, Slinn," he said, with a sudden decisiveness, "my pay-roll of the men around here don't run short of a hundred and fifty dollars a day, and yet I could n't get a hand to help me bring this truck over for my Christmas dinner."

"Of course," said Slinn gloomily.

"Of course; so it oughter be," returned Mulrady shortly. "Why, it's only their one day out of 364; and I can have 363 days off, as I am their boss. I don't mind a man's being independent," he continued, taking off his coat and beginning to unpack his sack — a common "gunny bag" — used for potatoes. "We're independent ourselves, ain't we, Slinn?"

His good spirits, which had been at first labored and affected, had become natural. Slinn, looking at his brightened eye and fresher color, could not help thinking he was more like his own real self at this moment than in his counting-house and offices — with all his simplicity as a capitalist. A less abstracted and more observant critic than Slinn would have seen in this patient aptitude for real work, and the recognition of the force of petty detail, the dominance of the old market-gardener in his former humble, as well as his later more ambitious successes.

"Heaven keep us from being dependent upon our children!" said Slinn darkly.

"Let the young ones alone to-night; we can get along without them, as they can without us," said Mulrady, with a slight twinge as he thought of his reflections on the hill-side. "But look here, there's some champagne and them sweet cordials that women like; there's jellies and such like stuff, about as good as they make 'em, I reckon; and pre-serves, and tongues, and spiced beef — take your pick! Stop, let's spread them out." He dragged the table to the middle of the floor, and piled the provisions upon it. They certainly were not deficient in quality or quantity. "Now, Slinn, wade in."

"I don't feel hungry," said the invalid, who had lapsed again into a chair before the fire.

"No more do I," said Mulrady; "but I reckon it's the right thing to do about this time. Some folks think they can't be happy without they're getting outside o' suthin', and my directors down at 'Frisco can't do any business without a dinner. Take some champagne, to begin with."

He opened a bottle, and filled two tumblers. "It's past twelve o'clock, old man, so here's a Merry Christmas to you, and both of us ez is here. And here's another to our families — ez is n't."

They both drank their wine stolidly. The rain beat against the windows sharply, but without the hollow echoes of the house on the hill. "I must write to the old woman and Mamie, and say that you and me had a high old time on Christmas Eve."

"By ourselves," added the invalid.

Mr. Mulrady coughed. "Nat'rally — by ourselves. And her provisions," he added, with a laugh. "We're really beholden to *her* for 'em. If she had n't thought of having them" —

"For somebody else, you would n't have had them — would you?" said Slinn slowly, gazing at the fire.

"No," said Mulrady dubiously. After a pause he began

more vivaciously, and as if to shake off some disagreeable thought that was impressing him. "But I must n't forget to give you *your* Christmas, old man, and I 've got it right here with me." He took the folded envelope from his pocket, and, holding it in his hand with his elbow on the table, continued : "I don't mind telling you what idea I had in giving you what I 'm goin' to give you now. I 've been thinking about it for a day or two. A man like you don't want money — you would n't spend it. A man like you don't want stocks or fancy investments, for you could n't look after them. A man like you don't want diamonds and jewellery, nor a gold-headed cane, when it 's got to be used as a crutch. No, sir. What you want is suthin' that won't run away from you ; that is always there before you and won't wear out, and will last after you 're gone. That 's land ! And if it was n't that I have sworn never to sell or give away this house and that garden, if it was n't that I 've held out agin the old woman and Mamie on that point, you should have *this* house and *that* garden. But, mebbe, for the same reason that I 've told you, I want that land to keep for myself. But I 've selected four acres of the hill this side of my shaft, and here 's the deed of it. As soon as you 're ready, I 'll put you up a house as big as this — that shall be yours, with the land, as long as you live, old man ; and after that your children's."

"No ; not theirs ! " broke in the old man passionately. "Never ! "

Mulrady recoiled for an instant in alarm at the sudden and unexpected vehemence of his manner. "Go slow, old man ; go slow," he said soothingly. "Of course, you 'll do with your own as you like." Then, as if changing the subject, he went on cheerfully : "Perhaps you 'll wonder why I picked out that spot on the hillside. Well, first, because I reserved it after my strike in case the lead should run that way, but it did n't. Next, because when you first came here you seemed to like the prospect. You used to sit there looking at it, as if it reminded you of something. You never said it did. They say you was sitting on that boulder there when you had that last attack, you know; but," he added gently, "you've forgotten all about it."

"I have forgotten nothing," said Slinn, rising, with a choking voice. "I wish to God I had; I wish to God I could!"

He was on his feet now, supporting himself by the table. The subtle generous liquor he had drunk had evidently shaken his self-control, and burst those voluntary bonds he had put upon himself for the last six months; the insidious stimulant had also put a strange vigor into his blood and nerves. His face was flushed, but not distorted; his eyes were brilliant, but not fixed; he looked as he might have looked to Masters in his strength three years before on that very hillside.

"Listen to me, Alvin Mulrady," he said, leaning over him with burning eyes. "Listen, while I have brain to think and strength to utter, why I have learnt to distrust, fear, and hate them! You think you know my story. Well, hear the truth from *me* to-night, Alvin Mulrady, and do not wonder if I have cause."

He stopped, and, with pathetic inefficiency, passed the fingers and inward-turned thumb of his paralyzed hand across his mouth, as if to calm himself. "Three years ago I was a miner, but not a miner like you! I had experience, I had scientific knowledge, I had a theory, and the patience and energy to carry it out. I selected a spot that had all the indications, made a tunnel, and, without aid, counsel, or assistance of any kind, worked it for six months, without rest or cessation, and with scarcely food enough to sustain my body. Well, I made a strike; not like you, Mulrady, not a blunder of good luck, a fool's fortune — there, I don't blame you for it — but in perfect demonstration of my theory, the reward of my labor. It was no pocket, but a vein, a lead, that I had regularly hunted down and found — a fortune !

"I never knew how hard I had worked until that morning ; I never knew what privations I had undergone until that moment of my success, when I found I could scarcely think or move ! I staggered out into the open air. The only human soul near me was a disappointed prospector, a man named Masters, who had a tunnel not far away. I managed to conceal from him my good fortune and my feeble state, for I was suspicious of him — of any one ; and as he was going away that day I thought I could keep my secret until he was gone. I was dizzy and confused, but I remember that I managed to write a letter to my wife, telling her of my good fortune, and begging her to come to me ; and I remember that I saw Masters go. I don't remember anything else. They picked me up on the road, near that boulder, as you know."

"I know," said Mulrady, with a swift recollection of the stage-driver's account of his discovery.

"They say," continued Slinn tremblingly, " that I never recovered my senses or consciousness for nearly three years ; they *say* I lost my memory completely during my illness, and that by God's mercy, while I lay in that hospital, I knew no more than a babe ; they say, because I could not speak or move, and only had my food as nature required it, that I was an imbecile, and that I never really came to my senses until after my son found me in the hospital. They *say* that — but I tell you to-night, Alvin Mulrady," he said, raising his voice to a hoarse outcry, "I tell you that it is a lie ! I came to my senses a week after I lay on that hospital cot ; I kept my senses and memory ever after during the three years that I was there, until Harry brought his cold, hypocritical face to my bedside and recognized me. Do you understand ? I, the possessor of millions, lay there a pauper ! Deserted by wife and children — a spectacle for the curious, a sport for the doctors — *and I knew it !* I heard them speculate on the cause of my helplessness. I heard them talk of excesses and indulgences — I, that never knew wine or woman ! I heard a preacher speak of the finger of God, and point to me. May God curse him ! ”

“ Go slow, old man ; go slow,” said Mulrady gently.

“ I heard them speak of me as a friendless man, an outcast, a criminal, — a being whom no one would claim. They were right ; no one claimed me. The friends of others visited them ; relations came and took away their kindred ; a few lucky ones got well ; a few, equally lucky, died ! I alone lived on, uncared for, deserted.

“ The first year,” he went on more rapidly, “ I prayed for their coming. I looked for them every day. I never lost hope. I said to myself, ‘ She has not got my letter ; but when the time passes she will be alarmed by my silence, and then she will come or send some one to seek me.’ A young student got interested in my case, and, by studying my eyes, thought that I was not entirely imbecile and unconscious. With the aid of an alphabet, he got me to spell my name and town in Illinois, and promised by signs to write to my family. But in an evil moment I told him of my cursed fortune, and in that moment I saw that he thought me a fool and an idiot. He went away, and I saw him no more. Yet I still hoped. I dreamed of their joy at finding me, and the reward that my wealth would give them. Perhaps I was a little weak still, perhaps a little flighty, too, at times ; but I was quite happy that year, even in my disappointment, for I still had hope ! ”

He paused, and again composed his face with his paralyzed hand ; but his manner had become less excited, and his voice was stronger.

“ A change must have come over me the second year, for

I only dreaded their coming now and finding me so altered. A horrible idea that they might, like the student, believe me crazy if I spoke of my fortune made me pray to God that they might not reach me until after I had regained my health and strength — and found my fortune. When the third year found me still there — I no longer prayed for them — I cursed them! I swore to myself that they should never enjoy my wealth ; but I wanted to live, and let them know I had it. I found myself getting stronger ; but as I had no money, no friends, and nowhere to go, I concealed my real condition from the doctors, except to give them my name, and to try to get some little work to do to enable me to leave the hospital and seek my lost treasure. One day I found out by accident that it had been discovered ! You understand — my treasure ! — that had cost me years of labor and my reason ; had left me a helpless, forgotten pauper. That gold I had never enjoyed had been found and taken possession of by another ! "

He checked an exclamation from Mulrady with his hand. "They say they picked me up senseless from the floor, where I must have fallen when I heard the news — I don't remember — I recall nothing until I was confronted, nearly three weeks after, by my son, who had called at the hospital, as a reporter for a paper, and had accidentally discovered me through my name and appearance. He thought me crazy, or a fool. I did n't undeceive him. I did not tell him the story of the mine to excite his doubts and derision, or, worse (if I could bring proof to claim it), have it perhaps pass into his ungrateful hands. No ; I said nothing. I let him bring me here. He could do no less, and common decency obliged him to do that."

" And what proof could you show of your claim ? " asked Mulrady gravely.

"If I had that letter — if I could find Masters," began Slinn vaguely.

" Have you any idea where the letter is, or what has become of Masters ? " continued Mulrady, with a matter-of-fact gravity that seemed to increase Slinn's vagueness and excite his irritability.

" I don't know — I sometimes think " — He stopped, sat down again, and passed his hands across his forehead. " I have seen the letter somewhere since. Yes," he went on with sudden vehemence, " I know it, I have seen it ! I " — His brows knitted, his features began to work convulsively ; he suddenly brought his paralyzed hand down, partly opened, upon the table. " I *will* remember where."

" Go slow, old man ; go slow."

" You asked me once about my visions. Well, that is one of them. I remember a man somewhere showing me that letter. I have taken it from his hands and opened it, and knew it was mine by the specimens of gold that were in it. But where — or when — or what became of it, I cannot tell. It will come to me — it *must* come to me soon."

He turned his eyes upon Mulrady, who was regarding him with an expression of grave curiosity, and said bitterly, " You think me crazy. I know it. It needed only this."

" Where is this mine ? " asked Mulrady, without heeding him.

The old man's eyes swiftly sought the ground.

" It is a secret, then ? "

" No."

" You have spoken of it to any one ? "

" No."

" Not to the man who possesses it ? "

" No."

" Why ? "

" Because I would n't take it from him."

" Why would n't you ? "

" Because that man is yourself ! "

In the instant of complete silence that followed they could hear that the monotonous patter of rain on the roof had ceased.

" Then all this was in *my* shaft, and the vein I thought I struck there was *your* lead, found three years ago in *your* tunnel. Is that your idea ? "

" Yes."

" Then I don't sabe why you don't want to claim it."

" I have told you why I don't want it for my children. I go further, now, and I tell you, Alvin Mulrady, that I was willing that your children should squander it, as they were doing. It has only been a curse to me; it could only be a curse to them ; but I thought you were happy in seeing it feed selfishness and vanity. You think me bitter and hard. Well, I should have left you in your fool's paradise, but that I saw to-night, when you came here, that your eyes had been opened like mine. You, the possessor of my wealth, my treasure, could not buy your children's loving care and company with your millions, any more than I could keep mine in my poverty. You were to-night lonely and forsaken, as I was. We were equal, for the first time in our lives. If that cursed gold had dropped down the shaft between us into the hell from which it sprang, we might have clasped hands like brothers across the chasm."

Mulrady, who in a friendly show of being at his ease had not yet resumed his coat, rose in his shirt-sleeves, and, standing before the hearth, straightened his square figure by drawing down his waistcoat on each side with two powerful thumbs. After a moment's contemplative survey of the floor between him and the speaker, he raised his eyes to Slinn. They were small and colorless; the forehead above them was low, and crowned with a shock of tawny reddish hair ; even the rude strength of his lower features was enfeebled by a long, straggling, goat-like

Go slow, old man ; go slow

beard ; but for the first time in his life the whole face was impressed and transformed with a strong and simple dignity.

"Ez far ez I kin see, Slinn," he said gravely, " the pint between you and me ain't to be settled by our children, or wot we allow is doo and right from them to us. Afore we preach at them for playing in the slumgullion, and gettin' themselves splashed, perhaps we mout ez well remember that that thar slumgullion comes from our own sluice-boxes, where we wash our gold. So we 'll just put *them* behind us, so," he continued, with a backward sweep of his powerful hand towards the chimney, "and goes on. The next thing that crops up ahead of us is your three years in the hospital, and wot you went through at that time.   I ain't sayin' it was n't rough on you, and that you did n't have it about as big as it 's made ; but ez you 'll allow that you 'd hev had that for three years, whether I 'd found your mine or whether I had n't, I think we can put *that* behind us, too.   There 's nothin' now left to prospect but your story of your strike. Well, take your own proofs.   Masters is not here ; and if he was, accordin' to your own story, he knows nothin' of your strike that day, and could only prove you were a disappointed prospector in a tunnel ; your letter — that the person you wrote to never got — *you* can't produce ; and if you did, would be only your own story without proof ! There is not a business man ez would look at your claim ; there is n't a friend of yours that would n't believe you were crazy, and dreamed it all ; there is n't a rival of yours ez would n't say ez you 'd invented it. Slinn, I 'm a business man — I am your friend — I am your rival — but I don't think you 're lyin' — I don't think you 're crazy — and I 'm not sure your claim ain't a good one !

"Ef you reckon from that that I 'm goin' to hand you **over the mine to-morrow**," he went on, after a pause, raising his hand with a deprecating gesture, " you 're mistaken. For your own sake, and the sake of my wife and children, you 've got to prove it more clearly than you hev; but I promise you that from this night forward I will spare neither time nor money to help you to do it. I have more than doubled the amount that you would have had, had you taken the mine the day you came from the hospital. When you prove to me that your story is true — and we will find some way to prove it, if it *is* true — that amount will be yours at once, without the need of a word from law or law-yers. If you want my name to that in black and white, come to the office to-morrow, and you shall have it."

" And you think I 'll take it now ? " said the old man passionately. " Do you think that your charity will bring back my dead wife, the three years of my lost life, the love and respect of my children ? Or do you think that your own wife and children, who deserted you in your wealth, will come back to you in your poverty ? No ! Let the mine stay, with its curse, where it is — I 'll have none of it ! "

"Go slow, old man; go slow," said Mulrady quietly, putting on his coat. " You will take the mine if it is yours; if it is n't I 'll keep it. If it is yours, you will give your children a chance to show what they can do for you in your sudden prosperity, as I shall give mine a chance to show how they can stand reverse and disappointment. If my head is level — and I reckon it is — they 'll both pan out all right."

He turned and opened the door. With a quick revulsion of feeling, Slinn suddenly seized Mulrady's hand between both of his own, and raised it to his lips. Mulrady smiled, disengaged his hand gently, and saying soothingly, " Go slow, old man ; go slow," closed the door behind him, and passed out into the clear Christmas dawn.

For the stars, with the exception of one that seemed to sparkle brightly over the shaft of his former fortunes, were slowly paling.   A burden seemed to have fallen from his square shoulders as he stepped out sturdily into the morning air.   He had already forgotten the lonely man behind him, for he was thinking only of his wife and daughter.   And at the same moment they were thinking of him ; and in their elaborate villa overlooking the blue Mediterranean at Cannes were discussing, in the event of Mamie's marriage with Prince Rosso e Negro, the possibility of Mr. Mulrady's paying two hundred and fifty thousand dollars, the gambling debts of that unfortunate but deeply conscientious nobleman.

CHAPTER VI

WHEN Alvin Mulrady reëntered his own house, he no longer noticed its loneliness. Whether the events of the last few hours had driven it from his mind, or whether his late reflections had repeopled it with his family under pleasanter auspices, it would be difficult to determine. Destitute as he was of imagination, and matter-of-fact in his judgments, he realized his new situation as calmly as he would have considered any business proposition. While he was decided to act upon his moral convictions purely, he was prepared to submit the facts of Slinn's claim to the usual patient and laborious investigation of his practical mind. It was the least he could do to justify the ready and almost superstitious assent he had given to Slinn's story.

When he had made a few memoranda at his desk by the growing light, he again took the key of the attic, and ascended to the loft that held the tangible memories of his past life. If he was still under the influence of his reflections, it was with very different sensations that he now regarded them. Was it possible that these ashes might be warmed again, and these scattered embers rekindled? His practical sense said No! whatever his wish might have been. A sudden chill came over him ; he began to realize the terrible change that was probable, more by the impossibility of his accepting the old order of things than by his voluntarily abandoning the new. His wife and children would never submit. They would go away from this place, far away, where no reminiscence of either former wealth or

former poverty could obtrude itself upon them. Mamie —
his Mamie — should never go back to the cabin, since
desecrated by Slinn's daughters, and take their places. No!
Why should she? — because of the half-sick, half-crazy
dreams of an old vindictive man?

He stopped suddenly. In moodily turning over a heap
of mining clothing, blankets, and india-rubber boots, he had
come upon an old pickaxe — the one he had found in the
shaft; the one he had carefully preserved for a year, and
then forgotten! Why had he not remembered it before?
He was frightened, not only at this sudden resurrection of
the proof he was seeking, but at his own fateful forgetfulness. Why had he never thought of this when Slinn was
speaking? A sense of shame, as if he had voluntarily withheld it from the wronged man, swept over him. He was
turning away, when he was again startled.

This time it was by a voice from below — a voice calling
him — Slinn's voice. How had the crippled man got here
so soon, and what did he want? He hurriedly laid aside
the pick, which, in his first impulse, he had taken to the
door of the loft with him, and descended the stairs. The
old man was standing at the door of his office awaiting him.

As Mulrady approached, he trembled violently, and clung
to the door-post for support.

"I had to come over, Mulrady," he said in a choked
voice; "I could stand it there no longer. I 've come to
beg you to forget all that I have said; to drive all thought
of what passed between us last night out of your head and
mine forever! I 've come to ask you to swear with me
that neither of us will ever speak of this again forever. It
is not worth the happiness I have had in your friendship
for the last half-year; it is not worth the agony I have
suffered in its loss in the last half-hour."

Mulrady grasped his outstretched hand. "P'r'aps," he
said gravely, "there may n't be any use for another word,

if you can answer one now.   Come with me.   No matter,"
he added, as Slinn moved with difficulty ; " I will help
you."

He half supported, half lifted the paralyzed man up the
three flights of stairs, and opened the door of the loft.
The pick was leaning against the wall, where he had left it.
" Look around, and see if you recognize anything."

The old man's eyes fell upon the implement in a half-
frightened way, and then lifted themselves interrogatively
to Mulrady's face.

" Do you know that pick ? "

Slinn raised it in his trembling hands.   " I think I do ;
and yet " —

" Slinn ! is it yours ? "

" No," he said hurriedly.

" Then what makes you think you know it ? "

" It has a short handle like one I have seen."

" And it is n't yours ? "

" No.   The handle of mine was broken and spliced.   I
was too poor to buy a new one."

" Then you say that this pick which I found in my shaft
is not yours ? "

" Yes."

" Slinn ! "

The old man passed his hand across his forehead, looked
at Mulrady, and dropped his eyes.   " It is not mine," he
said simply.

" That will do," said Mulrady gravely.

" And you will not speak of this again ? " said the old
man timidly.

" I promise you — not until I have some more evidence."

He kept his word, but not before he had extorted from
Slinn as full a description of Masters as his imperfect
memory and still more imperfect knowledge of his former

neighbor could furnish. He placed this, with a large sum of money and the promise of a still larger reward, in the hands of a trustworthy agent. When this was done he resumed his old relations with Slinn, with the exception that the domestic letters of Mrs. Mulrady and Mamie were no longer a subject of comment, and their bills no longer passed through his private secretary's hands.

Three months passed; the rainy season had ceased, the hillsides around Mulrady's shaft were bridal-like with flowers; indeed, there were rumors of an approaching fashionable marriage in the air, and vague hints in the " Record " that the presence of a distinguished capitalist might soon be required abroad. The face of that distinguished man did not, however, reflect the gayety of nature nor the anticipation of happiness ; on the contrary, for the past few weeks, he had appeared disturbed and anxious, and that rude tranquillity which had characterized him was wanting. People shook their heads ; a few suggested speculations ; all agreed on extravagance.

One morning, after office hours, Slinn, who had been watching the careworn face of his employer, suddenly rose and limped to his side.

" We promised each other," he said in a voice trembling with emotion, " never to allude to our talk of Christmas Eve again unless we had other proofs of what I told you then. We have none ; I don't believe we 'll ever have any more. I don't care if we never do, and I break that promise now because I cannot bear to see you unhappy and know that this is the cause."

Mulrady made a motion of deprecation, but the old man continued : —

" You are unhappy, Alvin Mulrady. You are unhappy, because you want to give your daughter a dowry of two hundred and fifty thousand dollars, and you will not use the fortune that you think may be mine."

"Who's been talking about a dowry?" asked Mulrady, with an angry flush.

"Don Cæsar Alvarado told my daughter."

"Then that is why he has thrown off on me since he returned," said Mulrady, with sudden small malevolence, "just that he might unload his gossip because Mamie would n't have him. The old woman was right in warnin' me agin him."

The outburst was so unlike him, and so dwarfed his large though common nature with its littleness, that it was easy to detect its feminine origin, although it filled Slinn with vague alarm.

"Never mind him," said the old man hastily; "what I wanted to say now is that I abandon everything to you and yours. There are no proofs; there never will be any more than what we know, than what we have tested and found wanting. I swear to you that, except to show you that I have not lied and am not crazy, I would destroy them on their way to your hands. Keep the money, and spend it as you will. Make your daughter happy, and, through her, yourself. You have made me happy through your liberality; don't make me suffer through your privation."

"I tell you what, old man," said Mulrady, rising to his feet, with an awkward mingling of frankness and shame in his manner and accent, "I should like to pay that money for Mamie, and let her be a princess, if it would make her happy. I should like to shut the lantern jaws of that Don Cæsar, who 'd be too glad if anything happened to break off Mamie's match. But I should n't touch that capital — unless you 'd lend it to me. If you 'll take a note from me, payable if the property ever becomes yours, I 'd thank you. A mortgage on the old house and garden, and the lands I bought of Don Cæsar, outside the mine, will screen you."

"If that pleases you," said the old man, with a smile

"have your way; and if I tear up the note, it does not concern you."

It did please the distinguished capitalist of Rough-and-Ready; for the next few days his face wore a brightened expression, and he seemed to have recovered his old tranquillity. There was, in fact, a slight touch of consequence in his manner, the first ostentation he had ever indulged in, when he was informed one morning at his private office that Don Cæsar Alvarado was in the counting-house, desiring a few moments' conference. "Tell him to come in," said Mulrady shortly. The door opened upon Don Cæsar — erect, sallow, and grave. Mulrady had not seen him since his return from Europe, and even his inexperienced eyes were struck with the undeniable ease and grace with which the young Spanish-American had assimilated the style and fashion of an older civilization. It seemed rather as if he had returned to a familiar condition than adopted a new one.

"Take a cheer," said Mulrady.

The young man looked at Slinn with quietly persistent significance.

"You can talk all the same," said Mulrady, accepting the significance. "He's my private secretary."

"It seems that for that reason we might choose another moment for our conversation," returned Don Cæsar haughtily. "Do I understand you cannot see me now?"

Mulrady hesitated. He had always revered and recognized a certain social superiority in Don Ramon Alvarado; somehow his son — a young man of half his age, and once a possible son-in-law — appeared to claim that recognition also. He rose, without a word, and preceded Don Cæsar upstairs into his drawing-room. The alien portrait on the wall seemed to evidently take sides with Don Cæsar, as against the common intruder, Mulrady.

"I hoped the Señora Mulrady might have saved me this

interview," said the young man stiffly ; " or at least have
given you some intimation of the reason why I seek it.   As
you just now proposed my talking to you in the presence
of the unfortunate Señor Esslinn himself, it appears she has
not."

" I don't know what you're driving at, or what Mrs.
Mulrady 's got to do with Slinn or you," said Mulrady in
angry uneasiness.

" Do I understand," said Don Cæsar sternly, " that
Señora Mulrady has not told you that I entrusted to her an
important letter, belonging to Señor Esslinn, which I had
the honor to discover in the wood six months ago, and which
she said she would refer to you ? "

" Letter ? " echoed Mulrady slowly ; " my wife had a
letter of Slinn's ? "

Don Cæsar regarded the millionaire attentively.   " It is
as I feared," he said gravely.   " You do not know, or you
would not have remained silent."   He then briefly recounted
the story of his finding Slinn's letter, his exhibition of it to
the invalid, its disastrous effect upon him, and his innocent
discovery of the contents.   " I believed myself at that time
on the eve of being allied with your family, Señor Mulrady," he said haughtily ; " and when I found myself in
possession of a secret which affected its integrity and good
name, I did not choose to leave it in the helpless hands of
its imbecile owner, or his sillier children, but proposed to
trust it to the care of the señora, that she and you might
deal with it as became your honor and mine.   I followed
her to Paris, and gave her the letter there.   She affected to
laugh at any pretension of the writer, or any claim he might
have on your bounty; but she kept the letter, and, I fear,
destroyed it.   You will understand, Señor Mulrady, that
when I found that my attentions were no longer agreeable to
your daughter, I had no longer the right to speak to you on
the subject, nor could I, without misapprehension, force her

to return it.   I should have still kept the secret to myself, if I had not since my return here made the nearer acquaintance of Señor Esslinn's daughters.   I cannot present myself at his house as a suitor for the hand of the Señorita Vashti, until I have asked his absolution for my complicity in the wrong that has been done to him.   I cannot, as a caballero, do that without your permission.   It is for that purpose I am here."

It needed only this last blow to complete the humiliation that whitened Mulrady's face.   But his eye was none the less clear and his voice none the less steady as he turned to Don Cæsar.

"You know perfectly the contents of that letter ? "

"I have kept a copy of it."

"Come with me."

He preceded his visitor down the staircase and back into his private office.   Slinn looked up at his employer's face in unrestrained anxiety.   Mulrady sat down at his desk, wrote a few hurried lines, and rang a bell.   A manager appeared from the counting-room.

"Send that to the bank."

He wiped his pen as methodically as if he had not at that moment countermanded the order to pay his daughter's dowry, and turned quietly to Slinn.

"Don Cæsar Alvarado has found the letter you wrote your wife on the day you made your strike in the tunnel that is now my shaft.   He gave the letter to Mrs. Mulrady ; but he has kept a copy."

Unheeding the frightened gesture of entreaty from Slinn, equally with the unfeigned astonishment of Don Cæsar, who was entirely unprepared for this revelation of Mulrady's and Slinn's confidences, he continued : "He has brought the copy with him.   I reckon it would be only square for you to compare it with what you remember of the original."

In obedience to a gesture from Mulrady, Don Cæsar mechanically took from his pocket a folded paper, and handed it to the paralytic. But Slinn's trembling fingers could scarcely unfold the paper; and as his eyes fell upon its contents, his convulsive lips could not articulate a word.

"P'r'aps I'd better read it for you," said Mulrady gently. "You kin follow me and stop me when I go wrong."

He took the paper, and, in a dead silence, read as follows: —

"DEAR WIFE, — I've just struck gold in my tunnel, and you must get ready to come here with the children, at once. It was after six months' hard work; and I'm so weak I . . . It's a fortune for us all. We should be rich even if it were only a branch vein dipping west towards the next tunnel, instead of dipping east, according to my theory" —

"Stop!" said Slinn in a voice that shook the room.

Mulrady looked up.

"It's wrong, ain't it?" he asked anxiously; "it should be *east* towards the next tunnel."

"No! *It's right! I* am wrong! We're all wrong!"

Slinn had risen to his feet, erect and inspired. "Don't you see," he almost screamed, with passionate vehemence, "it's *Masters's abandoned tunnel* your shaft has struck? Not mine! It was Masters's pick you found! I know it now!"

"And your own tunnel?" said Mulrady, springing to his feet in his excitement. "And *your* strike?"

"Is still there!"

The next instant, and before another question could be asked, Slinn had darted from the room. In the exaltation of that supreme discovery he regained the full control of his mind and body. Mulrady and Don Cæsar, no less excited, followed him precipitately, and with difficulty kept up with his feverish speed. Their way lay along the base of the hill below Mulrady's shaft, and on a line with Masters's abandoned tunnel. Only once he stopped to snatch a pick from the hand of an astonished Chinaman at work in a ditch, as he still kept on his way, a quarter of a mile beyond the shaft. Here he stopped before a jagged hole in the hillside. Bared to the sky and air, the very openness of its abandonment, its unpropitious position, and distance from the strike in Mulrady's shaft had no doubt preserved its integrity from wayfarer or prospector.

"You can't go in there alone, and without a light," said Mulrady, laying his hand on the arm of the excited man. "Let me get more help and proper tools."

"I know every step in the dark as in the daylight," returned Slinn, struggling. "Let me go, while I have yet strength and reason! Stand aside!"

He broke from them, and the next moment was swallowed up in the yawning blackness. They waited with bated breath until, after a seeming eternity of night and silence, they heard his returning footsteps, and ran forward to meet him. As he was carrying something clasped to his breast, they supported him to the opening. But at the same moment the object of his search, and his burden, a misshapen wedge of gold and quartz, dropped with him, and both fell together with equal immobility to the ground. He had still strength to turn his fading eyes to the other millionaire of Rough-and-Ready, who leaned over him.

"You — see," he gasped brokenly, "I was not — crazy!"

No. He was dead!

A DRIFT FROM REDWOOD CAMP

THEY had all known him as a shiftless, worthless crea
ture. From the time he first entered Redwood Camp, carrying his entire effects in a red handkerchief on the end of
a long-handled shovel, until he lazily drifted out of it on a
plank in the terrible inundation of '56, they never expected
anything better of him. In a community of strong men
with sullen virtues and charmingly fascinating vices, he was
tolerated as possessing neither — not even rising by any
dominant human weakness or ludicrous quality to the importance of a butt. In the *dramatis personæ* of Redwood
Camp he was a simple "super" — who had only passive,
speechless rôles in those fierce dramas that were sometimes
unrolled beneath its green-curtained pines. Nameless and
penniless, he was overlooked by the census and ignored by
the tax-collector, while in a hotly contested election for
sheriff, when even the headboards of the scant cemetery
were consulted to fill the poll-lists, it was discovered that
neither candidate had thought fit to avail himself of his
actual vote. He was debarred the rude heraldry of a nick-
name of achievement, and in a camp made up of "Euchre
Bills," "Poker Dicks," "Profane Pete," and "Snap-shot
Harry," was known vaguely as "him," "Skeesicks," or
"that coot." It was remembered long after, with a feeling
of superstition, that he had never even met with the dignity of an accident, nor received the fleeting honor of a
chance shot meant for somebody else in any of the liberal
and broadly comprehensive encounters which distinguished
the camp. And the inundation that finally carried him

out of it was partly anticipated by his passive incompetency; for while the others escaped — or were drowned in escaping — he calmly floated off on his plank without an opposing effort.

For all that, Elijah Martin — which was his real name — was far from being unamiable or repellent. That he was cowardly, untruthful, selfish, and lazy, was undoubtedly the fact; perhaps it was his peculiar misfortune that, just then, courage, frankness, generosity, and activity were the dominant factors in the life of Redwood Camp. His submissive gentleness, his unquestioned modesty, his half refinement, and his amiable exterior consequently availed him nothing against the fact that he was missed during a raid of the Digger Indians, and lied to account for it; or that he lost his right to a gold discovery by failing to make it good against a bully, and selfishly kept this discovery from the knowledge of the camp. Yet this weakness awakened no animosity in his companions, and it is probable that the indifference of the camp to his fate in this final catastrophe came purely from a simple forgetfulness of one who at that supreme moment was weakly incapable.

Such was the reputation and such the antecedents of the man who, on the 15th of March, 1856, found himself adrift in a swollen tributary of the Minyo. A spring freshet of unusual volume had flooded the adjacent river until, bursting its bounds, it escaped through the narrow, wedge-shaped valley that held Redwood Camp. For a day and a night the surcharged river poured half its waters through the straggling camp. At the end of that time every vestige of the little settlement was swept away; all that was left was scattered far and wide in the country, caught in the hanging branches of water-side willows and alders, embayed in sluggish pools, dragged over submerged meadows, and one fragment — bearing up Elijah Martin —

pursuing the devious courses of an unknown tributary fifty
miles away. Had he been a rash, impatient man, he would
have been speedily drowned in some earlier desperate attempt to reach the shore ; had he been an ordinarily bold
man, he would have succeeded in transferring himself to
the branches of some obstructing tree ; but he was neither,
and he clung to his broken raft-like berth with an endurance that was half the paralysis of terror and half the patience of habitual misfortune. Eventually he was caught
in a side current, swept to the bank, and cast ashore on an
unexplored wilderness.

His first consciousness was one of hunger that usurped
any sentiment of gratitude for his escape from drowning.
As soon as his cramped limbs permitted, he crawled out of
the bushes in search of food. He did not know where he
was ; there was no sign of habitation — or even occupation
— anywhere. He had been too terrified to notice the direction in which he had drifted — even if he had possessed the
ordinary knowledge of a backwoodsman, which he did not.
He was helpless. In his bewildered state, seeing a squirrel
cracking a nut on the branch of a hollow tree near him, he
made a half-frenzied dart at the frightened animal, which
ran away. But the same association of ideas in his torpid
and confused brain impelled him to search for the squirrel's
hoard in the hollow of the tree. He ate the few hazel-nuts
he found there ravenously. The purely animal instinct
satisfied, he seemed to have borrowed from it a certain
strength and intuition. He limped through the thicket not
unlike some awkward, shy quadrumane, stopping here and
there to peer out through the openings over the marshes
that lay beyond. His sight, hearing, and even the sense of
smell had become preternaturally acute. It was the latter
which suddenly arrested his steps with the odor of dried
fish. It had a significance beyond the mere instincts of
hunger — it indicated the contiguity of some Indian en-

campment. And as such — it meant danger, torture, and death.

He stopped, trembled violently, and tried to collect his scattered senses. Redwood Camp had embroiled itself needlessly and brutally with the surrounding Indians, and only held its own against them by reckless courage and unerring marksmanship. The frequent use of a casual wandering Indian as a target for the practicing rifles of its members had kept up an undying hatred in the heart of the aborigines and stimulated them to terrible and isolated reprisals. The scalped and skinned dead body of Jack Trainer, tied on his horse and held hideously upright by a cross of wood behind his saddle, had passed, one night, a slow and ghastly apparition, into camp ; the corpse of Dick Ryner had been found anchored on the river-bed, disemboweled and filled with stone and gravel. The solitary and unprotected member of Redwood Camp who fell into the enemy's hands was doomed.

Elijah Martin remembered this, but his fears gradually began to subside in a certain apathy of the imagination, which perhaps dulled his apprehensions and allowed the instinct of hunger to become again uppermost. He knew that the low bark tents, or wigwams, of the Indians were hung with strips of dried salmon, and his whole being was now centred upon an attempt to stealthily procure a delicious morsel. As yet he had distinguished no other sign of life or habitation ; a few moments later, however, and grown bolder with an animal-like trustfulness in his momentary security, he crept out of the thicket and found himself near a long, low mound or burrow-like structure of mud and bark on the river-bank. A single narrow opening, not unlike the entrance of an Esquimau hut, gave upon the river. Martin had no difficulty in recognizing the character of the building. It was a " sweat-house," an institution common to nearly all the aboriginal tribes of California.

Half a religious temple, it was also half a sanitary asylum, was used as a Russian bath or superheated vault, from which the braves, sweltering and stifling all night, by smothered fires, at early dawn plunged, perspiring, into the ice-cold river. The heat and smoke were further utilized to dry and cure the long strips of fish hanging from the roof, and it was through the narrow aperture that served as a chimney that the odor escaped which Martin had detected. He knew that, as the bathers only occupied the house from midnight to early morn, it was now probably empty. He advanced confidently toward it.

He was a little surprised to find that the small open space between it and the river was occupied by a rude scaffolding, like that on which certain tribes exposed their dead, but in this instance it only contained the feathered leggings, fringed blanket, and eagle-plumed head-dress of some brave. He did not, however, linger in this plainly visible area, but quickly dropped on all fours and crept into the interior of the house. Here he completed his feast with the fish, and warmed his chilled limbs on the embers of the still smouldering fires. It was while drying his tattered clothes and shoeless feet that he thought of the dead brave's useless leggings and moccasins, and it occurred to him that he would be less likely to attract the Indians' attention from a distance and provoke a ready arrow, if he were disguised as one of them. Crawling out again, he quickly secured, not only the leggings, but the blanket and head-dress, and, putting them on, cast his own clothes into the stream. A bolder, more energetic, or more provident man would have followed the act by quickly making his way back to the thicket to reconnoitre, taking with him a supply of fish for future needs. But Elijah Martin succumbed again to the recklessness of inertia; he yielded once more to the animal instinct of momentary security. He returned to the interior of the hut, curled himself again on the ashes, and, weakly resolving to sleep until moonrise, and as weakly hesitating, ended by falling into uneasy but helpless stupor.

When he awoke, the rising sun, almost level with the low entrance to the sweat-house, was darting its direct rays into the interior, as if searching it with fiery spears. He had slept ten hours. He rose tremblingly to his knees. Everything was quiet without; he might yet escape. He crawled to the opening. The open space before it was empty, but the scaffolding was gone. The clear, keen air revived him. As he sprang out, erect, a shout that nearly stunned him seemed to rise from the earth on all sides. He glanced around him in a helpless agony of fear. A dozen concentric circles of squatting Indians, whose heads were visible above the reeds, encompassed the banks around the sunken base of the sweat-house with successive dusky rings. Every avenue of escape seemed closed. Perhaps for that reason the attitude of his surrounding captors was passive rather than aggressive, and the shrewd, half-Hebraic profiles nearest him expressed only stoical waiting. There was a strange similarity of expression in his own immovable apathy of despair. His only sense of averting his fate was a confused idea of explaining his intrusion. His desperate memory yielded a few common Indian words. He pointed automatically to himself and the stream. His white lips moved.

" I come — from — the river ! "

A guttural cry, as if the whole assembly were clearing their throats, went round the different circles. The nearest rocked themselves to and fro and bent their feathered heads toward him. A hollow-cheeked, decrepit old man arose and said simply : —

" It is he ! The great chief has come ! "

.   .   .   .

He was saved. More than that, he was recreated. For by signs and intimations he was quickly made aware that since the death of their late chief, their medicine-men had prophesied that his perfect successor should appear miraculously before them, borne noiselessly on the river *from the sea*, in the plumes and insignia of his predecessor. This mere coincidence of appearance and costume might not have been convincing to the braves had not Elijah Martin's actual deficiencies contributed to their unquestioned faith in him. Not only his inert possession of the sweat-house and his apathetic attitude in their presence, but his utter and complete unlikeness to the white frontiersmen of their knowledge and tradition — creatures of fire and sword and malevolent activity — as well as his manifest dissimilarity to themselves, settled their conviction of his supernatural origin. His gentle, submissive voice, his yielding will, his lazy helplessness, the absence of strange weapons and fierce explosives in his possession, his unwonted sobriety — all proved him an exception to his apparent race that was in itself miraculous. For it must be confessed that, in spite of the cherished theories of most romances and all statesmen and commanders, that *fear* is the great civilizer of the savage barbarian, and that he is supposed to regard the prowess of the white man and his mysterious death-dealing weapons as evidence of his supernatural origin and superior creation, the facts have generally pointed to the reverse. Elijah Martin was not long in discovering that when the Minyo hunter, with his obsolete bow, dropped dead by a bullet from a viewless and apparently noiseless space, it was *not* considered the lightnings of an avenging Deity, but was traced directly to the ambushed rifle of Kansas Joe, swayed by a viciousness quite as human as their own; the spectacle of Blizzard Dick, verging on delirium tremens, and riding "amuck" into an Indian village with a revolver in each hand, did *not* impress them as a supernatural act, nor excite their respectful awe as much as the less harmful frenzy of one of their own medicine-men; they were *not* influenced by implacable white gods, who relaxed only to drive hard bargains and exchange mildewed flour and shoddy blankets for their fish and furs. I am afraid they regarded these raids of Christian civilization as they looked upon grasshopper plagues, famines, inundations, and epidemics; while an utterly impassive God washed his hands of the means he had employed, and even encouraged the faithful to resist and overcome his emissaries — the white devils! Had Elijah Martin been a student of theology, he would have been struck with the singular resemblance of these theories — although the application thereof was reversed — to the Christian faith. But Elijah Martin had neither the imagination of a theologian nor the insight of a politician. He only saw that he, hitherto ignored and despised in a community of half-barbaric men, now translated to a community of men wholly savage, was respected and worshiped!

It might have turned a stronger head than Elijah's. He was at first frightened, fearful lest his reception concealed some hidden irony, or that, like the flower-crowned victim of ancient sacrifice, he was exalted and sustained to give importance and majesty to some impending martyrdom. Then he began to dread that his innocent deceit — if deceit it was — should be discovered; at last, partly from meekness and partly from the animal contentment of present security, he accepted the situation. Fortunately for him it was purely passive. The Great Chief of the Minyo tribe was simply an expressionless idol of flesh and blood. The previous incumbent of that office had been an old man, impotent and senseless of late years through age and disease. The chieftains and braves had consulted in council before him, and perfunctorily submitted their decisions, like offerings, to his unresponsive shrine. In the same way, all material events — expeditions, trophies, industries — were supposed to pass before the dull, impassive eyes of the great chief, for direct acceptance. On the second day of Elijah's accession, two of the braves brought a bleeding human scalp before him. Elijah turned pale, trembled, and averted his head, and then, remembering the danger of giving way to his weakness, grew still more ghastly. The warriors watched him with impassioned faces. A grunt — but whether of astonishment, dissent, or approval, he could not tell — went round the circle. But the scalp was taken away and never again appeared in his presence.

An incident still more alarming quickly followed. Two captives, white men, securely bound, were one day brought before him on their way to the stake, followed by a crowd of old and young squaws and children. The unhappy Elijah recognized in the prisoners two packers from a distant settlement who sometimes passed through Redwood Camp. An agony of terror, shame, and remorse shook the pseudo-chief to his crest of high feathers, and blanched his face beneath its paint and yellow ochre. To interfere to save them from the torture they were evidently to receive at the hands of those squaws and children, according to custom, would be exposure and death to him as well as themselves; while to assist by his passive presence at the horrible sacrifice of his countrymen was too much for even his weak selfishness. Scarcely knowing what he did as the lugubrious procession passed before him, he hurriedly hid his face in his blanket and turned his back upon the scene. There was a dead silence. The warriors were evidently unprepared for this extraordinary conduct of their chief. What might have been their action it was impossible to conjecture, for at that moment a little squaw, perhaps impatient for the sport and partly emboldened by the fact that she had been selected, only a few days before, as the betrothed of the new chief, approached him slyly from the other side. The horrified eyes of Elijah, momentarily raised from his blanket, saw and recognized her. The feebleness of a weak nature, that dared not measure itself directly with the real cause, vented its rage on a secondary object. He darted a quick glance of indignation and hatred at the young girl. She ran back in startled terror to her companions, a hurried consultation followed, and in another moment the whole bevy of girls, old women, and children were on the wing, shrieking and crying, to their wigwams.

"You see," said one of the prisoners coolly to the other, in English, "I was right. They never intended to do anything to us. It was only a bluff. These Minyos are a different sort from the other tribes. They never kill anybody if they can help it."

"You're wrong," said the other excitedly. "It was that big chief there, with his head in a blanket, that sent those dogs to the right-about. Hell! did you see them run at just a look from him ? He's a big and mighty feller, you bet. Look at his dignity!"

"That's so — he ain't no slouch," said the other, gazing at Elijah's muffled head critically. "D—d if he ain't a born king."

The sudden conflict and utter revulsion of emotion that those simple words caused in Elijah's breast was almost incredible. He had been at first astounded by the revelation of the peaceful reputation of the unknown tribe he had been called upon to govern ; but even this comforting assurance was as nothing compared to the greater revelations implied in the speaker's praise of himself. He, Elijah Martin! the despised, the rejected, the worthless outcast of Redwood Camp, recognized as a "born king," a leader; his power felt by the very men who had scorned him! And he had done nothing — stop! had he actually done *nothing?* Was it not possible that he was *really* what they thought him? His brain reeled under the strong, unaccustomed wine of praise ; acting upon his weak selfishness, it exalted him for a moment to their measure of his strength, even as their former belief in his inefficiency had kept him down. Courage is too often only the memory of past success. This was his first effort; he forgot he had not earned it, even as he now ignored the danger of earning it. The few words of unconscious praise had fallen like the blade of knighthood on his cowering shoulders; he had risen ennobled from the contact. Though his face was still muffled in his blanket, he stood erect and seemed to have gained in stature.

The braves had remained standing irresolute, and yet watchful, a few paces from their captives. Suddenly Elijah, still keeping his back to the prisoners, turned upon the braves, with blazing eyes, violently throwing out his hands with the gesture of breaking bonds. Like all sudden demonstrations of undemonstrative men, it was extravagant, weird, and theatrical. But it was more potent than speech — the speech that, even if effective, would still have betrayed him to his countrymen. The braves hurriedly cut the thongs of the prisoners; another impulsive gesture from Elijah, and they, too, fled. When he lifted his eyes cautiously from his blanket, captors and captives had dispersed in opposite directions, and he was alone — and triumphant!

From that moment Elijah Martin was another man. He went to bed that night in an intoxicating dream of power; he arose a man of will, of strength. He read it in the eyes of the braves, albeit at times averted in wonder. He understood, now, that although peace had been their habit and custom, they had nevertheless sought to test his theories of administration with the offering of the scalps and the captives, and in this detection of their common weakness he forgot his own. Most heroes require the contrast of the unheroic to set them off; and Elijah actually found himself devising means for strengthening the defensive and offensive character of the tribe, and was himself strengthened by it.

Meanwhile the escaped packers did not fail to heighten the importance of their adventure by elevating the character and achievements of their deliverer; and it was presently announced throughout the frontier settlements that the hitherto insignificant and peaceful tribe of Minyos, who inhabited a large territory bordering on the Pacific Ocean, had developed into a powerful nation, only kept from the warpath by a more powerful but mysterious chief. The Government sent an Indian agent to treat with them, in its usual half-paternal, half-aggressive, and wholly inconsistent policy. Elijah, who still retained the imitative sense and adaptability to surroundings which belong to most lazy, impressible natures, and in striped yellow and vermilion features looked the chief he personated, met the agent with silent and becoming gravity. The council was carried on by signs. Never before had an Indian treaty been entered into with such perfect knowledge of the intentions and designs of the whites by the Indians, and such profound ignorance of the qualities of the Indians by the whites. It need scarcely be said that the treaty was an unquestionable Indian success. They did not give up their arable lands; what they did sell to the agent they refused to exchange for extravagant-priced shoddy blankets, worthless guns, damp powder, and mouldy meal. They took pay in dollars, and were thus enabled to open more profitable commerce with the traders at the settlements for better goods and better bargains; they simply declined beads, whiskey, and Bibles at any price. The result was that the traders found it profitable to protect them from their countrymen, and the chances of wantonly shooting down a possible valuable customer stopped the old indiscriminate rifle-practice. The Indians were allowed to cultivate their fields in peace. Elijah purchased for them a few agricultural implements. The catching, curing, and smoking of salmon became an important branch of trade. They waxed prosperous and

rich ; they lost their nomadic habits — a centralized settlement bearing the external signs of an Indian village took
the place of their old temporary encampments, but the huts
were internally an improvement on the old wigwams.   The
dried fish were banished from the tent-poles to long sheds
especially constructed for that purpose.   The sweat-house
was no longer utilized for worldly purposes.   The wise and
mighty Elijah did not attempt to reform their religion, but
to preserve it in its integrity.

That these improvements and changes were due to the
influence of one man was undoubtedly true, but that he
was necessarily a superior man did not follow.   Elijah's
success was due partly to the fact that he had been enabled
to impress certain negative virtues, which were part of his
own nature, upon a community equally constituted to receive them.   Each was strengthened by the recognition in
each other of the unexpected value of those qualities ; each
acquired a confidence begotten of their success.   "*He-hides-
his-face*," as Elijah Martin was known to the tribe after
the episode of the released captives, was really not so much
of an autocrat as many constitutional rulers.

.   .   .   .

Two years of tranquil prosperity passed.   Elijah Martin,
foundling, outcast, without civilized ties or relationship of
any kind, forgotten by his countrymen, and lifted into alien
power, wealth, security, and respect, became — homesick !

It was near the close of a summer afternoon.   He was
sitting at the door of his lodge, which overlooked, on one
side, the far-shining levels of the Pacific, and, on the other,
the slow descent to the cultivated meadows and banks of
the Minyo River, that debouched through a waste of salt-
marsh, beach-grass, sand-dunes, and foamy estuary into the
ocean.   The headland, or promontory — the only eminence
of the Minyo territory — had been reserved by him for his
lodge, partly on account of its isolation from the village at

its base, and partly for the view it commanded of his territory. Yet his wearying and discontented eyes were more often found on the ocean, as a possible highway of escape from his irksome position, than on the plain and the distant range of mountains, so closely connected with the nearer past and his former detractors. In his vague longing he had no desire to return to them, even in triumph; in his present security there still lingered a doubt of his ability to cope with the old conditions. It was more like his easy, indolent nature — which revived in his prosperity — to trust to this least practical and remote solution of his trouble. His homesickness was as vague as his plan for escape from it; he did not know exactly what he regretted, but it was probably some life he had not enjoyed, some pleasure that had escaped his former incompetency and poverty.

He had sat thus a hundred times, as aimlessly blinking at the vast possibilities of the shining sea beyond, turning his back upon the nearer and more practicable mountains, lulled by the far-off beating of monotonous rollers, the lonely cry of the curlew and plover, the drowsy changes of alternate breaths of cool, fragrant reeds and warm, spicy sands that blew across his eyelids, and succumbed to sleep, as he had done a hundred times before. The narrow strips of colored cloth, insignia of his dignity, flapped lazily from his tent-poles, and at last seemed to slumber with him; the shadows of the leaf-tracery thrown by the bay-tree, on the ground at his feet, scarcely changed its pattern. Nothing moved but the round, restless, berry-like eyes of Wachita, his child-wife, the former heroine of the incident with the captive packers, who sat near her lord, armed with a willow wand, watchful of intruding wasps, sand-flies, and even the more ostentatious advances of a rotund and clerical-looking humble-bee, with his monotonous homily. Content, dumb, submissive, vacant, at such times, Wachita, debarred her husband's confidences through the native customs and his own indifferent taciturnity, satisfied herself by gazing at him with the wondering but ineffectual sympathy of a faithful dog. Unfortunately for Elijah, her purely mechanical ministration could not prevent a more dangerous intrusion upon his security.

He awoke with a light start, and eyes that gradually fixed upon the woman a look of returning consciousness. Wachita pointed timidly to the village below.

"The Messenger of the Great White Father has come to-day, with his wagons and horses; he would see the chief of the Minyos, but I would not disturb my lord."

Elijah's brow contracted. Relieved of its characteristic metaphor, he knew that this meant that the new Indian agent had made his usual official visit, and had exhibited the usual anxiety to see the famous chieftain.

"Good!" he said. "White Rabbit [his lieutenant] will see the Messenger and exchange gifts. It is enough."

"The white messenger has brought his wangee [white] woman with him. They would look upon the face of him who hides it," continued Wachita dubiously. "They would that Wachita should bring them nearer to where my lord is, that they might see him when he knew it not."

Elijah glanced moodily at his wife, with the half suspicion with which he still regarded her alien character. "Then let Wachita go back to the squaws and old women, and let her hide herself with them until the wangee strangers are gone," he said curtly. "I have spoken. Go!"

Accustomed to these abrupt dismissals, which did not necessarily indicate displeasure, Wachita disappeared without a word. Elijah, who had risen, remained for a few moments leaning against the tent-poles, gazing abstractedly toward the sea. The bees droned uninterruptedly in his ears, the far-off roll of the breakers came to him distinctly; but suddenly, with greater distinctness, came the murmur of a woman's voice.

" He don't look savage a bit ! Why, he's real hand-some."

"Hush ! you " — said a second voice in a frightened whisper.

" But if he *did* hear he could n't understand," returned the first voice. A suppressed giggle followed.

Luckily, Elijah's natural and acquired habits of repression suited the emergency. He did not move, although he felt the quick blood fly to his face, and the voice of the first speaker had suffused him with a strange and delicious anticipation. He restrained himself, though the words she had naïvely dropped were filling him with new and tremulous suggestion. He was motionless, even while he felt that the vague longing and yearning which had possessed him hitherto was now mysteriously taking some unknown form and action.

The murmuring ceased. The humble-bee's drone again became ascendant — a sudden fear seized him. She was *going ;* he should never see her ! While he had stood there a dolt and sluggard, she had satisfied her curiosity and stolen away. With a sudden yielding to impulse, he darted quickly in the direction where he had heard her voice. The thicket moved, parted, crackled, and rustled, and then undulated thirty feet before him in a long wave, as if from the passage of some lithe, invisible figure. But at the same moment a little cry, half of alarm, half of laughter, broke from his very feet, and a bent manzanita bush, relaxed by frightened fingers, flew back against his breast. Thrusting it hurriedly aside, his stooping, eager face came almost in contact with the pink, flushed cheeks and tangled curls of a woman's head. He was so near, her moist and laughing eyes almost drowned his eager glance ; her parted lips and white teeth were so close to his that her quick breath took away his own.

She had dropped on one knee, as her companion fled, ex-

pecting he would overlook her as he passed, but his direct
onset had extracted the feminine outcry. Yet even then
she did not seem greatly frightened.

"It's only a joke, sir," she said, coolly lifting herself to
her feet by grasping his arm. "I'm Mrs. Dall, the Indian
agent's wife. They said you wouldn't let anybody see you
— and *I* determined I would. That's all!" She stopped,
threw back her tangled curls behind her ears, shook the
briers and thorns from her skirt, and added: "Well, I
reckon you aren't afraid of a woman, are you? So no
harm's done. Good-by!"

She drew slightly back as if to retreat, but the elasticity
of the manzanita against which she was leaning threw her
forward once more. He again inhaled the perfume of her
hair; he saw even the tiny freckles that darkened her upper
lip and brought out the moist, red curve below. A sudden
recollection of a playmate of his vagabond childhood flashed
across his mind; a wild inspiration of lawlessness, begotten
of his past experience, his solitude, his dictatorial power,
and the beauty of the woman before him, mounted to his
brain. He threw his arms passionately around her, pressed
his lips to hers, and with a half-hysterical laugh drew back
and disappeared in the thicket.

Mrs. Dall remained for an instant dazed and stupefied.
Then she lifted her arm mechanically, and with her sleeve
wiped her bruised mouth and the ochre-stain that his paint
had left, like blood, upon her cheek. Her laughing face
had become instantly grave, but not from fear; her dark
eyes had clouded, but not entirely with indignation. She
suddenly brought down her hand sharply against her side
with a gesture of discovery.

"That's no Injun!" she said, with prompt decision.
The next minute she plunged back into the trail again,
and the dense foliage once more closed around her. But
as she did so the broad, vacant face and the mutely wonder-

ing eyes of Wachita rose, like a placid moon, between the branches of a tree where they had been hidden, and shone serenely and impassively after her.

.   .   .   .

A month elapsed.   But it was a month filled with more experience to Elijah than his past two years of exaltation. In the first few days following his meeting with Mrs. Dall, he was possessed by terror, mingled with flashes of desperation, at the remembrance of his rash imprudence.   His recollection of extravagant frontier chivalry to womankind, and the swift retribution of the insulted husband or guardian, alternately filled him with abject fear or extravagant recklessness.   At times prepared for flight, even to the desperate abandonment of himself in a canoe to the waters of the Pacific, at times he was on the point of inciting his braves to attack the Indian agency and precipitate the war that he felt would be inevitable.   As the days passed, and there seemed to be no interruption to his friendly relations with the agency, with that relief a new, subtle joy crept into Elijah's heart.   The image of the agent's wife framed in the leafy screen behind his lodge, the perfume of her hair and breath mingled with the spicing of the bay, the brief thrill and tantalization of the stolen kiss still haunted him.   Through his long, shy abstention from society, and his two years of solitary exile, the fresh beauty of this young Western wife, in whom the frank artlessness of girlhood still lingered, appeared to him like a superior creation. He forgot his vague longings in the inception of a more tangible but equally unpractical passion.   He remembered her unconscious and spontaneous admiration of him; he dared to connect it with her forgiving silence.   If she had withheld her confidences from her husband, he could hope — he knew not exactly what!

One afternoon Wachita put into his hand a folded note. With an instinctive presentiment of its contents, Elijah

turned red and embarrassed in receiving it from the woman
who was recognized as his wife. But the impassive, submissive manner of this household drudge, instead of touching his conscience, seemed to him a vulgar and brutal acceptance of the situation that dulled whatever compunction he
might have had. He opened the note and read hurriedly
as follows : —

"You took a great freedom with me the other day, and
I am justified in taking one with you now. I believe you
understand English as well as I do. If you want to explain
that, and your conduct to me, I will be at the same place
this afternoon. My friend will accompany me, but she need
not hear what you have to say."

Elijah read the letter, which might have been written
by an ordinary schoolgirl, as if it had conveyed the veiled
rendezvous of a princess. The reserve, caution, and shyness which had been the safeguard of his weak nature were
swamped in a flow of immature passion. He flew to the
interview with the eagerness and inexperience of first love.
He was completely at her mercy. So utterly was he sub-
jugated by her presence that she did not even run the risk
of his passion. Whatever sentiment might have mingled
with her curiosity, she was never conscious of a necessity
to guard herself against it. At this second meeting she
was in full possession of his secret. He had told her
everything ; she had promised nothing in return — she
had not even accepted anything. Even her actual after-
relations to the dénouement of his passion are still shrouded
in mystery.

Nevertheless, Elijah lived two weeks on the unsubstantial memory of this meeting. What might have followed
could not be known, for at the end of that time an outrage — so atrocious that even the peaceful Minyos were
thrilled with savage indignation — was committed on the
outskirts of the village. An old chief, who had been spe-

cially selected to deal with the Indian agent, and who kept a small trading outpost, had been killed and his goods despoiled by a reckless Redwood packer. The murderer had coolly said that he was only "serving out" the tool of a fraudulent imposture on the Government, and that he dared the arch-impostor himself, the so-called Minyo chief, to help himself. A wave of ungovernable fury surged up to the very tent-poles of Elijah's lodge and demanded vengeance. Elijah trembled and hesitated. In the thralldom of his selfish passion for Mrs. Dall he dared not contemplate a collision with her countrymen. He would have again sought refuge in his passive, non-committal attitude, but he knew the impersonal character of Indian retribution and compensation, — a sacrifice of equal value, without reference to the culpability of the victim, — and he dreaded some spontaneous outbreak. To prevent the enforced expiation of the crime by some innocent brother packer, he was obliged to give orders for the pursuit and arrest of the criminal, secretly hoping for his escape or the interposition of some circumstance to avert his punishment. A day of sullen expectancy to the old men and squaws in camp, of gloomy anxiety to Elijah alone in his lodge, followed the departure of the braves on the war-path. It was midnight when they returned. Elijah, who, from his habitual reserve and the accepted etiquette of his exalted station, had remained impassive in his tent, only knew from the guttural rejoicings of the squaws that the expedition had been successful and the captive was in their hands. At any other time he might have thought it an evidence of some growing skepticism of his infallibility of judgment and a diminution of respect that they did not confront him with their prisoner. But he was too glad to escape from the danger of exposure and possible arraignment of his past life by the desperate captive, even though it might not have been understood by the spectators. He reflected that the omission might have arisen from their recollection of his previous aversion to a retaliation on other prisoners. Enough that they would wait his signal for the torture and execution at sunrise the next day.

The night passed slowly. It is more than probable that the selfish and ignoble torments of the sleepless and vacillating judge were greater than those of the prisoner, who dozed at the stake between his curses. Yet it was part of Elijah's fatal weakness that his kinder and more human instincts were dominated even at that moment by his lawless passion for the Indian agent's wife, and his indecision as to the fate of his captive was as much due to this preoccupation as to a selfish consideration of her relations to the result. He hated the prisoner for his infelicitous and untimely crime, yet he could not make up his mind to his death. He paced the ground before his lodge in dishonorable incertitude. The small eyes of the submissive Wachita watched him with vague solicitude.

Toward morning he was struck by a shameful inspiration. He would creep unperceived to the victim's side, unloose his bonds, and bid him fly to the Indian agency. There he was to inform Mrs. Dall that her husband's safety depended upon his absenting himself for a few days, but that she was to remain and communicate with Elijah. She would understand everything, perhaps; at least she would know that the prisoner's release was to please her, but even if she did not, no harm would be done, a white man's life would be saved, and his real motive would not be suspected. He turned with feverish eagerness to the lodge. Wachita had disappeared — probably to join the other women. It was well; she would not suspect him.

The tree to which the doomed man was bound was, by custom, selected nearest the chief's lodge, within its sacred inclosure, with no other protection than that offered by its reserved seclusion and the outer semicircle of warriors' tents before it. To escape, the captive would therefore have to pass beside the chief's lodge to the rear and descend the hill toward the shore. Elijah would show him the way, and make it appear as if he had escaped unaided. As he glided into the shadow of a group of pines, he could dimly discern the outline of the destined victim, secured against one of the larger trees in a sitting posture, with his head fallen forward on his breast as if in sleep. But at the same moment another figure glided out from the shadow and approached the fatal tree. It was Wachita !

He stopped in amazement. But in another instant a flash of intelligence made it clear. He remembered her vague uneasiness and solicitude at his agitation, her sudden disappearance ; she had fathomed his perplexity, as she had once before. Of her own accord she was going to release the prisoner ! The knife to cut his cords glittered in her hand. Brave and faithful animal !

He held his breath as he drew nearer. But, to his horror, the knife suddenly flashed in the air and darted down, again and again, upon the body of the helpless man. There was a convulsive struggle, but no outcry, and the next moment the body hung limp and inert in its cords. Elijah would himself have fallen, half-fainting, against a tree, but, by a revulsion of feeling, came the quick revelation that the desperate girl had rightly solved the problem ! She had done what he ought to have done — and his loy-alty and manhood were preserved. That conviction and the courage to act upon it — to have called the sleeping braves to witness his sacrifice — would have saved him, but it was ordered otherwise.

As the girl rapidly passed him he threw out his hand and seized her wrist. "Who did you do this for ? " he demanded.

"For you," she said stupidly.

"And why ? "

"Because you no kill him — you love his squaw."

" *His* squaw ! " He staggered back. A terrible suspicion flashed upon him. He dashed Wachita aside and ran to the tree. It was the body of the Indian agent! Aboriginal justice had been satisfied. The warriors had not caught the *murderer*, but, true to their idea of vicarious retribution, had determined upon the expiatory sacrifice of a life as valuable and innocent as the one they had lost.

.   .   .   .

" So the Gov'r'ment hev at last woke up and wiped out them cussed Digger Minyos," said Snap-shot Harry, as he laid down the newspaper, in the brand-new saloon of the brand-new town of Redwood. " I see they 've stampeded both banks of the Minyo River, and sent off a lot to the reservation. I reckon the soldiers at Fort Cass got sick o' sentiment after those hounds killed the Injun agent, and are beginning to agree with us that the only ' good Injun ' is a dead one."

" And it turns out that that wonderful chief, that them two packers used to rave about, woz about as big a devil ez any, and tried to run off with the agent's wife, only the warriors killed her. I 'd like to know what become of him. Some says he was killed, others allow that he got away. I 've heerd tell that he was originally some kind of Methodist preacher ! — a kind o' saint that got a sort o' spiritooal holt on the old squaws and children."

" Why don't you ask old Skeesicks ? I see he 's back here agin — and grubbin' along at a dollar a day on tailin's. He 's been somewhere up north, they say."

" What, Skeesicks ? that shiftless, o'n'ry cuss ! You bet he wus n't anywhere where there was danger or fighting. Why, you might as well hev suspected *him* of being the big chief himself ! There he comes — ask him."

And the laughter was so general that Elijah Martin — alias Skeesicks — lounging shyly into the bar-room, joined in it weakly.

CAPTAIN JIM'S FRIEND

I

HARDLY one of us, I think, really believed in the auriferous probabilities of Eureka Gulch. Following a little stream, we had one day drifted into it, very much as we imagined the river-gold might have done in remoter ages, with the difference that *we* remained there, while the river-gold to all appearances had not. At first it was tacitly agreed to ignore this fact, and we made the most of the charming locality, with its rare watercourse that lost itself in tangled depths of manzanita and alder, its laurel-choked pass, its flower-strewn hillside, and its summit crested with rocking pines.

"You see," said the optimistic Rowley, "water's the main thing after all. If we happen to strike river-gold, thar's the stream for washing it; if we happen to drop into quartz — and that thar rock looks mighty likely — thar ain't a more natural-born site for a mill than that right bank, with water enough to run fifty stamps. That hillside is an original dump for your tailings, and a ready found inclined road for your trucks, fresh from the hands of Providence; and that road we're kalkilatin' to build to the turnpike will run just easy along that ridge."

Later, when we were forced to accept the fact that finding gold was really the primary object of a gold-mining company, we still remained there, excusing our youthful laziness and incertitude by brilliant and effective sarcasms upon the unremunerative attractions of the gulch. Nevertheless, when Captain Jim, returning one day from the nearest settlement and post-office, twenty miles away, burst upon us with "Well, the hull thing 'll be settled now, boys; Lacy Bassett is coming down yer to look round," we felt considerably relieved.

And yet, perhaps, we had as little reason for it as we had for remaining there. There was no warrant for any belief in the special divining power of the unknown Lacy Bassett, except Captain Jim's extravagant faith in his general superiority, and even that had always been a source of amused skepticism to the camp. We were already impatiently familiar with the opinions of this unseen oracle; he was always impending in Captain Jim's speech as a fragrant memory or an unquestioned authority. When Captain Jim began, "Ez Lacy was one day tellin' me," or, "Ez Lacy Bassett allows," or more formally, when strangers were present, "Ez a partickler friend o' mine, Lacy Bassett — maybe ez you know him — sez," the youthful and lighter members of the Eureka Mining Company glanced at each other in furtive enjoyment. Nevertheless no one looked more eagerly forward to the arrival of this apocryphal sage than these indolent skeptics. It was at least an excitement; they were equally ready to accept his condemnation of the locality or his justification of their original selection.

He came. He was received by the Eureka Mining Company lying on their backs on the grassy site of the prospective quartz mill, not far from the equally hypothetical "slide" to the gulch. He came by the future stage road — at present a thickset jungle of scrub-oaks and ferns. He was accompanied by Captain Jim, who had gone to meet him on the trail, and for a few moments all critical inspection of himself was withheld by the extraordinary effect he seemed to have upon the faculties of his introducer.

Anything like the absolute prepossession of Captain Jim by the stranger we had never imagined. He approached us

running a little ahead of his guest, and now and then returning assuringly to his side with the expression of a devoted
Newfoundland dog, which in fluffiness he generally resembled. And now, even after the introduction was over,
when he made a point of standing aside in an affectation of
carelessness, with his hands in his pockets, the simulation
was so apparent, and his consciousness and absorption in his
friend so obvious, that it was a relief to us to recall him
into the conversation.

As to our own first impressions of the stranger, they were
probably correct. We all disliked him; we thought him
conceited, self-opinionated, selfish, and untrustworthy. But
later, reflecting that this was possibly the result of Captain
Jim's over-praise, and finding none of these qualities as yet
offensively opposed to our own selfishness and conceit, we
were induced, like many others, to forget our first impression.
We could easily correct him if he attempted to impose
upon *us*, as he evidently had upon Captain Jim. Believing, after the fashion of most humanity, that there was
something about *us* particularly awe-inspiring and edifying
to vice or weakness of any kind, we good-humoredly yielded
to the cheap fascination of this showy, self-saturated, over-
dressed, and underbred stranger. Even the epithet of
"blower" as applied to him by Rowley had its mitigations;
in that Trajan community a bully was not necessarily a
coward, nor florid demonstration always a weakness.

His condemnation of the gulch was sweeping, original,
and striking. He laughed to scorn our half-hearted theory
of a gold deposit in the bed and bars of our favorite stream.
We were not to look for auriferous alluvium in the bed of
any present existing stream, but in the "cement" or dried-
up bed of the original prehistoric rivers that formerly
ran parallel with the present bed, and which — he demonstrated with the stem of Pickney's pipe in the red dust —
could be found by sinking shafts at right angles with the

stream. The theory was to us, at that time, novel and attractive. It was true that the scientific explanation, although full and gratuitous, sounded vague and incoherent. It was true that the geological terms were not always correct, and their pronunciation defective, but we accepted such extraordinary discoveries as " ignus fatuus rock," " splendiferous drift," " mica twist " (recalling a popular species of tobacco), " iron pirates," and " discomposed quartz " as part of what he not inaptly called a " tautological formation," and were happy. Nor was our contentment marred by the fact that the well-known scientific authority with whom the stranger had been intimate, — to the point of " sleeping together " during a survey, — and whom he described as a bent old man with spectacles, must have aged considerably since one of our party saw him three years before as a keen young fellow of twenty-five. Inaccuracies like those were only the carelessness of genius. " That 's my opinion, gentlemen," he concluded, negligently rising, and with pointed preoccupation whipping the dust of Eureka Gulch from his clothes with his handkerchief, " but of course it ain't nothin' to me."

Captain Jim, who had followed every word with deep and trustful absorption, here repeated, " It ain't nothing to him, boys," with a confidential implication of the gratuitous blessing we had received, and then added, with loyal encouragement to him, " It ain't nothing to you, Lacy, in course," and laid his hand on his shoulder with infinite tenderness.

We, however, endeavored to make it something to Mr. Lacy Bassett. He was spontaneously offered a share in the company and a part of Captain Jim's tent. He accepted both after a few deprecating and muttered asides to Captain Jim, which the latter afterwards explained to us was the giving up of several other important enterprises for our sake. When he finally strolled away with Rowley to look over the gulch, Captain Jim reluctantly tore himself away from him only for the pleasure of reiterating his praise to us as if in strictest confidence and as an entirely novel proceeding.

"You see, boys, I did n't like to say it afore *him*, we bein' old friends; but, between us, that young feller ez worth thousands to the camp. Mebbe," he continued, with grave *naïveté*, "I ain't said much about him afore, mebbe, bein' old friends and accustomed to him — you know how it is, boys, — I have n't appreciated him as much ez I ought, and ez you do. In fact, I don't ezakly remember how I kem to ask him down yer. It came to me suddent, one day only a week ago Friday night, thar under that buckeye; I was thinkin' o' one of his sayin's, and sez I — thar 's Lacy, if he was here he 'd set the hull thing right. It was the ghost of a chance my findin' him free, but I did. And there *he* is, and yer *we* are settled! Ye noticed how he just knocked the bottom outer our plans to work. Ye noticed that quick sort o' sneerin' smile o' his, did n't ye — that 's Lacy! I 've seen him knock over a heap o' things without sayin' anythin' — with jist that smile."

It occurred to us that we might have some difficulty in utilizing this smile in our present affairs, and that we should have probably preferred something more assuring, but Captain Jim's faith was contagious.

"What is he, anyway?" asked Joe Walker lazily.

"Eh!" echoed Captain Jim in astonishment. "What is Lacy Bassett?"

"Yes, what is he?" repeated Walker.

"Wot *is* — he?"

"Yes."

"I 've knowed him now goin' as four year," said Captain Jim, with slow, reflective contentment. "Let 's see. It was in the fall o' '54 I first met him, and he 's allus been the same ez you see him now."

"But what is his business or profession? What does he do?"

Captain Jim looked reproachfully at his questioner.

" Do ? " he repeated, turning to the rest of us as if dis-
daining a direct reply. " Do ? — why, wot he's doin' now.
He's allus the same, allus Lacy Bassett."

Howbeit, we went to work the next day under the super-
intendence of the stranger with youthful and enthusiastic
energy, and began the sinking of a shaft at once.   To do
Captain Jim's friend justice, for the first few weeks he did
not shirk a fair share of the actual labor, replacing his
objectionable and unsuitable finery with a suit of service-
able working clothes got together by general contribution of
the camp, and assuring us of a fact we afterwards had cause
to remember, that " he brought nothing but himself into
Eureka Gulch."   It may be added that he certainly had
not brought money there, as Captain Jim advanced the
small amounts necessary for his purchases in the distant
settlement, and for the still smaller sums he lost at cards,
which he played with characteristic self-sufficiency.

Meantime the work in the shaft progressed slowly but
regularly.   Even when the novelty had worn off and the
excitement of anticipation grew fainter, I am afraid that we
clung to this new form of occupation as an apology for
remaining there ; for the fascinations of our vagabond and
unconventional life were more potent than we dreamed of.
We were slowly fettered by our very freedom ; there was a
strange spell in this very boundlessness of our license that
kept us from even the desire of change ; in the wild and
lawless arms of Nature herself we found an embrace as
clinging, as hopeless and restraining, as the civilization from
which we had fled.   We were quite content after a few
hours' work in the shaft to lie on our backs on the hillside
staring at the unwinking sky, or to wander with a gun
through the virgin forest in search of game scarcely less
vagabond than ourselves.   We indulged in the most extravagant and dreamy speculations of the fortune we should

eventually discover in the shaft, and believed that we were practical. We broke our " saleratus bread " with appetites unimpaired by restlessness or anxiety ; we went to sleep under the grave and sedate stars with a serene consciousness of having fairly earned our rest; we awoke the next morning with unabated trustfulness, and a sweet obliviousness of even the hypothetical fortunes we had perhaps won or lost at cards overnight. We paid no heed to the fact that our little capital was slowly sinking with the shaft, and that the rainy season — wherein not only " no man could work," but even such play as ours was impossible — was momentarily impending.

In the midst of this, one day Lacy Bassett suddenly emerged from the shaft before his " shift " of labor was over with every sign of disgust and rage in his face and inarticulate with apparent passion. In vain we gathered round him in concern ; in vain Captain Jim regarded him with almost feminine sympathy, as he flung away his pick and dashed his hat to the ground.

" What 's up, Lacy, old pard ? What 's gone o' you ? " said Captain Jim tenderly.

" Look ! " gasped Lacy at last, when every eye was on him, holding up a small fragment of rock before us and the next moment grinding it under his heel in rage. " Look ! To think that I 've been fooled agin by this blanked fossiliferous trap — blank it ! To think that after me and Professor Parker was once caught jist in this way up on the Stanislaus at the bottom of a hundred-foot shaft by this rotten trap — that yer I am — bluffed agin ! "

There was a dead silence ; we looked at each other blankly.

" But, Bassett," said Walker, picking up a part of the fragment, " we 've been finding this kind of stuff for the last two weeks."

" But how ? " returned Lacy, turning upon him almost

fiercely. " Did ye find it superposed on quartz, or did you find it *not* superposed on quartz ? Did you find it in volcanic drift, or did ye find it in old red-sandstone or coarse illuvion ? Tell me that, and then ye kin talk. But this yer blank fossiliferous trap, instead o' being superposed on top, is superposed on the bottom. And that means " —

" What ? " we all asked eagerly.

" Why — blank it all — that this yer convulsion of nature, this prehistoric volcanic earthquake, instead of acting laterally and chuckin' the stream to one side, has been revolutionary and turned the old river-bed bottom-side up, and yer d—d cement hez got half the globe atop of it ! Ye might strike it from China, but nowhere else."

We continued to look at one another, the older members with darkening faces, the younger with a strong inclination to laugh. Captain Jim, who had been concerned only in his friend's emotion, and who was hanging with undisguised satisfaction on these final convincing proofs of his superior geological knowledge, murmured approvingly and confidingly, " He's right, boys ! Thar ain't another man livin' ez could give you the law and gospil like that ! Ye can tie to what he says. That's Lacy all over."

Two weeks passed. We had gathered, damp and disconsolate, in the only available shelter of the camp. For the long summer had ended unexpectedly to us ; we had one day found ourselves caught like the improvident insect of the child's fable with gauzy and unseasonable wings wet and bedraggled in the first rains, homeless and hopeless. The scientific Lacy, who lately spent most of his time as a bar-room oracle in the settlement, was away, and from our dripping canvas we could see Captain Jim returning from a visit to him, slowly plodding along the trail towards us.

" It's no use, boys," said Rowley, summarizing the result of our conference, " we must speak out to him ; and if nobody else cares to do it I will. I don't know why we should be more mealy-mouthed than they are at the settlement. They don't hesitate to call Bassett a dead-beat, whatever Captain Jim says to the contrary."

The unfortunate Captain Jim had halted irresolutely before the gloomy faces in the shelter. Whether he felt instinctively some forewarning of what was coming I cannot say. There was a certain doglike consciousness in his eye and a half-backward glance over his shoulder as if he were not quite certain that Lacy was not following. The rain had somewhat subdued his characteristic fluffiness, and he cowered with a kind of sleek storm-beaten despondency over the smoking fire of green wood before our tent.

Nevertheless, Rowley opened upon him with a directness and decision that astonished us. He pointed out briefly that Lacy Bassett had been known to us only through Captain Jim's introduction. That he had been originally invited there on Captain Jim's own account, and that his later connection with the company had been wholly the result of Captain Jim's statements. That, far from being any aid or assistance to them, Bassett had beguiled them by apocryphal knowledge and sham scientific theories into an expensive and gigantic piece of folly. That, in addition to this, they had just discovered that he had also been using the credit of the company for his own individual expenses at the settlement while they were working on his d—d fool shaft — all of which had brought them to the verge of bankruptcy. That, as a result, they were forced now to demand his resignation — not only on their general account, but for Captain Jim's sake — believing firmly, as they did, that he had been as grossly deceived in his friendship for Lacy Bassett as *they* were in their business relations with him.

Instead of being mollified by this, Captain Jim, to our greater astonishment, suddenly turned upon the speaker, bristling with his old canine suggestion.

"There! I said so! Go on! I'd have sworn to it afore you opened your lips. I knowed it the day you sneaked around and wanted to know wot his business was! I said to myself, Cap, look out for that sneakin' hound Rowley, he's no friend o' Lacy's. And the day Lacy so far demeaned himself as to give ye that splendid explanation o' things, I watched ye; ye didn't think it, but I watched ye. Ye can't fool me! I saw ye lookin' at Walker there, and I said to myself, Wot's the use, Lacy, . wot's the use o' your slingin' them words to such as *them?* Wot do *they* know? It's just their pure jealousy and ignorance. Ef you'd come down yer, and lazed around with us and fallen into our common ways, you'd ha' been ez good a man ez the next. But no, it ain't your style, Lacy, you're accustomed to high-toned men like Professor Parker, and you can't help showing it. No wonder you took to avoidin' us; no wonder I've had to foller you over the Burnt Wood Crossin' time and again, to get to see ye. I see it all now : ye can't stand the kempany I brought ye to! Ye had to wipe the slumgullion of Eureka Gulch off your hands, Lacy" — He stopped, gasped for breath, and then lifted his voice more savagely, "And now, what's this? Wot's this hogwash? this yer lyin' slander about his gettin' things on the kempany's credit? Eh, speak up, some of ye!"

We were so utterly shocked and stupefied at the degradation of this sudden and unexpected outburst from a man usually so honorable, gentle, self-sacrificing, and forgiving, that we forgot the cause of it and could only stare at each other. What was this cheap stranger, with his shallow swindling tricks, to the ignoble change he had worked upon the man before us. Rowley and Walker, both fearless fighters and quick to resent an insult, only averted their saddened faces and turned aside without a word.

"Ye dussen't say it! Well, hark to me then," he continued, with white and feverish lips. "*I* put him up to helpin' himself. *I* told him to use the kempany's name for credit. Ye kin put that down to *me*. And when ye talk of *his* resigning, I want ye to understand that *I* resign outer this rotten kempany and *take him with me!* Ef all the gold yer lookin' for was piled up in that shaft from its bottom in hell to its top in the gulch, it ain't enough to keep me here away from him! Ye kin take all my share — all *my* rights yer above ground and below it — all I carry," — he threw his buckskin purse and revolver on the ground, — " and pay yourselves what you reckon you've lost through *him*. But you and me is quits from to-day."

He strode away before a restraining voice or hand could reach him. His dripping figure seemed to melt into the rain beneath the thickening shadows of the pines, and the next moment he was gone. From that day forward Eureka Gulch knew him no more. And the camp itself somehow melted away during the rainy season, even as he had done.

II

Three years had passed. The pioneer stagecoach was
sweeping down the long descent to the pastoral valley of
Gilead, and I was looking towards the village with some
pardonable interest and anxiety. For I carried in my
pocket my letters of promotion from the box seat of the
coach — where I had performed the functions of treasure
messenger for the Excelsior Express Company — to the
resident agency of that company in the bucolic hamlet before me. The few dusty right-angled streets, with their
rigid and staringly new shops and dwellings, the stern formality of one or two obelisk-like meeting-house spires, the
illimitable outlying plains of wheat and wild oats beyond,
with their monotony scarcely broken by skeleton stockades,
corrals, and barrack-looking farm buildings, were all certainly unlike the unkempt freedom of the mountain fast-
nesses in which I had lately lived and moved. Yuba Bill,
the driver, whose usual expression of humorous discontent
deepened into scorn as he gathered up his reins as if to
charge the village and recklessly sweep it from his path,
indicated a huge, rambling, obtrusively glazed, and capital-
lettered building with a contemptuous flick of his whip as
we passed. " Ef you 're kalkilatin' we 'll get our partin'
drink there you 're mistaken. That 's wot they call a
temperance house — wot means a place where the licker ye
get underhand is only a trifle worse than the hash ye get
above-board. I suppose it 's part o' one o' the mysteries o'
Providence that wherever you find a dusty hole like this —
that 's naturally *thirsty* — ye run agin a ' temperance '

house. But never *you* mind! I should n't wonder if thar was a demijohn o' whiskey in the closet of your back office, kept thar by the feller you 're relievin' — who was a white man and knew the ropes."

A few minutes later, when my brief installation was over, we *did* find the demijohn in the place indicated. As Yuba Bill wiped his mouth with the back of his heavy buckskin glove, he turned to me not unkindly. " I don't like to set ye agin Gil-e-ad, which is a scrip-too-rural place, and a God-fearin' place, and a nice dry place, and a place ez I 've heard tell whar they grow beans and pertatoes and garden sass; but afore three weeks is over, old pard, you 'll be howlin' to get back on that box seat with me, whar you uster sit, and be ready to take your chances agin, like a little man, to get drilled through with buckshot from road agents. You hear me! I 'll give you three weeks, sonny, just three weeks, to get your butes full o' hayseed and straws in yer ha'r; and I 'll find ye wadin' the North Fork at high water to get out o' this." He shook my hand with grim tenderness, removing his glove — a rare favor — to give me the pressure of his large, soft, protecting palm, and strode away. The next moment he was shaking the white dust of Gilead from his scornful chariot-wheels.

In the hope of familiarizing myself with the local interests of the community, I took up a copy of the " Gilead Guardian " which lay on my desk, forgetting for the moment the usual custom of the country press to displace local news for long editorials on foreign subjects and national politics. I found, to my disappointment, that the " Guardian " exhibited more than the usual dearth of domestic intelligence, although it was singularly oracular on " The State of Europe," and " Jeffersonian Democracy." A certain cheap assurance, a copy-book dogmatism, a colloquial familiarity, even in the impersonal plural, and a series of inaccuracies and blunders here and there, struck some old chord in my memory. I was mutely wondering where and when I had become personally familiar with rhetoric like that, when the door of the office opened and a man entered. I was surprised to recognize Captain Jim.

I had not seen him since he had indignantly left us, three years before, in Eureka Gulch. The circumstances of his defection were certainly not conducive to any voluntary renewal of friendship on either side ; and although, even as a former member of the Eureka Mining Company, I was not conscious of retaining any sense of injury, yet the whole occurrence flashed back upon me with awkward distinctness. To my relief, however, he greeted me with his old cordiality ; to my amusement he added to it a suggestion of the large forgiveness of conscious rectitude and amiable toleration. I thought, however, I detected, as he glanced at the paper which was still in my hand and then back again at my face, the same uneasy canine resemblance I remembered of old. He had changed but little in appearance; perhaps he was a trifle stouter, more mature, and slower in his movements. If I may return to my canine illustration, his grayer, dustier, and more wiry *ensemble* gave me the impression that certain pastoral and agricultural conditions had varied his type, and he looked more like a shepherd's dog in whose brown eyes there was an abiding consciousness of the care of straying sheep, and possibly of one black one in particular.

He had, he told me, abandoned mining and taken up farming on a rather large scale. He had prospered. He had other interests at stake, "A flour-mill with some improvements — and — and " — here his eyes wandered to the " Guardian " again, and he asked me somewhat abruptly what I thought of the paper. Something impelled me to restrain my previous fuller criticism, and I contented myself by saying briefly that I thought it rather ambitious for the locality. "That 's the word," he said, with a look of gratified relief, " 'ambitious' — you've just hit it. And what's the matter with thet? Ye can't expect a high-toned man to write down to the level of every karpin' hound, ken ye now? That's what he says to me " — He stopped half confused, and then added abruptly : " That's one o' my investments."

" Why, Captain Jim, I never suspected that you " —

" Oh, I don't *write* it," he interrupted hastily. " I only furnish the money and the advertising, and run it gin'rally, you know; and I'm responsible for it. And I select the eddyter — and " — he continued, with a return of the same uneasy wistful look — " thar's suthin' in thet, you know, eh ? "

I was beginning to be perplexed. The memory evoked by the style of the editorial writing and the presence of Captain Jim was assuming a suspicious relationship to each other. " And who's your editor ? " I asked.

" Oh, he's — he's — er — Lacy Bassett," he replied, blinking his eyes with a hopeless assumption of careless-ness. " Let's see ! Oh yes ! You knowed Lacy down there at Eureka. I disremembered it till now. Yes, sir ! " he repeated suddenly and almost rudely, as if to preclude any adverse criticism, " he's the eddyter ! "

To my surprise he was quite white and tremulous with nervousness. I was very sorry for him; and as I really cared very little for the half-forgotten escapade of his friend except so far as it seemed to render *him* sensitive, I shook his hand again heartily and began to talk of our old life in the gulch — avoiding as far as possible any allusion to Lacy Bassett. His face brightened; his old simple cordiality and trustfulness returned, but unfortunately with it his old disposition to refer to Bassett. " Yes, they waz high old times ; and ez I waz sayin' to Lacy on'y yesterday, there is a kind o' freedom 'bout that sort o' life that runs civiliza-tion and noospapers mighty hard, however high-toned they

is. Not but what Lacy ain't right," he added quickly,
" when he sez that the opposition the ' Guardian ' gets here
comes from ignorant low-down fellers ez wos brought up
in played-out camps, and can't tell a gentleman and a
scholar and a scientific man when they sees him. No ! So
I sez to Lacy, ' Never you mind, it 's high time they did,
and they 've got to do it and to swaller the " Guardian,"
if I sink double the money I 've already put into the
paper.' "

I was not long in discovering from other sources that
the " Guardian " was not popular with the more intelligent readers of Gilead, and that Captain Jim's extravagant
estimate of his friend was by no means indorsed by the
community. But criticism took a humorous turn even in
that practical settlement, and it appeared that Lacy Bassett's
vanity, assumption, and ignorance were an unfailing and
weekly joy to the critical, in spite of the vague distrust
they induced in the more homely-witted, and the dull acquiescence of that minority who accepted the paper for its
respectable exterior and advertisements. I was somewhat
grieved, however, to find that Captain Jim shared equally
with his friend in this general verdict of incompetency,
and that some of the most outrageous blunders were put
down to *him*. But I was not prepared to believe that
Lacy had directly or by innuendo helped the public to this
opinion.

Whether through accident or design on his part, Lacy
Bassett did not personally obtrude himself upon my remembrance until a month later. One dazzling afternoon,
when the dust and heat had driven the pride of Gilead's
manhood into the surreptitious shadows of the temperance
hotel's back room, and had even cleared the express office of
its loungers, and left me alone with darkened windows in
the private office, the outer door opened and Captain Jim's
friend entered as part of that garish glitter I had shut out.

To do the scamp strict justice, however, he was somewhat subdued in his dress and manner, and, possibly through some gentle chastening of epigram and revolver since I had seen him last, was less aggressive and exaggerated. I had the impression, from certain odors wafted through the apartment and a peculiar physical exaltation that was inconsistent with his evident moral hesitancy, that he had prepared himself for the interview by a previous visit to the hidden fountains of the temperance hotel.

" We don't seem to have run agin each other since you 've been here," he said, with an assurance that was nevertheless a trifle forced, " but I reckon we 're both busy men, and there 's a heap too much loafing goin' on in Gilead. Captain Jim told me he met you the day you arrived ; said you just cottoned to the ' Guardian ' at once and thought it a deal too good for Gilead; eh ?   Oh, well, jest ez likely he *did n't* say it — it was only his gassin'. He 's a queer man — is Captain Jim."

I replied somehat sharply that I considered him a very honest man, a very simple man, and a very loyal man.

" That 's all very well," said Bassett, twirling his cane with a patronizing smile, " but, as his friend, don't you find him considerable of a darned fool ? "

I could not help retorting that I thought *he* had found that hardly an objection.

" *You* think so," he said querulously, apparently ignoring everything but the practical fact, — " and maybe others do ; but that 's where you 're mistaken. It don't pay. It may pay *him* to be runnin' me as his particular friend, to be quotin' me here and there, to be gettin' credit of knowin' me and my friends and ownin' me — by Gosh ! but I don't see where the benefit to *me* comes in. Eh ? Take your own case down there at Eureka Gulch ; did n't he send for me just to show me up to you fellers ? Did I want to have anything to do with the Eureka Company ?

Did n't he set me up to give my opinion about that shaft just to show off what I knew about science and all that? And what did he get me to join the company for? Was it for you? No! Was it for me? No! It was just to keep me there for *himself*, and kinder pit me agin you fellers and crow over you! Now that ain't my style! It may be *his* — it may be honest and simple and loyal, as you say, and it may be all right for him to get me to run up accounts at the settlement and then throw off on me — but it ain't my style. I suppose he let on that I did that. No? He did n't? Well, then, why did he want to run me off with him, and cut the whole concern in an underhand way and make me leave with nary a character behind me, eh? Now, I never said anything about this before — did I? It ain't like me. I would n't have said anything about it now, only you talked about *my* being benefited by his darned foolishness. Much I 've made outer *him*."

Despicable, false, and disloyal as this was, perhaps it was the crowning meanness of such confidences that his very weakness seemed only a reflection of Captain Jim's own, and appeared in some strange way to degrade his friend as much as himself. The simplicity of his vanity and selfishness was only equaled by the simplicity of Captain Jim's admiration of it. It was a part of my youthful inexperience of humanity that I was not above the common fallacy of believing that a man is "known by the company he keeps," and that he is in a manner responsible for its weakness; it was a part of that humanity that I felt no surprise in being more amused than shocked by this revelation. It seemed a good joke on Captain Jim!

"Of course *you* kin laugh at his darned foolishness; but, by Gosh, it ain't a laughing matter to me!"

"But surely he 's given you a good position on the 'Guardian,'" I urged. "That was disinterested, certainly."

" Was it ? I call that the cheekiest thing yet. When he found he could n't make enough of me in private life, he totes me out in public as *his* editor, — the man who runs *his* paper ! And has his name in print as the proprietor, the only chance he 'd ever get of being before the public. And don't know the whole town is laughing at him ! "

"That may be because they think *he* writes some of the articles," I suggested.

Again the insinuation glanced harmlessly from his vanity. "That could n't be, because *I* do all the work, and it ain't his style," he said, with naïve discontent. " And it 's always the highest style, done to please him, though between you and me it 's sorter castin' pearls before swine, — this 'Frisco editing, — and the public would be just as satisfied with anything I could rattle off that was peart and sassy, — something spicy or personal. I 'm willing to climb down and do it, for there 's nothin' stuck-up about me, you know ; but that darned fool Captain Jim has got the big head about the style of the paper, and darned if I don't think he 's afraid if there 's a lettin' down, people may think it 's him ! Ez if ! Why, you know as well as me that there 's a sort of snap *I* could give these things that would show it was me and no slouch did them, in a minute."

I had my doubts about the elegance or playfulness of Mr. Bassett's trifling, but from some paragraphs that appeared in the next issue of the " Guardian " I judged that he had won over Captain Jim — if indeed that gentleman's alleged objections were not entirely the outcome of Bassett's fancy. The social paragraphs themselves were clumsy and vulgar. A dull-witted account of a select party at Parson Baxter's, with a pointblank compliment to Polly Baxter his daughter, might have made her pretty cheek burn but for her evident prepossession for the meretricious scamp, its writer. But even this horse-play seemed more natural than the utterly artificial editorials with their pinchbeck glitter and cheap erudition ; and thus far it appeared harmless.

I grieve to say that these appearances were deceptive. One afternoon, as I was returning from a business visit to the outskirts of the village, I was amazed on reëntering the main street to find a crowd collected around the " Guardian " office, gazing at the broken glass of its windows and a quantity of type scattered on the ground. But my attention was at that moment more urgently attracted by a similar group around my own office, who, however, seemed more cautious, and were holding timorously aloof from the entrance. As I ran rapidly towards them, a few called out, " Look out — he 's in there ! " while others made way to let me pass. With the impression of fire or robbery in my mind, I entered precipitately, only to find Yuba Bill calmly leaning back in an armchair with his feet on the back of another, a glass of whiskey from my demijohn in one hand and a huge cigar in his mouth. Across his lap lay a stumpy shot-gun which I at once recognized as " the Left Bower," whose usual place was at his feet on the box during his journeys. He looked cool and collected, although there were one or two splashes of printer's ink on his shirt and trousers, and from the appearance of my lavatory and towel he had evidently been removing similar stains from his hands. Putting his gun aside and grasping my hand warmly without rising, he began, with even more than his usual lazy imperturbability : —

" Well, how 's Gilead lookin' to-day ? "

It struck me as looking rather disturbed, but, as I was still too bewildered to reply, he continued lazily : —

" Ez you did n't hunt me up, I allowed you might hev got kinder petrified and dried up down yer, and I reckoned to run down and rattle round a bit and make things lively for ye. I've jist cleared out a newspaper office over thar. They call it the 'Guar-di-an,' though it didn't seem to offer much pertection to them fellers ez was in it. In fact, it wasn't ez much a fight ez it orter hev been. It was rather monotonous for me."

"But what's the row, Bill? What has happened?" I asked excitedly.

"Nothin' to speak of, I tell ye," replied Yuba Bill reflectively. "I jest meandered into that shop over there, and I sez, 'I want ter see the man ez runs this yer mill o' literatoor an' progress.' Thar waz two infants sittin' on high chairs havin' some innocent little game o' pickin' pieces o' lead outer pill-boxes like, and as soon ez they seed me one of 'em crawled under his desk and the other scooted outer the back door. Bimeby the door opens again, and a fluffy coyote-lookin' feller comes in and allows that *he* is responsible for that yer paper. When I saw the kind of animal he was, and that he hadn't any weppings, I jist laid the Left Bower down on the floor. Then I sez, 'You allowed in your paper that I oughter hev a little sevility knocked inter me, and I'm here to hev it done. You ken begin it now.' With that I reached for him, and we waltzed oncet or twicet around the room, and then I put him up on the mantelpiece and on them desks and little boxes, and took him down again, and kinder wiped the floor with him gin-'rally, until the first thing I knowed he was outside the winder on the sidewalk. On'y blamed if I didn't forget to open the winder. Ef it hadn't been for that, it would hev been all quiet and peaceful-like, and nobody hev knowed it. But the sash being in the way, it sorter created a disturbance and unpleasantness *outside.*"

"But what was it all about?" I repeated. "What had he done to you?"

"Ye'll find it in that paper," he said, indicating a copy of the "Guardian" that lay on my table, with a lazy nod of his

head. " P'r'aps you don't read it ?   No more do I.   But
Joe Bilson sez to me yesterday : ' Bill,' sez he, ' they 're
goin' for ye in the " Guardian." '   ' Wot 's that ? ' sez I.
' Hark to this,' sez he, and reads out that bit that you 'll
find there."

I had opened the paper, and he pointed to a paragraph.
" There it is.   Pooty, ain't it ? "   I read with amazement
as follows : —

" If the Pioneer Stage Company want to keep up with
the times, and not degenerate into the old style ' one horse '
road-wagon business, they 'd better make some reform on
the line.   They might begin by shipping off some of the
old-time whiskey-guzzling drivers who are too high and
mighty to do anything but handle the ribbons, and are
above speaking to a passenger unless he 's a favorite or one
of their set.   Overpraise for an occasional scrimmage with
road agents and flattery from Eastern greenhorns have given
them the big head.   If the fool-killer were let loose on
the line with a big club, and knocked a little civility into
their heads, it would n't be a bad thing, and would be a
particular relief to the passengers for Gilead who have to
take the stage from Simpson's Bar."

" That 's my stage," said Yuba Bill quietly, when I had
ended ; " and that 's *me*."

" But it 's impossible," I said eagerly.   " That insult
was never written by Captain Jim."

" Captain Jim," repeated Yuba Bill reflectively.   " Captain Jim, — yes, that was the name o' the man I was playin'
with.   Shortish hairy feller, suthin' between a big coyote
and the old-style hair-trunk.   Fought pretty well for a hay-
footed man from Gil-e-ad."

" But you 've whipped the wrong man, Bill," I said.
" Think again !   Have you had any quarrel lately ? — run
against any newspaper man ? "   The recollection had flashed
upon me that Lacy Bassett had lately returned from a
visit to Stockton.

Yuba Bill regarded his boots on the other armchair for a few moments in profound meditation. "There was a sort o' gaudy insect," he began presently, "suthin' half-way betwixt a hoss-fly and a devil's darnin'-needle, ez crawled up onter the box seat with me last week, and buzzed! Now I think on it, he talked highfaluten' o' the inflooence of the press and sech. I may hev said ' shoo' to him when he was hummin' the loudest. I mout hev flicked him off oncet or twicet with my whip. It must be him. Gosh!" he said suddenly, rising and lifting his heavy hand to his forehead, "now I think agin, *he was the feller ez crawled under the desk when the fight was goin' on, and stayed there*. Yes, sir, that was *him*. His face looked sorter familiar, but I did n't know him moultin' with his feathers off." He turned upon me with the first expression of trouble and anxiety I had ever seen him wear. "Yes, sir, that's him. And I've kem — me, Yuba Bill! — kem *myself*, a matter of twenty miles, totin' a *gun* — a gun, by Gosh! — to fight that — that — that potatar-bug!" He walked to the window, turned, walked back again, finished his whiskey with a single gulp, and laid his hand almost despondingly on my shoulder. "Look ye, old — old fell, you and me's ole friends. Don't give me away. Don't let on a word o' this to any one! Say I kem down yer howlin' drunk on a gen'ral tear! Say I mistook that newspaper office for a cigar-shop, and — got licked by the boss! Say anythin' you like, 'cept that I took a gun down yer to chase a fly that had settled onter me. Keep the Left Bower in yer back office till I send for it. Ef you've got a back door somewhere handy, where I can slip outer this without bein' seen, I'd be thankful."

As this desponding suggestion appeared to me as the wisest thing for him to do in the then threatening state of affairs outside, — which, had he suspected it, he would have stayed to face, — I quickly opened a door into a courtyard that communicated through an alley with a side street. Here we shook hands and parted ; his last dejected ejaculation being, " That potatar-bug ! "   Later I ascertained that Captain Jim had retired to his ranch some four miles distant. He was not seriously hurt, but looked, to use the words of my informant, " ez ef he 'd been hugged by a playful b'ar." As the " Guardian " made its appearance the next week without the slightest allusion to the fracas, I did not deem it necessary to divulge the real facts.   When I called to inquire about Captain Jim's condition, he himself, however, volunteered an explanation.

"I don't mind tellin' you, ez an old friend o' mine and Lacy's, that the secret of that there attack on me and the ' Guardian ' was perlitikal.   Yes, sir !   There was a powerful orginization in the interest o' Halkins for assemblyman ez did n't like our high-toned editorials on caucus corruption, and hired a bully to kem down here and suppress us. Why, this yer Lacy spotted the idea to oncet ; yer know how keen he is."

" Was Lacy present ? " I asked as carelessly as I could.

Captain Jim glanced his eyes over his shoulder quite in his old furtive canine fashion, and then blinked them at me rapidly.   " He war !   And if it warn't for *his* pluck and *his* science and *his* strength, I don't know whar *I 'd* hev been now !   Howsomever, it 's all right.   I 've had a fair offer to sell the ' Guardian ' over at Simpson's Bar, and it 's time I quit throwin' away the work of a man like Lacy Bassett upon it.   And between you and me, I 've got an idea and suthin' better to put his talens into."

III

It was not long before it became evident that the "talens" of Mr. Lacy Bassett, as indicated by Captain Jim, were to grasp at a seat in the State legislature. An editorial in the "Simpson's Bar Clarion" boldly advocated his pretensions. At first it was believed that the article emanated from the gifted pen of Lacy himself, but the style was so unmistakably that of Colonel Starbottle, an eminent political "war-horse" of the district, that a graver truth was at once suggested, namely, that the "Guardian" had simply been transferred to Simpson's Bar, and merged into the "Clarion" solely on this condition. At least it was recognized that it was the hand of Captain Jim which guided the editorial fingers of the colonel, and Captain Jim's money that distended the pockets of that gallant political leader.

Howbeit Lacy Bassett was never elected; in fact, he was only for one brief moment a candidate. It was related that upon his first ascending the platform at Simpson's Bar a voice in the audience said lazily, "Come down!" That voice was Yuba Bill's. A slight confusion ensued, in which Yuba Bill whispered a few words in the colonel's ear. After a moment's hesitation the "war-horse" came forward, and in his loftiest manner regretted that the candidate had withdrawn. The next issue of the "Clarion" proclaimed with no uncertain sound that a base conspiracy gotten up by the former proprietor of the "Guardian" to undermine the prestige of the Great Express Company had been ruthlessly exposed, and the candidate, on learning it *himself* for the first time, withdrew his name from the canvass, as became a high-toned gentleman. Public opinion, ignoring Lacy Bassett completely, unhesitatingly denounced Captain Jim.

During this period I had paid but little heed to Lacy Bassett's social movements, or the successes which would naturally attend such a character with the susceptible sex. I had heard that he was engaged to Polly Baxter, but that they had quarreled in consequence of his flirtations with others, especially a Mrs. Sweeny, a profusely ornamented but reputationless widow. Captain Jim had often alluded with a certain respectful pride and delicacy to Polly's ardent appreciation of his friend, and had more than half hinted with the same reverential mystery to their matrimonial union later, and his intention of " doing the square thing" for the young couple. But it was presently noticed that these allusions became less frequent during Lacy's amorous aberrations, and an occasional depression and unusual reticence marked Captain Jim's manner when the subject was discussed in his presence. He seemed to endeavor to make up for his friend's defection by a kind of personal homage to Polly, and not unfrequently accompanied her to church or to singing-class. I have a vivid recollection of meeting him one afternoon crossing the fields with her, and looking into her face with that same wistful, absorbed, and uneasy canine expression that I had hitherto supposed he had reserved for Lacy alone. I do not know whether Polly was averse to the speechless devotion of these yearning brown eyes; her manner was animated, and the pretty cheek that was nearest me mantled as I passed ; but I was struck for the first time with the idea that Captain Jim loved her ! I was surprised to have that fancy corroborated in the remark of another wayfarer whom I met, to the effect, " That now that Bassett was out o' the running it looked ez if Captain Jim was makin' up for time ! " Was it possible that Captain Jim had always loved her ? I did not at first know whether to be pained or pleased for his sake. But I concluded that whether the

unworthy Bassett had at last found a *rival* in Captain Jim
or in the girl herself, it was a displacement that was for Captain Jim's welfare. But as I was about leaving Gilead for a
month's transfer to the San Francisco office, I had no opportunity to learn more from the confidences of Captain Jim.

I was ascending the principal staircase of my San Francisco hotel one rainy afternoon, when I was pointedly recalled to Gilead by the passing glitter of Mrs. Sweeny's
jewelry and the sudden vanishing behind her of a gentleman
who seemed to be accompanying her. A few moments
after I had entered my room I heard a tap at my door, and
opened it upon Lacy Bassett. I thought he looked a little
confused and agitated. Nevertheless, with an assumption
of cordiality and ease he said, "It appears we're neighbors. That's my room next to yours." He pointed to
the next room, which I then remembered was a sitting-room
en suite with my own, and communicating with it by a
second door, which was always locked. It had not been
occupied since my tenancy. As I suppose my face did not
show any extravagant delight at the news of his contiguity,
he added hastily, "There's a transom over the door, and
I thought I'd tell you you kin hear everything from the
one room to the other."

I thanked him, and told him dryly that, as I had no secrets to divulge and none that I cared to hear, it made no
difference to me. As this seemed to increase his confusion
and he still hesitated before the door, I asked him if Captain Jim was with him.

"No," he said quickly. "I haven't seen him for a
month, and don't want to. Look here, I want to talk to
you a bit about him." He walked into the room, and
closed the door behind him. "I want to tell you that me
and Captain Jim is played! All this runnin' o' me and
interferin' with me is played! I'm tired of it. You kin
tell him so from me."

" Then you have quarreled ? "

" Yes. As much as any man can quarrel with a darned fool who can't take a hint."

" One moment. Have you quarreled about Polly Baxter ? "

" Yes," he answered querulously. " Of course I have. What does he mean by interfering ? "

" Now listen to me, Mr. Bassett," I interrupted. " I have no desire to concern myself in your association with Captain Jim, but since you persist in dragging me unto it, you must allow me to speak plainly. From all that I can ascertain you have no serious intentions of marrying Polly Baxter. You have come here from Gilead to follow Mrs. Sweeny, whom I saw you with a moment ago. Now, why do you not frankly give up Miss Baxter to Captain Jim, who will make her a good husband, and go your own way with Mrs. Sweeny ? If you really wish to break off your connection with Captain Jim, that's the only way to do it."

His face, which had exhibited the weakest and most pitiable consciousness at the mention of Mrs. Sweeny, changed to an expression of absolute stupefaction as I concluded.

" Wot stuff are you tryin' to fool me with ? " he said at last roughly.

" I mean," I replied sharply, " that this double game of yours is disgraceful. Your association with Mrs. Sweeny demands the withdrawal of any claim you have upon Miss Baxter at once. If you have no respect for Captain Jim's friendship, you must at least show common decency to her."

He burst into a half-relieved, half-hysteric laugh. " Are you crazy ? " gasped he. " Why, Captain Jim's just huntin' *me* down to make *me* marry Polly. That's just what the row's about. That's just what he's interferin' for — just to carry out his darned fool ideas o' gettin' a wife for me; just his vanity to say *he's* made the match. It's *me* that he wants to marry to that Baxter girl, — not himself. He's too cursed selfish for that."

I suppose I was not different from ordinary humanity, for in my unexpected discomfiture I despised Captain Jim quite as much as I did the man before me. Reiterating my remark that I had no desire to mix myself further in their quarrels, I got rid of him with as little ceremony as possible. But a few minutes later, when the farcical side of the situation struck me, my irritation was somewhat mollified, without however increasing my respect for either of the actors. The whole affair had assumed a triviality that was simply amusing, nothing more, and I even looked forward to a meeting with Captain Jim and *his* exposition of the matter — which I knew would follow — with pleasurable anticipation. But I was mistaken.

One afternoon, when I was watching the slanting volleys of rain driven by a strong southwester against the windows of the hotel reading-room, I was struck by the erratic movements of a dripping figure outside that seemed to be hesitating over the entrance to the hotel. At times furtively penetrating the porch as far as the vestibule, and again shyly recoiling from it, its manner was so strongly suggestive of some timid animal that I found myself suddenly reminded of Captain Jim and the memorable evening of his exodus from Eureka Gulch. As the figure chanced to glance up to the window where I stood I saw to my astonishment that it *was* Captain Jim himself, but so changed and haggard that I scarcely knew him. I instantly ran out into the hall and vestibule, but when I reached the porch he had disappeared. Either he had seen me and wished to avoid me, or he had encountered the object of his quest, which I at once concluded must be Lacy Bassett. I was so much impressed and worried by his appearance and manner, that in this belief, I overcame my aversion to meeting Bassett, and even sought him through the public room and lobbies in the hope of finding Captain Jim with him. But in vain; possibly he had succeeded in escaping his relentless friend.

As the wind and rain increased at nightfall and grew into a tempestuous night, with deserted streets and swollen waterways, I did not go out again, but retired early, inexplicably haunted by the changed and brooding face of Captain Jim. Even in my dreams he pursued me in his favorite likeness of a wistful, anxious, and uneasy hound, who, on my turning to caress him familiarly, snapped at me viciously, and appeared to have suddenly developed a snarling rabid fury. I seemed to be awakened at last by the sound of his voice. For an instant I believed the delusion a part of my dream. But I was mistaken; I was lying broad awake, and the voice clearly had come from the next room, and was distinctly audible over the transom.

"I've had enough of it," he said, "and I'm givin' ye now — this night — yer last chance. Quit this hotel and that woman, and go back to Gilead and marry Polly. Don't do it and I'll kill ye, ez sure ez you sit there gapin' in that chair. If I can't get ye to fight me like a man, — and I'll spit in yer face or put some insult onto you afore that woman, afore everybody, ez would make a bigger skunk nor you turn, — I'll hunt ye down and kill ye in your tracks."

There was a querulous murmur of interruption in Lacy's voice, but whether of defiance or appeal I could not distinguish. Captain Jim's voice again rose, dogged and distinct.

"Ef *you* kill me it's all the same, and I don't say that I won't thank ye. This yer world is too crowded for yer and me, Lacy Bassett. I've believed in ye, trusted in ye, lied for ye, and fought for ye. From the time I took ye up — a feller-passenger to 'Fresco — believin' there wor the makin's of a man in ye, to now, you fooled me, — fooled me afore the Eureka boys; fooled me afore Gilead; fooled me afore *her;* fooled me afore God! It's got to end here.

Ye 've got to take the curse of that foolishness off o' me! You 've got to do one single thing that 's like the man I took ye for, or you 've got to die. Times waz when I 'd have wished it for your account — that 's gone, Lacy Bassett! You 've got to do it for *me*. You 've got to do it so I don't see 'd — d fool' writ in the eyes of every man ez looks at me."

He had apparently risen and walked towards the door. His voice sounded from another part of the room.

"I 'll give ye till to-morrow mornin' to do suthin' to lift this curse off o' me. Ef you refoose, then, by the living God, I 'll slap yer face in the dinin'-room, or in the office afore them all! You hear me!"

There was a pause, and then a quick sharp explosion that seemed to fill and expand both rooms until the windows were almost lifted from their casements, a hysterical inarticulate cry from Lacy, the violent opening of a door, hurried voices, and the tramping of many feet in the passage. I sprang out of bed, partly dressed myself, and ran into the hall. But by that time I found a crowd of guests and servants around the next door, some grasping Bassett, who was white and trembling, and others kneeling by Captain Jim, who was half lying in the doorway against the wall.

"He heard it all," Bassett gasped hysterically, pointing to me. "*He* knows that this man wanted to kill me."

Before I could reply, Captain Jim partly raised himself with a convulsive effort. Wiping away the blood that, oozing from his lips, already showed the desperate character of his internal wound, he said in a husky and hurried voice: "It 's all right, boys! It 's my fault. It was *me* who done it. I went for him in a mean underhanded way just now, when he had n't a weppin nor any show to defend himself. We gripped. He got a holt o' my derringer — you see that 's *my* pistol there, I swear it — and turned it agin me in self-defense, and sarved me right. I swear to God, gentlemen, it's so!" Catching sight of my face, he looked at me, I fancied half imploringly and half triumphantly, and added, "I might hev knowed it! I allers allowed Lacy Bassett was game! — game, gentlemen — and he was. If it's my last word, I say it — he was game!"

And with this devoted falsehood upon his lips and something of the old canine instinct in his failing heart, as his head sank back he seemed to turn it towards Bassett, as if to stretch himself out at his feet. Then the light failed from his yearning upward glance, and the curse of foolishness was lifted from him forever.

So conclusive were the facts, that the coroner's jury did not deem it necessary to detain Mr. Bassett for a single moment after the inquest. But he returned to Gilead, married Polly Baxter, and probably on the strength of having "killed his man," was unopposed on the platform next year, and triumphantly elected to the legislature!

THE HERITAGE OF DEDLOW MARSH

I

THE sun was going down on the Dedlow Marshes. The tide was following it fast as if to meet the reddening lines of sky and water in the west, leaving the foreground to grow blacker and blacker every moment, and to bring out in startling contrast the few half-filled and half-lit pools left behind and forgotten. The strong breath of the Pacific fanning their surfaces at times kindled them into a dull glow like dying embers. A cloud of sandpipers rose white from one of the nearer lagoons, swept in a long eddying ring against the sunset, and became a black and dropping rain to seaward. The long sinuous line of channel, fading with the light and ebbing with the tide, began to give off here and there light puffs of gray-winged birds like sudden exhalations. High in the darkening sky the long arrow-headed lines of geese and "brant" pointed towards the upland. As the light grew more uncertain the air at times was filled with the rush of viewless and melancholy wings, or became plaintive with far-off cries and lamentations. As the Marsh grew blacker the far-scattered tussocks and accretions on its level surface began to loom in exaggerated outline, and two human figures, suddenly emerging erect on the bank of the hidden channel, assumed the proportion of giants.

When they had moored their unseen boat, they still appeared for some moments to be moving vaguely and aimlessly round the spot where they had disembarked. But as the eye became familiar with the darkness it was seen that they were really advancing inland, yet with a slowness of progression and deviousness of course that appeared inexplicable to the distant spectator. Presently it was evident that this seemingly even, vast, black expanse was traversed and intersected by inky creeks and small channels, which made human progression difficult and dangerous. As they appeared nearer and their figures took more natural proportions, it could be seen that each carried a gun; that one was a young girl, although dressed so like her companion in shaggy pea-jacket and sou'wester as to be scarcely distinguished from him above the short skirt that came halfway down her high india-rubber fishing-boots. By the time they had reached firmer ground, and turned to look back at the sunset, it could be also seen that the likeness between their faces was remarkable. Both had crisp, black, tightly curling hair; both had dark eyes and heavy eyebrows; both had quick vivid complexions, slightly heightened by the sea and wind. But more striking than their similarity of coloring was the likeness of expression and bearing. Both wore the same air of picturesque energy; both bore themselves with a like graceful effrontery and self-possession.

The young man continued his way. The young girl lingered for a moment looking seaward, with her small brown hand lifted to shade her eyes, — a precaution which her heavy eyebrows and long lashes seemed to render utterly gratuitous.

"Come along, Mag. What are ye waitin' for?" said the young man impatiently.

"Nothin'. Lookin' at that boat from the Fort." Her clear eyes were watching a small skiff, invisible to less keen-sighted observers, aground upon a flat near the mouth of the channel. "Them chaps will have a high ole time gunnin' thar, stuck in the mud, and the tide goin' out like sixty!"

"Never you mind the sodgers," returned her companion aggressively, "they kin take care o' their own precious skins, or Uncle Sam will do it for 'em, I reckon. Anyhow the people — that's you and me, Mag — is expected to pay for their foolishness. That's what they're sent yer for. Ye oughter to be satisfied with that," he added, with deep sarcasm.

"I reckon they ain't expected to do much off o' dry land, and they can't help bein' queer on the water," returned the young girl, with a reflecting sense of justice.

"Then they ain't no call to go gunnin', and wastin' Guv'nment powder on ducks instead o' Injins."

"Thet's so," said the girl thoughtfully. "Wonder ef Guv'nment pays for them frocks the Kernel's girls went cavortin' round Logport in last Sunday — they looked like a cirkis."

"Like ez not the old Kernel gets it outer contracts — one way or another. We pay for it all the same," he added gloomily.

"Jest the same ez if they were my clothes," said the girl, with a quick, fiery, little laugh, "ain't it? Wonder how they'd like my sayin' that to 'em when they was prancin' round, eh, Jim?"

But her companion was evidently unprepared for this sweeping feminine deduction, and stopped it with masculine promptitude.

"Look yer — instead o' botherin' your head about what the Fort girls wear, you'd better trot along a little more lively. It's late enough now."

"But these darned boots hurt like pizen," said the girl, limping. "They swallowed a lot o' water over the tops while I was wadin' down there, and my feet go swashin' around like in a churn every step."

"Lean on me, baby," he returned, passing his arm around her waist, and dropping her head smartly on his shoulder. "Thar!" The act was brotherly and slightly contemptuous, but it was sufficient to at once establish their kinship.

They continued on thus for some moments in silence, the girl, I fear, after the fashion of her sex, taking the fullest advantage of this slightly sentimental and caressing attitude. They were moving now along the edge of the Marsh, parallel with the line of rapidly fading horizon, following some trail only known to their keen youthful eyes. It was growing darker and darker. The cries of the sea-birds had ceased; even the call of a belated plover had died away inland; the hush of death lay over the black funereal pall of marsh at their side. The tide had run out with the day. Even the sea-breeze had lulled in this dead slack-water of all nature, as if waiting outside the bar with the ocean, the stars, and the night.

Suddenly the girl stopped and halted her companion. The faint far sound of a bugle broke the silence, if the idea of interruption could have been conveyed by the two or three exquisite vibrations that seemed born of that silence itself, and to fade and die in it without break or discord. Yet it was only the "retreat" call from the Fort two miles distant and invisible.

The young girl's face had become irradiated, and her small mouth half opened as she listened. "Do you know, Jim," she said, with a confidential sigh, "I allus put words to that when I hear it — it 's so pow'ful pretty. It allus goes to me like this: 'Goes the day, Far away, With the light, And the night Comes along — Comes along — Comes along — Like a-a so-o-ong.'" She here lifted her voice, a sweet, fresh, boyish contralto, in such an admirable imitation of the bugle that her brother, after the fashion of more select auditors, was for a moment quite convinced that the words meant something. Nevertheless, as a brother, it was his duty to crush this weakness. "Yes; and it says:

'Shut your head, Go to bed,'" he returned irascibly; "and *you'd* better come along, if we're goin' to hev any supper. There's Yeller Bob hez got ahead of us over there with the game already."

The girl glanced towards a slouching burdened figure that now appeared to be preceding them, straightened herself suddenly, and then looked attentively towards the Marsh.

"Not the sodgers again?." said her brother impatiently.

"No," she said quickly; "but if that don't beat anythin'! I'd hev sworn, Jim, that Yeller Bob was somewhere behind us. I saw him only jest now when 'Taps' sounded, somewhere over thar." She pointed with a half-uneasy expression in quite another direction from that in which the slouching Yellow Bob had just loomed.

"Tell ye what, Mag, makin' poetry outer bugle-calls hez kinder muddled ye. *That's* Yeller Bob ahead, and ye orter know Injins well enuff by this time to remember that they allus crop up jest when ye don't expect them. And there's the bresh jest afore us. Come!"

The "bresh," or low bushes, was really a line of stunted willows and alders that seemed to have gradually sunk into the level of the plain, but increased in size farther inland, until they grew to the height and density of a wood. Seen from the channel it had the appearance of a green cape or promontory thrust upon the Marsh. Passing through its tangled recesses, with the aid of some unerring instinct, the two companions emerged upon another and much larger level that seemed as illimitable as the bay. The strong breath of the ocean lying just beyond the bar and estuary they were now facing came to them salt and humid as another tide. The nearer expanse of open water reflected the after-glow, and lightened the landscape. And between the two wayfarers and the horizon rose, bleak and startling, the strange outlines of their home.

At first it seemed a ruined colonnade of many pillars, whose base and pediment were buried in the earth, supporting a long parallelogram of entablature and cornices. But a second glance showed it to be a one-storied building, upheld above the Marsh by numberless piles placed at regular distances; some of them sunken or inclined from the perpendicular, increasing the first illusion. Between these pillars, which permitted a free circulation of air, and, at extraordinary tides, even the waters of the bay itself, the level waste of marsh, the bay, the surges of the bar, and finally the red horizon line, were distinctly visible. A railed gallery or platform, supported also on piles, and reached by steps from the Marsh, ran around the building, and gave access to the several rooms and offices.

But if the appearance of this lacustrine and amphibious dwelling was striking, and not without a certain rude and massive grandeur, its grounds and possessions, through which the brother and sister were still picking their way, were even more grotesque and remarkable. Over a space of half a dozen acres the flotsam and jetsam of years of tidal offerings were collected, and even guarded with a certain care. The blackened hulks of huge uprooted trees, scarcely distinguishable from the fragments of genuine wrecks beside them, were securely fastened by chains to stakes and piles driven in the marsh, while heaps of broken and disjointed bamboo orange crates, held together by ropes of fibre, glistened like ligamented bones heaped in the dead valley. Masts, spars, fragments of shell-encrusted boats, binnacles, round-houses and galleys, and part of the after-deck of a coasting schooner had ceased their wanderings and found rest in this vast cemetery of the sea. The legend on a wheel-house, the lettering on a stern or bow, served for mortuary inscription. Wailed over by the trade-winds, mourned by lamenting sea-birds, once every year the tide visited its lost dead and left them wet with its tears.

To such a spot and its surroundings the atmosphere of tradition and mystery was not wanting. Six years ago Boone Culpepper had built the house, and brought to it his wife — variously believed to be a gypsy, a Mexican, a bright mulatto, a Digger Indian, a South Sea princess from Tahiti, somebody else's wife — but in reality a little Creole woman from New Orleans, with whom he had contracted a marriage, with other gambling debts, during a winter's vacation from his home in Virginia. At the end of two years she had died, succumbing, as differently stated, from perpetual wet feet, or the misanthropic idiosyncrasies of her husband, and leaving behind her a girl of twelve and a boy of sixteen to console him. How futile was this bequest may be guessed from a brief summary of Mr. Culpepper's peculiarities. They were the development of a singular form of aggrandizement and misanthropy. On his arrival at Logport he had bought a part of the apparently valueless Dedlow Marsh from the Government at less than a dollar an acre, continuing his singular investment year by year until he was the owner of three leagues of amphibious domain. It was then discovered that this property carried with it the *water-front* of divers valuable and convenient sites for manufactures and the commercial ports of a noble bay, as well as the natural embarcaderos of some "lumbering" inland settlements. Boone Culpepper would not sell. Boone Culpepper would not rent or lease. Boone Culpepper held an invincible blockade of his neighbors, and the progress and improvement he despised — granting only, after a royal fashion, occasional license, revocable at pleasure, in the shape of tolls, which amply supported him, with the game he shot in his kingfisher's eyrie on the Marsh. Even the Government that had made him powerful was obliged to "condemn" a part of his property at an equitable price for the purposes of Fort Redwood, in which the adjacent town of Logport shared. And Boone Culpep-

per, unable to resist the act, refused to receive the compensation or quitclaim the town. In his scant intercourse
with his neighbors he always alluded to it as his own, showed
it to his children as part of their strange inheritance, and
exhibited the starry flag that floated from the Fort as a
flaunting insult to their youthful eyes. Hated, feared, and
superstitiously shunned by some, regarded as a madman by
others, familiarly known as "The Kingfisher of Dedlow,"
Boone Culpepper was one day found floating dead in his
skiff, with a charge of shot through his head and shoulders.
The shot-gun lying at his feet at the bottom of the boat
indicated the "accident" as recorded in the verdict of the
coroner's jury — but not by the people. A thousand
rumors of murder or suicide prevailed, but always with the
universal rider, "Served him right." So invincible was
this feeling that but few attended his last rites, which took
place at high water. The delay of the officiating clergyman lost the tide ; the homely catafalque — his own boat —
was left aground on the Marsh, and deserted by all mourners except the two children. Whatever he had instilled
into them by precept and example, whatever took place
that night in their lonely watch by his bier on the black
marshes, it was certain that those who confidently looked
for any change in the administration of the Dedlow Marsh
were cruelly mistaken. The old Kingfisher was dead, but
he had left in the nest two young birds, more beautiful
and graceful, it was true, yet as fierce and tenacious of beak
and talon.

Arriving at the house, the young people ascended the outer flight of wooden steps, which bore an odd likeness to the companionway of a vessel, and the gallery, or " deck," as it was called — where a number of nets, floats, and buoys thrown over the railing completed the nautical resemblance. This part of the building was evidently devoted to kitchen, dining-room, and domestic offices; the principal room in the centre serving as hall or living-room, and communicating on the other side with two sleeping apartments. It was of considerable size, with heavy lateral beams across the ceiling, — built, like the rest of the house, with a certain maritime strength, — and looked not unlike a saloon cabin. An enormous open Franklin stove between the windows, as large as a chimney, blazing with driftwood, gave light and heat to the apartment, and brought into flickering relief the boarded walls hung with the spoils of sea and shore, and glittering with gun-barrels. Fowling-pieces of all sizes, from the long ducking-gun mounted on a swivel for boat use to the light single-barrel or carbine, stood in racks against the walls; game-bags, revolvers in their holsters, hunting and fishing knives in their sheaths, depended from hooks above them. In one corner stood a harpoon; in another, two or three Indian spears for salmon. The carpetless floor and rude chairs and settles were covered with otter, mink, beaver, and a quantity of valuable seal-skins, with a few larger pelts of the bear and elk. The only attempt at decoration was the displayed wings and breasts of the wood and harlequin duck, the

muir, the cormorant, the gull, the gannet, and the femi-
ninely delicate half mourning of petrel and plover, nailed
against the wall.   The influence of the sea was dominant
above all, and asserted its saline odors even through the
spice of the curling driftwood smoke that half veiled the
ceiling.

A berry-eyed old Indian woman with the complexion of
dried salmon ; her daughter, also with berry eyes, and
with a face that seemed wholly made of a moist laugh ;
" Yellow Bob," a Digger " buck," so called from the prevailing ochre markings of his cheek, and " Washooh," an ex-
chief ; a nondescript in a blanket, looking like a cheap and
dirty doll whose fibrous hair was badly nailed on his carved
wooden head, composed the Culpepper household.   While
the two former were preparing supper in the adjacent dining-
room, Yellow Bob, relieved of his burden of game, appeared on the gallery and beckoned mysteriously to his
master through the window.   James Culpepper went out,
returned quickly, and, after a minute's hesitation and an
uneasy glance towards his sister, who had meantime pushed
back her sou'wester from her forehead, and without taking
off her jacket had dropped into a chair before the fire with
her back towards him, took his gun noiselessly from the
rack, and, saying carelessly that he would be back in a
moment, disappeared.

Left to herself, Maggie coolly pulled off her long boots
and stockings, and comfortably opposed to the fire two very
pretty feet and ankles, whose delicate purity was slightly
blue-bleached by confinement in the tepid sea-water.   The
contrast of their waxen whiteness with her blue woolen
skirt, and with even the skin of her sunburnt hands and
wrists, apparently amused her, and she sat for some moments
with her elbows on her knees, her skirts slightly raised,
contemplating them, and curling her toes with evident satisfaction.   The firelight playing upon the rich coloring of her

face, the fringe of jet-black curls that almost met the thick
sweep of eyebrows, and left her only a white strip of forehead, her short upper lip and small chin, rounded but
resolute, completed a piquant and striking figure. The
rich brown shadows on the smoke-stained walls and ceiling,
the occasional starting into relief of the scutcheons of brilliant plumage, and the momentary glitter of the steel barrels made a quaint background to this charming picture.
Sitting there, and following some lingering memory of her
tramp on the Marsh, she hummed to herself a few notes of
the bugle-call that had impressed her — at first softly, and
finally with the full pitch of her voice.

Suddenly she stopped.

There was a faint and unmistakable rapping on the
floor beneath her. It was distinct, but cautiously given,
as if intended to be audible to her alone. For a moment
she stood upright, her feet still bare and glistening, on the
otter skin that served as a rug. There were two doors to
the room, one from which her brother had disappeared,
which led to the steps, the other giving on the back gallery, looking inland. With a quick instinct she caught up
her gun and ran to that one, but not before a rapid scram-
ble near the railing was followed by a cautious opening of
the door. She was just in time to shut it on the extended
arm and light blue sleeve of an army overcoat that pro-
truded through the opening, and for a moment threw her
whole weight against it.

" A dhrop of whiskey, Miss, for the love of God."

She retained her hold, cocked her weapon, and stepped
back a pace from the door. The blue sleeve was followed
by the rest of the overcoat, and a blue cap with the infantry blazoning, and the letter H on its peak. They were
for the moment more distinguishable than the man beneath
them — grimed and blackened with the slime of the Marsh.
But what could be seen of his mud-stained face was more

grotesque than terrifying.   A combination of weakness and
audacity, insinuation and timidity struggled through the
dirt for expression.   His small blue eyes were not ill-
natured, and even the intruding arm trembled more from
exhaustion than passion.

"On'y a dhrop, Miss," he repeated piteously, "and av
ye pleeze, quick! afore I'm stharved with the cold en-
toirely."

She looked at him intently — without lowering her gun.
"Who are you?"

"Thin, it's the truth I'll tell ye, Miss — whisth then!"
he said in a half whisper; "I'm a desarter!"

"Then it was *you* that was doggin' us on the Marsh?"

"It was the sarjint I was lavin', Miss."

She looked at him hesitatingly.

"Stay outside there; if you move a step into the room,
I'll blow you out of it."

He stepped back on the gallery.   She closed the door,
bolted it, and, still holding the gun, opened a cupboard,
poured out a glass of whiskey, and, returning to the door,
opened it and handed him the liquor.

She watched him drain it eagerly, saw the fiery stimulant put life into his shivering frame, trembling hands, and
kindle his dull eye — and — quietly raised her gun again.

"Ah, put it down, Miss, put it down!   Fwhot's the
use?   Sure the bullets ye carry in them oiyes of yours is
more deadly!   It's out here oi'll sthand, glory be to
God, all night, without movin' a fut till the sarjint comes
to take me, av ye won't levil them oiyes at me like that.
Ah, whirra! look at that now! but it's a goddess she is
— the livin' Jaynus of warr, standin' there like a statoo,
wid her alybaster fut put forward."

In her pride and conscious superiority, any suggestion of
shame at thus appearing before a common man and a men-
dicant was as impossible to her nature as it would have

been to a queen or the goddess of his simile. His presence
and his compliment alike passed her calm modesty unchal-
lenged. The wretched scamp recognized the fact and felt
its power, and it was with a superstitious reverence assert-
ing itself through his native extravagance that he raised
his grimy hand to his cap in military salute and became
respectfully rigid.

"Then the sodgers were huntin' *you* ?" she said thoughtfully, lowering her weapon.

"Thrue for you, Miss — they worr, and it 's meself
that was lyin' flat in the ditch wid me faytures makin' an
illigant cast in the mud — more betoken, as ye see even
now — and the sarjint and his daytail thrampin' round
me. It was thin that the mortial cold sthruck through me
mouth, and made me wake for the whiskey that would
resthore me."

"What did you desert fer ?"

"Ah, list to that now ! Fwhat did I desart fer ? Shure
ev there was the ghost of an inemy round, it 's meself that
would be in the front now ! But it was the letthers from
me ould mother, Miss, that is sthruck wid a mortial illness
— long life to her ! — in County Clare, and me sisthers
in Ninth Avenue in New York, fornint the daypo, that is
brekken their harruts over me listin' in the Fourth Infan-
thry to do duty in a haythen wilderness. Av it was the
cavalry — and it 's me own father that was in the Innish-
killen Dthragoons, Miss — oi would n't moind. Wid a
horse betune me legs, it 's on parade oi 'd be now, Miss,
and not wandhering over the bare flure of the Marsh,
stharved wid the cold, the thirst, and hunger, wid the mud
and the moire thick on me ; facin' an illigant young leddy
as is the ekal ov a Fayld Marshal's darter — not to sphake
ov Kernal Preston's — ez could n't hold a candle to her."

Brought up on the Spanish frontier, Maggie Culpepper
was one of the few American girls who was not familiar

with the Irish race. The rare smile that momentarily lit up her petulant mouth seemed to justify the intruder's praise. But it passed quickly, and she returned dryly : —

"That means you want more drink, suthin' to eat, and clothes. Suppose my brother comes back and kctches you here ? "

"Shure, Miss, he's just now hunten me, along wid his two haythen Diggers, beyond the laygoon there. It worr the yellar one that sphotted me lyin' there in the ditch ; it worr only your own oiyes, Miss — more power to their beauty for that ! — that saw me folly him unbeknownst here ; and that desaved them, ye see ! "

The young girl remained for an instant silent and thoughtful.

"We 're no friends of the Fort," she said finally, " but I don't reckon for that reason my brother will cotton to *you*. Stay out thar where ye are, till I come to ye. If you hear me singin' again, you 'll know he 's come back, and ye 'd better scoot with what you 've already got, and be thankful."

She shut the door again and locked it, went into the dining-room, returned with some provisions wrapped in paper, took a common wicker flask from the wall, passed into her brother's bedroom, and came out with a flannel shirt, overalls, and a coarse Indian blanket, and, reopening the door, placed them before the astonished and delighted vagabond. His eye glistened ; he began, " Glory be to God," but for once his habitual extravagance failed him. Nature triumphed with a more eloquent silence over his well-worn art. He hurriedly wiped his begrimed face and eyes with the shirt she had given him, and, catching the sleeve of her rough pea-jacket in his dirty hand, raised it to his lips.

"Go ! " she said imperiously. " Get away while you can."

" Av it vas me last words — it 's speechless oi am," he stammered, and disappeared over the railing.

She remained for a moment holding the door half open, and gazing into the darkness that seemed to flow in like a tide. Then she shut it, and going into her bedroom resumed her interrupted toilet. When she emerged again she was smartly stockinged and slippered, and even the blue serge skirt was exchanged for a bright print, with a white fichu tied around her throat. An attempt to subdue her rebellious curls had resulted in the construction from their ruins of a low Norman arch across her forehead with pillared abutments of ringlets. When her brother returned a few moments later she did not look up, but remained, perhaps a little ostentatiously, bending over the fire.

" Bob allowed that the Fort boat was huntin' *men* — deserters, I reckon," said Jim aggrievedly. " Wanted me to believe that he *saw* one on the Marsh hidin'. On'y an Injin lie, I reckon, to git a little extra fire-water, for toting me out to the bresh on a fool's errand."

" Oh, *that 's* where you went ! " said Maggie, addressing the fire. " Since when hev you tuk partnership with the Guv'nment and Kernel Preston to hunt up and take keer of their property ? "

" Well, I ain't goin' to hev such wreckage as they pick up and enlist set adrift on our marshes, Mag," said Jim decidedly.

" What would you hev done had you ketched him ? " said Maggie, looking suddenly into her brother's face.

" Given him a dose of snipe-shot that he 'd remember, and be thankful it was n't slugs," said Jim promptly. Observing a deeper seriousness in her attitude, he added, " Why, if it was in war-time he 'd get a *ball* from them sodgers on sight."

" Yes ; but *you* ain't got no call to interfere," said Maggie.

"Ain't I? Why, he's no better than an outlaw. I ain't sure that he has n't been stealin' or killin' somebody over theer."

"Not *that* man!" said Maggie impulsively.

"Not what man?" said her brother, facing her quickly.

"Why," returned Maggie, repairing her indiscretion with feminine dexterity, "not *any* man who might have knocked you and me over on the marshes in the dusk, and grabbed our guns."

"Wish he'd hev tried it," said the brother, with a superior smile, but a quickly rising color. "Where d' ye suppose *I'd* hev been all the while?"

Maggie saw her mistake, and for the first time in her life resolved to keep a secret from her brother — over night. "Supper's gettin' cold," she said, rising.

They went into the dining-room — an apartment as plainly furnished as the one they had quitted, but in its shelves, cupboards, and closely fitting boarding bearing out the general nautical suggestion of the house — and seated themselves before a small table on which their frugal meal was spread. In this *tête-à-tête* position Jim suddenly laid down his knife and fork and stared at his sister.

"Hello!"

"What's the matter?" said Maggie, starting slightly. "How you do skeer one."

"Who's been prinkin', eh?"

"My ha'r was in kinks all along o' that hat," said Maggie, with a return of higher color, "and I had to straighten it. It's a boy's hat, not a girl's."

"But that necktie and that gown — and all those frills and tuckers?" continued Jim, generalizing, with a rapid twirling of his fingers over her. "Are you expectin' Judge Martin or the Expressman this evening?"

Judge Martin was the lawyer of Logport, who had proven her father's will, and had since raved about his single interview with the Kingfisher's beautiful daughter; the Expressman was a young fellow who was popularly supposed to have left his heart while delivering another valuable package on Maggie in person, and had " never been the same man since." It was a well-worn fraternal pleasantry that had done duty many a winter's evening, as a happy combination of moral admonition and cheerfulness. Maggie usually paid it the tribute of a quick little laugh and a sisterly pinch, but that evening those marks of approbation were withheld.

" Jim dear," said she, when their Spartan repast was concluded and they were reëstablished before the living-room fire, " what was it the Redwood Mill Kempany offered you for that piece near Dead Man's Slough ? "

Jim took his pipe from his lips long enough to say, "Ten thousand dollars," and put it back again.

" And what do ye kalkilate all our property, letting alone this yer house, and the driftwood front, is worth all together ? "

" Includin' wot the Gov'nment owes us ? — for that's all ours, ye know ? " said Jim quickly.

" No — leavin' that out — jest for greens, you know," suggested Maggie.

" Well nigh onter a hundred and seventy-five thousand dollars, I reckon, by and large."

" That 's a heap o' money, Jim ! I reckon old Kernel Preston would n't raise that in a hundred years," continued Maggie, warming her knees by the fire.

" In five million years," said Jim, promptly sweeping away further discussion. After a pause he added, " You and me, Mag, kin see anybody's pile, and go 'em fifty thousand better."

There were a few moments of complete silence, in which Maggie smoothed her knees, and Jim's pipe, which seemed to have become gorged and apoplectic with its owner's wealth, snored unctuously.

"Jim dear, what if — it's on'y an idea of mine, you know — what if you sold that piece to the Redwood Mill, and we jest tuk that money and — and — and jest lifted the ha'r offer them folks at Logport? Jest astonished 'em! Jest tuk the best rooms in that new hotel, got a hoss and buggy, dressed ourselves, you and me, fit to kill, and made them Fort people take a back seat in the Lord's Tabernacle, oncet for all. You see what I mean, Jim," she said hastily, as her brother seemed to be succumbing, like his pipe, in apoplectic astonishment, "jest on'y to *show* 'em what we *could* do if we keerd. Lord! when we done it and spent the money we'd jest snap our fingers and skip back yer ez nat'ral ez life! Ye don't think, Jim," she said, suddenly turning half fiercely upon him, "that I'd allow to *live* among 'em — to stay a menet after that!"

Jim laid down his pipe and gazed at his sister with stony deliberation. "And — what — do — you — kalkilate — to make by all that?" he said, with scornful distinctness.

"Why, jest to show 'em we *have* got money, and could buy 'em all up if we wanted to," returned Maggie, sticking boldly to her guns, albeit with a vague conviction that her fire was weakened through elevation, and somewhat alarmed at the deliberation of the enemy.

"And you mean to say they don't know it now," he continued with slow derision.

"No," said Maggie. "Why, theer's that new schoolmarm over at Logport, you know, Jim, the one that wanted to take your picter in your boat for a young smuggler or fancy pirate or Eyetalian fisherman, and allowed that you're handsomed some, and offered to pay you for sittin' — do you reckon *she'd* believe you owned the land her schoolhouse was built on? No! Lots of 'em don't. Lots of 'em thinks we're poor and low down — and them ez does n't, thinks" —

"What?" asked her brother sharply.

"That we 're *mean*."

The quick color came to Jim's cheek. "So," he said, facing her quickly, "for the sake of a lot of riff-raff and scum that 's drifted here around us — jest for the sake of cuttin' a swell before them — you 'll go out among the hounds ez allowed your mother was a Spanish nigger or a kanaka, ez called your father a pirate and landgrabber, ez much as allowed he was shot by some one or killed himself a purpose, ez said you was a heathen and a loony because you did n't go to school or church along with their trash, ez kept away from maw's sickness ez if it was smallpox, and dad's fun'ral ez if he was a hoss-thief, and left you and me to watch his coffin on the marshes all night till the tide kem back. And now you — *you* that jined hands with me that night over our father lyin' there cold and despised — ez if he was a dead dog thrown up by the tide — and swore that ez long ez that tide ebbed and flowed it could n't bring you to them, or them to you agin! You now want — what? What? Why, to go and cast your lot among 'em, and live among 'em, and join in their God-forsaken holler foolishness, and — and — and" —

"Stop! It 's a lie! I *did n't* say that. Don't you dare to say it!" said the girl, springing to her feet, and facing her brother in turn, with flashing eyes.

For a moment the two stared at each other — it might have been as in a mirror, so perfectly were their passions reflected in each line, shade, and color of the other's face. It was as if they had each confronted their own passionate and willful souls, and were frightened. It had often occurred before, always with the same invariable ending. The young man's eyes lowered first; the girl's filled with tears.

"Well, ef ye did n't mean that, what did ye mean?" said Jim, sinking, with sullen apology, back into his chair.

"I — only — meant it — for — for — revenge!" sobbed Maggie.

"Oh!" said Jim, as if allowing his higher nature to be touched by this noble instinct. "But I didn't jest see where the revenge kem in."

"No? But, never mind now, Jim," said Maggie, ostentatiously ignoring, after the fashion of her sex, the trouble she had provoked; "but to think — that — that — you thought" — (sobbing).

"But I didn't, Mag" — (caressingly).

With this very vague and impotent conclusion, Maggie permitted herself to be drawn beside her brother, and for a few moments they plumed each other's ruffled feathers, and smoothed each other's lifted crests, like two beautiful young specimens of that halcyon genus to which they were popularly supposed to belong. At the end of half an hour Jim rose, and, yawning slightly, said in a perfunctory way : —

"Where's the book?"

The book in question was the Bible. It had been the self-imposed custom of these two young people to read aloud a chapter every night as their one vague formula of literary and religious discipline. When it was produced, Maggie, presuming on his affectionate and penitential condition, suggested that to-night he should pick out "suthin' interestin'." But this unorthodox frivolity was sternly put aside by Jim — albeit, by way of compromise, he agreed to "chance it," *i. e.*, open its pages at random.

He did so. Generally he allowed himself a moment's judicious pause for a certain chaste preliminary inspection necessary before reading aloud to a girl. To-night he omitted that modest precaution, and in a pleasant voice, which in reading was singularly free from colloquial infelicities of pronunciation, began at once : —

"'Curse ye Meroz, said the angel of the Lord, curse ye bitterly the inhabitants thereof ; because they came not to

Suthin' interestin'

the help of the Lord, to the help of the Lord against the mighty.' ''

" Oh, you looked first," said Maggie.

" I did n't now — honest Injin !   I just opened."

" Go on," said Maggie, eagerly shoving him and inter-posing her neck over his shoulder.

And Jim continued Deborah's wonderful song of Jael and Sisera to the bitter end of its strong monosyllabic climax.

" There," he said, closing the volume, " that 's what *1* call revenge.   That 's the real Scripture thing — no fancy frills theer."

" Yes ; but, Jim dear, don't you see that she treated him first — sorter got round him with free milk and butter, and reg'larly blandished him," argued Maggie earnestly.

But Jim declined to accept this feminine suggestion, or to pursue the subject further, and after a fraternal embrace they separated for the night.   Jim lingered long enough to look after the fastening of the door and windows, and Maggie remained for some moments at her casement, look-ing across the gallery to the Marsh beyond.

The moon had risen, the tide was half up.   Whatever sign or trace of alien footprint or occupation had been there was already smoothly obliterated ; even the configuration of the land had changed.   A black cape had disappeared, a level line of shore had been eaten into by teeth of glisten-ing silver.   The whole dark surface of the Marsh was be-ginning to be streaked with shining veins as if a new life was coursing through it.   Part of the open bay before the Fort, encroaching upon the shore, seemed in the moonlight to be reaching a white and outstretched arm towards the nest of the Kingfisher.

III

THE reveille at Fort Redwood had been supplemented full five minutes by the voice of Lieutenant George Calvert's servant, before that young officer struggled from his bed. His head was splitting, his tongue and lips were dry and feverish, his bloodshot eyes were shrinking from the insufferable light of the day, his mind a confused medley of the past night and the present morning, of cards and wild revelry, and the vision of a reproachfully trim orderly standing at his door with reports and orders which he now held composedly in his hand. For Lieutenant Calvert had been enjoying a symposium variously known as "Stag Feed" and "A Wild Stormy Night" with several of his brother officers, and a sickening conviction that it was not the first or the last time he had indulged in these festivities. At that moment he loathed himself, and then after the usual derelict fashion cursed the fate that had sent him, after graduating, to a frontier garrison — the dull monotony of whose duties made the Border horse-play of dissipation a relief. Already he had reached the miserable point of envying the veteran capacities of his superiors and equals. "If I could drink like Kirby or Crowninshield, or if there was any other cursed thing a man could do in this hole," he had wretchedly repeated to himself, after each misspent occasion, and yet already he was looking forward to them as part of a "sub's" duty and worthy his emulation. Already the dream of social recreation fostered by West Point had been rudely dispelled. Beyond the garrison circle of Colonel Preston's family and two officers' wives, there was no society.   The vague distrust and civil jealousy with which some frontier communities regard the Federal power, heightened in this instance by the uncompromising attitude the Government had taken towards the settlers' severe Indian policy, had kept the people of Logport aloof from the Fort.   The regimental band might pipe to them on Saturdays, but they would not dance.

Howbeit, Lieutenant Calvert dressed himself with uncertain hands but mechanical regularity and neatness, and, under the automatic training of discipline and duty, managed to button his tunic tightly over his feelings, to pull himself together with his sword-belt, compressing a still cadet-like waist, and to present that indescribable combination of precision and jauntiness which his brother officers too often allowed to lapse into frontier carelessness.   His closely clipped light hair, yet dripping from a plunge in the cold water, had been brushed and parted with military exactitude, and when surmounted by his cap, with the peak in an artful suggestion of extra smartness tipped forward over his eyes, only his pale face — a shade lighter than his little blonde mustache — showed his last night's excesses.   He was mechanically reaching for his sword and staring confusedly at the papers on his table when his servant interrupted : —

" Major Bromley arranged that Lieutenant Kirby takes your sash this morning, as you 're not well, sir ; and you 're to report for special to the colonel," he added, pointing discreetly to the envelope.

Touched by this consideration of his superior, Major Bromley, who had been one of the veterans of last night's engagement, Calvert mastered the contents of the envelope without the customary anathema of specials, said, " Thank you, Parks," and passed out on the veranda.

The glare of the quiet sunlit quadrangle, clean as a well-swept floor, the whitewashed walls and galleries of the barrack buildings beyond, the white and green palisade of officers' cottages on either side, and the glitter of a sentry's bayonet, were for a moment intolerable to him. Yet, by a kind of subtle irony, never before had the genius and spirit of the vocation he had chosen seemed to be as incarnate as in the scene before him. Seclusion, self-restraint, cleanliness, regularity, sobriety, the atmosphere of a wholesome life, the austere reserve of a monastery without its mysterious or pensive meditation, were all there. To escape which, he had of his own free will successively accepted a fool's distraction, the inevitable result of which was the viewing of them the next morning with tremulous nerves and aching eyeballs.

An hour later, Lieutenant George Calvert had received his final instructions from Colonel Preston to take charge of a small detachment to recover and bring back certain deserters, but notably one, Dennis M'Caffrey of Company H, charged additionally with mutinous solicitation and example. As Calvert stood before his superior, that distinguished officer, whose oratorical powers had been considerably stimulated through a long course of " returning thanks for the Army," slightly expanded his chest and said paternally : —

" I am aware, Mr. Calvert, that duties of this kind are somewhat distasteful to young officers, and are apt to be considered in the light of police detail ; but I must remind you that no one part of a soldier's duty can be held more important or honorable than another, and that the fulfillment of any one, however trifling, must, with honor to himself and security to his comrades, receive his fullest devotion. A sergeant and a file of men might perform your duty, but I require, in addition, the discretion, courtesy, and consideration of a gentleman who will command an equal respect from those with whom his duty brings him in contact. The unhappy prejudices which the settlers

show to the military authority here render this, as you are
aware, a difficult service, but I believe that you will, without forgetting the respect due to yourself and the Government you represent, avoid rousing these prejudices by any
harshness, or inviting any conflict with the civil authority.
The limits of their authority you will find in your written
instructions; but you might gain their confidence, and impress them, Mr. Calvert, with the idea of your being their
auxiliary in the interests of justice — you understand.
Even if you are unsuccessful in bringing back the men,
you will do your best to ascertain if their escape has been
due to the sympathy of the settlers, or even with their preliminary connivance. They may not be aware that inciting enlisted men to desert is a criminal offense; you will
use your own discretion in informing them of the fact or
not, as occasion may serve you. I have only to add, that
while you are on the waters of this bay and the land covered
by its tides, you have no opposition of authority, and are
responsible to no one but your military superiors. Good-
by, Mr. Calvert. Let me hear a good account of you."

Considerably moved by Colonel Preston's manner, which
was as paternal and real as his rhetoric was somewhat perfunctory, Calvert half forgot his woes as he stepped from
the commandant's piazza. But he had to face a group of
his brother officers, who were awaiting him.

"Good-by, Calvert," said Major Bromley; "a day or
two out on the grass won't hurt you — and a change from
commissary whiskey will put you all right. By the way,
if you hear of any better stuff at Westport than they 're
giving us here, sample it and let us know. Take care of
yourself. Give your men a chance to talk to you now and
then, and you may get something from them, especially
Donovan. Keep your eye on Ramon. You can trust your
sergeant straight along."

"Good-by, George," said Kirby. "I suppose the old

man told you that, although no part of a soldier's duty was better than another, your service was a very delicate one, just fitted for you, eh ? He always does when he's cut out some hellish scrub-work for a chap. And told you, too, that as long as you did n't go ashore, and kept to a dispatch-boat, or an eight-oared gig, where you could n't deploy your men, or dress a line, you 'd be invincible."

"He did say something like that," smiled Calvert, with an uneasy recollection, however, that it was *the* part of his superior's speech that particularly impressed him.

"Of course," said Kirby gravely, "*that*, as an infantry officer, is clearly your duty."

"And don't forget, George," said Rollins still more gravely, "that, whatever may befall you, you belong to a section of that numerically small but powerfully diversified organization — the American Army. Remember that in the hour of peril you can address your men in any language, and be perfectly understood. And remember that when you proudly stand before them, the eyes not only of your own country, but of nearly all the others, are upon you ! Good-by, Georgey. I heard the major hint something about whiskey. They say that old pirate, Kingfisher Culpepper, had a stock of the real thing from Robertson County laid in his shebang on the Marsh just before he died. Pity we are n't on terms with them, for the cubs cannot drink it, and might be induced to sell. Should n't wonder, by the way, if your friend M'Caffrey was hanging round somewhere there ; he always had a keen scent. You might confiscate it as an 'incitement to desertion,' you know. The girl's pretty, and ought to be growing up now."

But haply at this point the sergeant stopped further raillery by reporting the detachment ready ; and drawing his sword, Calvert, with a confused head, a remorseful heart, but an unfaltering step, marched off his men on his delicate mission.

It was four o'clock when he entered Jonesville. Following a matter-of-fact idea of his own, he had brought his men the greater distance by a circuitous route through the woods, thus avoiding the ostentatious exposure of his party on the open bay in a well-manned boat to an extended view from the three leagues of shore and marsh opposite. Crossing the stream, which here separated him from the Dedlow Marsh, by the common ferry, he had thus been enabled to halt unperceived below the settlement and occupy the two roads by which the fugitives could escape inland. He had deemed it not impossible that, after the previous visit of the sergeant, the deserters hidden in the vicinity might return to Jonesville in the belief that the visit would not be repeated so soon. Leaving a part of his small force to patrol the road and another to deploy over the upland meadows, he entered the village. By the exercise of some boyish diplomacy and a certain prepossessing grace, which he knew when and how to employ, he became satisfied that the objects of his quest were not *there* — however their whereabouts might have been known to the people. Dividing his party again, he concluded to take a corporal and a few men and explore the lower marshes himself.

The preoccupation of duty, exercise, and perhaps, above all, the keen stimulus of the iodine-laden salt air seemed to clear his mind and invigorate his body. He had never been in the Marsh before, and enjoyed its novelty with the zest of youth. It was the hour when the tide of its feathered life was at its flood. Clouds of duck and teal passing from the fresh water of the river to the salt pools of the marshes perpetually swept his path with flying shadows; at times it seemed as if even the uncertain ground around him itself arose and sped away on dusky wings. The vicinity of hidden pools and sloughs was betrayed by startled splashings; a few paces from their marching feet arose the sunlit pinions of a swan. The air was filled with multitudinous small cries and pipings. In this vocal confusion it was some minutes before he recognized the voice of one of his out-flankers calling to the other.

An important discovery had been made. In a long tongue of bushes that ran down to the Marsh they had found a mud-stained uniform, complete even to the cap, bearing the initial of the deserter's company.

"Is there any hut or cabin hereabouts, Schmidt?" asked Calvert.

"Dot vos schoost it, Lefdennun," replied his corporal. "Dot vos de shanty from der Kingvisher — old Gulbebber. I pet a dollar, py shimminy, dot der men haf der gekommt."

He pointed through the brake to a long, low building that now raised itself, white in the sunlight, above the many blackened piles. Calvert saw in a single reconnoitring glance that it had but one approach — the flight of steps from the Marsh. Instructing his men to fall in on the outer edge of the brake and await his orders, he quickly made his way across the space and ascended the steps. Passing along the gallery he knocked at the front door. There was no response. He repeated his knock. Then the window beside it opened suddenly, and he was confronted with a double-muzzle of a long ducking-gun. Glancing instinctively along the barrels, he saw at their other extremity the bright eyes, brilliant color, and small set mouth of a remarkably handsome girl. It was the fact, and to the credit of his training, that he paid more attention to the eyes than to the challenge of the shining tubes before him.

"Jest stop where you are — will you!" said the girl determinedly.

Calvert's face betrayed not the slightest terror or surprise. Immovable as on parade, he carried his white gloved hand to his cap, and said gently, "With pleasure."

"Oh yes," said the girl quickly; "but if you move a step I'll jest blow you and your gloves offer that railin' inter the Marsh."

"I trust not," returned Calvert, smiling.

"And why?"

"Because it would deprive me of the pleasure of a few moments' conversation with you — and I've only one pair of gloves with me."

He was still watching her beautiful eyes — respectfully, admiringly, and strategically. For he was quite convinced that if he *did* move she would certainly discharge one or both barrels at him.

"Where's the rest of you?" she continued sharply.

"About three hundred yards away, in the covert, not near enough to trouble you."

"Will they come here?"

"I trust not."

"You trust not?" she repeated scornfully. "Why?"

"Because they would be disobeying orders."

She lowered her gun slightly, but kept her black brows leveled at him. "I reckon I'm a match for *you*," she said, with a slightly contemptuous glance at his slight figure, and opened the door. For a moment they stood looking at each other. He saw, besides the handsome face and eyes that had charmed him, a tall, slim figure, made broader across the shoulders by an open pea-jacket that showed a man's red flannel shirt belted at the waist over a blue skirt, with the collar knotted by a sailor's black handkerchief, and turned back over a pretty though sunburnt throat. She saw a rather undersized young fellow in a jaunty undress uniform, scant of gold braid, and bearing only the single gold shoulder-bars of his rank, but scrupulously neat and well fitting. Light-colored hair cropped close, the smallest of light mustaches, clear and penetrating blue eyes, and a few freckles completed a picture that did not prepossess her. She was therefore the more inclined to resent the perfect ease and self-possession with which the stranger carried off these manifest defects before her.

She laid aside the gun, put her hands deep in the pockets of her pea-jacket, and, slightly squaring her shoulders, said curtly, " What do you want ? "

" A very little information, which I trust it will not trouble you to give me.   My men have just discovered the uniform belonging to a deserter from the Fort lying in the bushes yonder.   Can you give me the slightest idea how it came there ? "

" What right have you traipsing over our property ? " she said, turning upon him sharply, with a slight paling of color.

" None whatever."

" Then what did you come for ? "

" To ask that permission, in case you would give me no information."

" Why don't you ask my brother, and not a woman ? Were you afraid ? "

" He could hardly have done me the honor of placing me in more peril than you have," returned Calvert, smiling. " Then I have the pleasure of addressing Miss Culpepper ? "

" I 'm Jim Culpepper's sister."

" And, I believe, equally able to give or refuse the permission I ask."

" And what if I refuse ? "

" Then I have only to ask pardon for having troubled you, go back, and return here with the tide.   You don't resist *that* with a shot-gun, do you ? " he asked pleasantly.

Maggie Culpepper was already familiar with the accepted theory of the supreme jurisdiction of the Federal Sea. She half turned her back upon him, partly to show her contempt, but partly to evade the domination of his clear, good-humored, and self-sustained little eyes.

" I don't know anythin' about your deserters, nor what rags o' theirs happen to be floated up here," she said angrily, " and don't care to.   You kin do what you like."

"Then I'm afraid I should remain here a little longer, Miss Culpepper; but my duty " —

"Your wot?" she interrupted disdainfully.

"I suppose I *am* talking shop," he said smilingly. "Then my business " —

"Your business — pickin' up half-starved runaways!"

"And, I trust, sometimes a kind friend," he suggested, with a grave bow.

"You *trust?* Look yer, young man," she said, with her quick, fierce, little laugh, "I reckon you *trust* a heap too much!" She would like to have added, "with your freckled face, red hair, and little eyes " — but this would have obliged her to face them again, which she did not care to do.

Calvert stepped back, lifted his hand to his cap, still pleasantly, and then walked gravely along the gallery down the steps, and towards the cover. From her window, unseen, she followed his neat little figure moving undeviatingly on, without looking to the left or right, and still less towards the house he had just quitted. Then she saw the sunlight flash on cross-belt plates and steel barrels, and a light blue line issued from out the dark green bushes, round the point, and disappeared. And then it suddenly occurred to her what she had been doing! This, then, was her first step towards that fancy she had so lately conceived, quarreled over with her brother, and lay awake last night to place anew, in spite of all opposition! This was her brilliant idea of dazzling and subduing Logport and the Fort! Had she grown silly, or what had happened? Could she have dreamed of the coming of this whippersnapper, with his insufferable airs, after that beggarly deserter? I am afraid that for a few moments the miserable fugitive had as small a place in Maggie's sympathy as the redoubtable whipper-snapper himself. And now the cherished dream of triumph and conquest was over! What a " loony " she had been ! Instead of inviting him in, and outdoing him in " company manners," and " fooling " him about the deserter, and then blazing upon him afterwards at Logport in the glory of her first spent wealth and finery, she had driven him away !

And now " he 'll go and tell — tell the Fort girls of his hairbreadth escape from the claws of the Kingfisher's daughter ! "

The thought brought a few bitter tears to her eyes, but she wiped them away. The thought brought also the terrible conviction that Jim was right, that there could be nothing but open antagonism between them and the traducers of their parents, as she herself had instinctively shown ! But she presently wiped that conviction away also, as she had her tears.

Half an hour later she was attracted by the appearance from the windows of certain straggling blue spots on the upland that seemed moving diagonally towards the Marsh. She did not know that it was Calvert's second " detail " joining him, but believed for a moment that he had not yet departed, and was strangely relieved. Still later the frequent disturbed cries of coot, heron, and marsh-hen, recognizing the presence of unusual invaders of their solitude, distracted her yet more, and forced her at last, with increasing color and an uneasy sense of shyness, to steal out to the gallery for a swift furtive survey of the Marsh. But an utterly unexpected sight met her eyes, and kept her motionless.

The birds were rising everywhere and drifting away with querulous perturbation before a small but augmented blue detachment that was moving with monotonous regularity towards the point of bushes where she had seen the young officer previously disappear. In their midst, between two soldiers with fixed bayonets, marched the man whom even at that distance she instantly recognized as the deserter of the preceding night, in the very clothes she had given him. To complete her consternation, a little to the right marched the young officer also, but accompanied by, and apparently on the most amicable terms with, Jim — her own brother!

To forget all else and dart down the steps, flying towards the point of bushes, scarcely knowing why or what she was doing, was to Maggie the impulse and work of a moment. When she had reached it the party were not twenty paces away. But here a shyness and hesitation again seized her, and she shrank back in the bushes with an instinctive cry to her brother inarticulate upon her lips. They came nearer, they were opposite to her; her brother Jim keeping step with the invader, and even conversing with him with an animation she had seldom seen upon his face — they passed! She had been unnoticed except by one. The roving eye of the deserter had detected her handsome face among the leaves, slightly turned towards it, and poured out his whole soul in a single swift wink of eloquent but indescribable confidence.

When they had quite gone, she crept back to the house, a little reassured, but still tremulous. When her brother returned at nightfall, he found her brooding over the fire, in the same attitude as on the previous night.

"I reckon ye might hev seen me go by with the sodgers," he said, seating himself beside her, a little awkwardly, and with an unusual assumption of carelessness.

Maggie, without looking up, was languidly surprised. He had been with the soldiers — and where?

"About two hours ago I met this yer Leftenant Calvert," he went on with increasing awkwardness, "and — oh, I say, Mag — he said he saw you, and hoped he had n't troubled ye, and — and — ye saw him, did n't ye?"

Maggie, with all the red of the fire concentrated in her cheek as she gazed at the flame, believed carelessly "that she had seen a shrimp in uniform asking questions."

"Oh, he ain't a bit stuck up," said Jim quickly; "that's what I like about him. He's ez nat'ral ez you be, and tuck my arm, walkin' around, careless-like, laffen at what he was doin', ez ef it was a game, and he was n't sole commander of forty men. He's only a year or two older than me — and — and " — he stopped and looked uneasily at Maggie.

"So ye 've bin craw-fishin' agin?" said Maggie in her deepest and most scornful contralto.

"Who's craw-fishin'?" he retorted angrily.

"What's this backen out o' what you said yesterday? What's all this trucklin' to the Fort now?"

"What? Well now, look yer," said Jim, rising suddenly, with reproachful indignation, "darned if I don't jest tell ye everythin'. I promised *him* I would n't. He allowed it would frighten ye."

"*Frighten me!*" repeated Maggie contemptuously, nevertheless with her cheek paling again. "Frighten me — with what?"

"Well, since yer so cantankerous, look yer. We 've been robbed!"

"Robbed?" echoed Maggie, facing him.

"Yes, robbed by that same deserter. Robbed of a suit of my clothes, and my whiskey-flask, and the darned skunk had 'em on. And if it had n't bin for that Leftenant Calvert, and my givin' him permission to hunt him over the Marsh, we would n't have caught him."

"Robbed?" repeated Maggie again vaguely.

"Yes, robbed! Last night, afore we came home. He must hev got in yer while we was comin' from the boat."

"Did, did that Leftenant say so?" stammered Maggie.

"Say it, of course he did! and so do I," continued Jim impatiently. "Why, there were my very clothes on his back, and he dare n't deny it. And if you 'd hearkened to me jest now, instead of flyin' off in tantrums, you'd see that *that's* jest how we got him, and how me and the Leftenant joined hands in it. I did n't give him permission to hunt deserters, but *thieves*. I did n't help him to ketch the man that deserted from *him*, but the skunk that took *my* clothes. For when the Leftenant found the man's old uniform in the bush, he nat'rally kalkilated he must hev got some other duds near by in some underhand way. Don't you see? eh? Why, look, Mag. Darned if you ain't skeered after all! Who'd hev thought it? There now — sit down, dear. Why, you're white ez a gull."

He had his arm round her as she sank back in the chair again with a forced smile.

"There now," he said with fraternal superiority, "don't mind it, Mag, any more. Why, it's all over now. You bet he won't trouble us agin, for the Leftenant sez that now he's found out to be a thief, they'll jest turn him over to the police, and he's sure o' getten six months' state prison fer stealin' and burglarin' in our house. But" — he stopped suddenly and looked at his sister's contracted face; "look yer, Mag, you're sick, that's what's the matter. Take suthin'" —

"I'm better now," she said with an effort; "it's only a kind o' blind chill I must hev got on the Marsh last night. What's that?"

She had risen, and, grasping her brother's arm tightly, had turned quickly to the window. The casement had suddenly rattled.

"It's only the wind gettin' up. It looked like a sou'-wester when I came in. Lot o' scud flyin'. But *you* take some quinine, Mag. Don't *you* go now and get down sick like maw."

Perhaps it was this well-meant but infelicitous reference that brought a moisture to her dark eyes, and caused her lips to momentarily quiver. But it gave way to a quick

determined setting of her whole face as she turned it once
more to the fire, and said slowly : —

"I reckon I'll sleep it off, if I go to bed now.   What
time does the tide fall ?"

"About three, unless this yer wind piles it up on the
Marsh afore then.   Why ?"

"I was only wonderin' if the boat wus safe," said Maggie,
rising.

"You'd better hoist yourself outside some quinine, instead o' talken about those things," said Jim, who preferred
to discharge his fraternal responsibility by active medication.
"You are n't fit to read to-night."

"Good-night, Jim," she said suddenly, stopping before
him.

"Good-night, Mag."   He kissed her with protecting
and amiable toleration, generously referring her hot hands
and feverish lips to that vague mystery of feminine complaint which man admits without indorsing.

They separated ; Jim, under the stimulus of the late
supposed robbery, ostentatiously fastening the doors and
windows with assuring comments, calculated to inspire confidence in his sister's startled heart.   Then he went to bed.
He lay awake long enough to be pleasantly conscious that
the wind had increased to a gale, and to be lulled again to
sleep by the cosy security of the heavily timbered and
tightly sealed dwelling that seemed to ride the storm like
the ship it resembled.   The gale swept through the piles
beneath him and along the gallery as through bared spars
and over wave-washed decks.   The whole structure, attacked
above, below, and on all sides by the fury of the wind,
seemed at times to be lifted in the air.   Once or twice the
creaking timbers simulated the sound of opening doors and
passing footsteps, and again dilated as if the gale had forced
a passage through.   But Jim slept on peacefully, and
was at last only aroused by the brilliant sunshine staring

through his window from the clear wind-swept blue arch
beyond.

Dressing himself lazily, he passed into the sitting-room
and proceeded to knock at his sister's door, as was his custom ; he was amazed to find it open and the room empty.
Entering hurriedly, he saw that her bed was undisturbed,
as if it had not been occupied, and was the more bewildered
to see a note ostentatiously pinned upon the pillow, addressed in pencil, in a large school-hand, " To Jim."

Opening it impatiently, he was startled to read as follows : —

Don't be angry, Jim dear — but it was all my fault —
and I did n't tell you.   I knew all about the deserter, and
I gave him the clothes and things that they say he stole.
It was while you was out that night, and he came and
begged of me, and was mournful and hidjus to behold.   I
thought I was helping him, and getting our revenge on the
Fort, all at the same time.   Don't be mad, Jim dear, and
do not be frighted fer me.   I 'm going over thar to make it
all right — to free *him* of stealing — to have *you* left out of
it all — and take it all on myself.   Don't you be a bit feared
for me.   I ain't skeert of the wind or of going.   I 'll close
reef everything, clear the creek, stretch across to Injen
Island, hugg the Point, and bear up fer Logport.   Dear Jim
— don't get mad — but I could n't bear this fooling of you
nor *him* — and that man being took for stealing any longer !
— Your loving sister,   MAGGIE.

With a confused mingling of shame, anger, and sudden fear
he ran out on the gallery.   The tide was well up, half the
Marsh had already vanished, and the little creek where he
had moored his skiff was now an empty shining river.
The water was everywhere — fringing the tussocks of salt
grass with concentric curves of spume and drift, or tumul-

tuously tossing its white-capped waves over the spreading expanse of the lower bay. The low thunder of breakers in the farther estuary broke monotonously on the ear. But his eye was fascinated by a dull shifting streak on the horizon, that, even as he gazed, shuddered, whitened along its whole line, and then grew ghastly gray again. It was the ocean bar.

IV

"WELL, I must say," said Cicely Preston, emphasizing the usual feminine imperative for perfectly gratuitous statement, as she pushed back her chair from the commandant's breakfast table, "I *must* really say that I don't see anything particularly heroic in doing something wrong, lying about it just to get other folks into trouble, and then rushing off to do penance in a high wind and an open boat. But she's pretty, and wears a man's shirt and coat, and of course *that* settles anything. But why earrings and wet white stockings and slippers? And why that Gothic arch of front and a boy's hat? That's what I simply ask;" and the youngest daughter of Colonel Preston rose from the table, shook out the skirt of her pretty morning dress, and, placing her little thumbs in the belt of her smart waist, paused witheringly for a reply.

"You are most unfair, my child," returned Colonel Preston gravely. "Her giving food and clothes to a deserter may have been only an ordinary instinct of humanity towards a fellow creature who appeared to be suffering, to say nothing of M'Caffrey's plausible tongue. But her periling her life to save him from an unjust accusation, and her desire to shield her brother's pride from ridicule, is altogether praiseworthy and extraordinary. And the moral influence of her kindness was strong enough to make that scamp refuse to tell the plain truth that might implicate her in an indiscretion, though it saved him from state prison."

"He knew you wouldn't believe him if he had said the clothes were given to him," retorted Miss Cicely, "so I

don't see where the moral influence comes in. As to her
periling her life, those Marsh people are amphibious anyway, or would be in those clothes. And as to her motive,
why, papa, I heard you say in this very room, and afterwards to Mr. Calvert, when you gave him instructions, that
you believed those Culpeppers were capable of enticing
away deserters; and you forget the fuss you had with her
savage brother's lawyer about that water front, and how
you said it was such people who kept up the irritation between the Civil and Federal power."

The colonel coughed hurriedly. It is the fate of all
great organizers, military as well as civil, to occasionally
suffer defeat in the family circle.

"The more reason," he said soothingly, "why we should
correct harsh judgments that spring from mere rumors.
You should give yourself at least the chance of overcoming
your prejudices, my child. Remember, too, that she is
now the guest of the Fort."

"And she chooses to stay with Mrs. Bromley! I'm
sure it's quite enough for you and mamma to do duty —
and Emily, who wants to know why Mr. Calvert raves
so about her — without *my* going over there to stare."

Colonel Preston shook his head reproachfully, but eventually retired, leaving the field to the enemy. The enemy,
a little pink in the cheeks, slightly tossed the delicate rings
of its blonde crest, settled its skirts again at the piano, but
after turning over the leaves of its music book, rose, and
walked pettishly to the window.

But here a spectacle presented itself that for a moment
dismissed all other thoughts from the girl's rebellious
mind.

Not a dozen yards away, on the wind-swept parade, a
handsome young fellow, apparently halted by the sentry,
had impetuously turned upon him in an attitude of indig-
nant and haughty surprise. To the quick fancy of the girl

it seemed as if some disguised rustic god had been startled by the challenge of a mortal.   Under an oilskin hat, like the *petasus* of Hermes, pushed back from his white forehead, crisp black curls were knotted around a head whose beardless face was perfect as a cameo cutting.   In a close-fitting blue woolen jersey under his open jacket the clear outlines and youthful grace of his upper figure were revealed as clearly as in a statue.   Long fishing-boots reaching to his thighs scarcely concealed the symmetry of his lower limbs. Cricket and lawn-tennis, knickerbockers and flannels had not at that period familiarized the female eye to unfettered masculine outline, and Cicely Preston, accustomed to the artificial smartness and regularity of uniform, was perhaps the more impressed by the stranger's lawless grace.

The sentry had repeated his challenge ; an angry flush was deepening on the intruder's cheek.   At this critical moment Cicely threw open the French windows and stepped upon the veranda.

The sentry saluted the familiar little figure of his colonel's daughter with an explanatory glance at the stranger. The young fellow looked up — and the god became human.

" I 'm looking for my sister," he said half awkwardly, half defiantly ;   " she 's here, somewhere."

" Yes — and perfectly safe, Mr. Culpepper, I think," said the arch-hypocrite with dazzling sweetness ;   " and we 're all so delighted.   And so brave and plucky and skillful in her to come all that way — and for such a purpose."

" Then — you know — all about it " — stammered Jim, more relieved than he had imagined — " and that I " —

" That you were quite ignorant of your sister helping the deserter.   Oh yes, of course," said Cicely, with bewildering promptitude.   " You see, Mr. Culpepper, we girls are *so* foolish.   I dare say *I* should have done the same thing in her place, only *I* should never have had the cour-

age to do what she did afterwards. You really must forgive her. But won't you come in — *do*." She stepped
back, holding the window open with the half-coaxing air of
a spoiled child. "This way is quickest. *Do* come." As
he still hesitated, glancing from her to the house, she added,
with a demure little laugh, "Oh, I forget — this is Colonel
Preston's quarters, and I 'm his daughter."

And this dainty little fairy, so natural in manner, so
tasteful in attire, was one of the artificial over-dressed
creatures that his sister had inveighed against so bitterly!
Was Maggie really to be trusted? This new revelation
coming so soon after the episode of the deserter staggered
him. Nevertheless he hesitated, looking up with a certain
boyish timidity into Cicely's dangerous eyes.

"Is — is — my sister there?"

"I 'm expecting her with my mother every moment,"
responded this youthful but ingenious diplomatist sweetly;
"she might be here now; but," she added with a sudden
heart-broken flash of sympathy, "I know *how* anxious you
both must be. *I'll* take you to her now. Only one moment, please." The opportunity of leading this handsome
savage as it were in chains across the parade, before everybody, her father, her mother, her sister, and *his* — was not
to be lost. She darted into the house, and reappeared with
the daintiest imaginable straw hat on the side of her head,
and demurely took her place at his side. "It 's only over
there, at Major Bromley's," she said, pointing to one of the
vine-clad cottage quarters; "but you are a stranger here,
you know, and might get lost."

Alas! he was already that. For keeping step with those
fairy-like slippers, brushing awkwardly against that fresh
and pretty skirt, and feeling the caress of the soft folds,
looking down upon the brim of that beribboned little hat,
and more often meeting the upturned blue eyes beneath it,
Jim was suddenly struck with a terrible conviction of his

own contrasting coarseness and deficiencies. How hideous those oiled canvas fishing-trousers and pilot jacket looked beside this perfectly fitted and delicately gowned girl! He loathed his collar, his jersey, his turned-back sou'wester, even his height, which seemed to hulk beside her — everything, in short, that the girl had recently admired. By the time that they had reached Major Bromley's door he had so far succumbed to the fair enchantress and realized her ambition of a triumphant procession, that when she ushered him into the presence of half a dozen ladies and gentlemen he scarcely recognized his sister as the centre of attraction, or knew that Miss Cicely's effusive greeting of Maggie was her first one. "I knew he was dying to see you after all you had *both* passed through, and I brought him straight here," said the diminutive Machiavelli, meeting the astonished gaze of her father and the curious eyes of her sister with perfect calmness, while Maggie, full of gratitude and admiration of her handsome brother, forgot his momentary obliviousness, and returned her greeting warmly. Nevertheless, there was a slight movement of reserve among the gentlemen at the unlooked-for irruption of this sunburnt Adonis, until Calvert, disengaging himself from Maggie's side, came forward with his usual frank imperturbability and quiet tact, and claimed Jim as his friend and honored guest.

It then came out with that unostentatious simplicity which characterized the brother and sister, and was their secure claim to perfect equality with their entertainers, that Jim, on discovering his sister's absence, and fearing that she might be carried by the current towards the bar, had actually *swum the estuary* to Indian Island, and in an ordinary Indian canoe had braved the same tempestuous passage she had taken a few hours before. Cicely, listening to this recital with rapt attention, nevertheless managed to convey the impression of having fully expected it from the first. "Of course he'd have come here; if she'd only waited," she said, *sotto voce*, to her sister Emily.

"He's certainly the handsomer of the two," responded that young lady.

"Of course," returned Cicely with a superior air, "don't you see she *copies* him?"

Not that this private criticism prevented either from vying with the younger officers in their attentions to Maggie, with perhaps the addition of an open eulogy of her handsome brother, more or less invidious in comparison to the officers. "I suppose it's an active out-of-door life gives him that perfect grace and freedom," said Emily, with a slight sneer at the smartly belted Calvert. "Yes; and he don't drink or keep late hours," responded Cicely significantly. "His sister says they always retire before ten o'clock, and that although his father left him some valuable whiskey he seldom takes a drop of it." "Therein," gravely concluded Captain Kirby, "lies *our* salvation. If, after such a confession, Calvert does n't make the most of his acquaintance with young Culpepper to remove that whiskey from his path and bring it here, he's not the man I take him for."

Indeed, for the moment it seemed as if he was not. During the next three or four days, in which Colonel Preston had insisted upon detaining his guests, Calvert touched no liquor, evaded the evening poker parties at quarters, and even prevailed upon some of his brother officers to give them up for the more general entertainment of the ladies. Colonel Preston was politician enough to avail himself of the popularity of Maggie's adventure to invite some of the Logport people to assist him in honoring their neighbor. Not only was the old feud between the Fort and the people thus bridged over, but there was no doubt that the discipline of the Fort had been strengthened by Maggie's extravagant reputation as a mediator among the disaffected rank and file. Whatever characteristic license the grateful Dennis M'Caffrey — let off with a nominal punishment — may have taken in his praise of the "Quane of the Marshes," it is certain that the men worshiped her, and that the band pathetically begged permission to serenade her the last night of her stay.

At the end of that time, with a dozen invitations, a dozen appointments, a dozen vows of eternal friendship, much hand-shaking, and accompanied by a number of the officers to their boat, Maggie and Jim departed.   They talked but little on their way home ; by some tacit under-standing they did not discuss those projects, only recalling certain scenes and incidents of their visit.   By the time they had reached the little creek the silence and nervous apathy which usually follow excitement in the young seemed to have fallen upon them.   It was not until after their quiet frugal supper that, seated beside the fire, Jim looked up somewhat self-consciously in his sister's grave and thoughtful face.

"Say, Mag, what was that idea o' yours about selling some land, and taking a house at Logport ? "

Maggie looked up, and said passively, " Oh, *that* idea ? "

"Yes."

"Why ? "

"Well," said Jim somewhat awkwardly, "it *could* be done, you know.   I 'm willin'."

As she did not immediately reply, he continued uneasily, "Miss Preston says we kin get a nice little house that is near the Fort, until we want to build."

"Oh, then you *have* talked about it ? "

"Yes — that is — why, what are ye thinkin' of, Mag ? Was n't it *your* idea all along ? " he said, suddenly facing her with querulous embarrassment.   They had been sitting in their usual evening attitudes of Assyrian frieze profile, with even more than the usual Assyrian frieze similarity of feature.

"Yes ; but, Jim dear, do you think it the best thing

for — for us to do ? " said Maggie, with half-frightened
gravity.

At this sudden and startling exhibition of female inconsistency and inconsequence, Jim was for a moment speechless.   Then he recovered himself, volubly, aggrievedly, and
on his legs.   What *did* she mean ?   Was he to give up
understanding girls — or was it their sole vocation in life
to impede masculine processes and shipwreck masculine con-
clusions ?   Here, after all she said the other night, after
they had nearly " quo'lled " over her " set idees," after
she 'd " gone over all that foolishness about Jael and Sisera
— and there was n't any use for it — after she 'd let him
run on to them officers all he was goin' to do — nay, after
she herself, for he had heard her, had talked to Calvert
about it, she wanted to know *now* if it was best."   He
looked at the floor and the ceiling, as if expecting the
tongued and grooved planks to cry out at this crowning
enormity.

The cause of it had resumed her sad gaze at the fire.
Presently, without turning her head, she reached up her
long, graceful arm, and, clasping her brother's neck, brought
his face down in profile with her own, cheek against cheek,
until they looked like the double outlines of a medallion.
Then she said — to the fire : —

" Jim, do you think she 's pretty ? "

" Who ? " said Jim, albeit his color had already answered the question.

" You know *who*.   Do you like her ? "

Jim here vaguely murmured to the fire that he thought
her " kinder nice," and that she dressed mighty purty.
" Ye know, Mag," he said with patronizing effusion, " you
oughter get some gownds like hers."

" That would n't make me like her," said Maggie
gravely.

" I don't know about that," said Jim politely, but with

an appalling hopelessness of tone.   After a pause he added slyly, " 'Pears to me *somebody else* thought somebody else mighty purty — eh ? "

To his discomfiture she did not solicit further information.   After a pause he continued, still more archly : —

" Do you like *him*, Mag ? "

" I think he 's a perfect gentleman," she said calmly.

He turned his eyes quickly from the glowing fire to her face.   The cheek that had been resting against his own was as cool as the night wind that came through the open door, and the whole face was as fixed and tranquil as the upper stars.

V

FOR a year the tide had ebbed and flowed on the Dedlow Marsh unheeded before the sealed and sightless windows of the " Kingfisher's Nest." Since the young birds had flown to Logport, even the Indian caretakers had abandoned the piled dwelling for their old nomadic haunts in the "bresh." The high spring tide had again made its annual visit to the little cemetery of driftwood, and, as if recognizing another wreck in the deserted home, had hung a few memorial offerings on the blackened piles, softly laid a garland of grayish drift before it, and then sobbed itself out in the salt grass.

From time to time the faint echoes of the Culpeppers' life at Logport reached the upland, and the few neighbors who had only known them by hearsay shook their heads over the extravagance they as yet only knew by report. But it was in the dead ebb of the tide and the waning daylight that the feathered tenants of the Marsh seemed to voice dismal prophecies of the ruin of their old master and mistress, and to give themselves up to gloomiest lamentation and querulous foreboding. Whether the traditional " bird of the air " had intrusted his secret to a few ornithological friends, or whether from a natural disposition to take gloomy views of life, it was certain that at this hour the vocal expression of the Marsh was hopeless and despairing. It was then that a dejected plover, addressing a mocking crew of sandpipers on a floating log, seemed to bewail the fortune that was being swallowed up by the riotous living and gambling debts of Jim. It was then that the querulous crane rose, and testily protested against the selling of his favorite haunt in the sandy peninsula, which only six months of Jim's excesses had made imperative. It was then that a mournful curlew, who, with the preface that he had always been really expecting it, reiterated the story that Jim had been seen more than once staggering home with nervous hands and sodden features from a debauch with the younger officers; it was the same desponding fowl who knew that Maggie's eyes had more than once filled with tears at Jim's failings, and had already grown more hollow with many watchings. It was a flock of wrangling teal that screamingly discussed the small scandals, jealous heart-burnings, and curious backbitings that had attended Maggie's advent into society. It was the high flying brent who, knowing how the sensitive girl, made keenly conscious at every turn of her defective training and ingenuous ignorance, had often watched their evening flight with longing gaze, now "honked" dismally at the recollection. It was at this hour and season that the usual vague lamentings of Dedlow Marsh seemed to find at last a preordained expression. And it was at such a time, when light and water were both fading, and the blackness of the Marsh was once more reasserting itself, that a small boat was creeping along one of the tortuous inlets, at times half hiding behind the bank like a wounded bird. As it slowly penetrated inland it seemed to be impelled by its solitary occupant in a hesitating, uncertain way, as if to escape observation rather than as if directed to any positive bourn. Stopping beside a bank of reeds at last, the figure rose stoopingly, and drew a gun from between its feet and the bottom of the boat. As the light fell upon its face, it could be seen that it was James Culpepper! James Culpepper! hardly recognizable in the swollen features, bloodshot eyes, and tremulous hands of that ruined figure! James Culpepper, only retaining a single trace of his former self

in his look of set and passionate purpose! And that purpose was to kill himself — to be found dead, as his father
had been before him — in an open boat, adrift upon the
Marsh !

It was not the outcome of a sudden fancy. The idea had
first come to him in a taunting allusion from the drunken
lips of one of his ruder companions, for which he had
stricken the offender to the earth. It had since haunted
his waking hours of remorse and hopeless fatuity ; it had
seemed to be the one relief and atonement he could make
his devoted sister ; and, more fatuous than all, it seemed to
the miserable boy the one revenge he would take upon the
faithless coquette, who for a year had played with his simplicity, and had helped to drive him to the distraction of
cards and drink. Only that morning Colonel Preston had
forbidden him the house ; and now it seemed to him the
end had come. He raised his distorted face above the
reedy bank for a last tremulous and half-frightened glance
at the landscape he was leaving forever. A glint in the
western sky lit up the front of his deserted dwelling in the
distance, abreast of which the windings of the inlet had
unwittingly led him. As he looked he started, and involuntarily dropped into a crouching attitude. For to his superstitious terror, the sealed windows of his old home were
open, the bright panes were glittering with the fading light,
and on the outer gallery the familiar figure of his sister
stood, as of old, awaiting his return ! Was he really going
mad, or had this last vision of his former youth been pur-
posely vouchsafed him ?

But even as he gazed, the appearance of another figure in
the landscape beyond the house proved the reality of his
vision, and as suddenly distracted him from all else. For
it was the apparition of a man on horseback approaching
the house from the upland ; and even at that distance he
recognized its well-known outlines. It was Calvert ! Cal-

vert the traitor !   Calvert, the man whom he had long suspected as being the secret lover and destined husband of
Cicely Preston !   Calvert, who had deceived him with his
calm equanimity and his affected preference for Maggie, to
conceal his deliberate understanding with Cicely.   What
was he doing here ?   Was he a double traitor, and now
trying to deceive *her* — as he had him ?   And Maggie here !
This sudden return — this preconcerted meeting.   It was
infamy !

For a moment he remained stupefied, and then, with a
mechanical instinct, plunged his head and face in the lazy-
flowing water, and then once again rose cool and collected.
The half-mad distraction of his previous resolve had given
way to another, more deliberate, but not less desperate
determination.   He knew now *why* he came there — *why*
he had brought his gun — why his boat had stopped when
it did !

Lying flat in the bottom, he tore away fragments of the
crumbling bank to fill his frail craft, until he had sunk it
to the gunwale, and below the low level of the Marsh.
Then, using his hands as noiseless paddles, he propelled
this rude imitation of a floating log slowly past the line of
vision, until the tongue of bushes had hidden him from
view.   With a rapid glance at the darkening flat, he then
seized his gun, and springing to the spongy bank, half
crouching, half crawling through reeds and tussocks, he
made his way to the brush.   A foot and eye less experienced would have plunged its owner helpless in the black
quagmire.   At one edge of the thicket he heard hoofs trampling the dried twigs.   Calvert's horse was already there,
tied to a skirting alder.

He ran to the house, but, instead of attracting attention
by ascending the creaking steps, made his way to the piles
below the rear gallery and climbed to it noiselessly.   It was
the spot where the deserter had ascended a year ago, and,

like him, he could see and hear all that passed distinctly. Calvert stood near the open door as if departing. Maggie stood between him and the window, her face in shadow, her hands clasped tightly behind her. A profound sadness, partly of the dying day and waning light, and partly of some vague expiration of their own sorrow, seemed to encompass them. Without knowing why, a strange trembling took the place of James Culpepper's fierce determination, and a film of moisture stole across his staring eyes.

"When I tell you that I believe all this will pass, and that you will still win your brother back to you," said Calvert's sad but clear voice, "I will tell you why — although, perhaps, it is only a part of that confidence you command me to withhold. When I first saw you, I myself had fallen into like dissolute habits; less excusable than he, for I had some experience of the world and its follies. When I met *you*, and fell under the influence of your pure, simple, and healthy life; when I saw that isolation, monotony, misunderstanding, even the sense of superiority to one's surroundings, could be lived down and triumphed over, without vulgar distractions or pitiful ambitions; when I learned to love you — hear me out, Miss Culpepper, I beg you — you saved *me* — I, who was nothing to you, even as I honestly believe you will still save your brother whom you love."

"How do you know I did n't *ruin* him?" she said, turning upon him bitterly. "How do you know that it was n't to get rid of *our* monotony, *our* solitude, that I drove him to this vulgar distraction, this pitiful — yes, you were right — pitiful ambition?"

"Because it is n't your real nature," he said quietly.

"My real nature," she repeated with a half savage vehe-mence that seemed to be goaded from her by his very gentleness, "my real nature! What did *he* — what do *you* know of it? — My real nature! — I 'll tell you what it was," she went on passionately. "It was to be revenged on you all for your cruelty, your heartlessness, your wickedness to me and mine in the past. It was to pay you off for your slanders of my dead father — for the selfishness that left me and Jim alone with his dead body on the Marsh. That was what sent me to Logport — to get even with you — to — to fool and flaunt you! There, you have it now! And now that God has punished me for it by crushing my brother — you — you expect me to let you crush *me* too."

"But," he said eagerly, advancing toward her, "you are wronging me — you are wronging yourself cruelly."

"Stop," she said, stepping back, with her hands still locked behind her. "Stay where you are. There! That's enough!" She drew herself up and let her hands fall at her side. "Now, let us speak of Jim," she said coldly.

Without seeming to hear her, he regarded her for the first time with hopeless sadness.

"Why did you let my brother believe you were his rival with Cicely Preston?" she asked impatiently.

"Because I could not undeceive him without telling him I hopelessly loved his sister. You are proud, Miss Culpepper," he said, with the first tinge of bitterness in his even voice. "Can you not understand that others may be proud too?"

"No," she said bluntly; "it is not pride but weakness. You could have told him what you knew to be true: that there could be nothing in common between her folk and such savages as we; that there was a gulf as wide as that Marsh and as black between our natures, our training and theirs; and even if they came to us across it, now and then, to suit their pleasure, light and easy as that tide — it was still there to some day ground and swamp them! And if he doubted it, you had only to tell him your own story. You had only to tell him what you have just told me — that you yourself, an officer and a gentleman, thought you loved me, a vulgar, uneducated, savage girl, and that I, kinder to you than you to me or him, made you take it back across that tide, because I could n't let you link your life with me, and drag you in the mire."

"You need not have said that, Miss Culpepper," returned Calvert with the same gentle smile, "to prove that I am your inferior in all but one thing."

"And that?" she said quickly.

"Is my love."

His gentle face was as set now as her own as he moved back slowly towards the door. There he paused.

"You tell me to speak of Jim, and Jim only. Then hear me. I believe that Miss Preston cares for him as far as lies in her young and giddy nature. I could not, therefore, have crushed *his* hope without deceiving him, for there are as cruel deceits prompted by what we call reason as by our love. If you think that a knowledge of this plain truth would help to save him, I beg you to be kinder to him than you have been to me,— or even, let me dare to hope, to *yourself.*"

He slowly crossed the threshold, still holding his cap lightly in his hand.

"When I tell you that I am going away to-morrow on a leave of absence, and that in all probability we may not meet again, you will not misunderstand why I add my prayer to the message your friends in Logport charged me with. They beg that you will give up your idea of returning here, and come back to them. Believe me, you have made yourself loved and respected there, in spite — I beg pardon — perhaps I should say *because* of your pride. Good-night and good-by."

For a single instant she turned her set face to the window with a sudden convulsive movement, as if she would have called him back, but at the same moment the opposite door creaked and her brother slipped into the room. Whether a quick memory of the deserter's entrance at that door a year ago had crossed her mind, whether there was some strange suggestion in his mud-stained garments and weak, deprecating smile, or whether it was the outcome of some desperate struggle within her, there was that in her face that changed his smile into a frightened cry for pardon, as he ran and fell on his knees at her feet. But even as he did so her stern look vanished, and with her arm around him she bent over him and mingled her tears with his.

"I heard it all, Mag dearest! All! Forgive me! I have been crazy! — wild! — I will reform! — I will be better! I will never disgrace you again, Mag! Never, never! I swear it!"

She reached down and kissed him. After a pause, a weak, boyish smile struggled into his face.

"You heard what he said of *her*, Mag. Do you think it might be true?"

She lifted the damp curls from his forehead with a sad, half-maternal smile, but did not reply.

"And Mag, dear, don't you think *you* were a little — just a little — hard on *him?* No! Don't look at me that way, for God's sake! There, I did n't mean anything. Of course you knew best. There, Maggie dear, look up. Hark there! Listen, Mag, do!"

They lifted their eyes to the dim distance seen through the open door. Borne on the fading light, and seeming to fall and die with it over marsh and river, came the last notes of the bugle from the Fort.

"There! Don't you remember what you used to say, Mag?"

The look that had frightened him had quite left her face now.

"Yes," she smiled, laying her cold cheek beside his softly. "Oh yes! It was something that came and went, 'Like a song'— 'Like a song.'"

A KNIGHT-ERRANT OF THE FOOT-HILLS

I

As Father Felipe slowly toiled up the dusty road toward the Rancho of the Blessed Innocents, he more than once stopped under the shadow of a sycamore to rest his somewhat lazy mule and to compose his own perplexed thoughts by a few snatches from his breviary. For the good padre had some reason to be troubled. The invasion of Gentile Americans that followed the gold discovery of three years before had not confined itself to the plains of the Sacramento, but stragglers had already found their way to the Santa Cruz Valley, and the seclusion of even the mission itself was threatened. It was true that they had not brought their heathen engines to disembowel the earth in search of gold, but it was rumored that they had already speculated upon the agricultural productiveness of the land, and had espied "the fatness thereof." As he reached the higher plateau he could see the afternoon sea-fog — presently to obliterate the fair prospect — already pulling through the gaps in the Coast Range, and on a nearer slope — no less ominously — the smoke of a recent but more permanently destructive Yankee saw mill was slowly drifting towards the valley.

"Get up, beast!" said the father, digging his heels into the comfortable flanks of his mule with some human impatience, "or art *thou*, too, a lazy renegade? Thinkest thou, besotted one, that the heretic will spare thee more work than the Holy Church?"

The mule, thus apostrophized in ear and flesh, shook its
head obstinately as if the question was by no means clear
to its mind, but nevertheless started into a little trot, which
presently brought it to the low adobe wall of the courtyard
of "The Innocents," and entered the gate. A few lounging peons in the shadow of an archway took off their broad-
brimmed hats and made way for the padre, and a half-
dozen equally listless vaqueros helped him to alight. Accustomed as he was to the indolence and superfluity of his
host's retainers, to-day it nevertheless seemed to strike
some note of irritation in his breast.

A stout, middle-aged woman of ungirt waist and be-
shawled head and shoulders appeared at the gateway as if
awaiting him. After a formal salutation she drew him aside
into an inner passage.

"He is away again, your Reverence," she said.

"Ah — always the same ? "

"Yes, your Reverence — and this time to ' a meeting'
of the heretics at their pueblo, at Jonesville — where they
will ask him of his land for a road."

"At a *meeting?* " echoed the priest uneasily.

"Ah yes! at a meeting — where Tiburcio says they
shout and spit on the ground, your Reverence, and only one
has a chair and him they call a ' chairman ' because of it,
and yet he sits not, but shouts and spits even as the others
and keeps up a tapping with a hammer like a very pico.
And there it is they are ever ' resolving ' that which is not,
and consider it even as done."

"Then he is still the same," said the priest gloomily, as
the woman paused for breath.

"Only more so, your Reverence, for he reads naught but
the newspaper of the Americanos that is brought in the
ship, the ' New York 'errald ' — and recites to himself the
orations of their legislators. Ah ! it was an evil day when
the shipwrecked American sailor taught him his uncouth

tongue, which, as your Reverence knows, is only fit for
beasts and heathen incantation."

"Pray Heaven *that* were all he learned of him," said
the priest hastily; "for I have great fear that this sailor
was little better than an atheist and an emissary from Satan. But where are these newspapers and the fantasies
of publicita that fill his mind? I would see them, my
daughter."

"You shall, your Reverence, and more too," she replied
eagerly, leading the way along the passage to a grated door
which opened upon a small cell-like apartment, whose scant
light and less air came through the deeply embayed windows in the outer wall. "Here is his estudio."

In spite of this open invitation, the padre entered with
that air of furtive and minute inspection common to his
order. His glance fell upon a rude surveyor's plan of the
adjacent embryo town of Jonesville hanging on the wall,
which he contemplated with a cold disfavor that even included the highly colored vignette of the projected Jonesville Hotel in the left-hand corner. He then passed to a
supervisor's notice hanging near it, which he examined with
a suspicion heightened by that uneasiness common to mere
worldly humanity when opposed to an unknown and unfamiliar language. But an exclamation broke from his lips
when he confronted an election placard immediately below
it. It was printed in Spanish and English, and Father
Felipe had no difficulty in reading the announcement that
"Don José Sepulvida would preside at a meeting of the
Board of Education in Jonesville as one of the trustees."

"This is madness," said the padre.

Observing that Doña Maria was at the moment preoccupied in examining the pictorial pages of an illustrated
American weekly which had hitherto escaped his eyes, he
took it gently from her hand.

"Pardon, your Reverence," she said with slightly acidulous deprecation, "but thanks to the Blessed Virgin and your Reverence's teaching, the text is but gibberish to me and I did but glance at the pictures."

"Much evil may come in with the eye," said the priest sententiously, "as I will presently show thee. We have here," he continued, pointing to an illustration of certain college athletic sports, "a number of youthful cavaliers posturing and capering in a partly nude condition before a number of shameless women, who emulate the saturnalia of heathen Rome by waving their handkerchiefs. We have here a companion picture," he said, indicating an illustration of gymnastic exercises by the students of a female academy at "Commencement," "in which, as thou seest, even the aged of both sexes unblushingly assist as spectators with every expression of immodest satisfaction."

"Have they no bull-fights or other seemly recreation that they must indulge in such wantonness?" asked Doña Maria indignantly, gazing, however, somewhat curiously at the baleful representations.

"Of all that, my daughter, has their pampered civilization long since wearied," returned the good padre; "for see, this is what they consider a moral and even a religious ceremony." He turned to an illustration of a woman's rights convention; "observe with what rapt attention the audience of that heathen temple watch the inspired ravings of that elderly priestess on the dais. It is even this kind of sacrilegious performance that I am told thy nephew Don José expounds and defends."

"May the blessed saints preserve us; where will it lead to?" murmured the horrified Doña Maria.

"I will show thee," said Father Felipe, briskly turning the pages with the same lofty ignoring of the text until he came to a representation of a labor procession. "There is one of their periodic revolutions unhappily not unknown even in Mexico. Thou perceivest those complacent artisans marching with implements of their craft, accompanied by the military, in the presence of their own stricken masters. Here we see only another instance of the instability of all communities that are not founded on the principles of the Holy Church."

"And what is to be done with my nephew?"

The good father's brow darkened with the gloomy religious zeal of two centuries ago.

"We must have a council of the family, the alcalde, and the archbishop at *once*," he said ominously. To the mere heretical observer the conclusion might have seemed lame and impotent, but it was as near the Holy Inquisition as the year of grace 1852 could offer.

A few days after this colloquy the unsuspecting subject of it, Don José Sepulvida, was sitting alone in the same apartment. The fading glow of the western sky, through the deep embrasured windows, lit up his rapt and meditative face. He was a young man of apparently twenty-five, with a colorless satin complexion, dark eyes alternating between melancholy and restless energy, a narrow high forehead, long straight hair, and a lightly penciled mustache. He was said to resemble the well-known portrait of the Marquis of Monterey in the mission church, a face that was alleged to leave a deep and lasting impression upon the observers. It was undoubtedly owing to this quality during a brief visit of the famous viceroy to a remote and married ancestress of Don José at Leon that the singular resemblance may be attributed.

A heavy and hesitating step along the passage stopped before the grating. Looking up, Don José beheld, to his astonishment, the slightly inflamed face of Roberto, a vagabond American whom he had lately taken into his employment.

Roberto, a polite translation of "Bob the Bucker," cleaned out at a monte-bank in Santa Cruz, penniless and profligate, had sold his mustang to Don José and recklessly thrown himself in with the bargain. Touched by the rascal's extravagance, the quality of the mare, and observing that Bob's habits had not yet affected his seat in the saddle, but rather lent a demoniac vigor to his chase of wild cattle, Don José had retained rider and horse in his service as vaquero.

Bucking Bob, observing that his employer was alone, coolly opened the door without ceremony, shut it softly behind him, and then closed the wooden shutter of the grating. Don José surveyed him with mild surprise and dignified composure. The man appeared perfectly sober, — it was a peculiarity of his dissipated habits that, when not actually raving with drink, he was singularly shrewd and practical.

"Look yer, Don Kosay," he began in a brusque but guarded voice, "you and me is pards. When ye picked me and the mare up and set us on our legs again in this yer ranch, I allowed I 'd tie to ye whenever ye was in trouble — and wanted me. And I reckon that 's what 's the matter now. For from what I see and hear on every side, although you 're the boss of this consarn, you 're surrounded by a gang of spies and traitors. Your comings and goings, your ins and outs, is dogged and followed and blown upon. The folks you trust is playing it on ye. It ain't for me to say why or wherefore — what 's their rights and what 's yourn — but I 've come to tell ye that if you don't get up and get outer this ranch them d—d priests and your own flesh and blood — your aunts and your uncles and your cousins, will have you chucked outer your property, and run into a lunatic asylum."

"Me — Don José Sepulvida — a lunatico ! You are yourself crazy of drink, friend Roberto."

"Yes," said Roberto grimly, "but that kind ain't *illegal,* while your makin' ducks and drakes of your property and going into 'Merikin ideas and 'Merikin speculations they reckon is. And speakin' on the square, it ain't *nat'ral.*"

Don José sprang to his feet and began to pace up and down his cell-like study. " Ah, I remember now," he muttered, " I begin to comprehend : Father Felipe's homilies and discourses ! My aunt's too affectionate care ! My cousin's discreet consideration ! The prompt attention of my servants ! I see it all ! And you," he said, suddenly facing Roberto, " why come you to tell me this ? "

" Well, boss," said the American dryly, " I reckoned to stand by you."

" Ah," said Don José, visibly affected. " Good Roberto, come hither, child, you may kiss my hand."

" If ! it 's all the same to you, Don Kosay, — *that* kin slide."

" Ah, if — yes," said Don José, meditatively putting his hand to his forehead, " miserable that I am ! — I remembered not you were Americano. Pardon, my friend — embrace me — Conpañero y Amigo."

With characteristic gravity he reclined for a moment upon Robert's astonished breast. Then recovering himself with equal gravity he paused, lifted his hand with gentle warning, marched to a recess in the corner, unhooked a rapier hanging from the wall, and turned to his companion.

" We will defend ourselves, friend Roberto. It is the sword of the Comandante — my ancestor. The blade is of Toledo."

" An ordinary six-shooter of Colt's would lay over that," said Roberto grimly — " but that ain't your game just now, Don Kosay. You must get up and get, and at once. You must vamose the ranch afore they lay hold of you and have you up before the alcalde. Once away from here, they dare n't follow you where there 's 'Merikin law, and when you kin fight 'em in the square."

" Good," said Don José with melancholy preciseness.

"You are wise, friend Roberto. We may fight them later, as you say — on the square, or in the open Plaza. And you, camarado, *you* shall go with me — you and your mare."

Sincere as the American had been in his offer of service, he was somewhat staggered at this imperative command. But only for a moment. "Well," he said lazily, "I don't care if I do."

"But," said Don José with increased gravity, "you *shall* care, friend Roberto. We shall make an alliance, an union. It is true, my brother, you drink of whiskey, and at such times are even as a madman. It has been recounted to me that it was necessary to your existence that you are a lunatic three days of the week. Who knows? I myself, though I drink not of aguardiente, am accused of fantasies for all time. Necessary it becomes, therefore, that we should go *together*. My fantasies and speculations cannot injure you, my brother; your whiskey shall not empoison me. We shall go together in the great world of your American ideas of which I am much inflamed. We shall together breathe as one the spirit of Progress and Liberty. We shall be even as neophytes making of ourselves Apostles of Truth. I absolve and renounce myself henceforth of my family. I shall take to myself the sister and the brother, the aunt and the uncle, as we proceed. I devote myself to humanity alone. I devote *you*, my friend, and the mare — though happily she has not a Christian soul — to this glorious mission."

The few level last rays of light lit up a faint enthusiasm in the face of Don José, but without altering his imperturbable gravity. The vaquero eyed him curiously and half doubtfully.

"We will go to-morrow," resumed Don José with solemn decision, "for it is Wednesday. It was a Sunday that thou didst ride the mare up the steps of the Fonda and demanded that thy liquor should be served to thee in a pail. I remember it, for the landlord of the Fonda claimed twenty pesos for damage and the kissing of his wife. Therefore, by computation, good Roberto, thou shouldst be sober until Friday, and we shall have two clear days to fly before thy madness again seizes thee."

"They kin say what they like, Don Kosay, but *your* head is level," returned the unabashed American, grasping Don José's hand. "All right, then. Hasta mañana, as your folks say."

"Hasta mañana," repeated Don José gravely.

At daybreak next morning, while slumber still weighted the lazy eyelids of "the Blessed Innocents," Don José Sepulvida and his trusty squire Roberto, otherwise known as "Bucking Bob," rode forth unnoticed from the corral.

II

THREE days had passed. At the close of the third, Don José was seated in a cosy private apartment of the San Mateo Hotel, where they had halted for an arranged interview with his lawyer before reaching San Francisco. From his window he could see the surrounding park-like avenues of oaks and the level white highroad, now and then clouded with the dust of passing teams. But his eyes were persistently fixed upon a small copy of the American Constitution before him. Suddenly there was a quick rap on his door, and before he could reply to it a man brusquely entered.

Don José raised his head slowly, and recognized the landlord. But the intruder, apparently awed by the gentle, grave, and studious figure before him, fell back for an instant in an attitude of surly apology.

"Enter freely, my good Jenkinson," said Don José, with a quiet courtesy that had all the effect of irony. "The apartment, such as it is, is at your disposition. It is even yours, as is the house."

"Well, I'm darned if I know as it is," said the landlord, recovering himself roughly, "and that's jest what's the matter. Yer's that man of yours smashing things right and left in the bar-room and chuckin' my waiters through the window."

"Softly, softly, good Jenkinson," said Don José, putting a mark in the pages of the volume before him. "It is necessary first that I should correct your speech. He is not my '*man*,' which I comprehend to mean a slave, a hire-

ling, a thing obnoxious to the great American nation which
I admire and to which *he* belongs.   Therefore, good Jenkinson, say ' friend,' ' companion,' ' guide,' ' philosopher,' if
you will.   As to the rest, it is of no doubt as you relate.   I
myself have heard the breakings of glass and small dishes
as I sit here ; three times I have seen your waiters projected into the road with much violence and confusion.   To
myself I have then said, even as I say to you, good Jenkinson, ' Patience, patience, the end is not far.'   In four hours,"
continued Don José, holding up four fingers, " he shall
make a finish.   Until then, not."

" Well, I'm d—d," ejaculated Jenkinson, gasping for
breath in his indignation.

" Nay, excellent Jenkinson, not dam-ned, but of a possibility dam-*aged*.   That I shall repay when he have make a
finish."

" But, darn it all," broke in the landlord angrily.

" Ah," said Don José gravely, " you would be paid before !   Good ; for how much shall you value *all* you have
in your bar ? "

Don José's imperturbability evidently shook the landlord's faith in the soundness of his own position.   He
looked at his guest critically and audaciously.

" It cost me two hundred dollars to fit it up," he said
curtly.

Don José rose, and, taking a buckskin purse from his
saddle-bag, counted out four slugs [1] and handed them to
the stupefied Jenkinson.   The next moment, however, his
host recovered himself, and, casting the slugs back on the
little table, brought his fist down with an emphasis that
made them dance.

" But, look yer — suppose I want this thing stopped —
you hear me — *stopped* — now."

[1] Hexagonal gold pieces valued at $50 each, issued by a private firm as
coin in the early days.

"That would be interfering with the liberty of the subject, my good Jenkinson — which God forbid!" said Don José calmly. "Moreover, it is the custom of the Americanos — a habit of my friend Roberto — a necessity of his existence — and so recognized of his friends. Patience and courage, Señor Jenkinson. Stay — ah, I comprehend! you have — of a possibility — a wife?"

"No, I'm a widower," said Jenkinson sharply.

"Then I congratulate you. My friend Roberto would have kissed her. It is also of his habit. Truly you have escaped much. I embrace you, Jenkinson."

He threw his arms gravely around Jenkinson, in whose astounded face at last an expression of dry humor faintly dawned. After a moment's survey of Don José's impenetrable gravity, he coolly gathered up the gold coins, and, saying that he would assess the damages and return the difference, he left the room as abruptly as he had entered it.

But Don José was not destined to remain long in peaceful study of the American Constitution. He had barely taken up the book again and renewed his serious contemplation of its excellencies when there was another knock at his door. This time, in obedience to his invitation to enter, the new visitor approached with more deliberation and a certain formality.

He was a young man of apparently the same age as Don José, handsomely dressed, and of a quiet self-possession and gravity almost equal to his host's.

"I believe I am addressing Don José Sepulvida," he said with a familiar yet courteous inclination of his handsome head. Don José, who had risen in marked contrast to his reception of his former guest, answered: —

"You are truly making it him a great honor."

"Well, you're going it blind as far as *I'm* concerned certainly," said the young man, with a slight smile, "for you don't know *me*."

"Pardon, my friend," said Don José gently; "in this book, this great Testament of your glorious nation, I have read that you are all equal, one not above, one not below the other. I salute in you the Nation! It is enough!"

"Thank you," returned the stranger, with a face that, saving the faintest twinkle in the corner of his dark eyes, was as immovable as his host's, "but for the purposes of my business I had better say I am Jack Hamlin, a gambler, and am just now dealing faro in the Florida saloon round the corner."

He paused carelessly, as if to allow Don José the protest he did not make, and then continued : —

"The matter is this. One of your vaqueros, who is, however, an American, was round there an hour ago bucking against faro, and put up and *lost*, not only the mare he was riding, but a horse which I have just learned is yours. Now we reckon, over there, that we can make enough money playing a square game, without being obliged to take property from a howling drunkard, to say nothing of it not belonging to him, and I've come here, Don José, to say that if you'll send over and bring away your man and your horse, you can have 'em both."

"If I have comprehended, honest Hamlin," said Don José slowly, "this Roberto, who was my vaquero and is my brother, has approached this faro game by himself unsolicited?"

"He certainly did n't seem shy of it," said Mr. Hamlin with equal gravity. "To the best of my knowledge he looked as if he'd been there before."

"And if he had won, excellent Hamlin, you would have given him the equal of his mare and horse?"

"A hundred dollars for each, yes, certainly."

"Then I see not why I should send for the property which is truly no longer mine, nor for my brother, who will amuse himself after the fashion of his country in the company of so honorable a caballero as yourself. Stay! oh, imbecile that I am. I have not remembered. You would possibly say that he has no longer of horses! Play him; play him, admirable yet prudent Hamlin. I have two thousand horses! Of a surety he cannot exhaust them in four hours. Therefore play him, trust to me for recompensa, and have no fear."

A quick flush covered the stranger's cheek, and his eyebrows momentarily contracted. He walked carelessly to the window, however, glanced out, and then turned to Don José.

"May I ask, then," he said with almost sepulchral gravity, "is anybody taking care of you?"

"Truly," returned Don José cautiously, "there is my brother and friend Roberto."

"Ah! Roberto, certainly," said Mr. Hamlin profoundly. "Why do you ask, considerate friend?"

"Oh! I only thought, with your kind of opinions, you must often feel lonely in California. Good-by." He shook Don José's hand heartily, took up his hat, inclined his head with graceful seriousness, and passed out of the room. In the hall he met the landlord.

"Well," said Jenkinson, with a smile half anxious, half insinuating, "you saw him? What do you think of him?"

Mr. Hamlin paused and regarded Jenkinson with a calmly contemplative air, as if he were trying to remember first who he was, and secondly why he should speak to him at all. "Think of whom?" he repeated carelessly.

"Why him — you know — Don José."

"I did not see anything the matter with him," returned Hamlin with frigid simplicity.

"What? nothing queer?"

"Well, no — except that he's a guest in *your* house," said Hamlin with great cheerfulness. "But then, as you keep a hotel, you can't help occasionally admitting a — gentleman."

Mr. Jenkinson smiled the uneasy smile of a man who knew that his interlocutor's playfulness occasionally extended to the use of a derringer, in which he was singularly prompt and proficient; and Mr. Hamlin, equally conscious of that knowledge on the part of his companion, descended the staircase composedly.

But the day had darkened gradually into night, and Don José was at last compelled to put aside his volume. The sound of a large bell rung violently along the hall and passages admonished him that the American dinner was ready, and, although the viands and the mode of cooking were not entirely to his fancy, he had, in his grave enthusiasm for the national habits, attended the *table d'hôte* regularly with Roberto. On reaching the lower hall he was informed that his henchman had early succumbed to the potency of his libations, and had already been carried by two men to bed. Receiving this information with his usual stoical composure, he entered the dining-room, but was surprised to find that a separate table had been prepared for him by the landlord, and that a rude attempt had been made to serve him with his own native dishes.

"Señores y Señoritas," said Don José, turning from it and with grave politeness addressing the assembled company, "if I seem to-day to partake alone and in a reserved fashion of certain viands that have been prepared for me, it is truly from no lack of courtesy to your distinguished company, but rather, I protest, to avoid the appearance of greater discourtesy to our excellent Jenkinson, who has taken some pains and trouble to comport his establishment to what he conceives to be my desires. Wherefore, my friends, in God's name fall to, the same as if I were not present, and grace be with you."

A few stared at the tall, gentle, melancholy figure with some astonishment; a few whispered to their neighbors; but when, at the conclusion of his repast, Don José arose and again saluted the company, one or two stood up and smilingly returned the courtesy; and Polly Jenkinson, the landlord's youngest daughter, to the great delight of her companions, blew him a kiss.

After visiting the vaquero in his room, and with his own hand applying some native ointment to the various contusions and scratches which recorded the late engagements of the unconscious Roberto, Don José placed a gold coin in the hands of the Irish chamber-maid, and bidding her look after the sleeper, he threw his *serape* over his shoulders and passed into the road. The loungers on the veranda gazed at him curiously, yet half acknowledged his usual serious salutation, and made way for him with a certain respect. Avoiding the few narrow streets of the little town, he pursued his way meditatively along the highroad, returning to the hotel after an hour's ramble, as the evening stagecoach had deposited its passengers and departed.

"There's a lady waiting to see you upstairs," said the landlord with a peculiar smile. "She rather allowed it wasn't the proper thing to see you alone, or she wasn't quite ekal to it, I reckon, for she got my Polly to stand by her."

"Your Polly, good Jenkinson?" said Don José interrogatively.

"My darter, Don José."

"Ah, truly! I am twice blessed," said Don José, gravely ascending the staircase.

On entering the room he perceived a tall, large-featured woman with an extraordinary quantity of blond hair parted on one side of her broad forehead, sitting upon the sofa. Beside her sat Polly Jenkinson, her fresh, honest, and rather pretty face beaming with delighted expectation and mischief. Don José saluted them with a formal courtesy, which, however, had no trace of the fact that he really did not remember anything of them.

"I called," said the large-featured woman with a voice equally pronounced, "in reference to a request from you, which, though perhaps unconventional in the extreme, I have been able to meet by the intervention of this young lady's company. My name on this card may not be familiar to you — but I am 'Dorothy Dewdrop.'"

A slight movement of abstraction and surprise passed over Don José's face, but as quickly vanished as he advanced towards her and gracefully raised the tips of her fingers to his lips. "Have I then, at last, the privilege of beholding that most distressed and deeply injured of women! Or is it but a dream!"

It certainly was not, as far as concerned the substantial person of the woman before him, who, however, seemed somewhat uneasy under his words as well as the demure scrutiny of Miss Jenkinson. "I thought you might have forgotten," she said with slight acerbity, "that you desired an interview with the authoress of " —

"Pardon," interrupted Don José, standing before her in an attitude of the deepest sympathizing dejection, "I had not forgotten. It is now three weeks since I have read in the journal 'Golden Gate' the eloquent and touching poem of your sufferings, and your aspirations, and your miscomprehensions by those you love. I remember as yesterday that you have said that cruel fate have linked you to a soulless state — that — but I speak not well your own beautiful language — you are in tears at evenfall 'because that you are not understood of others, and that your soul recoiled from iron bonds, until, as in a dream, you sought succor and release in some true Knight of equal plight.'"

"I am told," said the large-featured woman with some satisfaction, "that the poem to which you allude has been generally admired."

"Admired! Señora," said Don José, with still darker sympathy, "it is not the word; it is *felt*. I have felt it.

When I read those words of distress, I am touched of compassion! I have said, This woman, so disconsolate, so oppressed, must be relieved, protected! I have wrote to you, at the 'Golden Gate,' to see me here."

"And I have come, as you perceive," said the poetess, rising with a slight smile of constraint; "and emboldened by your appreciation, I have brought a few trifles thrown off " —

"Pardon, unhappy Señora," interrupted Don José, lifting his hand deprecatingly without relaxing his melancholy precision, "but to a cavalier further evidence is not required — and I have not yet make finish. I have not content myself to *write* to you. I have sent my trusty friend Roberto to inquire at the 'Golden Gate' of your condition. I have found there, most unhappy and persecuted friend — that with truly angelic forbearance you have not told *all* — that you are *married*, and that of a necessity it is your husband that is cold and soulless and unsympathizing — and all that you describe."

"Sir!" said the poetess, rising in angry consternation.

"I have written to him," continued Don José, with unheeding gravity; "have appealed to him as a friend, I have conjured him as a caballero, I have threatened him even as a champion of the Right, I have said to him, in effect — that this must not be as it is. I have informed him that I have made an appointment with you even at this house, and I challenged him to meet you here — in this room — even at this instant, and, with God's help, we should make good our charges against him. It is yet early; I have allowed time for the lateness of the stage and the fact that he will come by another conveyance. Therefore, O Doña Dewdrop, tremble not like thy namesake as it were on the leaf of apprehension and expectancy. I, Don José, am here to protect thee. I will take these charges " — gently withdrawing the manuscripts from her astonished grasp —

"though even, as I related to thee before, I want them not, yet we will together confront him with them and make them good against him."

"Are you mad?" demanded the lady in almost stentorious accents, "or is this an unmanly hoax?" Suddenly she stopped in undeniable consternation. "Good heavens," she muttered, "if Abner should believe this. He is *such* a fool! He has lately been queer and jealous. Oh dear!" she said, turning to Polly Jenkinson with the first indication of feminine weakness, "*is* he telling the truth? is he crazy? what shall I do?"

Polly Jenkinson, who had witnessed the interview with the intensest enjoyment, now rose equal to the occasion.

"You have made a mistake," she said, uplifting her demure blue eyes to Don José's dark and melancholy gaze. "This lady is a *poetess!* The sufferings she depicts, the sorrows she feels, are in the *imagination*, in her fancy only."

"Ah!" said Don José gloomily; "then it is all false."

"No," said Polly quickly, "only they are not her *own*, you know. They are somebody else's. She only describes them for another, don't you see?"

"And who, then, is this unhappy one?" asked the Don quickly.

"Well — a — friend," stammered Polly hesitatingly.

"A friend!" repeated Don José. "Ah, I see, of possibility a dear one, even," he continued, gazing with tender melancholy into the untroubled cerulean depths of Polly's eyes, "even, but no, child, it could not be! *thou* art too young."

"Ah," said Polly, with an extraordinary gulp and a fierce nudge of the poetess, "but it *was* me."

"You, Señorita," repeated Don José, falling back in an attitude of mingled admiration and pity. "You, the child of Jenkinson!"

"Yes, yes," joined in the poetess hurriedly ; "but that is n't going to stop the consequences of your wretched blunder. My husband will be furious, and will be here at any moment. Good gracious ! what is that ? "

The violent slamming of a distant door at that instant, the sounds of quick scuffling on the staircase, and the uplifting of an irate voice had reached her ears and thrown her back into the arms of Polly Jenkinson. Even the young girl herself turned an anxious gaze towards the door. Don José alone was unmoved.

"Possess yourselves in peace, Señoritas," he said calmly. " We have here only the characteristic convalescence of my friend and brother, the excellent Roberto. He will ever recover himself from drink with violence, even as he precipitates himself into it with fury. He has been prematurely awakened. I will discover the cause."

With an elaborate bow to the frightened women, he left the room. Scarcely had the door closed when the poetess turned quickly to Polly. "The man 's a stark staring lunatic, but, thank Heaven, Abner will see it at once. And now let 's get away while we can. To think," she said, snatching up her scattered manuscripts, "that *that* was all the beast wanted."

" I 'm sure he 's very gentle and kind," said Polly, recovering her dimples with a demure pout ; "but stop, he 's coming back."

It was indeed Don José reëntering the room with the composure of a relieved and self-satisfied mind. " It is even as I said, Señora," he began, taking the poetess's hand, — " and *more*. You are *saved !* "

As the women only stared at each other, he gravely folded his arms and continued : " I will explain. For the instant I have not remember that, in imitation of your own delicacy, I have given to your husband in my letter, not the name of myself, but, as a mere *Don Fulano*, the

name of my brother Roberto — 'Bucking Bob.' Your
husband have this moment arrive! Penetrating the bedroom of the excellent Roberto, he has indiscreetly seize
him in his bed, without explanation, without introduction,
without fear! The excellent Roberto, ever ready for such
distractions, have respond! In a word, to use the language of the good Jenkinson — our host, our father —
who was present, he have 'wiped the floor with your husband,' and have even carried him down the staircase to the
street. Believe me, he will not return. You are free!"

"Fool! Idiot! Crazy beast!" said the poetess, dash-
ing past him and out of the door. "You shall pay for
this!"

Don José did not change his imperturbable and melancholy calm. "And now, little one," he said, dropping on
one knee before the half-frightened Polly, "child of Jenkinson, now that thy perhaps too excitable sponsor has, in
a poet's caprice, abandoned thee for some newer fantasy,
confide in me thy distress, to me, thy Knight, and tell the
story of thy sorrows."

"But," said Polly, rising to her feet and struggling between a laugh and a cry, "I have n't any sorrows. Oh,
dear! don't you see, it's only her *fancy* to make me seem
so. There's nothing the matter with me."

"Nothing the matter," repeated Don José slowly.
"You have no distress? You want no succor, no relief,
no protector? This, then, is but another delusion!" he
said, rising sadly.

"Yes, no — that is — oh, my gracious goodness!" said
Polly, hopelessly divided between a sense of the ridiculous
and some strange attraction in the dark, gentle eyes that
were fixed upon her half reproachfully. "You don't understand."

Don José replied only with a melancholy smile, and
then going to the door opened it with a bowed head and

respectful courtesy. At the act Polly plucked up courage again, and with it a slight dash of her old audacity.

"I'm sure I'm very sorry that I ain't got any love sorrows," she said demurely. "And I suppose it's very dreadful in me not to have been raving and broken-hearted over somebody or other as that woman has said. Only," she waited till she had gained the secure vantage of the threshold, "I never knew a gentleman to *object* to it before!"

With this Parthian arrow from her blue eyes she slipped into the passage and vanished through the door of the opposite parlor. For an instant Don José remained motionless and reflecting. Then, recovering himself with grave precision, he deliberately picked up his narrow black gloves from the table, drew them on, took his hat in his hand, and, solemnly striding across the passage, entered the door that had just closed behind her.

III

It must not be supposed that in the meantime the flight of Don José and his follower was unattended by any commotion at the rancho of the Blessed Innocents. At the end of three hours' deliberation, in which the retainers were severally examined, the corral searched, and the well in the courtyard sounded, scouts were dispatched in different directions, who returned with the surprising information that the fugitives were not in the vicinity. A trustworthy messenger was sent to Monterey for " custom-house paper," on which to draw up a formal declaration of the affair. The archbishop was summoned from San Luis, and Don Victor and Don Vincente Sepulvida, with the Doñas Carmen and Inez Alvarado, and a former alcalde, gathered at a family council the next day. In this serious conclave the good Father Felipe once more expounded the alienated condition and the dangerous reading of the absent man. In the midst of which the ordinary post brought a letter from Don José, calmly inviting the family to dine with him and Roberto at San Mateo on the following Wednesday. The document was passed gravely from hand to hand. Was it a fresh evidence of mental aberration — an audacity of frenzy — or a trick of the vaquero ? The archbishop and alcalde shook their heads — it was without doubt a lawless, even a sacrilegious and blasphemous *fête*. But a certain curiosity of the ladies and of Father Felipe carried the day. Without formally accepting the invitation it was decided that the family should examine the afflicted man, with a view of taking active measures hereafter. On the day appointed, the traveling carriage of the Sepulvidas, an equipage coeval with the beginning of the century, drawn by two white mules gaudily caparisoned, halted before the hotel at San Mateo and disgorged Father Felipe, the Doñas Carmen and Inez Alvarado and Maria Sepulvida; while Don Victor and Don Vincente Sepulvida, their attendant cavaliers on fiery mustangs, like outriders, drew rein at the same time. A slight thrill of excitement, as of the advent of a possible circus, had preceded them through the little town; a faint blending of cigarette smoke and garlic announced their presence on the veranda.

Ushered into the parlor of the hotel, apparently set apart for their reception, they were embarrassed at not finding their host present. But they were still more disconcerted when a tall full-bearded stranger, with a shrewd, amused-looking face, rose from a chair by the window, and, stepping forward, saluted them in fluent Spanish with a slight American accent.

"I have to ask you, gentlemen and ladies," he began, with a certain insinuating ease and frankness that alternately aroused and lulled their suspicions, " to pardon the absence of our friend Don José Sepulvida at this preliminary greeting. For to be perfectly frank with you, although the ultimate aim and object of our gathering is a social one, you are doubtless aware that certain infelicities and misunderstandings — common to most families — have occurred, and a free, dispassionate, unprejudiced discussion and disposal of them at the beginning will only tend to augment the good will of our gathering."

"The Señor without doubt is " — suggested the padre, with a polite interrogative pause.

"Pardon me! I forgot to introduce myself. Colonel Parker — entirely at your service and that of these charming ladies."

The ladies referred to allowed their eyes to rest with

evident prepossession on the insinuating stranger.   " Ah, a soldier," said Don Vincente.

" Formerly," said the American lightly ; " at present a lawyer, the counsel of Don José."

A sudden rigor of suspicion stiffened the company ; the ladies withdrew their eyes ; the priest and the Sepulvidas exchanged glances.

" Come," said Colonel Parker, with apparent unconsciousness of the effect of his disclosure, " let us begin frankly. You have, I believe, some anxiety in regard to the mental condition of Don José."

" We believe him to be mad," said Padre Felipe promptly, " irresponsible, possessed ! "

" That is your opinion ; good," said the lawyer quietly.

" And ours too," clamored the party, " without doubt."

" Good," returned the lawyer with perfect cheerfulness. " As his relations, you have no doubt had superior opportunities for observing his condition. I understand also that you may think it necessary to have him legally declared *non compos*, a proceeding which, you are aware, might result in the incarceration of our distinguished friend in a madhouse."

" Pardon, Señor," interrupted Doña Maria proudly ; " you do not comprehend the family. When a Sepulvida is visited of God we do not ask the Government to confine him like a criminal. We protect him in his own house from the consequences of his frenzy."

" From the machinations of the worldly and heretical," broke in the priest, " and from the waste and dispersion of inherited possessions."

" Very true," continued Colonel Parker, with unalterable good humor ; " but I was only about to say that there might be conflicting evidence of his condition. For instance, our friend has been here three days. In that time he has had three interviews with three individuals under singular cir-

cumstances." Colonel Parker then briefly recounted the
episodes of the landlord, the gambler, Miss Jenkinson, and
the poetess, as they had been related to him. "Yet," he
continued, "all but one of these individuals are willing to
swear that they not only believe Don José perfectly sane,
but endowed with a singularly sound judgment. In fact,
the testimony of Mr. Hamlin and Miss Jenkinson is remarkably clear on that subject."

The company exchanged a supercilious smile. "Do you
not see, O Señor Advocate," said Don Vincente compassionately, "that this is but a conspiracy to avail themselves
of our relative's weakness? Of a necessity they find him
sane who benefits them."

"I have thought of that, and am glad to hear you say
so," returned the lawyer still more cheerfully, "for your
prompt opinion emboldens me to be at once perfectly frank
with you. Briefly, then, Don José has summoned me here
to make a final disposition of his property. In the carrying
out of certain theories of his, which it is not my province
to question, he has resolved upon comparative poverty for
himself as best fitted for his purpose, and to employ his
wealth solely for others. In fact, of all his vast possessions
he retains for himself only an income sufficient for the bare
necessaries of life."

"And you have done this?" they asked in one voice.

"Not yet," said the lawyer.

"Blessed San Antonio, we have come in time!" ejaculated Doña Carmen. "Another day and it would have
been too late; it was an inspiration of the Blessed Innocents themselves," said Doña Maria, crossing herself. "Can
you longer doubt that this is the wildest madness?" said
Father Felipe with flashing eyes.

"Yet," returned the lawyer, caressing his heavy beard
with a meditative smile, "the ingenious fellow actually
instanced the vows of *your own order*, reverend sir, as an

example in support of his theory. But to be brief. Conceiving, then, that his holding of property was a mere accident of heritage, not admitted by him, unworthy his acceptance, and a relic of superstitious ignorance " —

"This is the very sacrilege of Satanic prepossession," broke in the priest indignantly.

"He therefore," continued the lawyer composedly, "makes over and reverts the whole of his possessions, with the exceptions I have stated, to his family and the Church."

A breathless and stupefying silence fell upon the company. In the dead hush the sound of Polly Jenkinson's piano, played in a distant room, could be distinctly heard. With their vacant eyes staring at him the speaker continued : —

"That deed of gift I have drawn up as he dictated it. I don't mind saying that in the opinion of some he might be declared *non compos* upon the evidence of that alone. I need not say how relieved I am to find that your opinion coincides with my own."

"But," gasped Father Felipe hurriedly, with a quick glance at the others, "it does not follow that it will be necessary to resort to these legal measures. Care, counsel, persuasion " —

"The general ministering of kinship — nursing, a woman's care — the instincts of affection," piped Doña Maria in breathless eagerness.

"Any light social distraction — a harmless flirtation — a possible attachment," suggested Doña Carmen shyly.

"Change of scene — active exercise — experiences — even as those you have related," broke in Don Vincente.

"I for one have ever been opposed to *legal* measures," said Don Victor. "A mere consultation of friends — in fact, a *fête* like this is sufficient."

"Good friends," said Father Felipe, who had by this

time recovered himself, taking out his snuff-box porten-
tously, "it would seem truly, from the document which
this discreet caballero has spoken of, that the errors of our
dear Don José are rather of method than intent, and that
while we may freely accept the one " —

"Pardon," interrupted Colonel Parker with bland per-
sistence, "but I must point out to you that what we call
in law 'a consideration' is necessary to the legality of a
conveyance, even though that consideration be frivolous
and calculated to impair the validity of the document."

"Truly," returned the good padre insinuatingly ; "but
if a discreet advocate were to suggest the substitution of
some more pious and reasonable consideration "—

"But that would be making it a perfectly sane and
gratuitous document, not only glaringly inconsistent with
your charges, my good friends, with Don José's attitude
towards you and his flight from home, but open to the
gravest suspicion in law. In fact, its apparent propriety
in the face of these facts would imply improper influence."

The countenances of the company fell. The lawyer's
face, however, became still more good-humored and sympathizing. "The case is simply this. If in the opinion of
judge and jury Don José is declared insane, the document
is worthless except as a proof of that fact or a possible indication of the undue influence of his relations, which
might compel the court to select his guardians and trustees
elsewhere than among them."

"Friend Abogado," said Father Felipe with extraordinary deliberation, "the document thou hast just described
so eloquently convinces me beyond all doubt that Don José
is not only perfectly sane but endowed with a singular discretion. I consider it as a delicate and high-spirited intimation to us, his friends and kinsmen, of his unalterable
and logically just devotion to his family and religion, whatever may seem to be his poetical and imaginative manner

of declaring it. I think there is not one here," continued the padre, looking around him impressively, " who is not entirely satisfied of Don José's reason and competency to arrange his own affairs."

" Entirely," " truly," " perfectly," eagerly responded the others with affecting spontaneity.

"Nay, more. To prevent any misconception, we shall deem it our duty to take every opportunity of making our belief publicly known," added Father Felipe.

The padre and Colonel Parker gazed long and gravely into each other's eyes. It may have been an innocent touch of the sunlight through the window, but a faint gleam seemed to steal into the pupil of the affable lawyer at the same moment that, probably from the like cause, there was a slight nervous contraction of the left eyelid of the pious father. But it passed, and the next instant the door opened to admit Don José Sepulvida.

He was at once seized and effusively embraced by the entire company with every protest of affection and respect. Not only Mr. Hamlin and Mr. Jenkinson, who accompanied him as invited guests, but Roberto, in a new suit of clothes and guiltless of stain or trace of dissipation, shared in the pronounced friendliness of the kinsmen. Padre Felipe took snuff, Colonel Parker blew his nose gently.

Nor were they less demonstrative of their new convictions later at the banquet. Don José, with Jenkinson and the padre on his right and left, preserved his gentle and half-melancholy dignity in the midst of the noisy fraternization. Even Padre Felipe, in a brief speech or exhortation proposing the health of their host, lent himself in his own tongue to this polite congeniality. " We have had also, my friends and brothers," he said in peroration, " a pleasing example of the compliment of imitation shown by our beloved Don José. No one who has known him during his friendly sojourn in this community but will be struck with the conviction that he has acquired that most marvelous faculty of your great American nation, the exhibition of humor and of the practical joke."

Every eye was turned upon the imperturbable face of Don José as he slowly rose to reply. "In bidding you to this *fête*, my friends and kinsmen," he began calmly, "it was with the intention of formally embracing the habits, customs, and spirit of American institutions by certain methods of renunciation of the past, as became a caballero of honor and resolution. Those methods may possibly be known to some of you." He paused for a moment as if to allow the members of his family to look unconscious. "Since then, in the wisdom of God, it has occurred to me that my purpose may be as honorably effected by a discreet blending of the past and the present — in a word, by the judicious combination of the interests of my native people and the American nation. In consideration of that purpose, friends and kinsmen, I ask you to join me in drinking the good health of my host Señor Jenkinson, my future father-in-law, from whom I have to-day had the honor to demand the hand of the peerless Polly, his daughter, as the future mistress of the Rancho of the Blessed Innocents."

The marriage took place shortly after. Nor was the free will and independence of Don José Sepulvida in the least opposed by his relations. Whether they felt they had already committed themselves, or had hopes in the future, did not transpire. Enough that the escapade of a week was tacitly forgotten. The only allusion ever made to the bridegroom's peculiarities was drawn from the demure lips of the bride herself on her installation at the "Blessed Innocents."

"And what, little one, didst thou find in me to admire?" Don José had asked tenderly.

"Oh, you seemed to be so much like that dear old Don Quixote, you know," she answered demurely.

"Don Quixote," repeated Don José with gentle gravity. "But, my child, that was only a mere fiction — a romance, of one Cervantes. Believe me, of a truth there never was any such person!"